Praise for *Soldiers in the Schoolhouse*

"A deeply researched and clearly written account of an understudied facet of military history."

—William A. Taylor, author of *Every Citizen a Soldier*

"Coumbe provides mature insight and historical context for one of the military's most far-reaching efforts at domestic engagement. Love it or hate it, Junior ROTC continues to influence American youth, and Coumbe's work will assist those who manage the program into the future."

—Lance Betros, author of *Carved from Granite: West Point since 1902*

"JROTC—its origins, goals, and outcomes—has long been understudied. In this important work, Arthur Coumbe sheds light on more than one hundred years of JROTC history—its achievements and controversies, the military services' guiding assumptions about its worth, and the unique ways it aims to connect society to its military."

—Heidi A. Urben, author of *Party, Politics, and the Post-9/11 Army*

"*Soldiers in the Schoolhouse* is a splendid and deeply informative history of the Junior ROTC. Arthur Coumbe not only masterfully chronicles the major developments and vicissitudes of the corps but also deftly analyzes the various ways it has contributed to the defense and civic culture of our republic."

—Donald Alexander Downs, Alexander Meiklejohn Professor Emeritus, University of Wisconsin–Madison

SOLDIERS IN THE SCHOOLHOUSE

AUSA Books

Series editor: Joseph Craig

SOLDIERS IN THE SCHOOLHOUSE

A MILITARY HISTORY OF THE JUNIOR ROTC

ARTHUR T. COUMBE

A note to the reader: Several of the quotations printed in this volume contain outdated or racially insensitive terminology. The original language is retained here to provide full historical context for the events under discussion. Discretion is advised.

Scholarly publisher for the Commonwealth, serving Bellarmine University, Berea College, Centre College of Kentucky, Eastern Kentucky University, The Filson Historical Society, Georgetown College, Kentucky Historical Society, Kentucky State University, Morehead State University, Murray State University, Northern Kentucky University, Spalding University, Transylvania University, University of Kentucky, University of Louisville, University of Pikeville, and Western Kentucky University.

Editorial and Sales Offices: The University Press of Kentucky
663 South Limestone, Lexington, Kentucky 40508-4008
www.kentuckypress.com

Cataloging-in-Publication data is available from the Library of Congress.

ISBN 978-1-9859-0233-6 (hardcover : alk. paper)
ISBN 978-1-9859-0234-3 (paperback : alk. paper)
ISBN 978-1-9859-0237-4 (epub)
ISBN 978-1-9859-0236-7 (pdf)

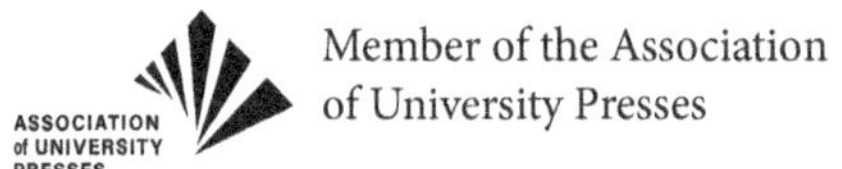

Member of the Association
of University Presses

For the untold thousands of students, instructors, and administrators who have taken part in one of the largest, most enduring, most popular, and most controversial experiments in domestic action ever undertaken by the military services.

To my wife
Deborah Coumbe

Contents

Abbreviations and Acronyms

A&NJ	*Army and Navy Journal*
AFB	air force base
AFQT	Armed Forces Qualification Test
AG	adjutant general
AGF	Army Ground Forces
AHEC	US Army Heritage and Education Center
AMSCUS	Association of Military Schools and Colleges of the United States
APT	Awareness Presentation Team
ASF	Army Service Forces
ASVAB	Armed Services Vocational Aptitude Battery
ATP	*Army Training Publication*
AUS	Army of the United States
AVF	all-volunteer force
AWC	Army War College
BCA	Budget Control Act
BCT	Basic Combat Training
BOB	Bureau of the Budget
CAR	Chief of Army Reserve
CBO	Congressional Budget Office
CCC	Civilian Conservation Corps
CG	commanding general
CME	Committee on Militarism in Education
CMH	Center of Military History
CMTC	Citizens' Military Training Camps
COEST	Committee on Education and Special Training
CONARC	Continental Army Command

Cong.	congressional
COS	chief of staff
CQ	*Congressional Quarterly*
CR	*Congressional Record*
CRS	Congressional Research Service
CSA	chief of staff of the army
CSIS	Center for Strategic and International Studies
CUL	Clemson University Libraries
DA	Department of the Army
DAP	Domestic Action Program
DAHSUM	*Department of the Army Historical Summary*
DAI	Department of the Army instructor
DCSPER	deputy chief of staff for personnel
DOD	Department of Defense
DODD	Department of Defense directive
DOE	Department of Education
DRC	Dean Rusk Collection
ER	enrollment report
ESTP	Enhanced Skills
FS	fact sheet
FY	fiscal year
GAR	Grand Army of the Republic
GC	general correspondence
GPO	Government Printing Office
GS	General Staff
HAI	Hispanic Access Initiative
HASC	House Armed Services Committee
HBCU	Historically Black College or University
HEW	Health, Education, and Welfare (Dept)
HS	high school
HSVUS	High School Volunteers of the United States
IP	information paper
JROTC	Junior Reserve Officers' Training Corps
LSUA	Louisiana State University Archives
M&RA	Manpower and Reserve Affairs
M&RF	Manpower and Reserve Forces
MJC	military junior college

MLDC	Military Leadership Diversity Commission
MMA	Massanutten Military Academy
NACP	National Archives at College Park
NCO	noncommissioned officer
NDA	National Defense Act
NDCC	National Defense Cadet Corps
NDEA	National Defense Education Act
NPS	Naval Postgraduate School
NYU	New York University
OBC	Officer Basic Course
ODCSROTC	Office of the Deputy Chief of Staff for ROTC
ORC	Officers' Reserve Corps
OSD	Office of the Secretary of Defense
PMS&T	professor of military science and training
POI	program of instruction
PPBS	Planning, Programming, and Budgeting System
PS	public school
RAI	report of army inspection
RBRC	Richard B. Russell Collection
RBRLPRS	Richard B. Russell Library for Political Research and Studies
RG	record group
ROA	Reserve Officers' Association
ROTC	Reserve Officers' Training Corps
SAI	senior army instructor
SASC	Senate Armed Services Committee
SC	subcommittee
SEC	section
SECWAR	secretary of war
SMEP	summary of major events and problems
SR	special regulation
SROTC	Senior Reserve Officers' Training Corps
STEM	science, technology, engineering, and mathematics
TA	TRADOC archives
TAG	the adjutant general
TD	Training Division
TRADOC	Training and Doctrine Command
UBBA	United Boys' Brigades of America

UGAL	University of Georgia Library
UMT	universal military training
USAAC	United States Army Accessions Command
USACC	United States Army Cadet Command
USACGSC	United States Army Command and General Staff College
USACMH	United States Army Center of Military History
USAWC	United States Army War College
USSGA	United States Spring Garden Army
VFW	Veterans of Foreign Wars
VMI	Virginia Military Institute
WCD	War College document
WDAR	*War Department Annual Report*
WPD	War Plans Division

1

Antecedents

This volume will look at the Junior Reserve Officers' Training Corps (JROTC) through the lens of the domestic engagement of the armed forces. In the past, scholars have viewed the JROTC from other perspectives—political, economic, social, and pedagogical. My history does not exclude these approaches but rather subsumes them. This work is essentially a military history, focusing on the JROTC as an arm of the defense establishment and written from the perspective of the military services.[1]

The National Defense Act (NDA) of 1916 launched the Reserve Officers' Training Corps (ROTC). It set up a two-division program, with each division targeting a distinct branch of the US educational system. The senior division (SROTC) was based in colleges and fixed on producing reserve officers for the army, while the junior division was rooted in secondary schools and had a more diffused focus.

Critics often represent the JROTC as a political and social aberration—an unwarranted and undemocratic injection of military influence into the nation's schools. As an institution established for national defense, they assert, the military has no business entangling itself in secondary education. Many military observers agree. They, too, believe that the armed forces should steer clear of such endeavors.[2] Using the services for civilian pursuits entangles them in social issues that not only are beyond their ken but hold the potential for drawing them into partisan political squabbles.

Nevertheless, the domestic use of the services has a long history in the United States. Since independence, the government has called on the military to assist the nation's economic development, promote its general welfare, ensure its internal stability, enable its westward expansion, and resolve pressing social problems.[3] The military's domestic roles have included exploration, weather forecasting, disaster relief, medical research, internal improvements, education, civil government, social welfare, counterdrug operations, air traffic control, internal order, mail delivery, traffic management, firefighting, ocean charting, topographical mapping, humanitarian aid, the administration of inland waterways, and the management of national parks. While the services have not always relished these roles, they have, for the most part, dutifully executed them.

From independence until World War II, the army was more active in domestic operations than in national defense. The lack of compelling external threats, the wide ocean barriers, the budgetary stringency, and an isolationist worldview militated against an exclusive focus on foreign foes and pushed the military into civilian roles. On occasion, there was no viable alternative to the military taking up a particular civic task. It alone had the organization, resources, and reach to accomplish what had to be done.

Historians have generally neglected the JROTC. In fact, there has been no book-length account that deals with the entirety of the program's history. The junior program has suffered neglect despite being one of the largest and most enduring domestic engagement efforts ever undertaken by the US military. At least part of this disregard stems from a general indifference toward the peacetime military in the historical community. Recent exceptions to this general trend include Brian Linn's *Real Soldiering*, which analyzes military life in the aftermath of war, Michael Neiberg's *Making Citizen Soldiers*, which investigates the origins and development of the Senior ROTC (SROTC), and Robert Wooster's, *The United States Army and the Making of America*, which chronicles the history of the army's contribution to building the nation in the eighteenth and nineteenth centuries.[4] Still, guns and boats sell books and attract attention, while accounts of soldiers during peacetime generally do neither.

My purpose in writing this book was to provide historical context for a program that has become, for better or worse, a key interface between the military establishment and society. The JROTC reaches into communities and touches segments of the population in ways that few other military programs can. This reach is, perhaps, more critical than ever, considering the nation's deep social fissures and the growing divide between the military and society.

This book will hopefully fill a void in the literature. It is not meant to be a definitive history. Rather, its aim is to broaden the lens through which the JROTC's complex evolution as an agency of the military establishment is viewed. Like most large federal bureaucracies, the program must navigate through a host of challenges and meet multiple objectives while trying to satisfy its many stakeholders. The process is necessarily fraught with opacity and ambiguity and requires a delicate balancing of goals.

This book departs from the general trend among the JROTC commentaries in that it explores the goals and purposes the military services have had for the program and the various ways they have used it. My focus is on policy and its implementation at the strategic (e.g., higher headquarters and Congress) not the tactical (e.g., schools and students) level. *Strategic*, in the sense I use it, connotes a lower level of geographic resolution and an extended time horizon, while *tactical* implies a more granular perspective and a shorter time frame.

I diverge from most students of the JROTC by framing my account in the context of military domestic engagement rather than viewing it through educational or other lenses. That said, while my focus is on military history, I cannot avoid larger societal issues since domestic engagement entails participation in a variety of essentially civil initiatives and projects. Over a span of more than a century, the JROTC has been in the forefront of the national debate about education, immigration policy, the maintenance of societal order, citizenship training, and other civil topics that intersect with national security. This has implicated the military in many controversies and troubled relationships, which is unavoidable when the services export their programs and methods to a domestic audience. It has also placed the services squarely in the middle of national debates about the sometimes strained relationship between citizenship and military service.

This work might not be of immediate value to all researchers of the JROTC. Professional educators might be disappointed because they will not get many insights into the issues with which they grapple. On the other hand, students of civil-military relations might find my account more useful since it delves into certain critical aspects of the defense establishment's interaction with society. Institutional military historians might also find it helpful, since it sheds light on a part of the defense establishment that gets relatively little attention.

COLONIAL AND ANTEBELLUM ANTECEDENTS

The tradition of school-based military training in North America stretches back to the early days of European colonization. It began with colonists providing basic military instruction in schools operating out of their homes.

Later, colonial governments became involved. During the great Narragansett War (1675–1676), the Connecticut court imposed a military training requirement on boys under sixteen years old. Other colonies adopted similar measures.[5] Life in colonial America with its omnipresent threat of conflict demanded that youth receive an early introduction to military training.[6]

While marksmanship and drill sufficed to prepare youth for service in the early colonial militias, the need for more specialized military education arose in the eighteenth century. The first type of educational institution in North America that offered instruction in the technical arms was the military subject matter school. Such schools covered subjects like fortification, gunnery, and military mathematics as a part of a regular academic curriculum.[7]

Schools with a distinct military focus began to crop up in early nineteenth-century America. Although the Military Academy at West Point (1802) was the most famous, the one founded by Captain Alden Partridge in Norwich, Vermont (1819), was the most relevant for this study. Partridge's institution—the American Scientific, Literary, and Military Academy (now Norwich University)—adopted a curriculum like West Point's, although with a wider array of courses. Partridge's cadets could study agriculture and the classics in addition to engineering and military tactics. Like other academies in antebellum America, the institute was something more than a secondary school and something less than a four-year college. Boys as young as twelve and men in their twenties could be found among its pupils.[8]

Scholars trace the philosophical roots of the ROTC back to the academy at Norwich. Its founder designed the school to promote the citizen-soldier ideal—an ideal reflecting the young nation's distrust of professional armies. Partridge, a disaffected former superintendent of the US Military Academy, envisaged his institute as a counterpoise to West Point's elitism. In his opinion, the nation's reliance on a standing army dominated by an elite, closely knit body of officers posed a threat to the republic. To avert this danger, he wanted to end the Military Academy's stranglehold on army commissions and revitalize the ineffectual state militias.[9]

This pioneer of military education considered civics or citizenship training to be a vital part of his program.[10] His emphasis on civic virtue, patriotic values, and the Constitution accorded with republican ideology and the educational orthodoxy of the day. Through such education, men like Partridge hoped to engender comity in a nation divided along ethnic and regional lines.[11] Partridge's vision of citizen-soldier education inspired both the Morrill Act of 1862, which established military training in land-grant colleges, and the NDA of 1916, which created the ROTC.[12]

After establishing Norwich, Partridge went on to found twenty-two more military schools, and his students started scores of others.[13] These institutions constituted only a fraction of the hundreds of private schools founded during the "Age of the Academies," which encompassed the years between the American Revolution and the Civil War. They flourished in an era in which the public high school was a rare phenomenon. It is difficult to determine the number of these schools because of the chaotic educational system that prevailed in antebellum America. This system, the historian Theodore Sizer noted, lacked precise boundaries: "The line between college and academy was blurred. No single articulated education ladder existed nor any clean concept of secondary education."[14]

Founders of military schools believed that military training developed valuable moral qualities and character traits, such as manliness, honor, self-control, and grace under adversity. The belief that military service engendered moral excellence and good citizenship had roots in the Anglo-Saxon fyrd and the Swiss militia system. The concept was very much alive in late eighteenth-century America, being espoused by such notables as Henry Knox, Alexander Hamilton, and George Clinton.[15]

A military format also fostered order in the classroom. The discipline it engendered induced "cheerful obedience" to and respect for the headmaster. These qualities were missing in many antebellum schools, which were plagued with brawls, riots, and rebellions. A teacher's ability to maintain order often counted for more than his mastery of subject matter.[16] Others prized military training for the beneficent effects it had on the health, vitality, and bearing of young people. According to Partridge, regular military exercises made students "healthy and vigorous," gave them a "good figure," and imparted a "manly and noble demeanor."[17]

There was considerable talk of integrating military education into common schools before the Civil War. Henry Knox, Washington's secretary of war, pushed this idea. Dismayed by militia shortcomings during the Revolution, he hoped to disseminate military skills throughout the population through school-based training. Major General Alexander Macomb, the army's commanding general; Colonel Joseph Swift, superintendent of West Point; and Representative (later president) William Henry Harrison were other proponents of this concept.

The hero of Tippecanoe was especially passionate. As governor of the Indiana Territory (1801–1813), Harrison pressed to have military training introduced in common schools. He continued to champion such training in the House of Representatives (1814–1821). As chair of the House Committee on Military Affairs, he drafted a bill (1817) calling for the introduction of military training "in every school in the United States." The proposed bill was part of Harrison's scheme to reinvigorate the nation's ill-organized militia units through classification and mandatory training.[18]

Various state governors championed drill in schools. In November 1835, South Carolina governor George McDuffie told the state legislature that military instruction should be regarded as "an essential part of the education of every citizen." Every student should devote "a portion of the time usually assigned to mere recreation, to the salutary and useful exercises of military training." This would infuse students with "sentiments of manliness and honor in every way conducive to the good order of the schools." Baltimore was one of the first large cities in the country to act on this idea. It introduced "military exercises" into its Central High School in 1852.[19]

The state of Virginia made provisions to implant military training in common schools when it established the Virginia Military Institute (VMI) in 1842. A cardinal purpose of the institute was to prepare cadets to become teachers. Subsidized graduates of VMI were obligated by law to perform for a minimum of two years "the duty of public instruction" in Virginia schools. They were to introduce a regimen like West Point's into their classrooms. Classes were to be small and arranged according to an order of merit list determined by periodic examinations. Discipline was to be enforced by a system of demerits, with punishments meted out on the basis of the number of violations accumulated. Drill was not to be neglected. The exactions of the drill master reputedly imparted the habit of "walking with an erect gait" in students and engendered the "full development" of their chests.[20]

VMI graduates taught in schools throughout the state. They brought into the classroom that "distinctive discipline which the [VMI] military system enjoined." Subsidized graduates of state-supported military academies in North Carolina, South Carolina, Alabama, and Georgia also incurred an obligation to teach in the *schools* of their respective states.[21]

Besides schools, there were other organizations in antebellum America that sponsored military drill for youth. Volunteer companies, which proliferated after the Mexican-American War, enrolled boys in their late teens, while their younger siblings joined juvenile auxiliaries. According to Marcus Cunliffe, this display of adolescent military ardor manifested the martial spirit then pervading American society.[22]

CIVIL WAR AND ITS AFTERMATH

The Civil War provided the first powerful impetus to military training in public schools. This was manifest in the North, where popular interest in school-based military instruction had hitherto been weak. At the outbreak of war, appeals for the introduction of drill appeared in periodicals throughout the region.[23] At a congressional hearing (March 1862), Senator Benjamin Wade of Ohio proudly reported that school-based units were proliferating "all over the country." His distrust of West Point kindled Wade's zeal for this training. He, like other Radical Republicans, regarded the academy as too aristocratic and expensive and wanted it replaced with more democratic institutions.[24]

Bangor, Maine, was one of the first Northern cities to adopt cadet training for its public school (December 2, 1861).[25] But it was in Massachusetts that such training gained the firmest hold. In 1863, a Brookline school began offering drill to all boys above ten years of age. In that same year, the Boston school board inserted "military gymnastics and drill [into its] public schools." Instruction began on a trial basis in all Boston high schools and grammar schools. Although training in grammar schools was dropped after a year, it continued in high schools and became a hallmark of the city's educational system.[26] In January 1864, a special committee of the Massachusetts Board of Education, impressed with Boston's results, urged that cadet training be expanded throughout the state.[27]

The Massachusetts cadet movement drew inspiration from the Swiss experience. In Switzerland, the training of school-age youth had a long history, stretching back to at least the sixteenth century. By the mid-1800s, drill was a part of the school routine in most Swiss cities and was compulsory for all able-bodied students between the ages of eleven and nineteen. It supposedly ensured domestic tranquility, buttressed national defense, and united the heterogeneous Swiss cantons into "one band of brothers." It also physically transformed boys, "making . . . their carriage erect, their bodies strong, their chests large, [and] their cheeks rosy."[28]

The experiment in Boston attracted national attention. The city soon gained a reputation for being the epicenter of school-based military training in the North. During both the Civil War and postbellum years, Boston authorities received countless letters from communities across the country inquiring about the city's military program.[29]

New Jersey also sponsored cadet programs. In 1862, it introduced military instruction at the state normal school, with the expectation that this would lead to the dissemination of military training to the state's public schools. It also subsidized the Eaglewood Collegiate and Military School, a private institute founded by one of Partridge's pupils (1861). Neighboring New York State was even more ambitious and drafted a plan to extend military instruction down to the elementary level.[30]

After the Civil War, cadet training slowly but steadily spread. Prussia's victory over France in the Franco-Prussian War of 1870 stimulated school-based drill. The Prussian combination of compulsory military service with a system of national education inspired admiration in the United States. While conscription was not a realistic option for the United States, similar results, it was believed, could be achieved by integrating drill into common schools. Henry Barnard, the US commissioner of education, thought so. In his nine-hundred-page tome on military education (1872), Barnard called for every public school in the nation to embrace military training.[31]

Veterans of the Civil War played a key part in the spread of military programs. Their expertise and prestige fueled public interest in cadet training. At Gloucester High School in Massachusetts, the principal, Albert W. Bacheler, who had served with distinction in the Civil War, organized a unit. In his school, teachers volunteered to become drill instructors, parents purchased uniforms, and funds raised by public subscription furnished rifles.[32]

The units that took root in the nation's capital were unusually robust. In 1882, George Manuel, a veteran and teacher at Central High School, founded the Washington High School Cadets, which consisted of students from the city's White high schools. Manuel's cadet corps came to public notice in May 1883 when it took part in a parade organized by the Grand Army of the Republic (GAR). Soon thereafter, the unit gained the backing of the War Department, which provided rifles for drill and marksmanship training. Congress officially recognized the corps in 1889. By the early 1890s, the Washington battalion had a membership of four hundred cadets and a National Guard officer as chief instructor.[33]

Black schools in Washington, DC, initiated military programs in the early 1890s. Minor Normal School was the first, forming its unit in 1893.

Another African American institution, Dunbar High School, introduced drill shortly afterward. Dunbar produced the first African American general in the US Army—Benjamin O. Davis Sr.[34]

Since most cadet corps were not administered by federal or state authorities, little documentation about them has survived. The rise of these units seems to have paralleled that of the public high school, whose enrollment more than doubled between 1870 and 1890. Enrollment in military programs grew pari passu.[35]

The postbellum years saw the creation of scores of private military schools. Sixty-five of these private institutes had a religious affiliation. The Episcopal, Presbyterian, Methodist, Baptist, Roman Catholic, Congregational, Mormon, Moravian, and Lutheran Churches all established military programs. Preparation for military service was not the purpose of these institutions. Few of their graduates entered the army. Rather, schools used military training to build character and enhance moral development.[36]

Some have linked the proliferation of denominational military institutes to the cult of Muscular Christianity. This cult, which promoted good health, vigor, and manliness, fed on fears that societal changes were eroding the nation's moral underpinnings and the masculinity of its young men. Urbanization, enervating office work, and waves of new immigrants were seemingly undermining traditional values and Anglo-Saxon ascendency. Politicians like Theodore Roosevelt and prominent clergymen like Josiah Strong urged Americans of northern European stock to "revitalize themselves by embracing a strenuous lifestyle replete with athleticism and aggressive male behavior."[37]

The character education movement was another enabler of military institutes. That movement drew strength from the growth of an industrial economy and the emergence of the corporation as the preferred business organization. These developments called for new approaches to education—approaches that emphasized teamwork and obedience. The ethos of rugged individualism seemed less relevant in a world dominated by large business conglomerates. With its emphasis on the subordination of the individual to the group, military training meshed well with the goals of character educators.[38]

Still others tie the ascent of military schools to the closing of the frontier. The frontier's demise represented an emblematic end to the "dream of endless space for manly self-assertion." Young men could no longer look to the West as a place to test their manhood. Military training offered a surrogate for the frontier experience.[39]

A military regimen appealed to the proprietors of military institutes because it fostered order in the classroom and facilitated control by the staff. With a military commandant responsible for conduct and discipline, a well-defined chain of command, and a system of rewards and punishments in place, teachers escaped many of their traditional disciplinary responsibilities. Some military institutes, however, elevated drill and discipline to such high importance that they overshadowed academics. These schools acquired the unenviable reputation of being for refractory adolescents.[40]

Military institutes received a boon in 1888 when Congress passed legislation granting them equipment and supplies, and authorizing the assignment of military officers to their faculties. This congressional largess gave military institutes a legitimacy they had heretofore lacked. In return, Congress required military institutes to maintain an enrollment of one hundred pupils over fifteen years of age and to devote three hours a week to military instruction.[41]

While assisting military schools, Congress refused to support cadet training in public high schools. It considered the costs prohibitive. Between 1887 and 1898, more than fifteen bills were introduced calling for the detailing of more officers to educational institutions. The three that affected colleges sailed through Congress with little opposition, while the eight that targeted public high schools foundered. Only one of the latter received serious consideration.[42]

The absence of congressional sanction did not deter two junior officers from forming a cadet unit in Omaha's public schools. Lieutenants Julius A. Penn and Harry Clement, stationed at nearby Fort Crook, founded the Omaha High School Cadets. Their combined tenure began in 1893 when they received the consent of the War Department to undertake the project. By 1897, the battalion enrolled 248 students. Instruction included setting up exercises, squad and company drills, lectures, and parades. The Omaha battalion limited drill to two hours per week, thus limiting academic conflicts and greatly pleasing local educators.[43]

School authorities credited drill with improving student deportment and lauded it as a valuable curricular supplement. They thought so highly of the program that they made it compulsory for all boys. The army also found much to admire. Inspectors marveled at the battalion's vibrancy even though it received neither arms nor equipment.[44]

The Omaha example invigorated the War Department's interest in high school training. As things stood, colleges with small military enrollments absorbed a large portion of a restricted supply of officers. If those officers served large urban high schools, the army would reap a greater return on its investment. In 1893, the army's adjutant general, Major General George Ruggles, proposed that officers be withdrawn from colleges with small military enrollments and assigned to large high schools, where "military instructors would be appreciated."[45] In 1894, Major General J. M. Schofield, the army's commanding general, urged that officers be assigned to normal schools and large metropolitan high schools. This would enable a volunteer force to be molded into "a reliable army in the shortest possible time" and justify an increase in the officer corps. Communities were as enthusiastic about cadet training as the army's leaders. They flooded the War Department with petitions asking that officers be detailed to their schools. When the army ruefully rejected these requests, many schools turned to the militia for instructors.[46]

New York City was a hotbed of cadet training at the end of the century. Its keenness for drill was evidenced at the centennial celebration of George Washington's inauguration in 1889. A marching unit of four thousand boys drawn from the city's schools was a prime attraction at the great industrial parade, the culminating event of the celebration. The unit's precision elicited "storms of applause" from onlookers. Its superb performance was attributed to the city's grammar school principals, most notably Robert Boyer, a noted advocate of military drill and one of the original architects of the cadet organization known as the American Guard.[47]

AMERICAN GUARD, BOYS' BRIGADES, AND NATIONALISTIC 1890S

In the 1890s, school-based military training floated on a wave of popular excitement, enjoying a "considerable vogue." This irritated the editor of the *Journal of Commerce*, who inveighed against the "remarkable fashion of hanging the flag over every schoolhouse and of giving boys military drill."[48] Two organizations, in particular, harnessed this enthusiasm. Of these, the GAR had the greatest reach and influence.

In 1893, the GAR launched its first American Guard unit in New York City. The unit drew from the city's grammar schools and adopted the West Point system of training. The city's board of education warmly supported the initiative. It created a military advisory council and invited the principals of grammar schools, commanders of GAR posts, and military officers stationed nearby to join. The response was electric, and the city soon became the center of the *American Guard* movement.[49]

In August 1893, the GAR's Lafayette Post, in New York City, called for the expansion of military training across the country "by all means possible."[50] Before long, "a favorable public sentiment" was aloft, propelling the cause of cadet training rapidly forward. In fact, the movement soon outgrew "the most sanguine hopes of its early promoters" and became an "important factor in American life." To direct this effort, the GAR created a special bureau in its headquarters.[51]

Influential GAR spokesmen like former president Benjamin Harrison touted the benefits that would accrue to the nation and individual students through such programs. Military drill, Harrison declared, developed "the whole man, head, chest, arms and legs . . . and [qualified] a man to serve his country."[52] Popular periodicals backed the GAR's crusade. Prominent among them were the *Century Magazine* and the *New York Tribune*, whose editor was a member of the GAR's Lafayette Post. Drill, the *Tribune* told its readers, developed the physique, sharpened the intellect, and strengthened the character of the young.[53]

In January 1895, the Lafayette Post hosted a conference for state governors. The goal was program expansion. The conference crystallized the American Guard movement into a concerted nationwide effort. Hundreds of local groups began lobbying state legislatures on behalf of cadet training. Units soon appeared throughout the country. New England led the way, with New Hampshire, Connecticut, Rhode Island, and Massachusetts being particularly active. In the west, Arizona and Colorado were the most ardent participants in the movement. The former made military training mandatory in all public schools in 1895.[54]

The GAR was not alone. Organizations hosting cadet corps proliferated in the late nineteenth century, with churches, YMCAs, juvenile reformatories, temperance societies, and other groups creating programs.[55] Of these organizations, the Boys' Brigades was perhaps the largest. Its founder was William Alexander Smith, an officer in the Volunteers and a Presbyterian Sunday school teacher in Glasgow. By combining drill, discipline, and uniforms with evangelism, Smith hoped to make church membership more attractive to young men. His program included social activities, physical exercise, and summer camps. Smith's model caught on and spread to Canada, Australia, the United States, and other countries.[56]

Smith's movement arrived in the United States in the late 1880s. A Presbyterian minister in San Francisco, John Quincy Adams, was the first to form a unit in his church (1889). The Boys' Brigades quickly spread across the country. In 1894, Protestant clergymen in Chicago founded the United Boys' Brigades of America (UBBA), which became a magnet for church-affiliated drill units. Not all churches joined this coalition. The Methodists (the Epworth Guards) and Roman Catholics maintained independent programs. The UBBA soon departed from the British model and militarized its program. It featured parades, inspections, drill competitions, and field exercises. Unlike the British, the Americans instituted an adult chain of command with colonels "commanding" at the local level, major generals at the state level, and a commanding general at the national level.

The Boys' Brigades achieved considerable, if transitory, success. By 1896, it reportedly had between twelve thousand and fifteen thousand members. It was not free from internal tension, though. David MacLeod estimates that about one-third of the Brigades' adult officers were guardsmen. Some churchmen suspected that these guardsmen were more interested in recruiting for the militia than they were in raising church membership. These churchmen consequently held the Boys Brigades at arm's length.[57]

Labor strife generated support for cadet training. Antilabor bias was evident in both the American Guard and the Boys' Brigades. Episodes like the Haymarket Affair and the Homestead Strike convinced conservatives that "national discipline" was lacking. A root cause of this upheaval was a severe economic depression. Triggered by the Panic of 1893, this four-year downturn brought economic and political turmoil in its wake. To inculcate discipline into the future workforce, the GAR resolved that "military instruction be made part of the common school system." It warned of the "increasing unrest between capital and labor" and offered military training "as a solvent in the enforcement of law and order."[58]

A heightened nationalism was another impulse behind military training. Industrial growth, the demand for new markets, the closing of the frontier, the race for empire, and the missionary impulse ignited a "jingoistic frenzy." At the end of the decade, the martial enthusiasm engendered by the Spanish-American War drove participation in cadet corps to a pre–World War I high. Marcus Cunliffe noted that passion for adolescent military training peaked when "war was a future possibility" or "a recent memory." The historical record seems to bear him out.[59]

Changes in the nation's educational system facilitated the growth of cadet training. Urban schools introduced graded classrooms in the mid-nineteenth century. Based on the industrial model, this system promoted an entire age cohort to the next higher grade at the same time. By the 1890s, age mixing in the classroom was the exception rather than the rule. The period of education lengthened as the growth of industrial employment created a need for the training and socialization provided in high school. Education became a screening device to manage the flow of workers into the workforce and equip them with the skills, habits, and attitudes necessary for industrial efficiency.[60] Military training aligned nicely with this development.

The citizen-soldier ideology likewise generated support for high school military training. Proponents of this ideology sought to bolster military preparedness while avoiding the danger and expense of militarism. The problem facing the nation, wrote a *New York Tribune* correspondent, was "how to become a people of military knowledge, prepared for emergencies, without being a nation in arms." The "most obvious solution" was "to begin with the children and give them at a receptive age such military training as will enable them to become good soldiers in later life."[61]

The GAR delivered a similar message: "It is contrary to the spirit of our republican institutions to maintain large standing armies. We look to the people for defense; and to make them quickly effective as soldiers, they must have military training . . . universal service is entirely out of the question with us. By causing military instruction to be given . . . in the schools, nothing is taken from the productive energies of the country."[62]

Cadet training did not go unchallenged. Peace and religious organizations strenuously opposed it. Alfred Love's Universal Peace Union denounced the GAR's campaign as "harmful, unchristian, and unnecessary." Labor leaders feared that it would "create an army" that would "threaten the liberties of the masses." Populists inveighed against the autocratic nature of cadet units.[63]

Well-known writers and intellectuals joined the protest. Felix Adler, William Dean Howells, and Henry George railed against a bill introduced in the New York legislature that sanctioned drill in public schools.[64] "The attempt to encourage in America the growth of the spirit of militarism which has done so much to hamper the civilization and prosperity of Europe," they asserted, was "a menace to true freedom."[65] Benjamin Trueblood, editor of the *Century Magazine*, claimed that drill was "entirely out of harmony with the purpose of the schools" and would "keep alive that excessive admiration of the soldier

TABLE 1
Distribution of Military Units in Public High Schools, 1894

Region	State	No. of Schools
Northeast	CT(2); ME(1); MA(11); NJ(1); NY(6); PA(3); RI(1)	25
Midwest	IL(2); KS(1); MI(1); MN(2); MO(2); NE(1); OH(4); WI(1)	14
South	DC(1); KY(1); LA(1)	3
West	CA(3); CO (1)	4

ideal which has been anything but a blessing to mankind."[66] The opponents of military training enjoyed some success. Their protests reportedly helped foil attempts to introduce units in Philadelphia and Providence, for example.[67] Still, it was clear that promoters of high school training had the upper hand.

Geographically, the footprint of cadet training began to change in the late nineteenth century. In the early 1890s, high school military units clustered in the Northeast, the region with the highest density of schools, students, and youth organizations (see table 1). That region hosted more than half of all military programs, with Massachusetts leading the way. The GAR's push to infiltrate public schools in the South was initially ineffectual. The legislatures of financially strapped southern states opposed projects that called for increased taxation. The GAR was not popular there in any case. Confederate veterans, incensed over GAR textbooks that painted Southerners as traitors, refused to cooperate.[68]

By the turn of the century, military training had mushroomed (see table 2) and made inroads even in southern public schools. Chancellor H. M. MacCracken of New York University noted the vibrancy of cadet training in South Carolina. While only 5 percent of the state's high schools offered drill, almost 30 percent of its male students participated in it—a rate exceeding that of Massachusetts. Half a decade earlier (1894), no public high school in that state hosted a cadet corps.[69]

At mid-decade, the GAR began to lobby Congress to create a national framework for cadet training in secondary schools. Bills advocating such training appeared on almost an annual basis. Opponents argued that federal support should be restricted to colleges, where military training was more "worth-while." There were "other things . . . children could learn in the public schools that would be more beneficial to them than military tactics."[70]

TABLE 2
Military Enrollment in High Schools, 1895–1900

Year	Enrollment	Public Schools	Private Schools
1895	12,049	5,812	6,237
1896	15,545	8,274	7,271
1897	15,309	8,661	6,648
1898	16,886	9,032	7,854
1899	18,855	10,396	8,459
1900	19,355	10,455	8,900

Marvin Kreidberg, *History of Military Mobilization in the US Army, 1775–1945* (Westport, CT: Greenwood, 1975), 211.

The most momentous motion put forward was the Carter Bill, introduced in the Senate in 1895 and 1897. It called for the creation of a uniform structure of high school military education encompassing the whole nation and the formation of a central federal bureau to monitor that system. It prefigured the creation of the ROTC. But the time was not ripe. This measure got no further than a favorable committee report.[71]

Agitation for cadet training reached a peak at the turn of the century. Drawing from nationalist fervor unleashed by the Spanish-American War and Europe's "embittered and outraged" response to escalating US tariffs, advocates redoubled their push for school-based military instruction. The GAR pressed Congress to act.[72] This time, Congress responded. It passed a law in 1901 that sanctioned the detail of retired officers to secondary schools. Another bill, passed in 1904, raised the limit on the number of retired officers authorized for detail.[73]

CADET TRAINING IN THE DOLDRUMS

These victories for cadet training might have produced notable results under more auspicious conditions. Such conditions did not exist in the first decade of the new century. After the victory over Spain, public enthusiasm for military training waned as nationalist ardor subsided, and social tension eased. The emergence of organizational rivals, like the Boy Scouts of America (1911), also drew boys away from cadet corps. In addition, there were several "tactical" reasons for the weakening of the cadet movement: the opposition of peace organizations, the requirement for boys to buy their own uniforms, the lack of pay for instructors, and a shortage of space for training. These factors did not stymie the movement in the jingoistic 1890s but loomed large in the less bellicose first decade of the new century.[74]

Cadet enrollment declined after the war. In absolute terms, that drop was moderate. But it occurred during a decade in which male enrollment in high schools more than doubled. Thus, in 1900, seventy-one of every thousand students attended military drill; by 1914, only twenty-eight of one thousand did. The number of public schools with military programs also fell—from 103 in 1906 to 82 in 1914. The early twentieth century witnessed the decay of the UBBA, which entered a period of stagnation in 1900 and of precipitous decline after 1909. Originally, the UBBA had accepted boys between twelve and eighteen years of age. Finding it hard to keep older boys in the program, it lowered the age limit to ten in 1912. This failed to revive the Brigades. Thereafter, the UBBA gradually disappeared from public view.[75]

Cadet training did not fall out of favor everywhere. It thrived in many high schools in California and Wyoming and in cities like Fort Worth, Omaha, Richmond, Salt Lake City, and Hartford.[76] Nevertheless, it was clear that the appetite for drill was diminishing.[77]

During this era, schools secured instructors from a variety of sources. They were eligible to have a retired army officer, although the possibility of that occurring was remote. Under the 1904 law, the War Department could detail one hundred officers to colleges and high schools. With this limitation, even the most populous states received only a handful of instructors. Priority went first to colleges and then to military schools. This left none for civilian high schools.[78]

Public schools that wanted retired or noncommissioned officers (NCOs) to staff their units had to find them on their own. Schools fortunate enough to get retirees were expected to pay them the difference between their active-duty salary and their retired pay. Schools unable to find retirees turned to the militia. As early as 1894, the War Department characterized the militia's involvement in high schools as "considerable." When militiamen weren't available, schools gave the job to their physical education director or another teacher.[79]

Even military institutes struggled to find qualified instructors. When the Baptist-affiliated Fork Union Academy became "essentially military in nature" in 1902, it appointed a reluctant Leslie Harvey Walton as commandant of cadets. "Major" Walton, a diminutive Baptist minister and language instructor, tried to turn down the position, protesting that he had no military experience or knowledge of military affairs. His pleas were fruitless. Reverend Walton spent the summer of 1902 in camp, trying to absorb as much knowledge as he could. Upon his return to campus, he set up a cadet battalion and military training program. Walton served as commandant until 1904, when he was replaced by an officer from the War Department.[80]

The military utility of cadet training had long been an open question. It remained so during this era. Many acknowledged its limitations. In his study of military education (1914), Captain Ira Reeves concluded that while such training benefited cadets, its value to the army was questionable. It certainly did not produce men capable of leading volunteer troops in war.[81]

Reeves's assessment struck a responsive chord within the army. Elihu Root, the secretary of war (1899–1904), was dismayed by the deficiencies revealed in the war with Spain. He set out to transform the army into *something* more than an America Indian–fighting constabulary by championing measures to enhance efficiency and professionalism. Now a world power, the nation needed a modern army capable of protecting its wide-ranging interests.[82] Root took Colonel Emory Upton's ideas as his guide for reorganization. Entranced with the Prussian military model, Upton wanted to build the country's defense system around a powerful and expansible regular force. He had little use for the unreliable levies of partially trained citizen-soldiers that the nation had relied on in the past. With the Uptonian model in the ascendant, the atmosphere was not propitious for cadet training. The image of cadet corps, quintessential expressions of the citizen-soldier ideal, clashed with the officer corps' growing sense of professionalism. Many officers recoiled at the amateurish nature of cadet training and the pretensions of cadets.[83]

PLATTSBURG, LEONARD WOOD, AND THE CREATION OF THE JROTC

The cause of cadet training revived after 1914. The war in Europe, the sinking of the *Lusitania*, and other incidents sparked an expansion of military programs that dwarfed all previous ones. Patriotic fervor combined with concern about the parlous state of the nation's defenses to galvanize state legislatures, municipal governments, and private citizens into action. It also energized the "preparedness movement" and the campaign to introduce universal military training. The most spectacular gains in high school training occurred between 1916 and 1918, when the number of public school units skyrocketed from 224 to 1,276, and enrollment increased from 25,000 to over 112,000 (15 percent of high school boys). Other quasi-military youth organizations—like the Boy Scouts, Junior Naval League, and US Spring Garden Army (USSGA)—saw their ranks swelled by the war.[84]

Various states initiated cadet training programs. In early 1916, the New York State Legislature passed a law, the Slater Bill, making drill compulsory for all male students between sixteen and nineteen years of age. At least seven other states—Arizona, Indiana, Louisiana, Michigan, New Hampshire, Oklahoma, and Oregon—made similar arrangements.[85] Not all states were as enthusiastic. State governments in New Jersey, Pennsylvania, and Massachusetts adjudged school-based military drill to have little training or recruiting value and provided it little encouragement.[86] Still, throughout most of the country, military programs thrived.[87]

The prototype for military programs came from Wyoming. In 1915, that state adopted a system of voluntary drill that attracted national attention. The architect of this system was Lieutenant Edgar Z. Steever, himself a product of the Washington, DC, cadet corps. At the time, he was an inspector-instructor for the Organized Militia of Wyoming. Steever had introduced his scheme into an existing unit at Cheyenne High School in 1911. He later convinced the state legislature to appropriate money to buy uniforms and create units across the state. At its peak, his organization enrolled about 90 percent of the state's high school boys. Steever's model elicited great interest. In September 1915 alone, Steever received 150 inquiries "from all parts of the country." His system soon spread. Cities as far away as Philadelphia, Chicago, and Louisville copied it.[88]

The Wyoming Plan embraced a conservative brand of citizenship education. Steever wanted to develop citizens who understood the value of national defense and were cognizant of the obligations of citizenship. He stressed that his program was not geared toward military service. True, Steever taught tactical skills. Drill, map reading, patrolling, scouting, woodcraft, and physical exercise were part of his program. So were summer camps. Steever insisted, however, that such training was not an end in itself but a device that enriched the regular academic curriculum, advanced the goals of educational leaders, and molded students into better citizens. By taking this tack, Steever overcame the opposition of parents, teachers, women's clubs, and labor unions and entrenched his program in Wyoming's system of public education.[89]

A distinguishing feature of the Wyoming Plan was its emphasis on athletic and academic competitions. Units were organized into teams, which competed in a variety of contests. Wall scaling was the preferred sport. Rifle matches were also popular. Academic competitions, conducted like spelling bees, encouraged students to hone their mastery of history, geography, and other subjects. Results were posted on bulletin boards, and winners received medals and certificates.[90]

Steever's stress on athletic competition reflected a wider national push for physical fitness. This drive, Garrett Gatzemeyer observes, involved more than building strength and stamina. It also aimed to develop young men in a more holistic way—making them more disciplined, resilient, morally upright, and assertive. Concerns about "overcivilized" men and the erosion of masculinity fed this enthusiasm for physical exercise. Military leaders introduced the instruments and ideology of martial physical training used in the army into schools, paramilitary programs, and summer camps. Not only did this make young men more masculine and productive, but it also prepared them for the rigors of modern war.[91]

Admirers praised the Wyoming Plan for its wondrous effects on students and schools. Reportedly, it made boys responsive to teachers, reduced truancy to negligible proportions, lowered the dropout rate, prevented juvenile delinquency, and discouraged teenage smoking.[92] The Wyoming experiment adumbrated many features of the modern JROTC. It downplayed the program's military aspects, emphasized citizenship training, and flaunted the program's ability to allay social and educational ills.[93]

Steever's foray into cadet training came at an opportune time. Military leaders were looking to harness the potential of schools to ready the nation for its entry into the European war. General Hugh Scott, the chief of staff of the army (CSA), believed Steever's system could facilitate this. "There is every reason," he declared, "why the 'Wyoming Plan' should be taken up by every high school in the nation."[94]

An article appearing in *Everybody's Magazine* (February 1916) ignited public interest in the Wyoming model. The article, titled "Wyoming's Answer to Militarism," extolled Steever's system and the remarkable effects it had on students. The author was George Creel, who would soon join the Committee on Public Information and become the country's chief propagandist during the war.[95]

Creel's article elicited a flood of commendatory letters from the magazine's readership. Impressed by this response, the magazine's editor, Howard Wheeler, developed a plan to expand the cadet movement. This resulted in the creation of the High School Volunteers of the United States (HSVUS). Wheeler provided office space for the new program in the magazine's New York headquarters. To launch the enterprise, Wheeler secured the endorsement of prominent public figures such as the secretary of war, Newton D. Baker, and the secretary of the interior, Frank K. Lane. Wheeler engaged Steever to write the program's manual.[96]

The HSVUS leaders implored the army to assign Steever to lead the effort. The army acceded to this request and assigned Steever to the Central Department, which encompassed several midwestern states, in December 1916. With the help of the four handpicked officers and sixteen NCOs, Steever implanted his "Wyoming System" in Chicago, Kansas City, Saint Louis, and "other centers."[97]

Steever set up his headquarters at the Culver Military Academy in Indiana. He convened a conference of educators to promote his model in January 1917. Representatives from seven states and twenty-three cities attended. Attendees left the confab committed to the project. Units soon sprang up throughout the region. Enthusiasm was greatest in the Chicago area, where Steever organized drill competitions in which hundreds of students took part. The popularity of his program among immigrants gratified Steever. He claimed that drill helped these students assimilate into American society.[98] When the war pulled Steever away in the spring of 1917, private organizations continued his work. By 1918, about one-third of the 112,000 cadets taking military training belonged to the HSVUS.[99]

Training took on a more military aspect during the war. Grenade throwing, bayonet drill, and tactical exercises replaced the wall scaling and academic competition favored by Steever. This more militaristic focus bothered the editors of *Everybody's Magazine*, who wanted to keep the emphasis on citizenship instruction. Local authorities, however, generally ignored them. Caught up in martial passion, they crafted their programs to imitate the training offered in army camps.[100]

It was within a context of growing public support for preparedness, expanding federal power, and the nation's emergence as a world power that the JROTC came into being.[101] Many military leaders and educators wanted to build on the inchoate training apparatus in colleges and secondary schools to fashion a national system of mobilization and defense. General Leonard Wood and secretary of war Henry L. Stimson were of this mind. By taking the existing system, upgrading instruction, adding summer camps, and requiring short tours of active duty for graduates, they believed, the nation's mobilization needs could be met. Their scheme appeared in a document titled *Organization of the Land Forces of the United States*, published as part of the War Department's annual report for 1912. High schools were included in their plans because they wanted to make commissions available to youths unable to attend college and spread military knowledge widely among the population. At the same time, the General Staff began to consult with schools and colleges to devise a reliable means to train reserve officers. As it was, schools had their own unique systems, which prevented most of them from securing commissions in the National Guard for their graduates. Soldiers and civilian educators agreed that the lack of standardization "was one of the greatest defects in the nation's military system."[102]

The army took the first tentative steps toward standardization when, in the summer of 1913, it conducted two experimental camps for college students. The training lasted six weeks and encompassed drill, marksmanship, field fortification, and other combat skills. Four camps were held in 1914. In 1915, feeding off the fervor generated by the sinking of the *Lusitania*, the army set up a camp in Plattsburg, New York, for an expanded audience. Instead of restricting participation to men between seventeen and thirty years old, it threw open the training to business and professional men and extended the maximum age to forty. This camp ignited a national crusade, which became known as the Plattsburg movement. Participation exploded in 1916, when sixteen thousand men attended training.[103]

Educators sought to garner the benefits of military camps for younger pupils. Starting in 1916, camps for boys between the ages of fourteen and seventeen sprang up across the nation. These boys' military training camps resembled those for older men and featured drill, trench digging, and guard duty, among other things. These Junior Plattsburghs, as they were called, were popular with the headmasters of elite preparatory schools, such as Groton, Saint Paul, Exeter, and Phillips Academy, who believed that the austerity and discipline of camp life mirrored the character-building regimen of their institutions.[104]

While Wood focused on summer camps, leaders from Ohio State University, led by President William O. Thompson and Dean Edward Orton Jr., elaborated an on-campus model of military education, which they presented at the 1913 annual convention of land-grant colleges. Orton, a reserve officer, proposed legislation setting minimum national standards for collegiate military training. Students completing this training, he recommended, should be commissioned as reserve officers and assigned to a reserve officer corps. Orton and Thompson's program benefited from the emerging consensus among college and military school presidents that the government was "not making all the use [it] could and should" of educational institutions "as military instruction centers."[105]

In 1915, the secretary of war, Lindley Garrison, crafted a proposal that rooted reserve officer training firmly in the US educational system. His design provided for a senior division, based in colleges, and a junior division, encompassing secondary institutions. Besides producing officers, his training corps would create a manpower pool that could fill the enlisted ranks of a mobilizing army. Leonard Wood enthusiastically supported Garrison. In his mind, Garrison's proposal offered a convenient and politically acceptable way to provide military training to a large number of young men in peacetime. Teaching basic military skills in school, Wood argued, would "greatly [reduce] the time required for the final intensive period of training" after a call to arms. Wood believed men who completed such training could be fashioned into effective soldiers in only three months.[106]

School-based training would also improve recruiting, Wood believed, by instilling in young men "a respect for the uniform and an appreciation of the importance of a soldier's duty." It could even serve as an attenuated form of national military service without inciting public opposition. Students would undergo training in school and not in the repressive atmosphere of the barracks or camp. The worries of labor unions, women's clubs, church groups, peace organizations, and parents would be allayed. The improvement of students' physiques, deportment, and discipline, "at home as well as in school," would turn skeptical parents into avid backers of military training.[107]

Wood viewed high school training as especially apposite for the United States. Such training used available "means and opportunities" to the best advantage while interfering "as little as possible with the educational and industrial careers of those affected."[108] Wood held up the Swiss and Australian models as examples to be emulated. Both systems, although differing in detail, taught basic military skills to teenage boys and conveyed social benefits. These extramilitary advantages generally fell under the label of civic socialization—fostering good citizenship, national cohesiveness, economic efficiency, and political stability.[109] Wood believed that civic socialization was particularly useful for the assimilation of immigrants. New arrivals were unfamiliar with American customs and ignorant of what responsible citizenship entailed. Military training would impart appropriate political and social attitudes to immigrants and fuse them "into one common mass of Americanism."[110]

This civic socialization role of military training figured prominently in the congressional debate on the NDA of 1916. Days before the passage of the act, one senator asserted that the primary purpose of the proposed officer reserve corps was to inculcate "high ideals and correct views on the duties of the citizen to the State." Although the training was military in content, the program would "encourage initiative and individuality, to correct defects and develop natural gifts, and to teach self-control by showing the value of obedience to superior authority." Those who learned to obey were preparing themselves to lead and "by practicing self-control [would] become imbued with the fundamental principle underlying good citizenship." Wilson's new secretary of war, Newton Baker, agreed. The former mayor of Cleveland also saw military training as an incubator of discipline and civic virtue.[111]

The War Department prized high school military training as a means to spread the gospel of preparedness. It was vital that the "peaceful and unmilitary" American people, who were but "dimly aware" of the nation's military needs, understood that the army was not a luxury but a public necessity. Through school-based training, thousands of young people would be exposed to the opinions of military officers, provided with a military perspective on national and world affairs, and given an appreciation of the army and its needs. It was critical that children of the volatile working classes received this training since it was the only practical way to instill proper political beliefs in potentially fractious elements of the population. As one officer put it, "There is no more effective way of arousing . . . support for the country's military than by enabling boys of the less privileged classes" to enroll in cadet corps.[112]

The NDA of 1916 (June 3) contained measures to shore up US defenses and create a force capable of rapid expansion; it increased the Regular Army, federalized and expanded the National Guard, doubled enrollment at West Point, and created a reserve corps. This corps was to be filled with discharged enlisted troops and officers produced through an ROTC. ROTC graduates were to be assigned to an Officers' Reserve Corps (ORC), where they could be pooled and regulated during peacetime.[113]

The new ROTC had a junior and a senior division. The senior division encompassed colleges, universities, and select military schools. The junior division included all other public and private institutions. Civilian high schools and "essentially military" secondary schools were assigned to this latter division.[114]

Civilian schools hosting units had to offer at least three hours of military instruction per week for three years, which normally meant grades ten through twelve. Military schools offered four years of instruction. Any JROTC graduate who completed a four-year course equating to that prescribed for the SROTC (four years) could receive a certificate of eligibility for a reserve commission to be honored at age twenty-one.[115] Only military schools offered such a curriculum. Consequently, only cadets from military schools could earn commissions.

The JROTC's agenda had appeared earlier in the epochal *Statement of a Proper Military Policy for the United States* (1915), prepared by the General Staff.[116] This statement outlined a plan for military training in public schools that stressed the military *and* civic education of youth. It praised Steever's system for imparting military skills that would expedite the mobilization of men in a national emergency and for educating "the young as to their future duties as citizens." The discipline and teamwork acquired from training would build better citizens, better workers, better family men, and a better, more cohesive nation. The document reflected the conservative progressive ideology then prevalent among military officers.[117]

Once the United States entered the war, there were few resources to spare for the JROTC. Between June 1916 and November 1918, the army established junior units at only thirty schools. It lacked the manpower to do more. Leavenworth High School in Kansas was the lone public high school to host a JROTC unit before the armistice. Even that unit was short-lived. The army created it on January 19, 1917, and disbanded it on October 10, 1917. War Department policy restricted the JROTC to military schools. The department's dissolution letter simply stated, "The World War and other emergencies pertaining to the Army necessitate the withdrawal of the detailed officers from high schools." Military training at the school continued under the auspices of the HSVUS for the remainder of the war.[118]

It was not until the waning months of the war that the army's interest in cadet training began to revive. In the summer of 1918, the War Department created a Committee on Education and Special Training to strengthen its articulation with the educational community. Initially, the committee concentrated on postsecondary institutions and vocational training. Before long, it extended its scope to high schools. The army created a Secondary School Division to improve the training given through the HSVUS and independent programs. Although it could not detail regular officers to units, it arranged for officers from the Canadian Army to serve as instructors and encouraged units to engage officers from Student Army Training Corps detachments on a part-time basis.[119]

Planning for the postwar expansion of the JROTC began during the final months of 1918. War Department leaders saw the JROTC as a means to engender public support for the army, stimulate recruiting, and address other issues affecting America's security. Accordingly, in the winter of 1918–1919, the army began to implant ROTC units in colleges and high schools.[120] By June 1919, military programs were operating in 191 colleges and 128 secondary schools. Nearly forty-five thousand secondary school students in forty-six cities were receiving instruction.[121]

The antecedents of the JROTC stretch back to the colonial era, when young men were expected to contribute to the defense of the community. This tradition was bolstered by republican and citizen-soldier ideologies, which closely intertwined military service, civic obligation, and republican principles. It was further strengthened by educationalists, who valued military training for the order it brought to the classroom and its utility in developing character, physical prowess, and republican virtues in students.

The Civil War gave a powerful impetus to high school military training in the North. At the outbreak of war, units began springing up throughout the region. The movement was strongest in New England, the region with the most developed and extensive public school system.

The 1890s saw another spurt of growth. The debate surrounding cadet units in this decade reflected competing visions of national defense and citizenship. Issues such as industrialization, urbanization, immigration, and imperial expansion were all bound up in this debate. So, too, was the question of what form of democracy should prevail in the United States: Was it one emphasizing social control and safeguarding property or one aiming at maximizing individual liberty and popular participation in government? The military's involvement in these issues reflected the growing power of the federal government and the expanding role of the War Department in the formulation of social policy. This was a role that the department was generally willing but not yet fully prepared to perform.

After a period of stasis following the Spanish-American War, cadet training revived with a vengeance after 1915, as the preparedness movement gained steam. By the end of World War I, a foundation had been laid for federally sponsored military training in the nation's high schools. These foundations shaped the goals and expectations that the federal government had for the JROTC in subsequent decades.

2

JROTC in the Aftermath of War, 1918–1929

After the armistice, the nation rushed to demobilize. The army shrank from nearly 4,000,000 men to about 230,000 by January 1920. The War Department lobbied for a permanent postwar force of 500,000 men along with the introduction of universal military training (UMT), which would obligate all physically able adult men to serve.[1] Congress and the American public, however, would have none of it. There was no serious foreign threat on the horizon. Without a clear-cut enemy, the traditional American distrust of foreign entanglements and standing armies reasserted itself. Added to this distrust was a desire for economy, a yearning for a return to normalcy, and a growing cynicism about the war and the motives of those who brought it about.[2]

The army underwent a major structural overhaul after the war. The National Defense Act (NDA) of 1920 laid the foundation for a citizen army. This legislation discarded Calhoun's expansible army concept, which had governed military organization for a century. In its place, the act created a force consisting of the Regular Army (RA) and four civilian components: the National Guard, the Officers' Reserve Corps (ORC), the Citizens' Military Training Camps (CMTCs), and the Reserve Officers' Training Corps (ROTC). The latter consisted of a junior and senior division.[3]

The National Guard was the army's principal reserve force. It provided fighting units to reinforce the RA. The Organized Reserve was a mobilization resource. It maintained skeletonized divisional headquarters, which could receive, process, and train conscripts in a crisis. Individual reservists went into the ORC and the Enlisted Reserve Corps (ERC), manpower pools created to flush out active formations. To manage the force, the army divided the country into nine corps areas, with each corps having one regular, two National Guard, and three reserve divisions.[4]

In keeping with American tradition, the RA remained small. The NDA capped it at 17,700 officers and 280,000 enlisted soldiers. Budgetary constraints prevented the active force from reaching even these modest levels. By 1922, the RA was down to about 110,000 men and 12,000 officers. At no time between 1921 and 1935 did the regular force exceed these limits.[5]

Training the civilian components became a core function of the RA. This was a major change for the army; it heretofore had relatively little to do with the reserves. In the new system, the ROTC became the largest source of reserve officers.[6] The army also tried to steer graduates of the junior division and one-year students in the senior division into the ERC. Because the mechanisms and incentives for enrolling in the ERC were weak, this aspect of the ROTC program was never very vibrant.

ORGANIZATION

The ROTC did not hold a monopoly on federal cadet training. Several federally sponsored training and rifle marksmanship programs existed alongside it. The most significant was the 55c program. The NDA of 1920 authorized the issuing of "arms, tentage and equipment" and the detailing of officers to schools that enrolled one hundred physically able male students who were at least fourteen years old. This authorization was contained in Section 55c of the law, hence the program's name. The War Department attached relatively little importance to 55c units. These units could not award reserve commissions unless they had an RA instructor assigned to them, which was unlikely.[7] Neither did they receive uniforms or textbooks. Most got only rifles, belts, and small amounts of ammunition.[8]

The Massanutten Military Academy converted from a 55c to a JROTC program in the early 1930s. Its experience is instructive. The army transformed the unit upon its redesignation, giving it two RA instructors (formerly it had none), initiating annual inspections, bolstering the military curriculum, and issuing new equipment, including Browning automatic rifles, machine guns, mortars, and fieldpieces. Massanutten emerged from this transformation ready to produce reserve officers.[9]

The army divided the JROTC schools into two categories: essentially military schools (class MS) and civilian high schools and other educational institutions (class CS). The former had a four-year curriculum and compulsory participation, while the latter offered a three-year course but left the terms of participation (voluntary vs. compulsory) to the school. Mandatory

CS programs existed in twenty of the fifty-three cities offering the JROTC in 1927.[10]

In military schools, cadets were "habitually in uniform" and "continually under military discipline." They also received more advanced military instruction than cadets in civilian schools. A few offered military programs "of so high a grade" that they were given senior division status. Graduates of MS programs received certificates of completion entitling them to a reserve commission when they reached twenty-one.[11]

The army expanded its system of honor schools (introduced in 1909).[12] A unit's rating depended on its performance in the annual inspection. Rated areas included the adequacy of material support and the appearance of cadets at the annual review. By regulation, only 10 percent of CS units in a corps area could be honor schools. The army imposed a ceiling of ten honor schools on MS programs. These latter units attached great importance to the honor designation because it afforded them perquisites, such as expanded access to West Point. Before long, the army began to receive urgent pleas from military school presidents whose institutions failed to win honor status, asking for reconsideration. The War Department found it difficult to deny these importunities. Thus, the limit on honor schools was steadily raised and, when this proved insufficient, ignored.[13]

Attaining the honor designation could be burdensome. To win this title, military schools had to devote considerable time preparing for the annual inspection. For several months, administrators, teachers, and cadets focused on this event. These elaborate and time-consuming preparations disrupted academic schedules and frustrated educators, who saw their efforts to ready their charges for college obstructed.[14]

The JROTC's organizational structure was very decentralized, with multiple agencies sharing responsibility for ROTC management. In 1919, the army disbanded the Committee on Education and Special Training (COEST), which administered the ROTC during the war. It transferred many of the committee's responsibilities to an ROTC Branch created within the General Staff's War Plans Division. To this branch fell the task of developing policies and regulations to govern the program. Another staff section, the Adjutant General's Office, presented ROTC budget requests to Congress and maintained enrollment records. The chiefs of the arms and services, operating under the Army G-3, developed the curriculum, appointed professors of military science and tactics (PMS&Ts), and conducted technical inspections.

Since all CS schools offered an infantry curriculum, the infantry branch handled these matters for the junior division. Finally, the corps area commands administered policy. The problem was that none of these organizations had the program as its principal focus. The JROTC was a sidelight.[15]

This decentralized chain of command spawned confusion and exasperation. There was no central office to which officials could go for guidance or answers. Confusion was inevitable when five separate divisions within the War Department had responsibility for discrete aspects of ROTC and no agency could speak with authority on the program as a whole. A bill presented in the House of Representatives in 1928 calling for a new agency to exercise centralized control over the ROTC failed to pass. Given the fiscal climate of the period, this bill was bound to founder. It would have consumed considerable manpower.[16]

While lines of authority were less muddled at the local level, ambiguities existed there also. Each junior unit had a dual reporting chain. The PMS&T reported to school authorities *and* the corps area commander. Pleasing two masters who had different priorities was not always easy.[17]

The minimum enrollment age emerged as an issue during the interwar period. Although the NDA set that mark at fourteen, in practice, younger students joined. Many students entered the ninth grade as thirteen-year-olds and witnessed the enrollment of classmates who were only a few weeks older than themselves. Some schools, put off by this anomalous restriction, ignored the age limit. A precocious Dean Rusk, a future secretary of state, joined the JROTC as a twelve-year-old at Atlanta's Central High School in the early 1920s.[18]

This age restriction posed few problems at civilian schools, which didn't host commissioning programs. Military schools, though, were more attentive to age limits because underage enrollment would likely be discovered when the student reached commissioning age or enrolled in the SROTC.[19] They chafed under this restriction because they believed it hurt enrollment. Without the prospect of earning commissions, many students would not attend their institutions.[20]

GROWTH

With the signing of the armistice, the popularity of independent cadet programs, like the High School Volunteers of the United States (HSVUS), dropped quickly. The JROTC, however, grew rapidly. Under the direction of the COEST, it began to expand as soon as hostilities ended. The COEST vigorously pushed the expansion with the hope of taking advantage of the temporary absence of a postwar military policy and extending the program beyond the bounds set by the NDA of 1916.[21] School districts responded eagerly, flooding the army with unit applications. The War Department accommodated as many schools as its budget and manpower would allow. It kicked off its postwar JROTC enlargement on December 29, 1919, with the opening of fifty JROTC units, encompassing more than 120 high schools.[22]

In the CS category, the War Department favored metropolitan areas and restricted new units to cities with populations above twenty-five thousand. Army leaders did not want to squander precious resources on small rural schools.[23] By 1920, the JROTC enrolled over forty-six thousand cadets, while its poorer cousin, the 55c program, grew to about fourteen thousand students.[24]

After its initial spurt of growth, the JROTC experienced a period of turbulence brought on by the postwar demobilization (see appendix A). The army hemorrhaged officers and saw its budget fall precipitously. This turbulence triggered a program contraction. Between 1920 and 1922, enrollment sank from over forty-six thousand to a little more than thirty-seven thousand as the army's emphasis shifted from encouraging growth to achieving economy. The army now concentrated on getting an "adequate return for funds expended." Since the JROTC was not a major source of reserve lieutenants or enlisted men, the army struggled to demonstrate a significant return on investment. Senior units could show a return and, therefore, received higher priority.[25]

The lack of growth did not reflect a lack of demand. The JROTC still enjoyed "widespread" popularity. Many large cities clamored for units. By 1922, the army had a sizable backlog of unit requests and had to contend with a "constant" stream of new applications, most of which had to be rejected.[26]

An officer shortage was behind this stagnation. The instructor pool shrank as the demobilization progressed. The JROTC lost half its officer strength between 1919 and 1923.[27] Dwindling appropriations and, after 1919, an erosion of surplus war stocks further complicated matters. These constraints forced units to purchase supplies and equipment they formerly received for free. Moreover, funding cuts compelled the army to restrict the size of existing units and reduce summer camp attendance. Cadets at military schools suffered most since summer camp attendance was a prerequisite for commissioning.[28]

By 1923, the disruption attendant to demobilization had abated, and the JROTC entered a period of stasis. Between 1923 and 1930, the program's institutional base changed little. Army policy was to establish no new units, only to replace ones that had been shuttered. Army leaders deviated from this policy only in a "few exceptional cases" because of "political considerations." Normally, this involved the personal intervention of influential Congress members or government officials on behalf of particular schools. Enrollment was also static, fluctuating moderately from time to time because of small changes in the army budget. Enrollment hovered around forty thousand until 1935. This meant that the JROTC's footprint in educational institutions atrophied since high school enrollment grew by more than 100 percent in the decade after 1923.[29]

The War Department imposed an enrollment ceiling in 1924 that remained in effect for most of the decade. There were not enough instructors, funds, supplies, or equipment to start new units or expand existing ones. Although military institutes maintained large stocks of equipment, most civilian units found themselves stretched thin. Some units made cadets purchase their own uniforms. This discouraged poor students from joining. Other units tried to compensate by scrounging from nearby reserve units, with varying degrees of success.[30]

OPPOSITION

As the JROTC became ensconced in schools after World War I, resistance to high school military training intensified. Fueled by growing isolationist and pacifist sentiment and disillusionment with the results of the war, strong anti-ROTC movements arose. They evidenced considerable strength in the Northeast. In 1926, a survey conducted by the state of Massachusetts, once the nation's center of cadet training, revealed a pervasive revulsion for the JROTC among educators. Three hundred of the 309 high school principals surveyed disapproved of military drill. New York, the birthplace of the American Guard, was another stronghold of anti-JROTC sentiment. New York City's school system reportedly employed large numbers of pacifists and radicals who demanded the elimination of cadet training.[31] The Midwest also experienced anti-JROTC agitation. Labor groups there pilloried the JROTC for being a tool of "industrial militarists" who used inflammatory rhetoric to create a market for armaments. Citizen groups denounced the program as a recruiting instrument for the National Guard.[32]

The most publicized incident involving anti-JROTC agitation occurred in Cleveland. That city had adopted a program of compulsory military training in 1918. By the mid-1920s, Cleveland was reconsidering its decision. In 1926, Cleveland's Board of Education held hearings to determine if the JROTC should be retained. The hearings precipitated a fiery debate. City officials and educators rose to the program's defense, arguing that the JROTC fostered good citizenship and self-discipline. Most board members, though, questioned the academic value of military training and expressed misgivings about the War Department's motives. An alliance of parent-teacher associations, women's groups, churches, and labor organizations supported the board.[33] In the end, the program's critics triumphed, and the city's JROTC units were terminated.

The crusade against military training enlisted the support of prominent personages. The renowned educator John Dewey and the eminent theologian Reinhold Niebuhr were both outspoken opponents of the JROTC. A group of distinguished legislators and social activists descended on Washington, DC, in late 1925 to consolidate opposition to cadet training. Jane Addams, Carrie Chapman Catt, and Senators William Borah, George Norris, and Robert La Follette were among its members.[34] A statement released by the group urged that military training be "rigidly excluded from the high schools . . . [because it did] not provide the best form of physical training; it [did] not teach constructive citizenship; [and] . . . it tend[ed] to impart . . . jingoistic notions."[35]

This assemblage of luminaries lent its support to the newly formed Committee on Militarism in Education (CME), which became one of the most influential anti-ROTC groups in the nation. The CME played a pivotal role in bringing the issue of school-based military training before Congress, helping to craft the Walsh-Frazier Bill of 1926 and the Nye-Kvale Bill of 1935. Both bills, while focused on compulsory programs, stimulated a wide-ranging public debate about the appropriateness of military training in general.[36]

These bills represented only two of the many attempts made in Congress to eliminate federal support for the JROTC. Every year from 1926 through 1937, legislators inserted in the annual army supply bills provisions targeting mandatory programs. None of these initiatives was successful. The Walsh-Frazier Bill did not even make it out of committee, and the insertions into the annual army supply bills were all voted down by sizable margins.[37]

These manifestations of public opposition left many instructors feeling besieged, convinced that they were being victimized by agents of an "aggressive and united" pacifism. All too often, they complained, influential "pacifists" and other "dissidents," inflamed with "decidedly humanitarian ideas," badgered weak-willed school principals and school boards into adopting policies inimical to military training. The publicity given to these dissidents, they averred, gave them legitimacy. The result was not only lower JROTC enrollment but growing disrespect for authority within entire school systems.[38]

A sense of beleaguerment was also on display in the War Department. Officials there railed against the "well-meaning but misguided" pawns of the radicals who agitated against military training and "undermine[d] the nation's ability to defend itself." They dismissed claims that ROTC bred militarism or made students "jingoistic." People who made such claims were at best wrongheaded and at worst traitorous. "If they [ROTC critics] have any patriotic feeling in their hearts," one War Department spokesperson declared, "they should not permit themselves to be misled by seditious propaganda but should . . . loyally support every agency created by the National Defense Act."[39]

Military officers pictured themselves as locked in an ideological battle with a hostile coalition of the uninformed, the credulous, the malevolent, and the disaffected. At stake were the minds of the American public, the loyalties of American youth, and ultimately the security of the United States; and the junior and senior divisions of the ROTC were on the front lines of this battle.[40] This intense opposition to the program was not without effect. The steady round of invective affected the way the army approached the program and pushed the War Department to be more cautious, tentative, and indirect than it might otherwise have been.

GOALS AND OBJECTIVES

The army's ambivalence about the objective of the JROTC invited criticism. Citizenship education, character development, Americanization, officer procurement, preinduction military training, and recruiting vied for top priority. Many JROTC backers were not satisfied with the diverse mix of goals contained in army regulations and policy statements. They urged the army to define the JROTC mission more precisely, prioritize its aims, and replace vague objectives like developing good citizenship with more concrete and measurable goals.

At a Citizenship Conference (1922) hosted by the War Department, one general officer observed that the army had not yet settled on a definite mission for the program. It vacillated between treating it as a training program, on the one hand, and a citizenship program, on the other. This ambivalence was manifest in the program's size and structure. The JROTC, with one hundred units and roughly forty thousand cadets, was too small to be an effective citizenship program. Its reach was too restricted. Nor was it configured to be a practicable officer-producing or military training program. It was too large and too sparsely staffed for those purposes. The program was a functional hybrid, ill-equipped to discharge any of its intended purposes particularly well.[41]

In March 1920, the War Department had convened a conference of educators and military leaders to forge a consensus about what the goals of the JROTC should be. In the end, the attendees came up with essentially the same list of objectives the army had been working with since 1916. Citizenship, discipline, character development, moral education, respect for authority, physical fitness, military training, and officer education all had their proponents. School principals from Cleveland, with a population that was 70 percent foreign born, were vocal advocates of Americanization. But as a body, school officials were as divided as military leaders on what the principal aim of the JROTC should be.[42]

This fuzziness about objectives frustrated C. R. Mann, an erstwhile academic, who was the chief adviser to the General Staff on matters relating to civilian education. With so many goals vying for priority, little could be accomplished. Mann pleaded with attendees to come to a working agreement on program objectives. They had to determine, he told them, whether the JROTC was for Americanization, education, military preparedness, or something else. If it encompassed multiple goals, then what were the components of each goal? Only when they solidified the program's objectives could the JROTC advocates approach Congress to ask for support.[43]

Mann's plea for clarity was logical but unrealistic. He underestimated the intractability of the many currents of thought and opinion that ran through public support for the JROTC. That support stemmed from a mottled, complex, and shifting mix of social, political, and military agendas, which defied prioritization or encapsulation in a neat bureaucratic formula or policy.

Mann's own solution was to orient the program toward national defense. Like other officials in this era, he entertained a broad conception of national defense, one that involved not only combat forces but elements like industrial strength, social cohesion, and national discipline. In the late war, the quality of inductees had been a problem. Many could not qualify for military service because of poor physical fitness, illiteracy, underdeveloped general intelligence, or a lack of technical skills. The army, he urged, should use the JROTC to obviate impediments to mobilization. Public schools should strengthen physical training, general education, technical training, and vocational guidance, while the army should define suitable standards of physical fitness, mental ability, and vocational training and instill a spirit of service and obedience in students.[44]

Mann thought the army's focus should be on ROTC in colleges, not in high schools. The senior program needed personnel and resources to produce lieutenants for the ORC. The junior division did not need personnel. Its inspirational and administrative functions could be done without full-time staff. The army should model its junior program on the 55c units operating in Washington, DC, which, he pointed out, drew minimal support from the federal government and hired their own instructors.[45]

Military Objectives

Military objectives had been paramount during the war. The Army General Staff identified the production of reserve officers as the principal purpose of the JROTC. It did not want the "true" purpose of the JROTC to be co-opted by organizations like the Military Training Camp Association (MTCA) and High School Volunteers of the United States (HSVUS), which saw the program as a vehicle to spread the gospel of preparedness and teach good citizenship rather than as a mechanism to produce officers and men for the army.[46]

After the war, the army set military goals for the JROTC. Some were spelled out; some were not. One objective was to prepare cadets for advanced placement in the SROTC. The JROTC graduates who earned a military proficiency certification could enter directly into the second year of the SROTC basic course and, thereby, earn reserve commissions before entering their senior year. A few units commissioned these students early and allowed them to serve as lieutenants on the SROTC staff. In other units, they were appointed cadet noncommissioned officers (NCOs) and only commissioned upon graduation.[47]

In practice, this use of the JROTC graduates proved only marginally effective. Most graduates who attended college failed to attain advanced standing. PMS&Ts were the arbiters of advanced placement. Usually, they "ignored or overlooked" high school military training. The JROTC graduates, even those who had been leaders in high school, often found themselves assigned to "rookie" squads alongside college freshmen who had never worn a uniform.[48]

There was another side to the issue, of course. Many RA officers were skeptical of the military proficiency of graduates. One complained that "relatively immature results were accomplished in tactical and technical training offered in most high schools." A lack of resources, the frequent rotation of officers, inadequate facilities, and neglect by the War Department combined to render such training inutile. Moreover, many graduates, having no standard against which to assess their military skills, entered college with an inflated estimate of their military proficiency. A war college study denounced the practice of allowing the JROTC graduates to skip the first year of the SROTC, avouching that it created "a false set of values." If they were not given advanced standing, the report lamented, they would not enroll.[49]

The JROTC also facilitated admission to West Point. In CS schools, recruiting for the Military Academy was informal and oblique, done through suggestion, persuasion, and exhortation. Despite the absence of formal inducements, the army enjoyed success in steering students toward the academy. In some instances, a JROTC unit opened an avenue of access into West Point where none had previously existed.[50]

In the case of MS institutions, the army embedded academy recruiting in regulations. It gave preference to "honor graduates" from "honor military schools" for admission. Honor students (one per honor school) did not take the standard mental examinations required of other applicants; this substantially enhanced their chances of acceptance. Instead, they were evaluated on their secondary school transcripts. The number of them admitted depended on the number of openings available. On average, these students constituted 2–3 percent of West Point's entering freshman class.[51]

The quality of honor graduates left much to be desired. Between 1935 and 1937, the academy admitted forty-one distinguished honor school graduates. Of these, almost half (twenty) failed their coursework and were dismissed. This prompted West Point's superintendent to change the admissions policy and require the JROTC cadets to pass the same mental examinations as other candidates.[52]

The JROTC remained a direct source of reserve commissions. Some officers considered this to be the program's principal mission even though only military schools performed this function.[53] The number of officers produced annually through the JROTC varied during the interwar years. From fewer than 60 lieutenants in the early 1920s, output rose to 309 in 1929. It trailed off thereafter, however. In the 1930s, annual output averaged about 230 officers. Altogether, between 1920 and 1939 the JROTC commissioned 3,706 lieutenants, or about 3.6 percent of the ROTC's total production.[54]

Many army officials considered the JROTC to be a huge disappointment. One General Staff officer labeled it a "failure" and saw "little justification" for its existence. A yield of only a few hundred lieutenants a year seemed a paltry return for the people, money, and equipment that the army poured into the junior division. Several army studies recommended that the high school division be pared down. The savings achieved could be applied to the senior division, which yielded greater dividends. Calls to eliminate or scale back the program increased after 1929 as the ORC dwindled, the international situation deteriorated, and mobilization requirements took on greater urgency.[55]

War Department officials hoped to reap more military benefits from the JROTC than additional commissions. One expected benefit was improved enlisted recruiting. The recruiting crisis of the early 1920s highlighted the importance of high school units. "The difficulty we have experienced in recruiting the ranks," the War Department noted, "makes it necessary to give earnest attention to the source from which they are derived." Exposure to military officers and NCOs and familiarity with the military lifestyle would, it was expected, induce students to enlist in the RA, the National Guard, and the ERC.[56]

To encourage reserve enlistment, the War Department offered advanced promotion to junior cadets. Students who completed two years of the program could enter the ERC at the seventh grade—the same grade given to college students who completed one year of the SROTC. To certify their eligibility, the JROTC graduates had to present training certificates signed by their PMS&T. Many PMS&Ts, however, did not issue these documents; they saw little point in doing so. The financial and vocational advantages of securing a one-grade accelerated promotion in the ERC was minimal.[57]

Another military goal of the JROTC was the diffusion of military knowledge in the general population. Students learned military skills and army organization, received physical training, and experienced military socialization. In an emergency, the army would have a large number of men with basic military skills who could be quickly turned into soldiers. General John Pershing and other senior officers thought of the program as a substitute for UMT. To be sure, the program, limited as it was to a few hundred high schools, touched only a fraction of the nation's adolescent boys. Still, it had the potential to build a sizable mobilization base if properly configured for that purpose.[58]

Medical screening was another benefit of the JROTC. During World War I, tens of thousands of young men were found physically or medically unfit for military service. This represented a tremendous waste of manpower. Many disqualifying defects could have been remedied if treated in time. Having the junior program vet thousands of potential recruits in peacetime with a required medical exam would immeasurably improve the efficiency and speed of the mobilization process.[59]

Domestic Engagement

After the war, the nation redirected its gaze back toward domestic issues. With this shift of focus, the army's social imperative, eclipsed by the war, took on new life. Military leaders strove to demonstrate that the army remained relevant and useful in an era of peace.

This is not to say that the social imperative was universally embraced by army officers. Some believed that the army's purpose was to fight the nation's wars, not instill discipline or develop character in unruly adolescents. Such tasks could be done more effectively by people trained to accomplish them; they only diverted attention away from the army's primary responsibility. Good citizenship, one officer commented, was not the purpose of an army. An army "exists to kill men, when ordered . . . irrespective of justice." The War Department should publicly recognize this and stop lying about the JROTC "being a school for citizenship or manual training, nor clutter up its drill grounds with disciples for these irrelevant arts."[60]

Public expressions of this nature, however, were relatively infrequent. Officers who forswore the JROTC's social and political missions were in the minority—or at least were less outspoken than those who believed otherwise. Articles appearing in military periodicals indicated solid support for the extramilitary roles of high school military training. Most professional officers understood that, in an era of industrial warfare, such missions played an important role in national security.

The War Department's acceptance of domestic missions was no mere ploy to maintain its budget or raise its popularity. It reflected genuine concern about domestic issues that imperiled national security. The United States faced a complex of internal threats, social problems, and economic challenges that threatened its political equilibrium. Army leaders understood the gravity of the dangers and willingly, if not always enthusiastically, employed the army's manpower and resources to allay them.

Thus, the JROTC pursued goals that went beyond narrow military objectives. Indeed, the program's political and social aims often overshadowed its military ones. A review of some of the problems confronting the nation will help the reader understand the urgency of extramilitary goals.[61]

A period of domestic upheaval followed World War I. In 1919, race riots enveloped Chicago, Saint Louis, and other cities. Dozens died, and hundreds were injured. The postwar period also witnessed the "Red Scare." A series of strikes and terrorist bombings suggested that foreign agents were at work inside the country. An anticommunist frenzy gripped the country, and legislators enacted harsh espionage and sedition laws that many felt transgressed the bounds of legality.[62]

A wave of xenophobia swept the nation. The continuing influx of southern and eastern Europeans into the country prompted this outburst. The indigent and largely Roman Catholic refugees were a source of dread for the nation's largely Protestant middle class. To stem this invasion, Congress passed a series of laws that progressively tightened immigration restrictions until the immigrant flow had been reduced to a trickle.

The nation's urban structure changed along with its ethnic composition. Foreign immigrants flowed into American cities. They congregated in ethnic ghettos, turning cities into cultural mosaics made up of dozens of ethnic enclaves, each of which spoke its own language, followed its own customs, and practiced its own religion. This occurred while rapid industrialization and agricultural mechanization drove millions of people from farm to factory. The impact of these population movements on urban school systems was enormous. Municipal authorities strained to find space to accommodate the extraordinary increases in student enrollment that accompanied these population shifts, and educators implemented new curricula to serve the needs of working-class children.

The army encapsulated many of its efforts to address social problems under the label of *citizenship training*—a term that had a wide currency among educators of the era. Citizenship programs could take on various forms and embrace a variety of subjects. In the 1920s, educators generally fell into one of two groups. One group conceived of citizenship education as a means to "encourage pupils to think for themselves about political and social issues." The other group believed that citizenship programs should "shape the minds of pupils for political and social purposes."[63]

The army's conception of a citizenship program accorded with that of the latter group. Like many educationalists, military officers believed that instilling appropriate attitudes, habits, and traits in students was as important as teaching them cognitive skills. Accordingly, they set out to inculcate in cadets the "habits of precision, orderliness, courtesy, correctness of posture and deportment, leadership, and respect for constituted authority." The end goal was to produce good soldiers, efficient employees, and loyal citizens.[64]

The JROTC's citizenship instruction encompassed moral training. As often happened in the wake of a great war, societal restraints loosened, and personal morals relaxed. Adolescents ignored traditional rules of personal conduct and manifested a disregard for established authority, or at least it appeared that way. One officer asserted, "The mob spirit is ever present in public schools and is even struggling for mastery. It is very difficult to control." A military regimen could counteract this breakdown of familial and national discipline. "The R.O.T.C., when thoroughly supported by the faculty," one officer noted, "seems to be the best practical moral training they have found to give the young American the discipline of which he stands so much in need."[65]

There was a strong economic component to the JROTC citizenship training. Many touted the efficacy of military training in preparing young men for the workforce by inculcating in them attention to detail, industriousness, and punctuality. This, in turn, engendered industrial productivity, economic efficiency, and a docile workforce.[66]

The JROTC also promoted social efficiency in a nation that was becoming increasingly urbanized, industrialized, and diverse. Through military training, students were introduced to the "right kind of ideal" and conditioned to be tractable citizens, ready to function as "cogs in the machinery of community living," as one high school principal put it. The program would help build an orderly and stable society capable of withstanding the dislocation wrought by rapid social and economic change.[67]

From the army's perspective, none of the JROTC's extramilitary benefits surpassed in importance that of public outreach, or, as some officers characterized it, "propaganda." In an age of isolationism and budgetary stringency, the War Department had to battle indifference on the part of a public that had "never been inculcated with any sound doctrine of national defense." Through the JROTC, the army could convince the public of the need for a "sane" defense policy.[68]

Their experiences in the Great War convinced army leaders that they could no longer ignore civil society as they had when the army was a frontier constabulary. A nation that waged total war could not afford this luxury. The military now had to elicit the active support of the citizenry.

Worried by the public's indifference about the nation's military posture, one General Staff officer asserted that "the most important work that must be accomplished under the leadership of the Army is the creation of an intelligent public opinion upon the question of adequate national preparedness." If this work was not done, he warned, then the army would "gradually disintegrate" to the point that the nation would "have little or no means of defense." To create public support for a proper military policy, he continued, "there must be scattered throughout the country large numbers of civilians sufficiently instructed and sufficiently interested to bring pressure to bear upon Congress from time to time."[69]

The ROTC was a convenient means by which the army could accomplish this task. To train "the popular public mind to the necessity and needs of an adequate defense," one officer opined, there was "no greater or better agency at our command." The program could shape the opinions of the rising generation on issues of national defense. Cadets would bring the ideas they picked up from military instructors back to the "family table" and forge "a direct connection between the War Department and the fireside." The army's emphasis on propaganda occasioned one critic to observe that the army seemed more intent on producing "a state of mind in favor of preparedness" than on "training for war conditions." There was a great deal of truth in this observation. Throughout the interwar period, the program's outreach function often overshadowed its other objectives.[70]

The army's outreach effort extended beyond military preparedness. The war had taught the army that national strength encompassed social cohesion, economic power, industrial might, and national efficiency. Therefore, the army's relationship with society had to transcend defense matters. In an era of mass citizen armies, the nation's military needed to be fully integrated into the body politic. The General Staff wanted the American people to "consider the Army as a vital and natural part of the social organism of the Nation . . . not [something] separate and distinct from American life, but as inevitably and permanently interwoven with the whole social fabric." The army's purpose was to "express essentially American ideals and to develop American men" accordingly. Machinery had been set up to foster this melding of the military and civilian sectors. And the JROTC was an important component of this machinery.[71]

The JROTC was also viewed as a useful tool in the Americanization campaign then underway. In 1921, the army's chief of staff described the program as "Americanization of the best form to the boys of foreign birth." The War Department's approach to assimilation resembled that of many private and civil government agencies. It encouraged students from immigrant families to adopt American customs, internalize Anglo-Saxon ideals, respect American institutions, venerate national symbols, speak the English language, and obey "constituted authority."[72]

The JROTC instructors believed they were "hastening the Americanization of America." Immigrants from countries with autocratic governments and rigid class distinctions had to be taught what effective civic participation meant in a democracy. Otherwise, they might fall prey to demagogues or embrace dangerous political philosophies. While critics accused them of erasing ethnic identities and exercising social control over the dispossessed, instructors saw themselves as cementing national cohesion and preserving "the most just and benign form of government on earth."[73]

Closely aligned with its Americanization effort was the JROTC's objective of combating the spread of political extremism. Convinced that it was confronting a "carefully organized[,] well-financed radical movement," the army monitored dissident groups as closely as its money and manpower would allow. There were some two hundred of these organizations in operation by 1924. The War Department considered such groups—though they represented a wide array of political orientations—"mediums for the projection of radical activities." Emboldened by Bolshevik success in Russia, these organizations sowed the "seeds of unrest and class distinction" among the public, undermined the military, and tried to oust the ROTC from high schools and colleges.[74]

Although radical groups posed no immediate threat to the RA, their agitation might impair manpower procurement in a national emergency by blocking the passage of a selective service law. And even if a conscription law were passed, they might interfere with the operation of the selective service apparatus or even nullify draft legislation by creating widespread opposition to its implementation.[75]

One officer called anti-ROTC agitation the "most dangerous phase of radical activities" since it was "inculcating the doctrine of internationalism and communism" in young people. Among the malleable students filling the nation's high schools and colleges, he noted, dissidents were finding a "fertile and receptive environment" for their ideas. Already, subversive organizations had implanted their agents in America's schools. Communists were well represented among public school teachers in large cities and on the faculties of leading universities.[76] The army had to help stem this invasion.

TRAINING METHODS

The JROTC's approach to citizenship training was not overt. In the 1920s, the JROTC curriculum did not include a single civics or citizenship course. The War Department incorporated one subcourse titled "The Obligations of Citizenship" into the curriculum in the early 1930s. But this single subcourse was the only explicit reference to citizenship training in the entire three-year curriculum.[77]

The dearth of formal courses led to charges that the JROTC's citizenship emphasis was a ploy to conceal more sinister purposes.[78] This is understandable. Leading educators like John Dewey and Peter Porter probably would not have discerned a connection between the subjects offered in the JROTC and citizenship instruction. Dismissing the JROTC citizenship training as a mere artifice, however, betrayed an ignorance of the army's conception of citizenship.

An examination of the army's citizenship manuals is edifying. The topics covered in these publications included army organization, military discipline, military law, army administration, inspections, military history, the US Constitution, the duty of the citizen, team play, the makers of the flag, army functions, and English. Military service, preparedness, and patriotism were inextricably bound up with the idea of citizenship conveyed in these manuals. Topics related to what academicians understood to be civics were present but inconspicuous.[79]

Usually, the army took an oblique approach to citizenship training. It normally presented citizenship instruction through casual interaction between the military faculty and cadets. Instructors engaged students about such topics as patriotism, the evils of communism, the dangers of the Washington Naval Conference, or the irrationality of the Kellogg-Briand Treaty outside the classroom. They would impart their views during breaks in training, before and after class, during visits to military installations, and in other informal venues.[80]

Some urged the army to use more direct methods to achieve their aims. They suggested that a comprehensive course in citizenship be introduced in the ROTC, the ORC, and the National Guard. Citizenship was already being taught at the CMTCs and in recruit training centers. Such training should be extended to programs that were even more closely connected to civil society. Such a scheme entailed risk, but the risk was worth it.[81]

When the War Department took a direct role in the propaganda war, however, the results were not always felicitous. Its most notorious attempt at active involvement ended in a public relations debacle. In 1928, the army's chief chaplain prepared a text on citizenship, the infamous *Citizenship Training Manual No. 2000–25*. This manual gave an embarrassingly simplistic and chauvinistic account of the nation's history, attacked public ownership and governmental regulation of property, exalted preparedness, denounced internationalism, and equated democracy with mobocracy. The document outraged many Congress members. A public outcry compelled the War Department to retract the manual, but not before substantial damage had been done to the army's public image.[82]

Learning from such missteps, War Department officials normally eschewed confronting their opponents head-on. Instead, they induced others to do their talking for them. Local notables, community leaders, prominent businessmen, and sympathetic teachers could promote the cause of high school military training more effectively than the JROTC instructors. The former were generally adept at communicating in the public square, while the latter were not. The army also enlisted the aid of sympathetic organizations to convey messages to cadets. The American Legion was among the most active of these. Local chapters provided lectures and pamphlets dealing with a wide range of topical issues.[83]

As its citizenship manuals suggested, army leaders believed vital lessons in citizenship inhered in military training. Drill, field exercises, uniforms, and the military chain of command all taught obedience, discipline, and courteous behavior. Close-order drill, derided by critics as the very apotheosis of mind-numbing routine, instilled in students the habit of "eager and intense obedience to the directions of a constituted leader." One contributor to a military periodical called the discipline of the drill field "the very bedrock of future government and the good citizenship which underlies it."[84]

Ritual and symbol were also used to teach citizenship. Parades and ceremonies featuring national symbols such as the American flag inspired patriotism and loyalty to the government. The army designed ceremonies to be stirring and imbued them with local significance whenever possible. In San Francisco, one JROTC unit routinely provided honor guards for naturalization ceremonies. Another cadet corps in Washington, DC, conducted a short military ceremony in front of the White House on Inauguration Day, saluting both the incoming and outgoing presidents.[85]

Summer training was an ideal setting to use symbol and ceremony to engender patriotic ideals. One officer wrote that there was "no better place to learn patriotism than in a camp with that symbol of American freedom—the Stars and Stripes waving in the breeze or borne honorably at the head of a marching column. . . . It was like a protecting spirit hovering on high, giving a sense of patriotism, security and well-being to all that behold it."[86] In this patriotic venue, "boys learn[ed] the true meaning of the flag and its symbolism." No student could undergo the camp experience "without becoming a stauncher, more patriotic American."[87]

ARMY-SCHOOL RELATIONS

Relations between schools and the JROTC were not always amicable. Upon his arrival at a school, the new military instructor had to adjust to a "marked change in working and living conditions" and face problems "sharply differentiated" from those he had encountered as a soldier. While some instructors adjusted swiftly to their new situation, others did not. The JROTC embodied a culture that at times clashed with the one in which it operated. Military instructors had different professional and educational experiences and harbored different philosophical beliefs than their civilian counterparts. They regarded civilian educators as impractical and naive academics, ignorant of international affairs and dismayingly optimistic about human nature. On their part, civilian educators looked upon military instructors as interlopers, appropriating privileges, benefits, and professional status to which they had no valid claim. They viewed military training as peripheral or even antithetical to the school's core academic mission. These differences in outlook bred disagreement and misunderstanding.

The scanty assistance given to the JROTC by schools was a bone of contention. Officers complained about the half-hearted support received from hostile or indifferent principals. Training was scheduled at inconvenient times—with classes and drill being relegated to the lunch hour or late afternoon. Instructors suspected that hostile motives were behind these moves. The lack of space was another issue. In some schools, units operated without an office or a storage room.[88]

One officer described the reception accorded a new instructor when he arrived at his unit: "Some officer receives a telegram assigning him to a school as a JROTC instructor. When he arrives, he discovers that the Board of Education has no office for him, not even a desk. He asks about hours and is told that his unit has from 12:00 to 1:00 for training. Major H—was one such officer. He was not given an office and had to share a desk with someone who occupied it almost all the time."[89]

This bare-bones backing had untoward consequences, including poor training, lackluster instruction, and low enrollment. Building a vigorous program in an environment of scarcity and indifference was an almost impossible task.

Another area of friction involved instructor duties. Some short-staffed schools treated the military faculty as additional manpower. Officers picked up responsibilities beyond those required by their official position. Some bore such a heavy burden of additional duties that it diverted them from their principal charge.

Many officers felt that the War Department should divest itself of schools that gave meager assistance and create units at schools that offered more generous support. One frustrated officer could not "see the sense of plugging along with schools that offer[ed] nothing in the way of space and facilities." No successful business would operate that way, and neither should the army.[90]

Despite the problems encountered, the JROTC units generally fit in well with host schools. When material support for the JROTC was exiguous, this was often due to budgetary shortfalls and limited space rather than ill will. Moreover, scheduling anomalies frequently reflected a packed academic agenda rather than hostility.

In fact, throughout most of the institutional base, professional educators and business leaders embraced high school military training. The JROTC's acceptance was largely due to its alignment with broader social and educational goals. Educationalists, industrialists, and military leaders aimed to facilitate the adjustment of immigrants and rural transplants to urban life, indoctrinate young people against political radicalism, foster economic and social efficiency, and cement national cohesion. They also shared the conviction that the rise of the modern industrial economy made respect for constituted authority among adolescents more important than ever.[91] Moreover, educators embraced Americanization as passionately as military officers did. Evidence of this can be seen in the forced assimilation programs and chauvinistic curricula that schools adopted. Even liberal organizations like the National Education Association endorsed compulsory Americanization programs and "English-only" classrooms.

Army officers had a special affinity for character educators, who placed obedience and Americanism at the core of their agenda. Both groups recognized the implications that economic and social changes had for schools; both advocated the civic approach to moral education; and both stressed the primacy of social cooperation and teamwork as curricular objectives. Moreover, the absolute moral code of character educators had a special appeal to army officers.

Educators and military men shared certain pedagogical beliefs, in addition to goals and objectives. Group assignments and service projects enjoyed wide popularity among both teachers and officers. Service projects were staples of many JROTC units. Such activities taught teamwork, social cooperation, and collective responsibility. Learning by doing was another shared preference. Army regulations directed the JROTC instructors to keep lectures to a minimum while employing hands-on training as much as practicable. This confluence of pedagogical predilections flowed from the common assumption that the principal aim of schooling was to condition students to their environment rather than to impart academic knowledge that many would never use.

Educators also embraced the military model of classroom management. The infamous Gary Plan featured marching between classes, rigid scheduling, and a platoon system of instruction. It evoked the image of a military training camp.[92] Perhaps the high priest of the military style of classroom organization was William Bagley, a professor of education at the University of Illinois. This noted authority on classroom superintendence prescribed a military regimen for the ills afflicting public schools. Although his writing focused on the elementary grades, his ideas had great currency among high school officials as well.[93]

Bagley, who considered social efficiency to be the principal aim of education, advised teachers to reduce the routine activities of the classroom "to the plane of automatism." This automatism was to be achieved through rigid discipline and "machine-like" organization. All movement was to be strictly controlled. Whenever students left the classroom, they were to march in step to their destination, maintaining complete silence. They were to rise, sit down, go to the blackboard, get their wraps, and even go to the bathroom upon command.[94]

In Bagley's system, order and obedience underpinned everything. He advised teachers to "drop everything else, if necessary, until order is secured." The "gravest of pedagogical crimes" was "to permit children to grow up in a constant attitude of disrespect for authority." Students owed "unquestioning obedience" to their teachers, and teachers owed unquestioning obedience to their superiors. The situation was "entirely analogous to that in any other organization [the army, navy, government, businesses]. Concentrated effort can be secured in no other way."[95]

Emily W. Elmore, a professor of education at the University of Wisconsin, also advocated the importation of military discipline into the classroom. She called her method "squads for discipline." Each row in her classroom formed a squad. The squad leader sat in the front of each row and was responsible for the actions of squad members. During physical education periods, squad leaders maintained order and assigned roles on teams. Squads competed against one another in various areas, such as deportment, drill, and posture. The teacher awarded points and tracked the results. Periodically, the winning squads received pennants or badges. Group punishment was meted out for breaches of discipline or unsatisfactory academic performance. Elmore believed that peer pressure would induce good behavior and compliance with school rules.[96]

The educational model posited by the likes of Bagley and Elmore had a wide appeal, not only among educators but among community and business leaders. Under this system, classrooms were tranquil and orderly, students obeyed their teachers and followed rules, and corporate leaders got tractable workers. This paradigm aligned with the vocational education movement, educational theory, and the "ethos of social efficiency, organization, and scientific management" that animated the worlds of business, education, and the military.[97]

The JROTC grew rapidly after the war. School districts eagerly sought units. The army accommodated as many schools as its resources would allow. The federal government was ambivalent about its goals for the JROTC. Citizenship education, character development, public outreach, workforce preparation, Americanization, officer procurement, preinduction training, enlisted recruiting, medical screening, and physical education all competed for top billing. Senior War Department officials were not satisfied with the diverse objectives pursued by the army and demanded that program goals be clarified.

While the JROTC was widely popular, hostility to high school military training grew after the war. Disillusionment with the results of the war, growing isolationist sentiment, and a determined pacifist movement spurred this opposition. War Department officials normally eschewed direct confrontations with critics and tried to induce others to speak for them. When they departed from this pattern, things often did not work out well.

Things changed in 1929 after the collapse of the stock market and the start of the Great Depression. While many strains of continuity remained, new conditions demanded adjustments. In the next chapter, the JROTC developments during the 1930s will be discussed.

3

Depression and War, 1930–1945

The Stock Market Crash of October 1929 marked the beginning of the largest economic downturn in US history. It initiated a decade of high unemployment, bank failures, homelessness, hunger, and, for the first time in US history, massive emigration. In this atmosphere of social disruption, radical political doctrines became more alluring. The nation seemed to be on the brink of revolution.

The nation's military policy in the 1930s remained essentially the same as it had been since 1920. That policy rested on the vision of a small Regular Army (RA) complemented by the civilian components (CC). The small RA was to serve as the nucleus around which a mass citizen army would be assembled in the event of war.

The military budget fell sharply as the government struggled to keep spending in balance with revenue. Military expenditures presented a tempting target for economy-minded Congress members. The cuts in the army budget began in 1930 and persisted for the next five years.[1]

These reductions were taken from an already shaky budgetary foundation. Although military spending had trended moderately upward after 1925, much of this increase was linked to the Air Corps Act of 1926 and the exhaustion of surplus equipment left over from the war. Supplies and equipment now had to be purchased.[2]

Modernization plans had to be modified or abandoned. By 1931, the renovation of the Air Corps was flagging, while mechanization was all but abandoned. Increasingly, the army struggled to supply its forces with even the most basic items. Its focus shifted from boosting security to minimizing damage to national defense.[3]

BUDGET PROBLEMS

The National Defense Act (NDA) of 1920 entailed expenses for new activities such as the Chemical Warfare Service, the Air Corps, and the CC, as well as for new equipment such as tanks, tractor-drawn artillery, and radios. These initiatives resulted in a doubling of the army's peacetime budget over a decade. In July 1929, President Herbert Hoover ordered a review of all military programs to effect savings. In conducting this review, the army sought to deflect charges that it was playing politics with the budget. The chief of staff of the army (CSA), General Charles Summerall, asked his budget officer whether the army's appropriations contained anything that had *political* value. That officer replied that military appropriations could be split into two types: one for the RA, which had few political implications, and one for the CC, which "unquestionably" had a political aspect.[4]

Summerall asked corps commanders and the army staff where savings should be realized. Three of the nine corps commanders advised him to curtail the CC. The army's inspector general recommended that the Citizens' Military Training Camps (CMTC) be abolished and that responsibility for *other* nonmilitary activities like the JROTC be transferred to agencies that had the appropriate expertise. The chief of the Militia Bureau urged the scaling down of the ROTC and CMTC with the savings used to expand the National Guard.[5]

Other senior officers rushed to the defense of the CC. The adjutant general (TAG) emphasized the ROTC's important training and recruiting functions and its critical role in mobilization plans. The army's chief financial officer opposed eliminating or transferring responsibility for the nonmilitary activities of the War Department. These activities, he reminded Summerall, were a source of valuable publicity for the army. The General Staff emerged as the most zealous protector of the CC, especially of the ROTC. It saw this program as a key element of the army's mobilization system; moreover, its elimination or curtailment would meet with a hostile reaction from high schools and colleges, which the army could not afford to alienate.[6]

Assessments of the JROTC's value must be understood in the context of contemporary assumptions about war. Most army leaders operated from the assumption that, in warfare, the human and not the machine was the decisive element. The General Staff felt this way. New weapons would soon become obsolete, while trained and capable manpower would retain its utility. While armaments could be quickly manufactured, skilled soldiers could not. Favoring weapons over manpower was foolhardy.[7]

There were those who prized equipment over manpower. People in this camp wanted to scrap the expensive mass army provided for in the NDA of 1920 and rely on a small, high-quality force armed with the most advanced weapons. The Democratic congressman Ross Collins was a powerful spokesman for this group. He attempted to reduce spending by cutting personnel assigned to the CC. Collins, an inveterate opponent of the JROTC and Committee on Militarism in Education adherent, feared that if Congress appropriated more money for the army, those funds would not be spent on tanks and planes but on the CC and more men for the RA.[8]

One of the most publicized assaults on army manpower occurred in 1932, when Democrats on the House Appropriations Committee attempted to cut the officer corps from twelve thousand to ten thousand, primarily by eliminating advisers and instructors assigned to the CC. They believed that this would nudge the War Department away from its fixation on the mass army toward a smaller, more technologically advanced force.[9]

Defenders of the CC successfully deflected this legislative assault. The secretary of war, Patrick Hurley, defended the ROTC as a bulwark of national defense and warned against any curtailment of the officer corps. Members of the House Military Affairs Committee backed Hurley and threatened to expose committee members who supported the cuts. Congress was bombarded with messages condemning the idea after the issue went public. Patriotic societies, college presidents, and high school principals vociferously denounced the proposal. In the end, Collins's démarche failed.[10]

THE DEPRESSION'S IMPACT

The Depression left its mark on the JROTC. As the fiscal situation worsened, the economy came to overshadow all other concerns. War Department officials struggled to cope with recurring bouts of budgetary belt-tightening. While the JROTC unit strength was stable, enrollment dropped steadily. When the army reached its fiscal nadir in 1933, it had to adopt extraordinary economy measures. It reduced the JROTC training, reimposed enrollment caps on the JROTC units, and eliminated five summer camps while shortening others. Cadets at military schools had to cancel or postpone their post-graduation plans since the completion of summer camp was a prerequisite for commissioning.[11]

High schools' ability to support the JROTC units suffered. A few schools dropped the program because of funding difficulties. Some smaller schools lost their units because they could not maintain the enrollment minimum of one hundred cadets. Many students withdrew to support their families.[12]

To compound the program's woes, the Franklin D. Roosevelt administration tasked the War Department to operate the Civilian Conservation Corps (CCC). The first CCC camp became operational in April 1933. By July, there were more than 1,400 camps in operation. This mission severely tested the army. To obtain the three thousand people needed to run the camps, the War Department pulled officers out of army professional schools and abruptly withdrew officers assigned to the Officers' Reserve Corps (ORC), National Guard, and JROTC. As a result, many schools had to suspend or temporarily close their units.[13]

Schools chafed at the withdrawal of their instructors. Their departure bred anxiety in the minds of school officials, created voids in instruction, and complicated planning for the next school year. Schools bitterly complained to federal authorities, who tried to placate the distraught officials as best they could.[14]

The situation improved gradually as the army substituted reserve officers for regulars at the CCC camps. This substitution began in October; by February 1934, most of the regulars were back in their old positions. While most regulars were away from their posts for only eight months, the episode left a bitter legacy of distrust of the War Department among school officials.[15]

Not all instructor shortages could be blamed on the CCC. The JROTC staffing rested on a formula introduced in 1923, which distributed instructors according to unit enrollment. In June 1923, there were 794 RA officers assigned to ROTC, of which 102 were retired. The appropriations bill of 1933 did not provide for the payment of these retirees, so they were released. Acute problems ensued. The G-3 urged that ROTC officer strength be raised from 566 to 675. Schools were battling pacifist agitation, and they needed more instructors to combat this danger. The G-1 balked at this proposal. He would agree to more support only if that assistance was "consistent with the efficient administration of other activities," which, he believed, it was not.[16]

In the fall of 1934, the army conducted another ROTC manpower review. From this review, the G-1 learned that teaching had suffered because of sparse staffing. Continued shortages would lead to a "general decay of the entire system." The G-1's solution was a more rational use of instructors; assignments should be based on unit training needs rather than on an arbitrary allotment of one instructor per so many students. Savings could be realized by combining officers assigned to the JROTC, ORC, and National Guard into a single manpower pool that could be drawn from when needed. School principals bristled at the thought of losing their full-time instructors and viewed this proposal as a symptom of the army's indifference toward the ROTC.[17]

The financial pinch hit the 55c program even harder than it did the JROTC. As school budgets flagged, hard-pressed school administrators found it difficult to sustain their units. Unit strength inevitably dipped. From a postwar high of fifty-nine units in 1929, the 55c program sank to forty-three units by 1935. The falloff in enrollment was even more dramatic. By 1935, that enrollment amounted to only 9,875, 40 percent below where it stood in 1929.[18]

Some blamed enrollment woes on the uniform issue, which was a long-standing problem that became more serious with the collapse of the economy. Without uniforms, cadet morale suffered. Some units responded by requiring cadets to buy their own uniforms. This placed an insuperable burden on poor students. Other schools formed nonuniformed companies, but a stigma clung to those students who chose this option.

The hiring of 55c instructors posed another difficulty. Some schools could not afford to employ a person solely as a military instructor. Accordingly, those hired for this job often had to serve triple duty as a military instructor, a coach, and a science teacher. Usually, the unit suffered in such arrangements.[19]

The declines in the JROTC and 55c enrollment after 1929 occurred while high school enrollment soared. This sharp rise in enrollment was due partly to government policy. Federal and state authorities tried to keep as many adolescents in high school as possible. The premature departure of students would swell the ranks of the unemployed. The concurrent decline in cadet enrollment and increase in secondary school enrollment resulted in the JROTC's school penetration rate reaching an interwar low, sinking from twenty-one students in every thousand in 1928 to nineteen in every thousand by 1933.[20]

THE JROTC'S REVIVAL

In the mid-1930s, JROTC's fortunes improved. A deteriorating international situation and a change in fiscal policy spurred another round of unit growth. Events overseas portended danger for the United States. Japan seized

Manchuria (1931), left the League of Nations (1933), and abrogated the Washington Naval Treaty (1934). In Germany, Adolf Hitler and his Nazi Party ascended to power in 1933. Hitler promptly inaugurated a program of rearmament, renounced the Treaty of Versailles, and withdrew Germany from the League of Nations. Meanwhile, Italy under Benito Mussolini built up its armed forces, made incendiary threats, and invaded Ethiopia in 1935.

Congress became more receptive to alarums of army officers who warned of the nation's parlous defense posture. In fiscal year 1935, it raised the army's end strength by 40 percent, increased West Point enrollment by 43 percent, and extended ROTC summer camps to the traditional six weeks. In addition, appropriations to replenish the army's war reserves and purchase modern equipment rose eighteenfold between 1934 and 1937.[21]

The JROTC shared in this "moderate rearmament." In fiscal year 1935, Congress set aside $1 million for the creation of more junior and senior ROTC units. With this money, the army added forty new JROTC units, a gain of 40 percent. Enrollment grew by 60 percent (see appendix A).[22]

The army enjoined corps commanders to observe strict economy in selecting new programs and to ensure that sufficient resources were available before establishing a unit. In the post–World War I expansion, commanders had proceeded hastily, spreading personnel and resources thinly across the institutional base and creating many weak and inefficient units. The army hoped to avoid repeating this mistake.[23]

The War Department's criteria for selecting new units included enrollment potential, drill grounds, facilities, proportionate unit distribution among states, school and community support, and "political interest." The last two factors were considered especially important.[24] The War Department believed that the wholehearted support of the local school was a prerequisite for success. It cited the case of one East Nashville public high school where a new and sympathetic school principal effected an "immense" improvement in his JROTC unit. The "excellent supervision and regulation" he provided presented a stark contrast with the indifference displayed by his predecessor and accounted for the transformation of an underperforming program into a "highly satisfactory" one.[25]

The support of the local community was another key to success. One inspector marveled about how the citizens of Gloucester, Massachusetts, turned the JROTC's annual field day into a local holiday. On that day, the citizens turned out en masse to observe the events and competitions. Veterans lent their support, as did patriotic organizations such as the American Legion and the Reserve Officers Association. These organizations provided valuable material support in the form of lectures, entertainment, and field trips.[26]

Conversely, lack of support shipwrecked units. War Department officials blamed the troubles of floundering programs on half-hearted backing by local authorities or school officials. Uncooperative principals lowered morale, hurt discipline, and diminished interest. The deleterious effect of an unsupportive administrator was a common theme running through interwar inspection reports.

Community opposition could also dim the JROTC's prospects. The unit at Jamaica High School in New York suffered because of "greatly divided sentiment" in the "community and [the] press" about the program. Units in Nashville, Carbondale, Sacramento, and other cities labored under similar conditions. Low enrollment, substandard training, and low morale were the inevitable results.[27]

The policy of establishing units where they were most welcome and abundantly provisioned clashed with the War Department's objective of achieving a proportional distribution of units among states. Although the army tried to balance these two objectives, receptivity usually won out over proportionality. This led to programs clustering in areas where they were most welcome.

The criterion of "political considerations" played a big part in the army's selection process. This term usually referred to the intervention of some prominent person or powerful organization on behalf of a school. The army was very vulnerable to this type of manipulation. When the army gave in to this pressure, the results were not always felicitous.[28]

An egregious case of a political establishment occurred in 1935 when the army succumbed to pressure applied by Senator Theodore G. Bilbo and opened a unit at Pearl River Junior College in Poplarville, Mississippi, the senator's hometown. The chief of staff planned to establish ten senior units to reduce the shortage of field artillery and engineer reserve officers. But the army chose to create three junior units "to meet the political aspects of the situation."[29]

Because the expansion occurred on a short timeline, some units, like the one at Pearl River, were launched hurriedly—in fact, "without first having been inspected."[30] The result was disastrous. One inspector described Pearl River as "the poorest school [he had] inspected. It [was] poor financially; poor in leadership and the students [were] . . . from a very poor class of white people." The conditions at the school were "unbelievable." Windowpanes in dormitories were broken, toilets exuded a terrible stench, halls were filled with trash, plumbing was out of order, and there was no heat or hot water. Student rooms were in disarray, with beds unmade, trash scattered on the floors, and "everything in wild disorder and confusion." The president of the school was "utterly incapable" and was not interested in improving conditions.[31] Army efforts to shutter the unit were unsuccessful.

Political establishments sometimes had ideological overtones. Some schools received programs because military leaders wanted to influence the political climate of a particular area. The War Department awarded a unit to Xavier High School in New York City because an army presence would supposedly bolster "the prestige of the ROTC in the metropolitan area" and "combat the pacifist and communist movements so prevalent in these [New York City] schools."[32]

Geographic proportionality triumphed over political expediency only when the payoff appeared substantial. Throughout most of the 1930s, neither North nor South Carolina hosted a single JROTC unit. The army planted programs in those states despite encountering strong local opposition. To the army, the units represented an opportunity to drive an "entering wedge" into the Carolinas. Their presence would awaken interest in military training and induce local and state authorities to become more solicitous of the army's needs. Students would profit from the "enormous . . . good accomplished in character building and physical development." The boost that the JROTC would give "to patriotic sentiment and loyal service" was certain to have "far-reaching" consequences.[33]

A school's racial makeup affected decisions to maintain or eliminate units. The Roosevelt administration showed more sensitivity to the interests of African American schools than its predecessor. This apparently rankled army officials who complained of being "constantly confronted [by the administration] with request(s) for equal educational opportunities for colored students." The administration pressed the army to spare Black units that failed to meet regulatory standards. The army reacted by either giving the units extra support to bolster enrollment or, if that didn't work, ignoring enrollment shortfalls. The unit at Bartlett Colored High School in Saint Joseph, Missouri, for example, escaped elimination despite its low enrollment—only thirty-two cadets—and lack of facilities. War Department officials had feared that the unit's closure would be "severely criticized" by the administration "for not providing the same type of opportunity for our colored high school" as it did for the white high schools.[34]

The Roosevelt administration did not exhibit the same benevolence toward Asian American citizens. In the 1930s, army officials anticipated a conflict with Japan and came to doubt the loyalty of Asian American people. They opposed the creation of more units in Hawaii because they did not want to provide an "opening wedge" for Asian American people to enter the ORC. When the army rejected unit applications submitted by three Hawaiian high schools in 1937, however, it listed the lack of storage facilities and a shortage of instructors as the reasons. In reality, the fear of a fifth column was the dominant concern. This fear manifested itself again in 1938 when the army rejected requests to raise enrollment in Hawaiian units, as it had elsewhere in the United States.[35]

THE EXPANSION PLATEAUS

Attempts to expand the program beyond the 141-unit legislative limit failed. To be sure, the demand for units remained "incessant." The waiting list was long, and congressional support remained strong. Congress repeatedly approved funds for more units in its annual appropriations bills. Nevertheless, the JROTC's institutional base did not grow. Every year from 1937 to 1940, the Office of the Budget and the War Department diverted funds earmarked for the JROTC growth to more critical priorities.[36]

The War Department cited a shortage of officers as the reason. Even before the expansion of the mid-1930s, there was an acute shortage of instructors. Subsequently, the situation became worse. General Malin Craig asserted that the enrollment increases of the mid-1930s placed the program in a "serious condition." The "only answer," he wrote, was an increase in the size of the officer corps since it was impossible to divert officers from other important duties.[37]

Despite the end of unit expansion, enrollment continued to rise. Average unit strength rose from 377 in 1936 to 476 in 1940. This placed existing units on a sounder footing.[38] Unit enlargement occurred without the army having to use more officers or noncommissioned officers (NCOs). In the cases of Detroit and Chicago schools, the army did this by detailing privates from nearby military posts to serve as instructors. The army would have preferred more mature instructors but had to bow to manpower constraints.[39]

In other instances, it leveraged multiple-school urban programs. One must recall that the JROTC had more high schools than units. In smaller communities and military institutes, the rule was that one school hosted one unit. But in major metropolitan areas, one unit could encompass an entire school system. In 1936, the JROTC maintained 141 units but was in 262 high schools. The Chicago unit, the largest in the country, included twenty-seven schools with 7,359 cadets and a staff of six officers and twenty-nine enlisted men.[40]

Because some urban programs encompassed entire school systems, the army could add a high school without creating a new unit. It had done this since the early 1920s but adopted it as an official policy only in 1936. In that year, the JROTC units in Fulton County, Georgia, and Omaha incorporated an additional high school. During the next several years, units in Detroit, Chicago, Fort Worth, Grand Rapids, and Sacramento followed suit. This type of intra-unit expansion was often done by redistribution—by spreading instructors more thinly across schools.[41]

THE JROTC'S CHANGING GEOGRAPHY

The geographical distribution of the JROTC units remained a problem for the army in the 1930s. In the Northeast, the JROTC was underrepresented, while in the West, South, and Midwest, it was slightly overrepresented. Eleven states—Connecticut, New Hampshire, Vermont, Delaware, Maryland, Pennsylvania, Ohio, Arkansas, North Dakota, New Mexico, and Montana—hosted no programs, while North and South Carolina were unitless until the late 1930s.[42]

The unit distribution pattern had shifted as the zeal for cadet training abated in the Northeast while growing in the South, the West, and the Midwest. The reasons for this shift are not entirely clear, although several plausible explanations have been suggested.

In the South, the growing presence of the JROTC units reflected the region's military tradition. The region's agrarian economic base, underdeveloped transportation network, history of incessant American Indian warfare, cult of romantic chivalry, fear of slave uprisings, and conservative political ideology supposedly created an atmosphere highly congenial to cadet programs.[43]

Economic forces were also at work. Poor regions of the country were more receptive to cadet programs than affluent ones. They were attracted by the material benefits the JROTC offered, such as instructors, uniforms, and weapons. The JROTC's decline in the Northeast has been ascribed to its commercial economy. The region became preoccupied with commerce, manufacturing, and other pursuits associated with an urban, industrial society. The austere life of a soldier had little appeal there. Moreover, the JROTC's material benefits had little salience in a region with strong tax bases, substantial education budgets, and abundant employment opportunities.[44]

The location of military bases may have been another contributing factor. World War I had spurred the creation of dozens of new bases in the South, many of which later became permanent installations. Climate, abundant training space, and inexpensive land drove this southward movement. By the 1930s, the southern half of the nation contained the preponderance of large military bases. Proximity to a post was a great boon to a unit, offering many practical benefits, such as supplies, training assistance, and space for summer camps.[45]

Finally, the movement of the country's demographic center to the South and West affected unit distribution. The shift started in the colonial period and continues to this day. Between 1870 and 1918, the nation's geographic center point moved from central Ohio to southern Indiana (near the Illinois border). The population moved southwest, and cadet training moved with it. Whatever the factors behind the shift may have been, by the 1930s, the geography of cadet training was very different from what it had been four decades earlier.

TRAINING AND THE CURRICULUM

In the 1930s, the objectives of the JROTC were to teach basic military skills, lay "the foundation for intelligent citizenship," and, "secondarily," prepare cadets for a "position of responsibility" in the event of induction.[46] It is noteworthy that in this time of international tension, military skills training was listed first.

In civilian high schools, the junior curriculum called for three hours of instruction each week for three years. The first two years concentrated on tasks appropriate to privates and NCOs in an infantry regiment. The third year focused on subjects relevant to junior officers. While the War Department provided subject guidelines, local school authorities and the professors of military science and training (PMS&Ts) had wide latitude in the allotment of instructional hours and selection of classes. Because they hosted commissioning programs, military institutes had more intensive four-year curricula, which included heavy doses of drill and military training. In the case of both military and civilian schools, however, the army decentralized authority as much as possible, standardization being inappropriate since conditions at each school differed so dramatically.[47]

The army's baseline curriculum changed little over the interwar period. Tweaks were constant, but substantial change was rare. The 1933 revision for civilian schools, for example, moved certain subjects from one year to another, regrouped others to achieve progressive development, and stopped dictating the number of hours allotted to each course. To keep cadets abreast of recent developments, the army occasionally introduced topical subjects. For example, the army inserted classes on mechanization into the schedule in 1939.[48]

The Infantry School produced the *JROTC Manual*, the program's basic text. The manual covered military history, weapons, drill, military administration, army organization, hygiene, and other topics. The narrow scope of the material invited condemnation from civilian critics, who berated the JROTC curriculum for being too narrow, too vocationally oriented, and too academically shallow.[49]

Army inspectors agreed, at least to a point. They took PMS&Ts to task for their overemphasis on drill and "woefully weak" theoretical instruction. Education, not training, they preached, should be the principal focus of the JROTC. Instead of pushing drill, instructors should concentrate on teaching cadets how "to think along logical lines" and organize their time.[50] Not all instructors accepted this critique. Many recognized that principals, parents, and local leaders prized the program for its disciplinary value. They did not want to jeopardize the JROTC's acceptance by pursuing fuzzy and irrelevant educational objectives.[51]

The War Department enjoined units to employ practical, hands-on instruction whenever possible. Lectures were to supplement, not substitute for, active learning activities. Many units did not attain this pedagogical ideal, but a significant minority of them did. This later group used senior cadets to present classes to underclassmen, to the delight of army inspectors.[52]

Competition remained a training mainstay. Intersquad drill, marksmanship, and athletic contests taught military skills, improved physical fitness, and fostered teamwork. They were also a boon to enrollment. Many cadets enrolled for these activities. Most units stressed the development of cadet officers since the army obtained its biggest payoffs from among these students. Seniors rotated through leadership positions in cadet battalions and learned how a military chain of command functioned.[53]

Summer training was an important event. Since most junior cadets could not attend federally funded camps, the army encouraged units to hold camps of their own, provided they were held at no expense to the government. This caveat greatly restricted the number of schools that could host camps and the number of cadets who could attend them. Camps varied in length from a few days to several weeks. The army issued no guidance for summer training; it assumed that local conditions determined what activities could be offered.[54]

The army set the normal tour of duty for an officer at three years. This policy irritated educators who insisted that three years was too brief a period for the instructor to become fully conversant with his responsibilities. Continuity in most units was provided by NCOs, who normally stayed on station much longer. In 1938, the army reported that of the more than 670 NCOs on ROTC duty, 21 percent had been with their unit for more than fifteen years, 18 percent for between ten and fifteen years, and 21 percent for between five and ten years.[55] Educators viewed the army's staffing solution as workable but far from ideal.

THE JROTC'S ROLES

The roles played by the JROTC in the 1920s retained their salience in the 1930s, although some assumed a different aspect. The importance attached to military training, for example, increased after 1935, as the nation took its first halting steps toward rearmament.[56]

Moral training took on a renewed importance with the collapse of the economy and family structure. Average family income plummeted by 35 percent in the four years of the Hoover administration. By 1933, an estimated 1.5 million people were homeless, and millions more were unemployed. Family structures and traditional parental roles were disrupted. Men who lost their jobs had to rely on handouts from the government or friends. Some had the dispiriting experience of depending on their working wives and children for support. This led to many men abandoning their families.[57]

Some JROTC instructors became virtual surrogate fathers, providing boys from fractured families both direction and discipline. One corps commander noted that the "tragic break-down of the home" compounded the nation's educational problems. He believed that, under the circumstances, instructors had to ramp up citizenship training: "I don't think you can do too much of it."[58] The fatherless family coupled with the dearth of male schoolteachers, it was feared, would lead to the feminization of adolescent boys. With their characters shaped by their mothers and a largely female corps of teachers, boys would become weak, effeminate, and submissive. A junior unit could combat feminization by giving boys tough, vigorous men to look up to and an all-male environment in which to cultivate their competitiveness.[59]

The JROTC remained an important agent of neutralizing pacifist and radical propaganda. The G-1 claimed that the JROTC could be employed to dispel the popular notion that the army was a militaristic organization bent on war and foreign conquest. It could likewise counteract the spread of pernicious political doctrines in schools, where naive and impressionable students were easy targets for agitators. This was critically important in large urban public schools, where many faculty members sympathized with the leftists.[60]

By injecting conservative beliefs into adolescents, the program also lowered attitudinal and ideological barriers to military service. This became important in the mid-1930s as wars broke out in Ethiopia and China. Subversive influences had cast "grave doubts" on the army's capacity to mobilize. The General Staff predicted a strong reaction against any attempt to recruit the million men needed for the initial mobilization force.[61] Opposition could be expected from pacifist and radical groups such as the Communist League and the National Council for Prevention of War. Their resistance would be formidable. Accordingly, the War Department staff urged that the 1933 Mobilization Plan be scrapped and a new one drafted—one that considered the likely effects of dissident agitation.[62]

The army sometimes became a bit too zealous in its battle against dissidents. One telling incident occurred in the early 1930s when the War Department dispatched officers to the capital city's public schools to lecture students on the dangers of radicalism. The initiative backfired. The sectarian harangues delivered by those officers disturbed the largely sympathetic audiences who heard them. Instead of striking a blow against communism, the effort confirmed popular stereotypes about the shallowness and fanaticism of professional military men.[63]

But such episodes were the exception, not the rule. The War Department continued to advise instructors to "refrain from directly attacking [dissident] individuals or groups" (see chap. 2). These groups could not be overcome by debate. Instructors were not equipped to succeed in such exchanges in any case. In any debate, they would "be arguing with a class of people whose training in the mechanics of argument [was] far better" than theirs. Public presentations were also discouraged because they were lightning rods for criticism and ridicule. Besides, little would be accomplished even if the officer succeeded in besting his opponents. The positive effect of such an outcome would be transitory at best.[64]

Arguing with critics was thus a waste of time; the less officers had to say about controversial issues, the better. They should counter the program's critics by becoming the most indispensable members of the faculty and forging personal contacts in the school and community. In public forums, instructors should use prominent citizens and sympathetic organizations such as the American Legion and the Veterans of Foreign Wars (VFW) to defend the JROTC interests and army policies.[65]

The War Department could do little to help instructors. Its public relations apparatus was too small to contest effectively against determined and articulate enemies. That apparatus consisted of a tiny cell in a "meagerly financed" intelligence division of the army staff.[66] Under the circumstances, an indirect approach was clearly the best strategy.

The ability of a cadet program to maintain order in the classroom had long attracted the attention of educators. It assumed new significance in the 1930s as high school enrollment soared. Youth who in an earlier era would have dropped their studies and found employment now remained in school. Many were shunted into commercial, vocational, or general tracks. As the number of students in nonacademic tracks mushroomed, the custodial function of the high school became more prominent. High schools became more absorbed in entertaining than in educating. The nation did not need more people competing for a limited number of jobs. The JROTC had an obvious attraction to educators struggling to keep their crowded classrooms under control.

THE JROTC IN WORLD WAR II

The outbreak of World War II did not spark an expansion of the JROTC. Between 1940 and 1945, the army established no new junior units. The freeze on unit growth did not reflect a slackening demand. The volume of school requests for new units remained large. Factors inhibiting growth included a lack of personnel and material resources and the War Department's focus on prosecuting the war, which made pre-induction military programs seem less urgent.[67]

With a moratorium on institutional expansion in effect, any growth had to occur within existing units. The army was open to this alternative since the marginal costs of incorporating more students into existing units were low. Thus, enrollment rose moderately after the outbreak of war. It reached a wartime peak of 77,300 students in 1943—10 percent above that of 1940.[68]

The JROTC had to contend with multiple constraints during the war. For one thing, the enlistment of thousands of high school seniors reduced the base from which cadets were drawn. Students rushed to the colors, afraid that they would be left out of the greatest event of their lifetime. Supply and equipment shortages also depressed enrollment. When the War Department replaced rifles with wooden dummies, esprit de corps plummeted. Instructors had to scrounge rifles from nearby reserve units if they wanted to take their cadets to the firing range. Moreover, the manpower demands of the war restricted the number of officers available for the JROTC duty. Turbulence ensued as the army abruptly pulled officers and NCOs out of schools to support the war effort. Some units experienced a turnover of instructors every year from 1940 through 1945. Others saw their instructors replaced with reservists, some of whom were superannuated and physically unfit.[69]

The 55c program experienced a minor resurgence during the war. After declining from thirty-six units to thirty between September 1939 and September 1943, it grew to fifty-three units by September 1944. At the same time, 55c enrollment rose by more than 44 percent (nine thousand to thirteen thousand).[70]

The War Department encouraged this growth. Three considerations moved it to sanction a 55c expansion. First, there were many high schools clamoring for units, and the army wanted to satisfy as many schools as it could. Second, the training given in 55c units was of some value to young men going into the army. Marksmanship training was especially useful. Finally, the 55c program was inexpensive. It required no active-duty instructors and consumed little money. In the 1943–1944 school year, the army spent only $8,900, or ninety-five cents per student, on 55c schools.[71]

The JROTC took on a more martial aspect during the war. The program's two main objectives became producing infantry reserve officers and providing preinduction military training for potential inductees. The militarization of the program was most pronounced at military schools, where training greatly intensified. Weapons training and physical conditioning took the place of military history. At Massanutten, officials curtailed vacations, eliminated holiday leaves, and introduced hand-to-hand combat and bayonet training. Similar transformations occurred at other military institutes.[72]

ROTC management underwent an extensive makeover. In 1941, the War Department created a new office—the Executive for Reserve and ROTC Affairs—to improve the administration of the CC. The general officer who led the new office performed supervisory and educational liaison functions. To assist him, the executive had an ROTC division, consisting of a colonel, six officers, and two civilian clerks.[73]

After the 1942 army reorganization, supervisory and policy-formulating responsibilities for the ROTC gravitated to the Office of the Director of Military Training in the newly created Army Service Forces (ASF). The director of training shared with the technical services and the Army Ground Forces (AGF) responsibility for curriculum development, personnel management, and technical training. In the new scheme, service commands supplanted corps area commands. While the new management arrangements were an improvement, lines of control and responsibility remained complicated and hazy.[74]

WARTIME PERFORMANCE

The junior division did not live up to the army's wartime expectations. The disappointment stemmed from the program's dismal record in producing reserve officers. Because civilian schools did not produce lieutenants, the army's displeasure fell primarily on military institutes. On the eve of the war, matters had looked promising. Military schools (MS) produced 672 lieutenants for the ORC in 1939 and 454 in 1940. Once war broke out, however, only a trickle of graduates attended Officer Candidate School (OCS), which became a prerequisite for commissioning.

This low attendance rate was brought on by a policy change. In March 1942, the army allotted an officer school quota to every MS-class institution. The next year, it rescinded that quota and reserved all OCS vacancies for the SROTC students. For military schools, this meant that their preferred commissioning status was at an end. The army's move disturbed the authorities at military institutes. Without special access into the officer corps, the viability of military schools was in jeopardy.[75]

The cancellation of officer quotas reflected the War Department's misgivings about the quality of military schools and their graduates. One PMS&T characterized military schools as mediocre academic institutions and the students attending them as "not of high quality." He viewed military schools as profit-making enterprises that the army should no longer subsidize. The ASF history of the wartime ROTC simply noted that military schools did not produce a "satisfactory product for the Army's purposes."[76]

The lackluster performance of graduates at OCS confirmed the army's misgivings. One hundred eleven military school graduates attended OCS classes 295 through 305. Only 31.5 percent of them passed the course. By comparison, enlisted candidates had a pass rate of 60.5 percent, while the graduation rate of the SROTC candidates was 67.5 percent. About one-third of military school graduates scored below the cutoff score of 110 on the Army General Classification Test (AGCT), and most of these failed the course. Age was not a factor. The average age of military school graduates was 19.6 years, the same as that of enlisted candidates.[77]

The large number of failures drew attention to the army's method of evaluating military institutes. An "exceedingly" large number of MS-class institutions, it was found, received the *honor* designation—twenty-five of thirty-eight in 1944. For all practical purposes, an ASF historian noted, the designation *honor military school* was equivalent to acceptable. The flawed evaluation process robbed the award of real significance.[78]

Within the army, many questioned the "propriety" of retaining the junior division. The attitude of army leaders ranged from tepid acceptance to outright disdain. The ASF's training director assessed the worth of civilian school units as "slight," although he conceded that they reinforced the "principle of military training for civilians" at small cost to the government. The ASF's official history of the ROTC observed, "It is difficult to justify the junior division.... It has been a misnomer to call it a reserve officer training program." The Executive for Reserve and ROTC Affairs agreed. In 1944, he recommended replacing the JROTC with a student training corps.[79]

Such negative assessments might be expected given the army's wartime focus. Winning the war was an all-consuming national passion. Inevitably, military organizations were evaluated on their impact on immediate military needs. And the JROTC, even its defenders had to admit, came up short in this regard.

THE VICTORY CORPS

At the outset of the war, the War Department discouraged the formation of independent cadet corps, claiming that they would be "impractical." More would be gained if students received "sound mental and physical training" in regular high school courses. Despite the coolness of military leaders, participation in high school military units skyrocketed. As in previous conflicts, nationalist enthusiasm stimulated public demand for military training.[80]

State governments, civic groups, and individual schools seized the initiative and began programs of their own. After being rebuffed by the army, the American Legion formed its own High School Military Training Program.[81] Among the states that initiated cadet programs, Louisiana stands out. Although the Louisiana High School Military Training Program, as it was called, was formally under the state's Department of Education, other organizations, like the American Legion, National Guard, and various colleges, helped administer and operate it.[82] Program objectives included reducing the dropout rate, improving discipline, creating an interest in military service, and giving preinduction military training. Louisiana billed cadet training as a citizenship program and operated under the premise that "a good citizen makes a good soldier, and the converse is equally true."[83]

The federal government eventually joined the effort and established the High School Victory Corps, by far the largest organization of its type during the war. This voluntary organization was headed by the Office of Education and assisted by the War Department, Navy Department, and Civil Aeronautics Administration (CAA). Its purpose was to orchestrate preinduction military training, teach good citizenship, harness the energies of students to perform essential services, and make adolescents feel part of the war effort. Announced in September 1942, it spread to 70 percent of US high schools by July 1943. According to the Office of Education, 22 percent of eligible students, which included boys and girls, enrolled in the corps within a year of its creation.[84]

When the Victory Corps was established, the services were experiencing "considerable difficulty" with inductees. They rejected half of the first two million men conscripted for medical reasons. No medical examination infrastructure was in place to help with the screening. In addition, many draftees were in terrible physical shape. They were "soft and flabby" and were not up to the rigors of basic training. The services spent considerable time bringing these men up to standard. Many men were also unprepared intellectually for military service. Inductees were "sadly deficient" in mathematics, basic sciences, and technical knowledge.[85]

Before the establishment of the High School Victory Corps, schools were getting mixed signals from the federal government about the types of skills and knowledge needed. The army told them one thing, the navy another, and the CAA still another. With the creation of the corps, the federal government could now speak with one voice.[86]

Through the Victory Corps, the government sponsored technical training and math, science, and language education. Instruction in these subjects reduced training time after induction and prepared students for work in war industries. In addition, the program promoted physical fitness, fostered appropriate attitudes, and provided community services. Salvage campaigns, bond drives, and farm labor were all part of the agenda.[87]

The War Department assisted the Office of Education in managing the Victory Corps, although its role was ambiguous. Confusion about the army's involvement was evident from the beginning. In March 1942, army officials declared their intention not to become involved in preinduction military training. Less than two months later, they established an organization—the Preinduction Training Section—to coordinate such training. This change stemmed from the growing recognition that total war had created a huge need for men with special technical skills, which few inductees had. Many did not have even the rudimentary skills and knowledge necessary for basic training. Eventually, the War Department realized the pressing need for preinduction preparation.[88]

The Victory Corps' organization consisted of a general membership section and five special divisions: land, sea, air, production, and community service. Students who selected the general membership option studied subjects related to the war effort, participated in at least one war-related activity, and took part in a physical fitness program. Students in one of the five special divisions were subject to stricter academic requirements and wore distinctive insignia. General membership was by far the most popular option; community service came in a distant second.[89]

The popularity of the Victory Corps proved evanescent. Although it was never intended as a permanent program, its demise was more rapid than anticipated. By the summer of 1944, the Victory Corps was a "dead duck." It lingered on in an attenuated form until the spring of 1945, when it was officially abolished. The corps' popularity waned as the urgency of the international threat subsided. A few Victory Corps units survived the war and continued as JROTC or 55c programs.[90]

The Victory Corps' record of achievement was "spotty," which was not surprising given its herculean tasks. Improving the science and math proficiency and physical fitness of youth was a daunting challenge in wartime.[91] Perhaps the program's greatest strength was that it allowed high school students to feel that they had a meaningful part in the war effort. Given the stresses of wartime and the pent-up energies of adolescents, this was no small achievement.

With the onset of the Great Depression, the JROTC entered a time of austerity. Funding, manpower, and resources were cut, and critics questioned its value. Although supporters rushed to its defense, the program experienced tough sledding.

The program began to revive in the late 1930s. A worsening international situation provided a powerful impetus to this recovery. Preinduction military training suddenly appeared more valuable. Other benefits of the program also became more evident. A burgeoning high school population, economic hardship, the weakening of the family structure, and social turmoil all highlighted the program's value as an instrument of citizenship education and moral training.

The US entry into World War II did not stimulate significant JROTC or 55c growth. Manpower, resources, and wartime priorities were the issues. While the JROTC was static, other school-based military programs mushroomed. The Victory Corps was the largest of these, but there were scores of others. These programs gave students service opportunities and cemented support for the war effort on the home front.

The JROTC emerged from the war with a sullied reputation within the War Department. Graduates had a high failure rate in officer-producing programs, while military school presidents made incessant demands on limited resources. Some War Department officials even called for the program's elimination. In the next chapter, will take up the JROTC's adjustment to the postwar world.

4

From Truman to Kennedy, 1945–1963

After the war, the armed services began a rapid demobilization. The Harry S. Truman administration, anxious to trim defense spending and avoid another depression, pared down the military from a little over 12 million men to just under 1.5 million men by 1950.[1] As the military shrank, the Soviet threat grew. A communist coup in Czechoslovakia (1948), the Berlin Blockade (1948–1949), the "fall" of China (1949), and other crises led to a growing suspicion of Soviet intentions. To meet this challenge, the army pushed for a system of universal military training (UMT). Modern technology had negated America's strategic advantages of distance and isolation. Huge reserves of trained manpower now had to be available upon the outbreak of hostilities. In late 1945, Truman asked Congress to approve legislation requiring all physically fit male citizens to undergo one year of military training. His proposal soon became bottled up in Congress, and the army, after a brief experiment with volunteerism, went back to selective service.[2]

The Cold War cast a pall over domestic relations. Escalating international tension fostered a preoccupation with internal security. Conspiracy theories about communist influence proliferated. State and federal legislatures investigated seditious activities and passed laws requiring loyalty oaths from public officials. Concerned citizens launched patriotic crusades to rid schools of subversive teachers and books.[3]

STAGNATION

Between World War II and the end of the Korean War, the JROTC's institutional base remained stable. In 1944, the JROTC encompassed 143 units. Nine years later, it had 142. While the unit base remained stable, enrollment dropped substantially. From a wartime high of nearly 77,000 in 1944, enrollment sank to 57,750 by 1950 (see appendix A).[4]

The enrollment decline stemmed from the ebbing of martial fervor, a decreasing propensity for military service, and a drop-off in high school enrollment, induced by a fall in the birth rate during the 1930s. With the decrease in the high school population, the JROTC's representation in schools held steady. At both the beginning and end of the decade, about ten in every thousand high school students were JROTC cadets.[5]

Army policy, too, limited the JROTC enrollment. Fearing recession, the Truman administration imposed fiscal restrictions on the Department of Defense (DOD).[6] Between 1945 and 1947, the army budget sank by a staggering 84 percent. Although defense spending rose again in 1950, there remained an imbalance between the army's budget and its expanded array of missions. This forced the army to make painful funding decisions. The JROTC, a non-officer-producing citizenship program, did not fare well in this process. Throughout the Truman administration, in fact, there was unremitting pressure on the program's budget.[7]

The prewar freeze on JROTC unit growth continued after 1945. The army's adjutant general formalized the no-growth policy in a policy letter (January 1947), which remained in effect for fifteen years. At the same time, the army restricted the ability of corps commanders to add schools to existing urban units and placed a cap on enrollment. In 1947, the Bureau of the Budget reduced the JROTC enrollment ceiling from eighty thousand to seventy thousand. In 1950, it cut that ceiling again—to sixty thousand.[8]

Within the ROTC, priority went to the senior program. The army needed more lieutenants. Since the JROTC did not produce officers, it was pushed aside. The 1947 letter announcing the no-growth policy stated that until the instructors and money become available to build up the SROTC to its authorized strength, no more junior units would be created.[9]

The JROTC's most critical shortage was manpower. Every officer assigned to the JROTC meant one less for the SROTC. In 1951, the junior division was absorbing one-third of the ROTC officer allocation, significantly reducing the SROTC's capacity to produce lieutenants.[10] The dearth of instructors became a contentious issue in 1952 when the army added twenty-five new units to the senior program to meet higher officer requirements. To staff the new units, the army drew from the JROTC. Overall, between 1952 and 1953, the junior division lost 121 officers—more than a third of its allotment—to college units. This angered high school officials, who saw the size of their faculties suddenly diminished, and irritated army leaders, who had to endure the complaints of disgruntled educators.[11]

From 1945 to 1953, there were calls for sharper reductions. In 1948, the DOD's Committee on Civilian Components (Gray Board) recommended that schools subsidize their own instructors.[12] Another DOD proposal (1949) called for assigning only one officer to each unit. This would cut officer staffing in half. Another suggestion urged the substitution of teachers with reserve commissions for active-duty instructors, which would slash the JROTC's officer requirements to zero; 55c schools had been doing this for years. The idea of shifting part of the instructor burden to the navy and air force was also broached. Those services benefited from the JROTC but contributed nothing to its support. Navy and air force leaders balked at the idea.[13]

There were even calls for the JROTC to be abolished. Pentagon officials considered the program unprofitable and "essentially superfluous" to army needs since it did not produce reserve officers. Studies analyzing the JROTC's effectiveness as an officer-producing program, the Army G-1 reported, had "failed to produce definitive results."[14]

In 1951, the deputy chief of staff of the army, Lieutenant General Maxwell Taylor, set out to eliminate the JROTC through normal attrition. Taylor, who branded the JROTC an expensive luxury, anticipated "strong resentment," so he proceeded cautiously. If he tightened up the no-growth policy, placed limits on enrollment, reduced funding, and closed inefficient units, he thought that this non-officer-producing program would eventually disappear.[15] He was soon disappointed.

COMMISSIONING AUTHORITY WITHDRAWN

A milestone occurred in 1942 when the army ceased tendering reserve commissions to graduates of military secondary schools. The army made this policy official in 1946. Henceforth, commissions came only through the senior program. Certainly, the junior division's dismal record of producing reserve officers weighed heavily in this decision.[16]

Some argued that, since the JROTC no longer offered commissions, it should be renamed and detached from the SROTC. The army rejected this proposal because the JROTC had become a trademark. Giving it a new name would have caused confusion and cost the army a large sum of money just to accommodate a superficial change.[17]

The army also kept the two programs linked organizationally despite the functional change that had occurred. It adduced five considerations to justify its decision: (1) historical precedence; (2) a common educational focus; (3) a common citizenship emphasis; (4) common public outreach functions; and (5) the JROTC's budgetary viability, since separation would inevitably result in resource cuts.[18]

CITIZENSHIP TRAINING

After the war, citizenship training gained salience in the public if not the military domain. The postwar campaign for UMT highlighted the civic value of military training. While military leaders had pushed UMT as a way to create an emergency manpower pool, others emphasized its potential for the moral, civic, and physical uplift of young men. President Truman felt this way. He expected the program "to develop skills that could be used in civilian life, to raise the physical standards of the nation's manpower, to lower the illiteracy rate, to develop citizenship responsibilities, and to foster the moral and spiritual welfare of male youth." Albeit never implemented, UMT underlined the connection between military training and the development of civic virtue.[19]

UMT was only one force behind the effort to teach citizenship and morality to men in uniform. That initiative also encompassed programs like character guidance, moral leadership, and, later, human self-development. One historian described this push as the "most massive, intensive, and carefully organized attempt at character building ever attempted under secular leadership."[20]

The army's Character Guidance program (1947) sought to provide religious and citizenship instruction to soldiers.[21] It gained strength from a growing public anxiety about immorality in the military. Newspapers told of rampant alcoholism and venereal disease among occupation forces in Europe. A congressional investigative team confirmed these reports. It found "staggering immorality" and an "appalling" level of alcohol use among service members.[22]

Another force behind citizenship training was the intensifying fear of communism. To protect troops against the blandishments of radical agitators, the army developed lectures that extolled the virtues of capitalism and democracy and denounced communist excesses.[23] The JROTC taught a version of citizenship that fit nicely within this campaign. One guard officer averred that by incorporating the junior program into this effort, "[they would] go a long way toward combating the communist infiltration which [was] getting stronger in this country every day."[24] The JROTC again took up the role of a bulwark against dangerous foreign ideologies.

The JROTC's character education function remained relevant. Its disciplinary benefits were invaluable in a country plagued with rising rates of juvenile crime. A senate judiciary subcommittee (1953) reported that cities across the nation were in the throes of an adolescent rebellion. In Philadelphia, the problem reached massive proportions; the city government imposed a curfew on all youths under seventeen. The subcommittee believed that the nation needed programs like the JROTC to combat the delinquency epidemic.[25]

Recruiting continued to be an important JROTC function. While the draft ensured a steady flow of inductees into the active force, filling the ranks of the reserve components was a problem. Hundreds of reserve units had been created as a hedge against a major war. The army struggled to fill these units. By the late 1940s, it suffered from severe reserve manpower shortages. To eliminate these shortfalls, the army turned to the JROTC.[26] In 1949, the chief of the Army Reserve (CAR) vetted a plan to increase JROTC input into the Enlisted Reserve Corps (ERC). He began to "coordinate" the JROTC and 55c units with the ERC, Officers' Reserve Corps (ORC), and SROTC to raise reserve enlistments and produce more reserve officers.[27] The army modified the JROTC goals accordingly. The JROTC objectives now included "to give basic military training which will be of use to the graduate and the service if he is inducted."[28]

One function that lost some of its urgency was public outreach. The nation was emerging from the largest war in its history, a war that had touched nearly every family in America. The United States retained a peacetime force of unprecedented magnitude, whose ranks were filled by the draft. With the country brimming with soldiers and veterans, the public no longer needed to be reminded of service needs and contributions to the extent it once did.

ELIMINATION OF THE JROTC?

The JROTC came under scrutiny in the late 1940s and early 1950s, when it appeared that a UMT law would be enacted.[29] The expected passage of the law presaged the program's demise since it presumably would make the

JROTC superfluous. The Army G-3 actually drew up plans for the JROTC's elimination, which he promised to release "at the appropriate time." That moment never came.[30]

The program's defenders resisted this closure attempt. The benefits of the program, they admitted, were of a general rather than concrete nature. Still, this did not make them less real. Prominent among its advantages was its ability to generate "military interest" in students. Contact with military officers and noncommissioned officers (NCOs) awakened this interest. The JROTC also provided valuable training. Its three-year program supposedly produced a soldier with a military proficiency equivalent to that of a junior NCO in the reserves. To its supporters, the program had proved its military worth in World War II, when it turned out large numbers of officers and NCOs. Paradoxically, it appeared even more valuable when it became clear that UMT legislation would not pass. It was then heralded as a partial substitute for UMT.[31]

THE JROTC'S DECLINE

Dwight D. Eisenhower's election ushered in eight years of budgetary stringency for the army. In 1953, the army had twenty divisions, 1.5 million men, and a budget of $13 billion. By 1958, it had fifteen divisions, 900,000 men, and a budget of $9 billion.[32] Declining manpower, limited funds, and an expanded mission presented challenges to the army and the JROTC. There was neither the money nor the manpower available to replace shuttered units, let alone create new ones. After remaining stable from 1941 to 1953, the program's institutional base began to contract, shrinking by 3 percent in the decade after Korea. DOD policy enabled this decline. The ban on institutional growth remained in effect. In fact, restrictions on growth became more severe. Under Eisenhower, the ban on unit creations was extended to the senior program (1953), while the practices of allowing multiple-school units to absorb new high schools and of replacing shuttered units with new ones were discontinued. Moreover, during the first year of Eisenhower's presidency, the army cut the JROTC's officer strength by another 22 percent as an economy measure.[33]

The decline in institutional strength was obfuscated by a change in the way the army counted units. Instead of grouping junior programs in large urban areas together in one comprehensive unit, the army began to list each high school separately. The purpose was to make the unit management process more transparent. The apparent unit increase in the mid-1950s was due to this change in tabulation methods, not to the establishment of any new units.[34]

Enrollment trends were more opaque than institutional developments. After 1952, enrollment dipped. This was due largely to the hard quotas imposed on the JROTC in August 1953. Previously, enrollment was regulated by "budget positions," a control method that gave managers flexibility. The new quotas established "formal, fixed" enrollment caps. Managers now had little wriggle room. In 1954, the army denied enrollment to 3,873 students because of the new restrictions. Simultaneously, the army more vigorously enforced its ban on growth *within* school systems. The JROTC administrators could no longer reshuffle instructors to found new programs.[35]

Conflicting pressures pummeled the JROTC after mid-decade. There were pressures to economize *and* to expand. In general, the government wanted to economize, while schools demanded more units. The growth of the high school population fueled this demand. Instructor availability remained the cardinal stumbling block for expansion. Army leaders struggled to find the manpower to support units amid an overall strength reduction. Something had to give, and the JROTC was the bill payer. In 1958, it suffered another manpower cut. This reduction was effected by closing units that did not meet enrollment minima and paring staffs at larger units.[36]

To achieve further savings, the army considered tapping alternative sources of instructors. Three suggested alternatives were reservists, retirees, and civilians. Replacing the JROTC with 55c units, however, was the most popular option. It would allow program extension at minimal cost.[37] None of these proposals generated much public support.

In May 1955, the CSA reported that he was under "constant and increasing pressure" from high schools for new units and the expansion of existing ones. The army had over five hundred requests for units on file and would have had more if it had not discouraged new applications.[38] The army's no-growth policy angered school officials. The superintendent of the Dallas school system wrote to Pentagon officials complaining about the "undue hardship" they had imposed on his growing school district. His district had twelve high schools, eight of which had JROTC units and four of which did not. Three of the four without a unit desperately wanted one.[39]

Dallas addressed its needs by "informally" enrolling students in the program. It had 325 unofficial cadets in 1954. The continued growth of the Dallas school system would eventually add hundreds more.[40] Informal enrollment was not new, nor was it limited to Dallas. In 1948, fifty-five units enrolled 3,277 unofficial cadets, most of whom were under fourteen years of age. While defense leaders objected to the practice, in the end they decided to live with it. The number of students involved was small, and the meager savings attained would be outweighed by the bad publicity that would result.[41]

CLOSING INEFFICIENT UNITS

Eliminating small and inefficient units was difficult because schools could harness the support of powerful backers. The Pentagon was very sensitive to this pressure and kept tabs on prominent individuals who might intervene on the JROTC's behalf. A Department of the Army (DA) memorandum (August 1962) identified proponents who would likely protest if the army attempted to eliminate or scale back the JROTC. In the Senate, John Carroll, Paul Douglas, Clair Engle, Barry Goldwater, Oren Long, Richard Russell, John Stennis, Herman Talmadge, Alexander Wiley, and Carl Hayden were identified, and in the House, William Bray, Jackson Betts, Jeffery Cohelan, William Cramer, E. L. Forrester, Daniel Inouye, George Miller, William Murphy, Barratt O'Hara, Carl Perkins, Melvin Price, Paul Rogers, Ashton Thompson, and Carl Vinson were named. One mayor—Richard J. Daley of Chicago—made this enemy list.[42]

Various interest groups could also be counted on to defend the program; they included the American Legion, the Reserve Officers' Association (ROA), the Veterans of Foreign Wars (VFW), the Association of the United States Army (AUSA), and the National Association for the Advancement of Colored People (NAACP). In many places, the Rotary and Kiwanis Clubs were among the program's most generous backers, contributing money to local units and passing resolutions for unit growth. Well-known newspapers were part of this JROTC lobby; the Hearst Newspapers and the *Chicago Tribune* were among the most zealous in their advocacy.[43]

Pressure to expand also came from uniformed supporters, who worried about the JROTC's shrinking demographic footprint. With the growth of the high school population, the JROTC was reaching a smaller percentage of students each year. In 1956, the army was in 260 high schools, which represented 5.4 percent of eligible institutions. The program's sixty thousand cadets represented only 2.3 percent of eligible students. By 1966, it was projected, the

JROTC would be in only 4.3 percent of eligible schools and enroll only 1.5 percent of male students. A bad situation would soon become worse.[44]

Officials worried that recruiting would suffer. One officer attributed both "the noticeable decline" in SROTC enrollment and "public apathy towards military service" to "the army's failure to reach the same number of impressionable young men as before." An enlargement of the JROTC seemed an obvious way to address this issue.[45]

Others argued that the JROTC had to provide more direct benefits to the army to merit support. As it was, those benefits were paltry. The army wasted money and resources on individuals who were not interested in military service. Students enrolled because the program was compulsory or because they enjoyed its activities. If the army restricted enrollment to students displaying a motivation and aptitude for military service, participation would grow, and new units could be created.[46]

The lack of convincing evidence showing positive program outcomes handicapped proponents of the program. The "direct [recruiting] benefits" derived from the JROTC, one officer noted, "[had] not and probably [could not] be measured." The army did not collect data showing how many JROTC graduates entered the SROTC, earned a commission, or enlisted. Even if it had such data, the results could not be directly linked to the JROTC. The "most cogent endorsement" of the program's worth, one study concluded, was the hundreds of schools on the waiting list for new units. It was not definitive evidence, but it was certainly suggestive.[47]

In the end, the army, faced with conflicting pressures and unable to forge an internal consensus about the JROTC's principal purpose, temporized. It approved a modest increase in the JROTC's budget but continued to chip away at JROTC manpower. It stuck with its no-growth policy but removed the enrollment caps on existing units. A staff study (1955) described the removal of restrictions as an "interim, token measure that did not solve the long-term problem"—namely, what to do about schools clamoring for a unit.[48]

Nevertheless, with enrollment restrictions lifted, membership rose by 23 percent between 1955 and 1959. This increase was misleading, however. In a relative sense, the JROTC enrollment declined, with the growth in high school enrollment outpacing program gains. High school enrollment, a product of the postwar baby boom, shot up 48 percent during the 1950s, while JROTC enrollment increased at less than half that rate. The JROTC's participation rate sank from about ten in every thousand to about eight in every thousand between 1950 and 1960.[49]

Enrollment numbers concealed other trends. One was the absolute decrease in the JROTC enrollment in civilian high schools (CS). By 1960, enrollment in CS stood at fifty-five thousand, a little less than it had been in 1951 and 25 percent below where it had been in 1940. The number of participating civilian schools also dropped, declining by 3 percent between 1956 and 1963.[50]

GROWTH OF MILITARY SCHOOLS

While JROTC enrollment in CS fell, enrollment in military schools mushroomed—280 percent between 1953 and 1963. Three factors accounted for this remarkable growth. First, high school enrollment soared by 120 percent between 1950 and 1960. Military schools benefited from this growth. Second, and more problematically, the army reorganized its ROTC management structure to focus attention on these institutions. More attention presumably translated into more vigorous programs. Finally, the army changed commissioning policies and incentivized students to matriculate at military schools.

One change in commissioning policy occurred just before the Korean War. Previously, the army regulated the admission of military junior college (MJC) graduates into Officer Candidate School (OCS) by quotas. Beginning in May 1950, these quotas vanished. Any MJC graduate who completed the four-year SROTC course and two years of college could attend OCS.[51]

In November 1950, the army broadened the path to commissions again. Now, the top 25 percent of each graduating cohort received certificates of eligibility that would allow the graduate, upon enlistment, to bypass basic training and enter directly into OCS. Military institute graduates received yet another boon in 1955 when the army declared that, henceforth, they would receive credit for the entire basic course of the SROTC, shortening their commissioning program from four to only two years.[52]

The reorganization of ROTC management took effect in 1955, when the army placed all MJCs and military institutes in a separate Military Schools Division within the Continental Army Command (CONARC) ROTC Directorate. The upshot was to give essentially military schools more visibility within the management hierarchy and greater power to resist personnel and budget cuts.[53]

The idea of creating a separate organization for military schools did not arise from within the army. The powerful Association of Military Schools and Colleges (AMSCUS), an organization dedicated to safeguarding the interests of military schools, pressured the army into doing it. The association was an irritant to the army. It flooded the Pentagon and Congress with "unpleasant and unnecessary correspondence" whenever it suspected that its members were being shortchanged.[54] The AMSCUS began lobbying for a separate division when it learned of army plans to achieve savings by downgrading military schools to JROTC status, which would result in their loss of instructors and conversion into non-officer-producing institutions.[55]

The army struggled to defend its position because it did not know how many military school graduates earned commissions. The AMSCUS took advantage of the army's lack of information. In 1954, it released a study claiming that between 1947 and 1952, 2,258 military school graduates received army or air force commissions, while 3,820 enrolled in the SROTC. The army had no data to counter these claims.[56]

In the end, the association got its way, and a Military Schools Division was created. This new division occupied an intermediate position between the JROTC, the citizenship program, and the SROTC, the officer-producing program. It was referred to as a partial officer-producing program.[57]

Along with the change in organization came a new mission for military schools. Citizenship training was dropped. The new remit was exclusively military: "To provide military training leading to qualification for a commission at such time as the student completes his college education; or if he should not complete college, to permit his early qualification as a non-commissioned officer in the active army or the army reserve." No longer fettered by the political constraints under which the JROTC operated, military schools were free to concentrate on military service and military training.[58]

NDCC GROWTH

Despite the decline in JROTC enrollment, participation in federally sponsored, school-based military training rose. This was due to the revivification of the 55c program. Both 55c enrollment and unit strength climbed between 1954 and 1964; enrollment more than doubled, while unit strength shot up by over 60 percent. Most new 55c units were in civilian institutions. Therefore, the character of the 55c base changed markedly. The program evolved from one that was about 50 percent military to one that was 75 percent civilian.[59]

The momentum for 55c expansion had been slow in developing. The program had never been popular. It offered no instructors and only meager resources. Things became even bleaker after World War II. The army, anxious to economize, discouraged the creation of new units until 1953, when it changed course and began inviting schools to apply for 55c units.[60]

This change in direction stemmed from several factors. One was a desire by congressional and army leaders to accommodate the demand for more units. Another was a renewed emphasis on the reserves. The Eisenhower administration's strategy of the New Look called for a greater dependence on nuclear weapons, a reduction of active-duty forces, and a bolstering, both quantitatively and qualitatively, of the Reserve Components (RC). Underlying the New Look was Eisenhower's conviction that economic strength was a vital component of national security. And since the president associated a healthy economy with fiscal restraint, cost cutting was at the heart of his national military strategy.

The emphasis on the reserves strengthened as the Korean War wound down. To bolster the RC, Congress passed the Reserve Forces Act of 1955. This act imposed a reserve commitment on discharged soldiers and provided for a six-month training program geared to the US Army Reserve (USAR) and National Guard (NG). Under this program, recruits underwent six months of basic training and then spent 7.5 years in an RC unit. Aided by such measures, reserve strength rose from 578,000 in June 1952 to 1,000,000 by June 1957, while active army strength dropped from 1.5 million to less than 900,000 people.[61]

Several problems plagued the RC. One was an officer shortage. In 1954, the army had a reserve officer deficit of fifty thousand. Consequently, the army quadrupled the number of state-sponsored NG OCS programs and expanded the SROTC. Inadequate training was a second problem. Both individual reservists and reserve units were unprepared for their enhanced role in national defense. To remedy this deficiency, the army afforded RC more opportunities to train with their active-duty counterparts and regulated reserve training more closely.[62]

A little-publicized facet of bolstering the RC entailed enlarging the 55c program. An expanded 55c program, it was expected, would yield more officer candidates, stimulate more reserve enlistments, and provide preinduction training to future soldiers. And it would do so at little cost. In 1951, it cost the army $10,000 a year ($0.90 per student) to run the 55c program. A decade later, its annual budget still amounted to only $100,000 ($4.50 per student).[63] The army knew that convincing schools to accept a 55c unit would be a hard sell. Of the five hundred applications for new JROTC units the army received and rejected between 1947 and 1956, only fourteen agreed to accept a 55c unit.[64]

Congress took a step toward rejuvenating the program when it passed legislation, PL 244 (1953), extending advanced placement credit to all 55c graduates entering the SROTC.[65] The army tried to broaden the program's appeal by enhancing its prestige, improving its curriculum, and funding it on "substantially the same basis" as it did the JROTC. In 1955, the army, prompted by the National Association of 55c Schools, created a 55c unit honor rating system, introduced a distinctive 55c sleeve insignia, and issued a new curriculum, with texts, films, and equipment. It also encouraged Regular Army (RA) and RC units to provide training and loan equipment to 55c units. Skeptical high school officials presumably would more readily accept 55c units if the army displayed more interest in them.[66]

Another step taken to widen the program's appeal was to give it a more dignified and meaningful name. Its official title bore little relation to its mission and meant nothing to the public. The term *55c school* invited the sobriquet *55-cent school*—hardly the image the army wanted to foster. After much debate, the army finally settled on the name National Defense Cadet Corps (NDCC), a name that it still bears today.[67] In 1957, the army further strengthened the NDCC by extending more recognition to schools and more benefits to cadets. It extended the enlistment incentive given to the JROTC cadets to NDCC cadets, provided flag streamers to NDCC honor schools, and reserved nominations to service academies for cadets from honor units.[68]

Army leaders were not sanguine about the results achieved. They expressed disappointment at the relatively small number of schools adopting the program—only sixty between 1954 and 1964. These seemed like paltry returns for the effort expended. The NDCC never became a significant aid to reserve recruiting, nor did it make more than a dent in the mountain of requests submitted for new units. The NDCC remained a poor substitute for the more generously endowed JROTC.[69]

While the JROTC saw only slight changes in its geographical balance after Korea, the orientation of NDCC units shifted decidedly to the South. Twenty-five of the thirty-three NDCC units established between 1958 and 1960 were in southern states. By 1964, the South had 60 percent of NDCC units, up from 38 percent in 1953. Most NDCC units would convert to JROTC after 1964, accelerating the latter program's southward drift.[70]

MANAGEMENT

Program management remained diffused and problematic. Many agencies had a hand in administering the JROTC. At the top stood the Civilian Components Policy Board (DOD). The board's writ was to develop policies for the NG, USAR, and ROTC. The Joint Advisory Panel on ROTC Affairs was a suboffice of the board that coordinated the JROTC policy and initiatives. It consisted of representatives from ten educational associations and the three services. Below the DOD were various DA organizations, including the Executive for Reserve and ROTC Affairs, Assistant Secretary of the Army for Manpower and Reserve Forces, the Special Assistant to the CSA for Civilian Component Affairs, the G-1, the G-2, the G-3, the G-4, the adjutant general (TAG), the chief of Army Field Forces (before 1956), the CONARC commander (after 1956), and the six Continental Army commanders. All these organizations were responsible for discrete aspects of the program. Because of the multiple layers separating the Pentagon and the individual unit, directives could take weeks or even months to wind their way through the bureaucracy to their ultimate destination.[71]

Bare-bones staffing likewise bedeviled management. The army published staffing guides, but army commanders determined actual personnel allocations. In three of the six armies, the ROTC staff consisted of one or two individuals. These staffs oversaw between 50 and 150 units spread over as many as ten states. Nowhere was staffing sufficient for adequate supervision.[72]

Withal, a lack of command attention plagued the program. Commanders who oversaw the program had more pressing duties. The JROTC was only one of their many responsibilities. These commanders were not "fully cognizant" of the JROTC's needs and did not accord it the requisite attention. A solution was to concentrate responsibility for the program in one office and flatten the chain of command, bringing the unit closer to the ultimate source of authority. Bureaucratic jurisdictional battles and a lack of consensus over the JROTC goals prevented this from happening.[73]

TRAINING

The JROTC's postwar training emphasized fundamental tactical skills, military knowledge, and hands-on activity. Military institutes still offered four-year and public schools three-year curricula. The heart of the program in CS units was the third year, when students assumed leadership roles, presented classes, supervised training, and organized activities. Because conditions varied greatly among high schools, the army accorded units great flexibility. Instructors could reduce the time allotted to any subject by 10 and later 25 percent.[74]

The army made only minor curricular revisions in the 1950s. It introduced an amended *JROTC Manual* in 1955. The manual consisted of three parts, one devoted to each grade level. Earlier manuals had not been so aligned.[75] Several revisions addressed emerging issues. In 1957, a two-hour class on atomic warfare was created for sophomores.[76] To boost recruiting, the army introduced a four-hour class for seniors on military "opportunities and benefits." Recruiting was also behind another new course called Achievements and Traditions of the Army. Through this course, the army hoped to interest cadets in military history and create an appreciation for the army's contribution to national development.[77]

Summer camps were not in the curriculum during this era. True, regulations sanctioned them, and units held them, but the army would not fund them, nor did it know much about them. When a congressman asked about JROTC summer training, an army spokesman responded that, as far as he knew, one camp had been conducted at Fort Leavenworth, Kansas; one at Camp Walters, Texas; and one at Camp Ashland, Nebraska, in the summer of 1955. The local parent-teacher association had funded the Texas camps, while the Nebraska NG had funded the Leavenworth training. Summer training clearly was not an army priority.[78]

One notable change that occurred was the abolition of weapons training. Until midcentury, some units, primarily military institutes, possessed stocks of arms comparable to those held by USAR and NG units. The New York Military Academy had an arsenal that included 105 mm howitzers, mortars, heavy machine guns, and Browning automatic rifles. In the early 1950s, units began to surrender these weapons and exchange their operational M-1 rifles for demilitarized versions.[79]

There were two cardinal reasons for this change. One was economy. Units with mortars, machine guns, and artillery pieces were very expensive to maintain. Another reason was the move away from the old branch-specific SROTC curriculum to the general military science (GMS) curriculum in the early 1950s. With the adoption of the GMS curriculum, every SROTC unit had a light infantry orientation. The JROTC graduates entering the senior program no longer required a familiarity with cannons.[80]

RECRUITING

The fiscally conservative Eisenhower administration pressed all army programs to realize concrete contributions to national defense. Citizenship and preinduction military training might be fine objectives, but they were not sufficient to satisfy budget managers. Defense officials wanted to see tangible returns on the money allotted to the program. More enlistments in the RC would meet those expectations.[81]

Accordingly, the army modified the JROTC objectives in the 1950s to emphasize recruiting for the RC. General Maxwell Taylor, while CSA, reinvigorated this effort. To be sure, regulations continued to list citizenship and military training at the top of the program's priorities. However, the army added a third objective that stressed the JROTC's procurement role: "To develop an appreciation of the Army in its role of national defense and to fully inform all students of the opportunities of service therein."[82]

The phrase "to fully inform all students of the opportunities of service," of course, was a euphemism for recruiting—but recruiting that went beyond the soft enlistment pitch that had always been present. Now, the army tried to make recruiting a more formal and systematic process. Taylor even imposed a reserve quota on subordinate commanders. In 1957, he instructed army commanders to "implement and execute aggressive recruiting programs" in JROTC units to "obtain the maximum number of enlistments and active participation with . . . the Army Reserve Program." He reminded commanders of the recent change in the program's mission that added recruiting to its list of functions.[83] Despite Taylor's exhortations and imposition of a reserve quota on JROTC, the stream of high school cadets into the RC did not noticeably increase. Local conditions and tradition exerted powerful influences on units; directives from above, when not accompanied by strong incentives and close supervision, often did not change unit behavior or performance.

The JROTC stagnated during the post–World War II era. Unit strength declined, while enrollment growth was anemic. By 1960, there were proportionally fewer students enrolled in the JROTC than there had been in 1950. Fiscal austerity during the Truman and Eisenhower administrations accounted for much of this. The 55c/NDCC program—a less expensive alternative to the JROTC—experienced a modest revival, but defense officials were disappointed with the results.

Program objectives changed little. Traditional staples such as good citizenship and character development remained salient. There were, of course, a few variations. Public outreach lost some of its luster in an era when conscription was in effect. The JROTC as a solution to juvenile delinquency surfaced as a popular theme after the war as adolescent crime became front-page news.

Recruiting remained a priority for the JROTC. Maxwell Taylor even tried to impose enlisted recruiting quotas on units, albeit to little avail. The JROTC's role as a direct commissioning source, never very productive, was eliminated after World War II. Because of its lack of concrete recruiting results, some defense officials lobbied to abolish the program. They were prevented from doing so by resistance organized by the JROTC's legion of supporters. In the next chapter, we will see how the program's backers managed to orchestrate the JROTC expansion that had been denied to them for so long.

5

McNamara and the Modern JROTC, 1963–1964

In 1961, Robert S. McNamara came to Washington determined to reform the management of the Department of Defense (DOD). Once ensconced as secretary of defense, this erstwhile Ford Motor Company executive launched initiatives that would transform the defense establishment. One of his most consequential moves involved a change in national strategy. Both McNamara and President John F. Kennedy rejected Eisenhower's doctrine of massive retaliation. They wanted options that went beyond "inglorious retreat or unlimited retaliation." Boosting conventional warfare capabilities gave them the flexibility they sought. This conventional buildup began in 1961 when, coincident with the outbreak of the Berlin Crisis, the United States increased its active forces by 217,000 troops.[1]

As part of his DOD overhaul, McNamara strengthened the link between the defense budget and national strategy. He deplored the existing accounting system, which did not capture the complete range of defense costs. McNamara instituted a budgeting methodology that treated defense requirements holistically rather than from the perspectives of the individual services. At the same time, he pressured the service chiefs to adopt modern business practices.[2]

The secretary's most momentous démarche was his introduction of systems analysis into defense planning. The Planning, Programming, and Budgeting System (PPBS) epitomized this approach. Through the PPBS, McNamara evaluated defense requirements systematically and produced a "long-term, program-oriented defense budget."[3]

The secretary believed that the nation could afford any amount needed for national security but that "this ability [did] not excuse us from applying strict standards of effectiveness and efficiency." Using systems analysis, he made several controversial decisions on weapons, canceling the B-70 bomber and Skybolt missile projects. Systems analysis also formed the basis of his cost-reduction program, which led to the closure of scores of military bases, the postponement of base construction projects, and the implementation of other cost-saving measures.[4]

ELIMINATION OF THE JROTC?

One of those cost-saving measures was the elimination of the JROTC. In January 1963, the secretary told the House Armed Service Committee (HASC) that the program cost more than $6 million a year. For McNamara, this was too much for a program that produced no officers and contributed nothing to military readiness. McNamara informed the committee that he intended to convert the JROTC into National Defense Cadet Corps (NDCC) units. To the defense secretary, it seemed a logical step. The missions of the two programs were identical, but the NDCC required an annual outlay of only $100,000. McNamara's submission for the fiscal year 1964 budget included no provision for JROTC funding, except for military schools.[5]

McNamara's initiative elicited a sharp congressional and public response and, paradoxically, led to the expansion, instead of the demise, of the JROTC. After McNamara unveiled his intentions, the public deluged Congress and the Pentagon with mail protesting the move. School principals, teachers, parents, and concerned citizens registered their displeasure. Approximately four hundred letters and telegrams poured into the Pentagon, and the vast majority of them heralded the JROTC as essential to the nation. McNamara's gambit incited the wrath of patriotic organizations such as the American Legion, Veterans of Foreign Wars (VFW), and Reserve Officers Association (ROA). The American Legion charged that the DOD had "subscribed to what the leftists and so-called pacifists" had preached for decades and was "playing directly into the hands of our deadly and implacable enemies."[6]

In the wake of McNamara's announcement, an irate Louisiana congressman, F. Edward Hebert, introduced legislation in February 1963 providing for the *expansion* of the junior program. This legislation (H.R. 4427 and 4444) proposed that the program be enlarged from 254 to 2,000 institutions. It also called for the extension of the JROTC to the navy and the air force and the absorption of the NDCC into the JROTC.[7]

In March 1963, the HASC held hearings on the DOD's proposal to shutter the program. The first witness to appear was Norman S. Paul, the assistant secretary of defense for manpower. Paul called for the program's dismantlement, arguing that the JROTC touched only a small fraction (1.6 percent) of the country's youth. He acknowledged the importance of developing discipline and patriotism in young people but contended that educational and civic organizations should shoulder the responsibility for "indoctrination and training in this general area." The DOD should not be involved.[8]

Service representatives also testified, presenting variations on the themes elaborated by McNamara and his assistant secretary of defense. The undersecretary of the navy, Paul B. Fay, emphasized the harm that expansion would inflict on the navy's operational readiness. "I can foresee," Fay told the HASC, "that millions of dollars would be needed to support JROTC." To guarantee proper management, some of the navy's best noncommissioned officers (NCOs) would have to be diverted to the program. This diversion would place a "drain on its manpower and . . . reduce its military effectiveness." The navy must remain, he declared, "basically a combat organization." The navy's aversion to the JROTC was not new. In 1945, a congressional proposal to extend the program to the navy had elicited a similar response. The navy then argued that it did not need the JROTC; it already had enough officer-producing programs to meet its needs.[9]

The navy's protests worked in 1945 but not in 1963. Its objections were drowned out by the voices of program advocates who turned Hebert's hearing into a forum about how best to expand the program. Educators and community leaders testified to the program's efficacy in reducing high school dropout rates, combating juvenile delinquency, teaching leadership, boosting recruiting, and developing character.[10]

Hebert excoriated defense officials for their testimony, expressing bewilderment at the "sudden cynical and shortsighted repudiation" of a program that had provided the nation with incalculable benefits for nearly fifty years. Many successful military leaders in the nation's last two wars had their leadership abilities honed in the JROTC. "Who," he asked, "would deny that thousands of young Americans are today better citizens for having been exposed to the JROTC and thereby contributed directly toward insuring a stronger and more resolute America?"[11]

Representative Herman Talmadge (D-Georgia) was another outspoken supporter of the program. He believed that any curtailment of it would be a "serious mistake." In April 1963, he wrote, "With the current emphasis of the [Kennedy] administration on youth, and the proposals for a domestic Peace Corps, and a Youth Conservation Corps, it is strange to me that there is even consideration of a cutback of [Junior] ROTC." Talmadge warmly endorsed a resolution passed by the Georgia State Assembly calling for the program's expansion.[12]

The Georgian representative believed that the JROTC could help solve two problems: the large number of young men who flunked the armed forces' entrance examination and the "appalling" high school dropout rate. In Georgia, more than half of the students who started high school did not finish, while about 60 percent of the men drafted could not meet induction standards; they failed either the mental exams or their physicals. The JROTC, by encouraging boys to stay in school, providing them with physical exercise, and imbuing them with self-discipline, could alleviate these problems.[13]

Faced with such strong opposition, the DOD agreed to postpone its decision on the JROTC's future until it conducted a thorough review. The review was to ascertain the JROTC's value to the services and to high schools. An Ad Hoc Committee of eleven members (nine military) conducted the study. It deliberated from April 30 to June 7, 1963. Committee members visited many high schools and interviewed scores of educators, government officials, and community leaders. They published their findings, "Future Operations of the Junior ROTC and National Defense Cadet Corps Programs," in June 1963.[14]

The report was a victory for Hebert and his allies. While it capped JROTC growth at 1,200 rather than 2,000 units, the report affirmed the program's importance to the nation's moral health and endorsed an expansion.[15] The report noted that further efforts to eliminate the program would lead to renewed public and congressional protests. Although the program did not fulfill an immediate military need, it provided more elusive benefits, such as cultivating favorable attitudes toward military service and fostering good citizenship in students. Indeed, the report deemed the development of good citizenship in youth "a national requirement." The committee's survey of school officials, community leaders, and parents revealed strong support for the expansion and a recognition of the JROTC's curricular merit. But to limit the costs of enlargement, the committee recommended reducing JROTC staffing requirements and hiring retirees as instructors.[16]

The committee's assessment of the NDCC was not as favorable. It lamented the debilitating effects of the program's scanty budget, which contained no funds to pay instructors, buy uniforms, or provide equipment. The results were commensurate with the resources expended on the program—that is, they were disappointing.[17]

REPORT OF THE AD HOC COMMITTEE

The following summary of the Ad Hoc Committee's report will illumine how the committee reached its conclusions and highlight the issues with which it grappled. The report was a milestone, heralding the birth of the modern JROTC and adumbrating its future course. If Hebert and his colleagues provided the vision for change, the committee provided the road map for its implementation.

The Ad Hoc Committee concluded that a "positive" demand existed for the expansion of cadet training. This demand stemmed from the JROTC's ability to address multiple needs, most of which related to "citizenship" training. The most frequently expressed developmental needs related to respect for authority, patriotism, military skills, discipline, personal honor, orderliness, and precision.[18]

The committee found that most stakeholders felt that the DOD was the logical governmental agency to oversee school-based military training. The need for DOD control stemmed from the nature of this training and not from any military requirement or direct military benefit. But while the DOD should provide the curriculum, texts, equipment, and instructors, the Department of Health, Education, and Welfare (HEW) should develop the citizenship and educational aspects of the program.[19]

Committee members agreed that schools should be accorded "maximum freedom" in administering the program. Local educators should fix the terms of participation (compulsory or elective), schedule courses, prescribe courses taught, determine instructor suitability, control unit activities, and align the JROTC curricula with school educational goals rather than prepare cadets for military service.[20]

The committee concurred with Hebert's plan to spread the program to the other services. Under existing law, all three service secretaries could operate the JROTC or NDCC units. However, apart from the navy's four honor schools, only the army did. This placed an "inequitable burden" on the army. If all services enjoyed the benefits of the program, then all services should share its burdens.[21]

The committee observed that extending the program to all services would enlarge the pool of institutions and participants. Schools that did not want an army unit might opt for a navy or air force program. Tri-service involvement would also enhance competition among units and burnish the image of the navy and air force. While the committee admitted that tri-service participation would mean greater costs, it reasoned that an improved public image would more than offset the additional expense.[22]

Among the services, the army was the most ardent advocate of making the JROTC a tri-service program; extending the program to the navy and air force would spread the burden of support wider and give students more options. The air force was less enthusiastic. It cautioned that any expansion should be kept within the budgetary and managerial capabilities of the services.

The navy was the least excited about the tri-service idea and offered the most stipulations regarding its adoption. It wanted to limit expansion, avoid large overhead costs, and keep material and financial support to a minimum. A naval spokesman observed that the navy's four honor schools used surplus government equipment. He hoped this arrangement would continue. The navy also wanted units to be located along a seaboard and near a naval installation so that the program would have a "naval flavor."[23]

Although they did not want to "fight the problem," navy leaders insisted that the optimal approach to expansion would be to shift responsibility for the program to a civilian organization. The JROTC units should be operated "by some other agency, with somebody else's money." Saddling the navy with JROTC responsibilities would detract from its principal mission of fighting the nation's wars.[24]

Hebert had originally set the JROTC expansion goal at two thousand schools. The committee was tasked to gauge that goal's feasibility. It first examined the existing application base. It found that nineteen applications for JROTC units and nine for NDCC units were pending. The frequently quoted number of 504 applications came from an army study conducted in 1955. That number reflected the total number of requests received from 1947 to 1955. Since that time, schools regarded the chances of getting a unit so dim that applications had almost dried up.[25]

Next, the committee tried to determine how many schools without a JROTC unit wanted one. One source of new units was the NDCC program. The committee found that most existing NDCC units wanted to convert to the JROTC. It also identified multiple-unit school districts within the

JROTC as a source of new programs. In these districts, some schools had units, while others did not. Many district superintendents wanted to extend the JROTC to all their schools. Finally, a survey revealed that about eight hundred schools with no previous JROTC ties desired units. The committee estimated that with pending applications, NDCC to JROTC conversions, the multiple-school district market, and eight hundred schools with no previous JROTC links, the expansion potential was 1,200–1,250 units. How much budgetary factors and DOD pressure figured into the committee's calculations is unclear. In the end, the committee discarded Hebert's original target of 2,000 units and adopted 1,200 units as its recommendation, which eventually prevailed.[26]

During congressional hearings, Hebert announced his intention to convert NDCC to JROTC units and essentially eliminate the NDCC program. The committee took up this matter and sought stakeholders' opinion of its advisability.[27] Public school officials were nearly unanimous in preferring the JROTC to the NDCC. Their schools did not have the wherewithal to erect facilities, hire instructors, or buy uniforms. Swiftly rising enrollments, declining tax millage, and rejections of school bond issues inhibited the creation of new NDCC units. For them, the NDCC was not an option.[28]

The preference for the JROTC was not universal. Some private school principals valued the NDCC because of the autonomy and flexibility it afforded. They did not want outsiders to control even a small portion of their faculty or curriculum. Moreover, private schools, with their high tuition rates, could better absorb the costs of instructors and uniforms than public schools. They gladly traded money for sovereignty.[29]

In the end, the committee concluded that the nation would be better served by having one program instead of two. Consolidation would simplify administration, centralize control, reduce confusion about objectives, and improve the curriculum. It would also remove inequities in material assistance. As it was, the wide disparity of support was unfair and divisive, and it left NDCC units underresourced.[30]

The committee amended two elements of Hebert's initial proposal. One was the requirement for all units to be compulsory.[31] More would be lost than gained if participation were mandatory. The compulsory feature would deter many schools from applying for a unit and prod schools with elective programs to drop the JROTC.[32] In addition, the immense student flow that would result from the extension of compulsory JROTC would raise costs, overburden school facilities, and increase staffing requirements. In its final report, the committee categorically rejected compulsory military training.[33]

The Ad Hoc Committee also labeled Hebert's proposal to eliminate officers and use NCOs as instructors "unacceptable." Such a misstep would create serious management problems, adversely affect school-army interaction, and damage the program's standing and prestige.[34] Most NCO instructors did not meet the teacher qualifications of state or regional accrediting agencies, and the courses they taught did not carry academic credit.[35]

The committee evaluated the idea of using part-time reserve component (RC) soldiers as instructors. School principals decidedly rejected this concept. They wanted full-time, active-duty officers who met certification standards. Only in a pinch would these educators accept reservists. Their main objection was the lack of control over faculty it would engender.[36]

The continued use of active personnel evoked a passionate response from the services. The services, the army especially, were overstretched by the flexible response strategy and the Berlin Crisis. The army had a shortage of six thousand midgrade NCOs—the personnel needed in the JROTC units—and a huge lieutenant deficit. Enlarging JROTC staff requirements under these conditions was "practically out of the question."[37] An army spokesman told the committee that the manpower "squeeze" was degrading military readiness. The services were being "required to do more and more but with the same number of personnel."[38]

The navy felt the same way. Even if the navy received more people and funds to conduct the expansion, one admiral stated, it would have difficulty maintaining suitable standards of instructor quality. Individuals performing semi-independent duty like the JROTC must be highly qualified people—personally, morally, and technically. The navy was already failing to meet quality demands in other programs. It would be placed under enormous strain if it was given four hundred JROTC units. Other programs would be in jeopardy.[39]

An air force representative told the committee that his service would participate in the expansion but would need additional money and manpower to do so. The Senior Air Force ROTC (AFROTC) program was not funded or manned sufficiently to supervise the JROTC. It was only producing 3,500 new lieutenants annually instead of its quota of 7,000. The air force's problem was maintaining the senior program while meeting the needs of the JROTC expansion.[40]

The services weighed in on solutions to the staffing problem. They rejected the NDCC model because it was ineffective. Many NDCC units could not find instructors. Neither were reservists a good option. If reservists were used, they would be counted against the authorized personnel strength, which would mean fewer officers and NCOs for other assignments. The army was open to using reservists but only if they served on an unpaid basis and were placed under the control of the active army.[41]

All services agreed that retirees were the best solution to the problem. These "mature individual[s]" fit the program's needs. Manpower supply would not be a problem. Retirees would "flock" to the program.[42] Acceptability was another advantage. Schools wanted to continue the program essentially as it was. The use of retired personnel would permit this. Like the traditional program, it would provide for full-time, carefully vetted instructors.[43] By relying on retirees, the services could draw from a larger pool of candidates and be more selective in hiring.[44] The navy preferred retirees over reservists because the former would not count against navy end strength but the latter would.[45] The DOD liked the retiree option because it allow the government to get more value out of young retirees. With the military's twenty-year retirement, individuals left the service in their late thirties or early forties, drawing half pay. Many considered this a waste of manpower and talent. The use of retirees in the JROTC would allay these concerns.[46]

CIVIC VALUE OF THE JROTC

The committee assessed the value of the JROTC as part of its review. This issue went to the heart of the matter since the imbroglio over the program began in response to DOD allegations that the benefits were not worth the costs. The committee gave the program a ringing endorsement, finding that it provided valuable benefits to the individual, the school, the family, the community, the state, the nation, and the services.[47]

The JROTC, the committee concluded, was accomplishing its primary objective of making cadets better citizens. It instilled habits of precision, discipline, respect for authority, and patriotism—habits essential to building strong families.[48] In addition, the program offered valuable services to schools, ranging from providing ushers at school events to proctoring examinations. Cadets were also exemplars for other students, demonstrating good citizenship and a service ethos.[49]

The discipline the JROTC brought to the classroom was a big selling point to school officials. A study by the Mershon Foundation found that schools with JROTC units had fewer disciplinary and delinquency problems than schools without them. Indeed, delinquency rates were "virtually zero" in schools with JROTC.[50]

Community leaders extolled the civic and social benefits provided by the JROTC. In Chicago, the annual ROTC parade aroused great excitement, brought neighborhoods together, and became a much-anticipated municipal event. The program was especially valuable in low-income areas, where the JROTC provided a structure in which students from poor families could develop "habits of personal leadership and achievement."[51] In addition, the JROTC gave students a social outlet. The JROTC balls and social gatherings gave poor students a social life they would not otherwise have had. Chicago's superintendent of schools, Benjamin Willis, declared that for these social reasons alone, expansion should be approved.[52]

The JROTC's ability to boost graduation rates was one of the program's most valued benefits. The Association of the US Army (AUSA) gave the committee a copy of its study of dropout rates among JROTC-affiliated schools. The study compared the dropout rate of cadets with that of other students. It found that cadets had a 50 percent lower attrition rate than their classmates.[53]

Some witnesses emphasized the advantages the program conferred on the nation. The attributes that the JROTC developed in cadets—physical fitness, leadership ability, integrity, discipline, and a respect for authority—were essential for fostering national efficiency, stability, and cohesiveness in America's diverse population.[54]

The JROTC delivered more immediate benefits as well. Local, state, and national authorities believed that units were valuable instruments of civil defense, a salient subject in the early 1960s. Schools that were designated as civil defense shelter areas often used the JROTC units as a ready force, charged with controlling ingress into buildings in case of emergency.[55] The assistant secretary of defense (civil defense) noted that cadets bolstered the civil defense effort at several levels. In an emergency, cadets could direct traffic, guide people to civil defense shelters, and exercise shelter control. He described cadets as men who, although young, would respond to direction from authority and accept responsibility, two vital elements in a crisis. Another official opined that the JROTC's usefulness in a crisis was underestimated. Its manpower, organization, and connections with the military would prove nearly indispensable in an emergency.[56]

General Lewis Hershey, director of selective service, acknowledged an obvious but unheralded advantage of the JROTC—namely, that it was already "in existence." It was "a lot easier to take something you've got and make something out of it than to create something new."[57] The program could address new tasks, adapt to new missions, and take on added responsibilities without the expenditure of extra funds, the use of additional people, or the creation of a new organization. It could do these things without laboriously navigating through the defense bureaucracy or hurdling legislative obstacles as would otherwise be necessary.

There were several discordant notes struck about the JROTC's value. HEW representatives were skeptical of the civil benefits. They questioned the program's effectiveness in combating juvenile delinquency. To be sure, it took "the blue jeans off and some of the long hair." But one should not assume, they warned, "that a program of this sort, or several such programs, [would] wipe out or solve delinquency or the problem of the underprivileged."[58] The HEW also feared that expansion would divert attention from more important initiatives. Congress was studying twenty-four amendments to the National Defense Education Act (NDEA) to improve instruction in math, foreign languages, and physical science. The HEW believed these amendments should have greater priority than Hebert's JROTC bill.[59]

The DOD proposal to have HEW fund expansion was conceivable, a HEW agent observed, but not appropriate. The educational objectives that benefited national defense were contained in the NDEA, not H.R. 4444. The academic requirements for national defense should be viewed in terms of educational objectives, not of personal, moral, or character development. In the opinion of HEW leaders, the JROTC expansion should not occur.[60]

MILITARY VALUE OF THE JROTC

The committee spent considerable time evaluating the military benefits of the JROTC, since it was its supposed lack of military value that moved the DOD to abolish the program in the first place. Members of the Ad Hoc Committee found that the opinion was split on the JROTC's military worth, with civilians being more convinced of the program's military utility than the services were. Civilian respondents pointed out that high schools were the source of most enlistees and that the JROTC was the army's passport into those institutions. They also noted that a high school diploma was a prerequisite for earning a commission. There was, therefore, a "considerable benefit if not a logical initial requirement" in establishing a recruiting base in high schools.[61]

School and community leaders identified other military benefits provided by the program. The acquisition of basic military skills was one. Armed with the skills learned in high school, the JROTC graduates who enlisted absorbed training more quickly and thus saved the government money. They also increased training efficiency by serving as leaders in Basic Combat Training (BCT).[62]

HEW officials rejected the notions that the JROTC prepared students for military service or that it substantially helped recruiting. Large number of cadets failed the armed forces' entrance exam. The JROTC could not remedy this problem. The main advantages of the program, from the HEW's perspective, lay in promoting discipline and order in the classroom.[63]

The Ad Hoc Committee asked the services to gauge the JROTC's worth as recruiting and training instruments and determine whether, if the JROTC did have training benefits, its graduates could be excused from portions of BCT.[64] The committee's inquiry rendered mixed results.

Of the services, the army was the most positive about the program's military value. It felt that students with JROTC experience were more likely than other students to enlist or enroll in the SROTC. An army general identified three main advantages. First, the JROTC gave a head start to students who entered the SROTC, providing them a base of professional knowledge. Second, the program prepared cadets for enrollment in the SROTC by conditioning them to a military environment. Third, the JROTC training made cadets good "NCO material" by providing them with rudimentary military skills and leadership training.[65] The Army G-1 thought the JROTC was a useful recruiting tool. His office conducted a survey of students at the Infantry, Signal, Air Defense, and Artillery Schools, polling 2,678 officers and 9,864 enlisted people. The survey found that 9.7 percent of the officers and 5.9 percent of the NCOs had participated in the JROTC. The G-1 deemed the results "quite significant."[66]

Some army witnesses were even more positive about the efficacy of cadet training. One asserted that basic training for the JROTC graduates could be abridged, albeit not completely waived, since marksmanship qualification was not offered in all units.[67] Nevertheless, the graduate did not need the prolonged orientation that the untrained recruit did.

The six Continental Army commanders were less enthusiastic about the JROTC training. To be sure, they believed that trainees with JROTC experience learned more rapidly than others and that former cadets were more suited for BCT leadership positions. Although there was no definitive evidence that graduates made better soldiers, their superior motivation suggested that this was the case. Nonetheless, the commanders did not believe graduates should forgo portions of basic training. Their training was not thorough or systematic enough to permit this.[68]

Richard Snyder of the army's Human Research Unit told the committee that the *draftees* (nonvolunteers) most interested in an army career were those with limited upward potential. Most had low scores on entrance tests and little civilian education. Among career-oriented *enlistees*, however, there were many with high test scores, good educational backgrounds, and the desired aptitudes. One group of enlistees exemplified the "very best type of career-oriented volunteer." That group was JROTC graduates. He could not say to what extent these men had been affected by their cadet experience. What he could say was that JROTC graduates were significantly more likely than other enlistees to enter the army as volunteers and that among volunteers, the JROTC graduates were more likely to reenlist than other inductees (28 percent versus 18 percent).[69]

The navy and air force were less positive about the JROTC's military benefits. From its limited contact with the program, the navy could see no direct need for the JROTC. There were undoubtedly indirect benefits, but it was impossible to measure them. Navy commanders were asked if enlistees with JROTC experience performed better at basic training. They claimed that, as a rule, the JROTC graduates were not awestruck by discipline, knew what to expect, and adapted readily to military life. However, these advantages were short-lived. It was difficult to distinguish graduates from nongraduates at the end of basic training. Basic training should not be abbreviated for the JROTC graduates, who, as a group, did not "excel in leadership ability." The JROTC training alone did not prepare them for the challenges they would face in the navy.[70]

Marine Corps respondents gave a similar assessment. They felt that graduates had "no marked superiority" over recruits with equivalent educational backgrounds. While they assumed that the JROTC training was of some value, it had not been demonstrated "to any significant degree." They did not believe graduates should receive advanced standing or rank while undergoing or after completing recruit training.[71]

The air force admitted that it had no conclusive statistical information about the ROTC's training outcomes. However, an air force spokesman noted, "It is the opinion of . . . people in the field that it's no help to us at all." Air force officials were more upbeat about the program's recruiting potential. They felt that it would have significant value as a feeder to the SROTC.[72]

The Ad Hoc Committee surveyed recruiting detachments in Atlanta, Chicago, Alexandria, Los Angeles, San Francisco, and Houston about the JROTC's recruiting potential. In every instance, detachment commanders stated that they could not see any appreciable effect of the program on procurement. In certain schools, units assisted recruiters in coordinating career-day programs. But beyond this, the JROTC did not render much aid. Regarding officer procurement, recruiters did not believe the JROTC had "any appreciable" effect. The only obvious benefit was that graduates got advanced placement in the SROTC.[73]

Despite reservations about the utility of the JROTC training, the services were open to awarding advanced rank to graduates upon enlistment. The army suggested that participants be awarded the grade of E-2 as soon as they were inducted. The air force recommended that graduates receive credit in basic training so the money spent on them in high school would not be wasted. This willingness to award advanced rank was predicated on the desire to induce enlistment, not on a recognition of the value of the training itself.[74]

Lobbying groups such as the AUSA and ROA insisted that the JROTC had substantial military worth. The former contended that it motivated students to enlist and provided a potential pool of NCOs for national emergencies.[75] The ROA touted the JROTC's great officer-recruiting potential, claiming that during World War II the JROTC graduates accounted for over one-third of those commissioned through Officer Candidate School (OCS).[76]

Civilian and military observers could agree on one benefit of the program—the value it had as a public relations tool. The JROTC cadets carried favorable impressions of the military back to their neighborhoods, creating a store of goodwill for the services. In addition, the program engendered an understanding of the military's role in national life. Even in an age of conscription, the military looked upon public outreach as a valuable, albeit not paramount, role of the JROTC.[77]

In the end, the Ad Hoc Committee did not find the military benefits of the program to be compelling. The committee noted rather weakly that a "positive" percentage of enlistees had military training in high school and that the

JROTC's impact on commissioning programs was large relative to its size. At the same time, it cautioned that it was impossible to determine if the program itself was responsible for these outcomes. Correlation said nothing about causation. The committee's assessment of the program's worth as a training vehicle was just as bland. It observed that the structure of existing basic training programs would preclude exempting the JROTC graduates from any part of them—a polite way of saying, perhaps, that the JROTC training could not substitute for real military training. In the end, the committee justified the JROTC's expansion by pointing to the many civic benefits it brought to the individual, school, and nation. The JROTC's true worth lay in its role as a citizenship training vehicle, not as a military training or recruiting instrument.[78]

ARMY ASSISTANCE

Another issue taken up by the committee was the support provided to the JROTC by reserve, National Guard, and active army units. Some wanted the active component (AC) and reserve component (RC) to provide more assistance to the program.[79] The committee noted that the reserves had not been formally given this task. Nevertheless, it found that cooperation occurred. Reserve units loaned equipment to schools, permitted the JROTC units to use their facilities, and helped with training. This type of aid was not widespread. It was spotty and varied with the attitude of the local reserve commander. It could never replace the existing paradigm. Local authorities would not tolerate such informal and erratic arrangements as substitutes for a formal, closely supervised program of military instruction.[80]

Neither could active military units provide regular support to the JROTC. Active units were too involved in their regular duties to provide anything more than intermittent assistance. Their use on "an additional duty basis" would not be of any great benefit.[81] It was clear that, while active and reserve units could be of occasional use to the JROTC units, they couldn't provide sustained support.

SOCIOLOGICAL AND GEOGRAPHIC PERSPECTIVES ON THE JROTC

In its report, the committee furnished a sociological and geographic snapshot of the program as it existed in the early 1960s. The program, it observed, was widely but not universally popular. The unevenness of its popularity manifested itself geographically. There were areas devoid of units. Connecticut, New Hampshire, New Jersey, Vermont, Delaware, Maryland, West Virginia, Arkansas, North Dakota, South Dakota, Montana, Oregon, and Alaska did not have any JROTC or NDCC units. Other states had dense concentrations of programs. The JROTC was well represented in the major cities of the Midwest, South, Southwest, and West, in that order.

Sociologically, too, support for the program was skewed. Support for military training was greatest in schools that drew their students from lower socioeconomic strata. Administrators and teachers there valued the program for the order it engendered and the extracurricular outlets it offered. Students liked it for its job opportunities, activities, and physical education credit. On the other hand, there was little demand for the JROTC in affluent areas. Educational authorities there were not keen on what it offered, and most students had little taste for military service.[82]

The services were not of one mind as to how the JROTC units should be distributed among the states. The air force, with the most widely dispersed installation pattern, wanted the program spread proportionately across the entire country. The navy wanted to locate units "within the orbit of naval installations," where it could best sustain the program and motivate boys to join its ranks.[83]

The Ad Hoc Committee observed how the civil rights movement affected cadet training. By 1963, desegregation was beginning to affect the JROTC's racial and ethnic balance. It was underway in many southern cities, where predominantly Black schools, after years of frustration, were finally being given programs. No great problems had been encountered, but some disruption of traditional practices was anticipated.[84]

The committee also touched on a trend that promised to alter the JROTC structure—namely, the changing anatomy of high schools. In the 1960s, more and more school districts were jettisoning junior high schools and three-year senior high schools and adopting the four-year educational model. Many thought it was time for the army to adjust to this trend. There was already a strong desire within the DOD and among host schools to transform the JROTC from a three-year to a four-year program. In some areas, this transformation had already taken place, in fact if not in name.[85] It would take another decade, however, for the services to officially adopt the four-year model.

INSTRUCTION, ATTRITION, AND NAME

Reservations about the quality of the JROTC instruction surfaced during the review. The army reported that the academic program was not on a par with civilian course offerings. Military instructors did not measure up to civilian faculty, nor did the content of military courses compare favorably with regular courses. The army's main contributions were in the areas of citizenship training and character development, both of which were taught by example, practice, and repetition rather than intellectual exploration.[86]

The extraordinarily high attrition rate of cadets was also analyzed. For decades, people had puzzled over why less than a third of sophomore cadets stayed with the program through their senior year. The attrition rate in voluntary programs was 70 percent in 1963. The NDCC's rate was slightly lower—65 percent. In both programs, the biggest inflection point occurred between the junior and senior years.[87]

For decades, the high attrition rates had perplexed military officials. The committee found that the principal reasons for attrition were (1) the movement of families to other areas; (2) deficiency in academic or military subjects; (3) academic overloads; (4) after-school employment; (5) dismissal for disciplinary infractions; (6) participation in physical education, band, athletics, or extracurricular activities; and (7) enrollment in difficult college preparation courses.[88]

The name of the program was another issue. Some favored changing that name to reflect the JROTC's actual missions, which no longer included the commissioning of officers. The army objected to this proposal. A spokesman argued that the designation JROTC had been used since 1916 and was embedded in schools across the country. Changing the name would cause confusion, disrupt continuity, and destroy tradition.[89]

But the army did not stand solely on tradition. It claimed that the name was appropriate. The title implied reserve officer training and thus signaled that the JROTC curriculum transcended academic subjects. Many classes focused on professional military education. True, it was introductory in nature, but it was professional education, nonetheless. Moreover, the JROTC did, indirectly at least, aid in recruiting and producing officers. While it was no longer a commissioning program itself, it sent hundreds of cadets off to earn commissions through West Point, ROTC, or OCS each year.[90]

The other services had no objection to the existing name. As far as the air force was concerned, the title given to the program was irrelevant. What was important was that some type of citizenship and national defense program be conducted in high schools. In the end, the committee recommended that the name JROTC should be retained.[91]

Kennedy entered office intent on discarding Eisenhower's strategy of massive retaliation and adopting a flexible strategy that balanced conventional against nuclear capabilities. To do this, he initiated a buildup of conventional forces. His defense secretary, Robert S. McNamara, went to the Pentagon determined to rationalize the management of the DOD and solidify the connection between the defense budget and national strategy. As part of this effort, he attempted to secure congressional approval for cost-saving measures. One such measure was the elimination of the JROTC. McNamara argued that the program cost more than $6 million a year to maintain but delivered few if any military benefits. He pushed to have all JROTC units converted into NDCC programs, which cost only a pittance to operate.

McNamara's démarche unleashed a firestorm. Opponents, led by Congressman Hebert, passionately defended the JROTC, arguing that it was a valuable citizenship program that performed useful services for communities, the services, students, and the nation. In the end, the JROTC supporters not only stopped the abolition of the JROTC but launched its expansion. Hebert deftly leveraged the enlargement of the SROTC to expand the high school program. Only grudgingly did the DOD relent and allow the expansion to go forward. However, at the DOD's request, Congress convened an Ad Hoc Committee to study the program and to give recommendations about its future. The study provided a revealing insight into the state of the program and established general guidelines for its future growth and operation. In the next chapter, we will see how this expansion occurred.

6

JROTC Expansion during the Vietnam War, 1964–1973

Three cardinal forces shaped the JROTC expansion during the Vietnam War. One was the enlargement of the armed forces, triggered by US involvement in Vietnam. Project 100,000, a program targeting disadvantaged people, was a controversial part of this manpower expansion.[1] The second was the civil rights struggle, which spurred profound changes throughout the military. The third was the widespread unrest fostered by antiwar sentiment, which precipitated a reevaluation of manpower policy. These developments made an indelible impression on society and shaped the perspectives of defense decision-makers.

Despite the passage of the ROTC Vitalization Act, the administration continued to resist expansion. Nevertheless, the public reaction to Robert S. McNamara's attempt to eliminate the program moved the Department of Defense (DOD) to moderate its position. By the time the Ad Hoc Committee's report was released, the focus of the debate had shifted. Defense officials now sought to circumscribe growth, not abolish the program.

One effort to curtail growth occurred in July 1964, when the deputy secretary of defense, Cyrus Vance, implored Congress to conduct the expansion on a permissive rather than mandatory basis. In the same petition, Vance requested that responsibility for citizenship education be transferred to schools and civic organizations, which were more suited to teach such controversial subjects.[2]

F. Edward Hebert and his allies parried these thrusts by tying their plans for the JROTC to the administration's push to upgrade the senior program—an upgrade essential for producing more officers. By conjoining the two in a single bill, they forced the administration's hand and virtually guaranteed a favorable outcome. With the opposition to expansion thus defanged, the expansion bill was passed on September 28, 1964.[3]

The expansion bill had encountered strong opposition when it came before the House in late 1963. Some representatives feared that, if the bill passed, the JROTC would proliferate among segregated southern high schools. This would necessarily entail the JROTC teaching citizenship "in schools where one of the most basic rights of citizenship [was] denied." A number of legislators vowed to oppose any legislation unless a civil rights amendment was attached to it.[4]

The opposition to JROTC growth subsided with the passage of the Civil Rights Bill in June 1964. The landmark legislation prohibited the use of federal funds on programs that discriminated on the basis of color, race, or national origin. With segregation eliminated as a bone of contention, the path was clear for the bill's passage.[5]

In a last-ditch effort to stop the expansion, Senator Gaylord Nelson of Wisconsin introduced an amendment to Hebert's bill, imposing a three-hundred-unit ceiling on growth. Nelson argued that the JROTC "had no valid purpose beyond helping fill officer shortages." He found few sympathetic listeners. Many of his colleagues viewed the expansion as a way to provide relief to financially stressed schools in their districts. In the end, the Senate rejected Nelson's amendment by a vote of 43–10.[6]

SPONSORS OF EXPANSION

Senator Richard Russell of Georgia led the expansion fight in the Senate. He saw in the bill "an opportunity to train some 600,000 or 700,000 young men in high schools and colleges . . . to give them some semblance of an idea as to discipline and order, and respect for authority, as well as improving their health." The senator claimed that the JROTC had military value although, he conceded, it did not serve a direct military need. Russell's ardor for expansion intensified after the creation of the Job Corps, a part of Lyndon B. Johnson's Great Society program that the senator bitterly opposed. Russell believed that more units would reduce the need for the president's expensive jobs program, which the Congress had "so blithely created . . . at a cost of $1 billion a year."[7]

While Russell led the fight in the Senate, Hebert was the linchpin of the JROTC expansion in the House. With some justification, he would later style himself as the father of the modern JROTC. Even as a senior at Jesuit High School in New Orleans, he had extolled cadet training in debates and papers. As a congressman, he was an indefatigable advocate who deftly levered his position on the House Armed Service Committee (HASC) to achieve his vision for the JROTC.[8]

Hebert regarded the JROTC as an effective vehicle for teaching citizenship. He drew a close connection between good citizenship and military service. That explains why the congressman recoiled at John F. Kennedy's Executive Order 1119 (September 1963), which allowed married men to escape military service. Hebert believed that the JROTC could make boys, "from the playground on up, conscious of their duty to their country and . . . motivated by the highest ideals of citizenship." They would not, as did the thousands of young people who took advantage of Kennedy's executive order, attempt to shirk their civic obligations.[9]

Even after Congress approved the bill, the administration continued to resist. The Bureau of the Budget wrote to President Johnson, reiterating its opposition to the JROTC growth and suggesting that he not sign the bill. The JROTC graduates did not "receive any meaningful degree of military training." The expansion would only divert manpower from operational forces and add $17 million annually to the program's cost. Bureau officials and DOD leaders rejected claims that the program's civic education value justified its growth. Neither group considered citizenship training to be an appropriate task for the military.[10]

THE ROTC VITALIZATION ACT

Eager to expedite the passage of those parts of the bill that enhanced the senior program's officer-production capacity, however, Johnson relented. On October 13, 1964, he signed PL 88–647, the ROTC Vitalization Act. Some dubbed it the Hebert Plan in recognition of the Louisiana congressman's crucial role in its passage.[11] This bill aimed to boost officer production by introducing Army and Air Force ROTC scholarships, increasing the ROTC stipend, creating a new two-year ROTC commissioning program, and expanding the JROTC.[12]

The Vitalization Act required each service to sponsor the JROTC units, set an expansion limit of 1,200 units, retained the minimum enrollment standard of one hundred US citizens, and prescribed the program's duration for both civilian high schools and military institutes. To reduce costs, the act encouraged schools to hire military retirees as instructors. Those retirees were to be paid by the school district an amount that, when added to their retired pay, equaled their active-duty base pay and allowances. Of the amount paid by the school, half would be reimbursed by the military departments.[13] While the bill did not give Hebert and his colleagues all they wanted, it was a substantial victory for them, nonetheless.

After the act's passage, McNamara wrote to remind Johnson that there was no hard evidence proving that the JROTC boosted enlistment. He urged the president to sign the bill because of its importance to the SROTC. At the same time, he advised Johnson to order a study to determine if the program could be made responsive to defense needs.[14]

Johnson accepted McNamara's counsel and issued a statement reflecting the defense secretary's misgivings. "Even though the program fulfills no direct military requirement," Johnson wrote, "it continues to occupy the full time of several hundred members of our active military personnel." The president then told McNamara to conduct the review.[15]

Johnson's comments spurred predictions that a squabble would erupt between the White House and Congress over the JROTC. Many doubted that expansion would occur. Their concerns proved illusory. Support for the program proved too strong.[16]

MECHANICS OF GROWTH

Key parts of the review ordered by Johnson appeared in a defense directive (1965). That directive ordered the development of a two-track curriculum, consisting of an academic and a technical track.[17] The academic option was for students following a college preparatory curriculum, while the technical track prepared students for a particular career field. Initially, only the army offered the technical option.[18] The directive also mandated that, in public institutions, instructors be employees of the school rather than of the DOD. It gave military departments the authority to set performance standards and qualification criteria for military faculty. Staffing in military institutes remained unchanged. Only the army continued to provide active-duty instructors to military schools, however.[19]

Finally, the directive required cadets to take physical education (PE) offered by their schools. Defense officials scoffed when schools allowed the JROTC to substitute for PE. School authorities, they complained, mistakenly assumed that close-order drill had significant physical-conditioning value. Neither the President's Council on Physical Fitness nor the DOD supported such a premise.[20]

The DOD's PE dictate proved difficult to implement. Forcing students to take PE in addition to the JROTC created insuperable scheduling problems. Moreover, since many students took the JROTC to *avoid* PE, instructors feared that enforcing the directive would precipitate a mass exodus of cadets. Principals were also skeptical. At many schools, students fulfilled their PE requirement through the JROTC. Complying with the directive would require hiring an additional teacher, an expensive proposition. Bombarded with protests from all angles, the services generally ignored this provision.[21]

When allocating units, the Pentagon gave the army 650 units, twice as many as the other services combined. Initially, it had intended to divide up the 1,200 units equally. But the army insisted that it needed more units to satisfy all National Defense Cadet Corps (NDCC) schools wishing to convert to the JROTC as well as the schools on its waiting list, some of which had been waiting for years.[22]

The DOD acceded to the army's entreaties. In the end, it gave the air force and the navy 275 units each. The navy, in turn, allotted forty-two of its units to the Marine Corps. Navy and air force officials did not object to the revised scheme since it allowed them to expand in a more orderly manner. Withal, many senior air force and navy officers doubted the JROTC's value and gladly gave some of their units to the army.[23]

The replacement of active duty with retired instructors began in July 1966. This posed no problem for the air force, navy, and Marine Corps; those services were starting anew. The army, on the other hand, underwent a wholesale staffing conversion. It did this gradually through normal instructor rotation. By July 1969, the conversion process was virtually complete. Instructor titles changed with the conversion; professor of military science (PMS) gave way to senior army instructor (SAI).[24]

The introduction of retirees created hiring issues. Applicants shunned schools that paid the minimum salary or were in high-cost-of-living areas. Schools remote from military installations also struggled to find staff; they lacked access to services available to retirees on military bases, such as medical care, commissary, and post exchange (PX).[25]

Two significant changes in the army's management structure occurred. Both took effect in July 1966. First, the army transferred general staff responsibility for the program from the reserve components (RC) to the G-1. This shift decoupled the JROTC from the reserves, gave it greater visibility, and aligned it more closely with recruiting. Second, the army transferred operational responsibility for the program to Continental Army Command (CONARC).[26] With this transfer, the army hoped to exercise tighter supervision over the program by moving the operational headquarters closer to the field. The army staff in the Pentagon retained responsibility only for general policy and certain critical functions, such as ensuring compliance with the Civil Rights Act.[27]

To carry out its extended mandate, CONARC's ROTC Directorate was enlarged. It grew from a division of eight people in 1965 to a directorate of eighty-nine people by 1967. To augment the program's clout, the army appointed a general officer to head the new office. It is an axiom of army management to appoint a general officer to head an organization whose importance senior leaders want to highlight. The ROTC staff at the five continental US armies (CONUSA) also grew, albeit to differing degrees. The Pentagon wanted to standardize ROTC management at the army level, but impassioned protests from the field derailed this plan. Army areas were so diverse and their span of control so large that any scheme to impose a uniform management structure on the JROTC was bound to founder.[28]

On January 1, 1966, President Johnson formally launched the JROTC's expansion. The goal was to expand to 1,200 schools and 240,000 cadets over five years. However, as the Vietnam War escalated, the DOD began diverting funds earmarked for the JROTC to higher-priority programs. In the end, budget shortages compelled the DOD to extend the activation timeline. The services did not reach the unit target until 1974 or the enrollment goal until 1983. Still, compared with the collegiate ROTC, the JROTC fared well. While JROTC enrollment grew by 54 percent between 1964 and 1974, enrollment in the senior program plummeted by 80 percent.[29] It was during this period that the JROTC overtook the SROTC in size and public visibility.

EXPANSION BEGINS

Growth of a sort occurred even before Johnson's announcement. It resulted from a reorganization of the army's ROTC management apparatus. To save manpower, CONARC disbanded its Military Schools Division. Military schools were again, as before 1955, conjoined with civilian high schools and counted as JROTC units. The thirty-four-unit increase between 1964 and 1965 thus reflected a reorganization rather than actual additions.[30]

The expansion began in earnest in the fall of 1966. The army's six selection criteria for new units were enrollment potential, date of application, capacity to host a unit, accreditation status, ability to meet statutory and contractual requirements, and a "fair and equitable distribution" of units among states. As one observer observed, this last criterion represented more of a "good intention" than a reality.[31]

The formal criteria did not include two factors of paramount importance. One factor was the "philosophy" of a school. Only schools that considered the JROTC to be a "desirable educational activity" could provide "a sound basis" for cooperation. This consideration gained saliency as antimilitary sentiment grew after 1967. NDCC status was another key factor. The army gave NDCC schools priority because of their proven commitment to cadet training. The initial burst of expansion was largely due to the conversion of NDCC to JROTC units; 81 of the 112 new units formed between 1965 and 1967 were former NDCC schools. As planned, the expansion signaled the virtual demise of the NDCC. By 1973, only seventeen NDCC units remained.[32]

In the expansion, schools used the practice of cross-enrollment to enable growth. This practice allowed students attending nonaffiliated schools to enroll in schools with JROTC. Instructors in new or struggling units seized on cross enrollment to attain the hundred-student minimum. Others used cross enrollment for securing additional instructors as staffing was based on enrollment.[33]

The army tempered its approval of cross enrollment with advisements and restrictions intended to hold down costs and forfend abuses. For example, it warned that cross-enrollment agreements did not constitute tacit promises of new units when vacancies occurred. Conceding such authority to instructors and school officials took control of growth away from the army and threatened to create more units than could be supported.[34]

DIVERSITY

The opening of the JROTC to African American people and other minorities gave a powerful impetus to expansion and changed the program's demographic makeup. Gains achieved after 1965 were largely due not to the program's increasing popularity among traditional constituents but to the inclusion of previously excluded schools and students. The army was particularly effective in attracting minorities. By 1970, the army's minority enrollment was more than twice that of the air force or the navy.

The influx of minorities into the JROTC came at a time when migrants, driven from rural areas by agricultural mechanization, flocked to cities in pursuit of economic opportunity. They congregated in the central city, where they foundered in unfamiliar surroundings. Between 1950 and 1966, the number of Black people living in inner cities almost doubled, while white people fled to the suburbs. The composition of urban schools changed along with that of cities. By the end of the 1970s, most school districts in large urban areas had Black or Hispanic majorities.

The federal government extended its role in protecting civil rights as the urban crisis deepened. Under Johnson, Congress passed several legislative landmarks that profoundly affected race relations. The most significant was the Civil Rights Act of 1964. This legislation proscribed discrimination based on race, color, or national origin in any program receiving federal funds and empowered federal officials to cut off funds from noncompliant programs.

Enhancing the power of the Civil Rights Act was a sharp increase in federal funding for education. The National Defense Education Act (NDEA, 1958) had increased the flow of federal dollars into the nation's educational system. By 1964, most educational institutions were receiving federal assistance. That aid grew after 1965 as federal programs attacking poverty and discrimination kicked into high gear. Schools became more dependent on federal aid and less able to resist federal policy. As Diane Ravitch noted, a school system that depended on federal support for even 10 percent of its revenues forfeited its autonomy.[35]

Race relations assumed greater urgency after World War II. Concerns about America's international image vis-à-vis the Soviet Union fed this development. By the early 1960s, however, the fear of social disorder had become the principal driver behind the equal rights struggle. Inner cities appeared to be tinderboxes of insurrection and revolution. This was seemingly confirmed by the outbreak of urban riots in the summer of 1963. The Johnson administration responded to this explosive situation by declaring a War on Poverty. Two cardinal planks of this war were the Economic Opportunity Act of 1964 and the Elementary and Secondary Education Act of 1965. The former established the Job Corps and Head Start and sanctioned federal financial aid for the educational uplift of "deprived children."[36]

The federal government reshuffled its educational priorities to deal with social tumult. The emphasis in the 1950s had been on raising academic standards, improving science and math education, and channeling high-aptitude youth into college. This emphasis reflected Cold War competition. As Diane Ravitch and Joel Springer noted, however, competition with the Soviets lost salience as race relations became the nation's preeminent concern. The push for academic excellence gave way to concern about the "underprivileged."[37]

As the federal stress on civil rights intensified, the Pentagon's role in civil rights broadened. While the department had worked to increase career opportunities for minorities, its commitment to civil rights seemed less than total. The DOD's tepidness concerning civil rights stemmed from a reluctance to offend local sensibilities and jeopardize its hold on strategically desirable real estate.[38]

Things changed in the summer of 1964 with the passage of the Civil Rights Act. The armed forces were suddenly thrust into the heart of the civil rights struggle. President Johnson pressed each federal department to put teeth into the new law. The DOD responded by launching assaults against discrimination in the National Guard, public schools near military bases, and off-base housing.

The DOD confronted discrimination in educational institutions when it issued a directive (April 1965) prohibiting the creation or maintenance of ROTC units at schools that practiced discrimination or segregation. Heretofore, few predominantly minority high schools had JROTC units. Those that did were concentrated in a handful of cities, with Chicago, Detroit, and Indianapolis being among the more notable. Black units were rare in the South, where authorities feared to train African American youth in firearms or military tactics.[39]

The push to open the program to minorities came from the bottom up as well as from the top down. Excluded from the program for decades, Black parents and school principals pressed to secure units for their communities. The demand reflected the popularity of military service among African American people, who generally viewed military service as a desirable career option.

The promise of order and discipline in the classroom was another powerful inducement. In many inner-city schools, teachers struggled to maintain order. Students were disruptive, and teachers were cynical. The psychologist Martin Deutsch found "an atmosphere of disorganization, an emphasis on disciplining, minimal academic teaching, and much emphasis on 'creative expression'" in inner-city schools. The principal aim of teachers was not to impart knowledge but to maintain control over unruly students. Up to 80 percent of classroom time was spent on discipline and administrative tasks, compared to roughly 30 percent in majority schools. Black parents deplored the chaotic conditions that prevailed in urban schools. They wanted their children to attend schools that were safe, orderly, and focused on traditional academic instruction. The JROTC seemed to promote this ideal.[40]

The growth of minority enrollment proceeded pari passu with the integration of southern schools. The active involvement of the Department of Health, Education, and Welfare (HEW) and a series of federal court rulings accelerated integration. The greatest advances occurred after 1968. The number of African American students attending integrated schools in the South rose from 2 percent in 1964 to 91 percent in 1972.[41]

The period between 1964 and 1972 was pivotal for the JROTC as minority enrollment steadily increased. While the DOD did not monitor the program's demographic composition before the late 1960s, the scant information available suggests that the army program's minority content was well below 10 percent in 1964. By 1972, non-Caucasian representation stood at 42 percent. Most of this growth occurred in the South as the Pentagon desegregated the JROTC and as inner-city schools became increasingly Black.[42]

ATLANTA PUBLIC SCHOOLS

The case of the Atlanta Public School System (APS) provides an example of how minorities came to be dominant in urban JROTC units. It is not a typical case since cities varied widely in their responses to the forces that were reshaping them. The Atlanta case, however, is one of the most well-documented instances of a makeover of an urban school system and can at least provide insight into how this transformation occurred elsewhere.

Atlanta had a long high school military training tradition. The city's first military unit was created on the eve of America's entry into World War I. By 1918, Atlanta had three programs in operation, none of which were affiliated with the JROTC. It was only after the war that the JROTC entered the city. Atlanta received its first unit in 1920. Thereafter, the program grew along with the APS. By the early 1960s, the city could boast of the third-largest JROTC program in the nation, with units in thirteen of its twenty-two high schools. Among the nation's cities, only Chicago and Detroit had more.[43]

Unlike many southern cities, Atlanta had been eager to implant the JROTC in Black schools before 1965. In fact, according to James C. Evans, a civilian assistant to the secretary of defense, the APS was the first public school system in the South to do so.[44] In February 1952, Ira Jarrell, APS superintendent, asked the army to approve two additional units for Atlanta's Black high schools. It was the policy of Atlanta's Board of Education to afford equal opportunities to all students, and it was thus "imperative" that Black schools had them.[45]

The army rebuffed this request, but in 1954, the Atlanta school board tried again. It sent a special committee to meet with the Third Army commander at Fort McPherson. The committee learned that budget shortfalls and the "changing needs of the army" precluded the creation of more units. It also discovered that there was to be a nationwide reduction of the JROTC. Undeterred, the board dispatched representatives to Washington to meet with congressional and DOD representatives. Once again, they were informed that budget constraints prevented growth.[46]

It wasn't until the fall of 1964 that the school board finally succeeded in embedding a unit at Booker T. Washington, a Black high school. This unit was one of two opened in Atlanta that year. Since this occurred before 1965, the army created the unit at Booker T. Washington under the old rule—a new unit could be created only after an existing program closed. Thus, only after Atlanta's Hoke Smith High School's unit closed did Washington get its program. Jeffrey Clement, an influential voice in Atlanta's Black community, played a key role in effecting the transfer from Hoke Smith to Washington. So, too, did a coalition of Black parents, which applied considerable pressure on city officials.[47]

The expansion of the 1960s extended the program throughout the APS. By 1968, the JROTC was operating in all of Atlanta's twenty-three high schools. At this point, the APS was well on its way to becoming a Black school system as the city's high schools went from being 70 percent white in 1958 to 85 percent Black in 1972. Atlanta's "chief problem," according to the National Education Association, "was not so much in desegregating a school as in keeping it desegregated." The JROTC transformed along with the APS. In 1960, it was an essentially white program. By 1970, it was an overwhelmingly Black one.[48]

The factors that made the JROTC appealing elsewhere were also at work in Atlanta. Its social opportunities appealed to students and its resources to school boards. Principals and teachers liked it because it fostered order in the classroom. And government officials supported it because it kept a lid on social tension in volatile inner cities. As elsewhere, the program in Atlanta served multiple functions and appealed to multiple audiences.

TURBULENCE AND RESISTANCE

The JROTC expansion of the 1960s was both less dramatic and more irregular than it is often portrayed. The picture is much different when the JROTC and NDCC are considered together. A look at table 3 reveals two trends. First, the rise in enrollment was not commensurate with the increase in unit strength; the average size of a unit fell by 31 percent between 1965 and 1972. Second, the trajectory of the JROTC growth was irregular.

The generally upward trend in enrollment and institutional strength was punctuated with declines. Factors that initially impelled the JROTC expansion forward—the dissolution of the Military Schools Division, the conversion of NDCC to JROTC, the large pool of schools on the waiting list for new units—either disappeared or contracted.[49]

While the army's experience was unique, all three JROTC programs were beset by the same issues. Coordinated resistance was one challenge. The core of anti-JROTC agitation consisted of a collection of loosely affiliated peace, religious, and anticonscription organizations.[50] These groups tended to employ moral, religious, and ideological arguments to combat the spread

TABLE 3

Size of the Army JROTC, School Years 1965–1966 to 1972–1973

School Year	Units JROTC	Units NDCC	Enrollment JROTC	Enrollment NDCC	Total Units	Total Enrollment
1965–1966	287	128	68,137	28,229	415	96,366
1966–1967	399	39	87,338	12,257	438	99,595
1967–1968	473	37	97,339	9,349	510	106,668
1968–1969	517	34	101,875	6,808	551	108,683
1969–1970	540	31	105,497	3,979	571	109,476
1970–1971	506	29	99,113	3,785	535	102,898
1971–1972	589	25	93,843	3,248	614	97,091
1972–1973	628	17	102,298	1,711	645	104,009

ER, AJROTC, FY1965–1973.

of the JROTC. Practical issues were not absent; observers still questioned the academic credentials of the JROTC instructors and program costs. But in an era in which the government was distrusted and deep fissures divided society, such questions were submerged under emotionally charged ones.[51]

Activists portrayed the JROTC as a part of the Pentagon's propaganda machine. Through the program, the DOD endeavored to impress students with the immediacy of the communist threat and instill in them a military worldview.[52] The citizenship training it offered was a sham. Its aim was to condition students to render "unquestioning obedience to governmental authority" and instill in them a patriotism of an intensely ethnocentric variety. The JROTC also allegedly exploited youths of color by inducing them to enlist.[53] The growing concentration of the JROTC units in minority communities "proved" the existence of an unwritten DOD policy of racial and ethnic exploitation.[54]

Activists also denounced the program's leadership training. The JROTC offered a "mechanistic, totalitarian model of leadership" that clashed with "the more complicated, Humanistic, democratic" paradigm offered in civilian courses. The product of such training resembled an "automaton." Marksmanship instruction elicited special condemnation. It predisposed students to seek violent solutions to problems and made gang violence in inner cities worse.[55]

Anti-JROTC sentiment sometimes manifested itself in the form of legislative and policy initiatives. At the national level, Representative Ron Dellums (D-California) introduced a bill calling for the elimination of the JROTC. That bill failed to pass, but less radical measures advanced at the state level took hold. In 1967, the New Jersey State Legislature passed a measure requiring school districts to submit proposals for new units to a referendum. In 1968, the Hawaii State Board of Education imposed a moratorium on new units in public schools. The board reaffirmed its moratorium in 1976, after a contentious hearing on the effects of cadet units in high schools.[56]

In New York, lawmakers blocked legislation overriding a law (1937) prohibiting military training during regular school hours. Beginning in 1969, New York State legislators attempted in four consecutive sessions to overturn this law. On each occasion, they were rebuffed by colleagues fearful of the educational and moral effects that military training would have on students. The debates over these bills were acrimonious and featured name-calling and obscenities.[57]

Local expressions of antimilitary sentiment posed the most immediate problems for units. The "disapproving attitude" prevalent in many universities, a Navy JROTC instructor noted, had "spilled over onto the high school level" and was an "obstacle" to unit growth. He was referring to the taunts, insults, and physical intimidation directed at cadets by "radical" activists.[58]

Military haircut and uniform standards exposed cadets to the obloquy of their peers. Cadets dreaded the days on which they wore their uniforms because of the harassment they incurred.[59] They suffered a range of indignities—having their hats "accidentally" knocked off and trampled on, their spit-shined shoes stepped on, or their dress coats soiled by the shoe prints other students impressed on their backs. Feeling harried and vulnerable, cadets wore uniforms only when attending the JROTC classes, donning them immediately before class and changing back into civilian garb immediately after. Cadets were especially vulnerable to the depredations of their fellows at drill, where they would be assailed by catcalls and ridicule without being able to respond or withdraw.[60]

One should not, though, overestimate the effect of antimilitary sentiment on growth. The JROTC largely escaped the intense antipathy directed at the SROTC. It operated, one official noted, "quietly . . . in the background," relative to the senior program. A survey by the National Association of Secondary School Principals found that 15 percent of JROTC-affiliated high schools experienced "major student disruptions" from 1969 to 1971, years when anti-ROTC protests on college campuses peaked. Only in 2 percent of these was the JROTC the principal focus of disruption. Battles over the JROTC were generally nonviolent, waged in school board and parent-teacher association meetings, not in the streets. Since most units were in conservative states, the relative paucity of opposition is understandable.[61]

There were also more prosaic forces at work dissuading students from joining the JROTC. The program's lackluster image was allegedly one of them. The JROTC had the reputation of being a haven for unpopular and troubled youths who existed on the periphery of student life. Students from the school's social mainstream were consequently deterred from enrolling. The military lifestyle was another repellent. There was a widespread perception that the JROTC entailed rigid discipline, stifled individuality, and appealed only to students who sought a military career.

School reorganization was another obstacle to growth. There were a staggering number of redistricting and consolidation initiatives between

1960 and 1973; the number of school districts in the United States fell by 60 percent. In many instances, mergers were undertaken as economy measures; in others, they were used to achieve integration. These reorganization moves led to the closure of some units and the disruption of others.[62]

Withal, the late 1960s and early 1970s were years of financial crisis in education. Financial difficulties plagued high schools and the JROTC "as never before." To save money, school districts cut their school days into fewer periods or adopted double sessions. With less elective time available, the scheduling of the JROTC classes became problematic. Budget shortages constrained growth. In 1971, 192 schools asked the army for financial relief because they were struggling to meet their portion of the JROTC instructor's salary. Some schools dropped the JROTC when told that no money was available. High schools planning to form new units likewise suffered from the financial crunch. Fifty high schools indicated that they wanted a unit but could not afford one. Another 162 schools said that they would sponsor a unit if the army provided more financial aid.[63]

Growing federal stringency exacerbated the financial crisis. Lawmakers, alarmed by spiraling inflation and huge deficits, demanded greater fiscal discipline from the administration. The JROTC felt the resultant squeeze more than other defense programs. Monies originally set aside for the JROTC were diverted to organizations with a higher priority. Consequently, many unit start-ups had to be postponed. Funds for advertising also dried up. The little advertising money available went to the SROTC. Only when it became clear that conscription would end did financial support for the JROTC begin to grow.[64]

DECLINE OF MILITARY SCHOOLS

Military institutes were especially hard hit by financial problems. Between 1965 and 1975, twenty-eight of these institutions either closed or dropped the JROTC. The army considered their demise a "great loss." The remaining institutes saw their collective enrollment drop by 56 percent. The decline of military institutes occurred at a time when enrollment in other private schools was exploding. The military schools that survived often did so by lowering admission standards or effecting partial demilitarization, which could entail admitting women or severing ties with the DOD. Even the Harvard School (Los Angeles), an original member of the JROTC, shed its military format in 1969.[65]

Institutes suffered from several disadvantages. One was their image. They had the reputation of being "dressed-up reform schools" that stressed spit and polish more than academics. Parades, rituals, and pageantry, elements that once bolstered the allure of military schools, appeared vapid by the late 1960s. Another major disadvantage was cost. Tuition at some institutes was as high as that charged by prestigious civilian preparatory schools. Few parents were willing to pay such a price for an education whose utility seemed questionable.[66]

Richard Davies, a faculty member at Culver Institute, attributed the decline of military schools to a fundamental change in the way the public perceived military service.[67] After World War II, military training increasingly was seen by the affluent and upwardly mobile to be irrelevant or even detrimental to the academic development and career prospects of students. A military regimen was too inflexible and narrow to develop a student's intellectual capabilities, which were keys to success in the emerging economy.[68]

The military sociologist Morris Janowitz noted the progressive "democratization" of the officer corps in the twentieth century. The gradual emergence of an information-based economy and its educational requirements gradually eroded the officer's societal standing and the military profession's cachet. The affluent and the abundantly talented became, as the century unfolded, less and less likely to enter a military career. As this occurred, military schools were progressively pushed to the margins of the educational mainstream.[69]

EROSION OF COMPULSORY JROTC

The trend away from compulsory JROTC contributed to enrollment difficulties. Between 1964 and 1974, the number of high schools with mandatory military programs fell by almost 30 percent. One of the most notable examples of the compulsory JROTC's demise occurred in 1971 at Bangor High School (Maine), whose unit traced its lineage back to the Civil War. Compulsory enrollment ended when a new and more liberal school board made the program voluntary and eliminated the JROTC as a graduation requirement.[70]

The compulsory NDCC program in Washington, DC, provided another example. Male students in that city had been automatically enrolled in the program since the 1890s. An escape hatch existed in the form of a 1907 municipal ordinance that permitted students to be excused if they produced a written parental request. A problem arose in October 1965, when the city's assistant superintendent for secondary schools, John D. Koontz, made it more difficult for students to evade participation. No longer, he declared, would boys be exempted from participation by producing a written request from home. Henceforth, parents would have to appear in person to have their sons excused. He wanted to prevent "hasty action" before the "full advantages of military training" could be made apparent. Koontz embraced the program because of the discipline it brought to the classroom. The NDCC, he believed, conditioned cadets to a "ready and cheerful obedience to orders" and developed in them "respect for constituted authority."[71]

The city's enrollment policy affected poorer schools the most. Schools serving the capital city's more affluent areas had a low percentage of their male students attending military training. Parents in these areas were more aware of their legal right to have their sons exempted. While JROTC enrollment rates in schools serving upper-income families were less than 25 percent, rates in some of the district's inner-city schools approached 100 percent. This did not seem equitable.[72]

Compulsory military training in Washington's high schools ended abruptly in March 1967, when the school system came under the scrutiny of the press and the attack of infuriated parents. Parents bombarded the school administration with complaints. A frustrated mother, who had already experienced an "annoying hassle" getting her eldest son released from a unit, alerted the press to these enrollment practices. When her youngest son, then a ninth grader, informed her that he had been automatically enrolled in the program, she turned to Susan Filson, a correspondent with the *Washington Post*. Filson wrote an article about the irregular methods used to compel attendance at military training. Public pressure finally induced Carl E. Hansen, the school system's superintendent, to rescind Koontz's directive requiring a parental conference and relax procedures for being excused from drill.[73]

The termination of mandatory participation resulted in a precipitous drop in enrollment. The percentage of students enrolled in the capital city's NDCC units sank from 73 percent in 1965 to 8 percent in 1973. Washington's experience was replicated in cities across the nation.[74]

ATTRITION

The program's struggles in the late 1960s and early 1970s refocused program managers on a perennial problem—the high attrition rate of the JROTC cadets. The services lost over 80 percent of each entering freshman class before graduation, with the bulk of the attrition occurring after the first year.

The reasons behind attrition were numerous. They included unsatisfactory academic performance, disciplinary infractions, and scheduling conflicts. College-bound students found it difficult to fit the JROTC into schedules filled with academically challenging courses such as chemistry, physics, and calculus. Military uniform and haircut standards also were disincentives. As students advanced in grade, they found personal-appearance restrictions increasingly burdensome. After the ninth grade, students left the program to accept after-school jobs, finding it impossible to reconcile the demands of the program with those of their employer. Still other students quit because they moved out of the area. Because the JROTC units tended to cluster around military installations with their highly mobile populations, this may have been a fairly important factor.[75]

The JROTC's high attrition rates should not be surprising. They were like those of other national youth organizations such as the Boy Scouts. The Boy Scouts, too, found it difficult to retain boys past the age of fourteen. The creation of the Cub Scouts in the mid-1940s was an acknowledgment of that reality. As adolescents mature, their interests become too volatile, their focus too broad, and their desire for autonomy and self-expression too strong for sustained commitment to organizations that impose restrictions on personal appearance and demand regimentation. The allure of the uniform slowly wears off as students advance in grade. What once appeared as a mark of distinction now symbolizes continued subjection to adult control.

CURRICULUM REVISION

After the passage of the Vitalization Act, the army revised the JROTC curriculum to align it with training offered in Basic Combat Training and the SROTC, making an already militarily oriented program even more military.[76] This did not resonate well in many high schools, so the army was forced back to the drawing board.[77] Meanwhile, units began tailoring their courses to fit more unobtrusively into the campus environment. Instructors downplayed, camouflaged, or eliminated the overtly military aspects of the program—scaling back or eliminating weapons training, reducing course requirements, curtailing tactical training and drill, and relaxing appearance and haircut policies to achieve "compatibility with the preferences of our youth."[78]

Weapons training emerged as a particularly contentious issue. Units stopped offering marksmanship instruction in many schools. The air force discouraged the use of rifles, except for ceremonial purposes and drill competitions. It cited the safety risks, costs, and the complexion of the Air Force JROTC curriculum as reasons. Air force managers also feared the openings such training gave to the JROTC's enemies. Weapons training was a rallying point for aggressive factions like the Students for a Democratic Society.[79]

The general educational environment, even when not overtly antimilitary, discouraged activities such as drill. Such activities drew the censure of teachers, parents, and local officials. Even principals well disposed toward the JROTC wanted their military unit to remain inconspicuous. On their part, cadets generally preferred anonymity to the spotlight. Their public presence in uniform invited harassment and ridicule.

The de-emphasis of military training had practical advantages. Foremost among them was that it reduced costs. The maintenance of rifle ranges required a considerable outlay of money, as did furnishing space to conduct drill and tactical training. Providing this support severely taxed poor institutions.[80]

In 1970, the army replaced its old curriculum with the *Junior Green Book*.[81] The new publication placed good citizenship and self-reliance at the top of the JROTC's list of objectives. That change represented yet another reorientation of the JROTC's focus. While McNamara's goal of making the JROTC more supportive of defense needs was not explicitly abandoned, it was no longer predominant. Instilling good citizenship and self-reliance in students now seemed more relevant than teaching military skills.[82]

The new program of instruction (POI) provided for greater curricular flexibility. It reduced the annual course load at military schools, authorized instructors to reduce the time spent on any one course by 25 percent, and decreased military instruction to that essential for understanding leadership problems. The *Junior Green Book* sanctioned the revisions already adopted by many units.[83]

Civilian educational trends affected the JROTC curriculum. In this period, traditional authority came under attack. Students bristled under constraints imposed by arbitrary rules and codes of conduct. Discipline eroded, absenteeism increased, and incidents of vandalism proliferated. Reformers pushed for less autocratic styles of classroom management. Schools responded by revamping their curricula to align with contemporary social forces. This involved lowering graduation requirements, introducing flexible scheduling, offering more topical subjects, and giving students a wider choice of courses. The Experimental Schools Program, introduced by the Richard Nixon administration in 1970, incentivized educators to be more innovative in their pedagogical practices. Reducing academic rigor, democratizing the classroom, and revising the curriculum to make it more socially relevant would supposedly mollify students and improve their behavior. The JROTC adjusted its program accordingly.[84]

AIR FORCE, NAVY, AND MARINE CORPS

The incorporation of the air force, navy, and Marine Corps into the JROTC was among the most momentous outcomes of the Vitalization Act. It made possible a larger program and increased the program's heterogeneity. Each service put its distinctive stamp on its program, although the resultant variations were more evident to military people than to civilians.

The air force and navy programs made their first appearance on the high school campus during the fall of 1965. They expanded slowly and deliberately. The air force, for example, created only twenty units in each of its first two years of existence. It picked up the pace in 1967 when it added fifty new schools. Because of social turbulence, budgetary stress, and institutional turnover, the air force did not reach its 275-unit target until 1973. By then, its 275 units were spread across forty-five states, Guam, and Europe (see appendix B).[85]

SERVICE DISTINCTIVENESS

The management structures of the navy and air force were more centralized than that of the army. While the latter's featured semiautonomous regional headquarters, the lines of authority in the air force and navy programs led to a single office. The smaller size of the air force and navy programs coupled with their lack of a JROTC tradition enabled them to construct their management arrangements on a more rational footing.

The new entrants to the program adopted distinctive curricula that diverged from the curriculum of the Army. The Air Force JROTC curriculum required a minimum of ninety-six hours of instruction per year. A typical program offered five one-hour classes per week over a nine-month academic year. Instructors devoted three hours to aerospace academics and two hours to leadership.[86] In military high schools, the air force provided a fourth year of instruction (AE4), which was a condensed version of the general military course in the SROTC.[87] The navy provided for two curricular tracks—a minimum program (one-half credit) with 96 instructional hours and a maximum program (one credit) with 120 hours.[88] In 1975, the navy began experimenting with a technical track, targeting students who did not plan to go to college.[89]

Service identities were manifest in the content of classes. The air force and navy instituted technical curricula, geared to their technology and missions. Air force cadets studied the principles of flight, propulsion, navigation, and the history of aviation. Subjects in the Navy JROTC curriculum included oceanography, meteorology, navigation, electronics, and the rules of the nautical road. The Marine Corps, like the army, featured leadership, military skills, and basic military knowledge.

More broadly, service identities were evident in attitudes toward and approaches to civic engagement. The roles and missions of the army historically had varied more than those of the other services. While the roles of the navy and air force were linked to their equipment—the ship and the airplane—the army's roles were bound up with the capabilities of soldiers.[90] The air and sea forces measured their strengths in airplanes and ships while the army measured its power in end strength, i.e., how many soldiers it had in its ranks. People were more malleable than technologies, a fact reflected in service ethos and culture. Moreover, the army's part in domestic engagement had historically been quite extensive. The variability of its missions, its size, its history, and the nature of its work conditioned it to be receptive to civil tasks. Participation in civil projects became engrained in the collective psyche of the army to a greater extent than it did in the more technology-centered services.

The air and sea services likewise differed from the army in their unit selection methodologies. The navy's selection criteria included breadth of curriculum, percentage of college-bound graduates, and school accreditation. Its emphasis on academic achievement and mental ability clearly set it apart from the army. The navy's need for technicians to understand, operate, and repair complex weapons systems and its mental requirements for enlistment help explain this orientation.[91] The air force stressed both academic ability and school size. It delineated this last criterion with more precision than the ground forces.[92] Its guiding rule was that a school should have at least five hundred male students enrolled in the tenth through twelfth grades to be eligible for a unit. This limited its presence in rural areas but mitigated, but by no means eliminated, it struggles with inefficient units.[93]

Instructor selection was another area of divergence. The air force stood on the most discriminating side of the spectrum, followed by the navy and army in that order. The air force required officer applicants to be holders of BS degrees who had been certified as teachers or were working toward certification. It also "highly encouraged" its instructor applicants to have graduate degrees.[94] Its emphasis on teacher certification, graduate education, and high school teaching experience enabled the air force to offer more rigorous classes and maintain a more credit-worthy program. That was, perhaps, why the air force could boast of being "well accepted by the academic community." The other services lagged behind the air force in terms of the educational and certification credentials of their instructors.

SERVICE SIMILARITIES

At the unit level, though, there was a basic commonality among the programs. Like the army, the other services devoted considerable time to drill and ceremonies, engaged in community service projects, conducted voluntary summer camps, and offered an array of extracurricular activities. They sponsored fundraisers for charities, participated in local parades, provided security at school assemblies, worked with students in elementary schools, sponsored drill and rifle teams, visited military bases, and offered social activities, such as open houses, potluck dinners, beach parties, and military balls.[95]

And like the army, the air force and navy found it expedient to adapt their programs to the contemporary educational environment. They relaxed appearance and discipline standards, demilitarized their curricula, encouraged the use of modern educational techniques, and adapted their curricula to "the individual desires of each participating school." Uniformity was out of the question. "We cannot come up with a [single] curriculum tailored to the needs of 160 schools spread throughout the country," observed one air force spokesman. Accordingly, instructors received pliable curricular guidelines, allowing them considerable leeway in the allocation of class time. There was, as one air force officer remarked, "little poured concrete" in the JROTC curriculum.[96]

Although each of the four programs had its own distinct flavor, societal pressures, the educational environment, federal priorities, and congressional and public expectations worked together to impose a degree of sameness across the JROTC. To be sure, the JROTC was more diverse in 1973 than in 1960. Still, to most observers, the four programs appeared to have more similarities than differences.[97]

The 1960s witnessed the birth of the modern JROTC. With the passage of the ROTC Vitalization Act of 1964, the JROTC absorbed the NDCC, replaced active-duty instructors with retirees, expanded the JROTC institutional base, and extended its reach to the navy, air force, and Marine Corps. While these new additions placed their own distinctive stamps on their units, interservice commonalities outweighed interservice differences.

McNamara threatened to liquidate the program in the early 1960s. He argued that it consumed a lot of resources but contributed little to national defense. An irate Congress not only repelled his foray but set the program on the road to expansion.

While he failed to block expansion, McNamara refocused the JROTC from citizenship to preinduction military training. Even this victory, however, was short-lived. Societal pressures in the late 1960s compelled the services to demilitarize their programs, with many units curtailing or de-emphasizing military training.

The JROTC entered a period of instability in the late 1960s as financial crises, antiwar sentiment, and education reform disrupted program growth. As the nation shifted toward a volunteer force, however, this turbulence abated, and the JROTC once again began to grow. By the mid-1970s, the JROTC's recent travails had been largely forgotten by a new set of defense leaders. In the next chapter, we will explore the evolution of the program in the decade after the US disengagement from Vietnam.

Gloucester High School cadets, Dale Avenue, spring 1888. Photograph by George H. Leck of Lawrence, Massachusetts. Gift of Mr. Arthur N. Smith, 1983. Courtesy of the Cape Ann Museum Library and Archives.

Cadets on parade, Gloucester, Massachusetts, ca. 1890s. Benham Collection. Gift of the Estate of Caroline Benham, 1994. Courtesy of the Cape Ann Museum Library and Archives.

Girls Squad in front of Babson School (then the high school), 1888, First High School Cadets. Eliot Rogers Collection. Gift of Mrs. Elliot Rogers, 1980. Courtesy of the Cape Ann Museum Library and Archives.

Gloucester High School ROTC band in parade, ca. 1936. Robert F. Holloran Collection. Courtesy of the Cape Ann Museum Library and Archives.

Captain Edgar Z. Steever, director of training of the High School Volunteers of the United States, addressing students of the Culver Military Academy, 1917. Courtesy of the Library of Congress.

Gloucester High School cadets in parade, ca. June 1907. Courtesy of the Cape Ann Museum Library and Archives.

Girl cadets at Dunbar High School, Washington, DC, at a competitive drill contest, 1943. Courtesy of the Library of Congress.

Cadets in the High School Victory Corps at Charlotte Amalie High School in the Virgin Islands, 1941. This group assists police and fire departments during blackouts and air raids. Courtesy of the Library of Congress.

District of Columbia Public Schools, high school cadets and military instructor, 1916. Courtesy of the Library of Congress.

Omaha High School and cadets, ca. 1914. Courtesy of the Library of Congress.

Portrait of Congressman F. Edward Hebert holding up papers, May 12, 1966. Hebert was called the "Father of the Modern JROTC." He was the leading congressional figure behind the expansion and reform of the JROTC in the 1960s. Courtesy of the Library of Congress.

Secretary of Defense Robert McNamara, June 1965. Courtesy of the Library of Congress.

7

The Advent of the AVF, 1973–1980

Between 1969 and 1973, the services executed their gradual withdrawal from Vietnam. Over this period, they saw their combined end strength fall by 1.2 million, or 37 percent. The army suffered the most, shrinking by a staggering 50 percent.[1] This vast reduction inevitably entailed institutional turbulence. Discipline, morale, and operational readiness all deteriorated as the military contracted.[2]

During this period, the armed forces transitioned to an all-volunteer force (AVF). To facilitate the transition, Congress granted substantial pay raises to service members.[3] At the same time, defense leaders strove to make military service more attractive by improving living conditions, relaxing haircut standards, and enhancing personal privacy.[4]

The transition coincided with a change in the international environment, which became more benign after President Richard Nixon announced the opening of an "era of negotiation" upon entering office in 1969. Relations between the United States and the two communist superpowers warmed, with détente reaching its heyday between 1972 and 1975.[5]

Domestically, things were far from serene. Civil and racial strife marred Nixon's first term. Antiwar protests reached a peak in 1970, portending a weakening of the nation's internal stability. Although racial rioting subsided after 1969, gang violence, crime, and poverty turned many inner cities into urban combat zones.[6]

The changing international scene and domestic turmoil fueled a heated debate over national priorities and prompted an examination of service missions. Pressure built to shift the focus of the military away from "the killing business" toward more socially productive roles.[7] Sensitive to charges that domestic ills stemmed from excessive defense spending, the Nixon administration redirected the gaze of the Pentagon toward internal matters. If the military failed to adjust, some feared, its societal standing might fall and its claim on national resources weaken.[8]

GROWTH RESUMES

After several years of stagnation, the JROTC expansion resumed (see appendix B).[9] Defense managers, buoyed by the new vitality, became more optimistic about the JROTC's prospects. Analysts ascribed the upturn to various causes. The waning of antimilitary sentiment was one. By 1972, much of the original force behind the antiwar movement had been spent. Hostility toward the JROTC changed to indifference. Aggressive protests became rare.[10]

There were even signs that public sentiment was turning in a positive direction. In 1973, the New York State Legislature overturned the ban on JROTC training during regular school hours, providing an opening for the air force and navy to create more units in New York City and suggesting that the nation was beginning to put the Vietnam imbroglio behind it.[11]

WOMEN AND GIRLS

The admission of women and girls into the JROTC gave it an enormous boost. A court ruling deemed the exclusion of women and girls from the JROTC to be discriminatory. The adoption of Title IX of the Education Amendments of 1972, which prohibited discrimination based on gender, gave teeth to this ruling. Women entered the JROTC in 1972, although it was not until the passage of PL 93–165 in November 1973 that they could be counted in official enrollment tallies.[12]

The inclusion of women was part of the military's transition to the AVF. By 1972, it had become apparent even to inveterate traditionalists that the Department of Defense (DOD) had to rely more heavily on women in a world without conscription. Women, who in this era had fewer dependents, represented both an untapped and economical recruiting market.[13]

The Nixon administration continued the federal effort to combat gender discrimination in the workplace and aggressively pushed to open more federal jobs to women. In March 1972, the Office of Management and Budget (OMB) director sent a stinging missive to Defense Secretary Melvin Laird denouncing the DOD's "less than full compliance toward the President's

TABLE 4
Female Enrollment in the Army JROTC
School Years 1971–1972 to 1978–1979

School Year	Male Enrollment	Female Enrollment	Total Enrollment
1971–1972	97,091	0 (0%)	97,091
1972–1973	96,201	7,808 (8%)	104,009
1973–1974	87,855	22,984 (21%)	110,839
1974–1975	81,449	33,573 (29%)	115,022
1975–1976	77,928	35,514 (31%)	113,442
1976–1977	74,072	34,634 (32%)	108,706
1977–1978	72,848	34,858 (32%)	107,706
1978–1979	70,454	34,689 (33%)	105,143

objective of full employment opportunity for women." Defense officials immediately responded to the president's wishes.[14]

The entry of women produced immediate effects. The thousands of them who flocked into units were a lifeline for the JROTC. They were largely responsible for the enrollment gains of the 1970s. This was very apparent in the army's program. See table 4.

While female representation rose, male enrollment steadily fell. Participation trends in the other services followed a similar trajectory. In the Air Force JROTC, for example, female representation rose from 8.6 percent in 1972 to 33 percent in 1979. Women did indeed, as one observer noted, provide the "margin of success" for the JROTC in the era of the AVF.[15]

The air force embraced female participation earlier than the other services. It maintained female auxiliary units and enrolled hundreds of girls as special students long before 1972.[16] The army also did so but tempered its assent to full-fledged female participation with reservations. It cautioned that curricular modifications had to be made, provisions for uniforms worked out, and policies about enlistment and commissioning options elaborated before female enrollment could be made official policy. The air force had similar concerns but considered them of little moment. Its opening of the Air Force ROTC to women in 1969 made their enrollment in the junior program seem less threatening.[17]

Air Force officials adduced several factors to explain the decline in male enrollment. First, instructors were eager to exploit a new market, leaving less time to recruit men. Second, to raise program quality, instructors jettisoned low-performing men in favor of more academically focused women. Finally, in schools plagued with limited space and packed schedules, any increase in female enrollment necessarily entailed a decrease in male participation.[18]

MINORITIES

Rising minority participation was another impetus to enrollment growth. Minorities constituted more than half of army enrollment by 1979. Minority gains were less dramatic in navy and air force units but were large enough to elicit the concern of the Air Force JROTC managers, who had misgivings about minorities being overrepresented. This concern reflected a wider fear among political and military leaders that the services were becoming demographically unbalanced by admitting too many minorities. In February 1978, air force instructors were told to advise their cadets that, when they entered the "adult working society," they would have "to function in a predominantly White society." The hope was that Black cadets would "recruit some Whites into [the] program [to] keep it properly integrated."[19]

Minority participation was a sensitive issue. Some critics scored the services for not recruiting enough minority officers, while others berated them for targeting minorities for recruitment. The services had to tread carefully, balancing the complaints of both parties as best they could.

FOUR-YEAR HIGH SCHOOLS

The progressive conversion of the JROTC from a three-year to a four-year format also helped growth by opening enrollment eligibility to more and younger students. In this period, a rising number of public high schools converted from three-year to four-year institutions. The number of four-year units grew accordingly. In 1964, about a quarter of the JROTC units were four-year programs. By 1979, more than two-thirds were.[20]

At first, the services resisted attempts at conversion. As late as 1972, changing from a three-year to a four-year format required extensive justification and the approval of higher headquarters. Budgetary concerns inspired this resistance; the addition of one year to the program entailed considerable costs.[21]

The services' resistance to the four-year model gradually abated as public education underwent a transformation. In the 1960s and 1970s, many school systems abandoned the junior high school and adopted the four-year paradigm. Originally, the purpose of junior high schools had been to encourage students to stay in school and earn their diplomas. Now that high school attendance was almost automatic, the need for such schools was no longer apparent. Before long, the four-year high school with grades nine through twelve became the norm. The JROTC's structure evolved pari passu with this trend.[22]

OVERSEAS UNITS

The expansion of the JROTC overseas gave a modest boost to enrollment. In 1964, the Panama Canal Zone was the only US territory with a unit. By 1979, the number of overseas units had grown fourfold; the JROTC now had a presence in West Germany, Puerto Rico, Guam, and Samoa in addition to the Canal Zone.[23] The largest gains occurred in West Germany, where units were embedded in DOD Dependents Schools, which served military families.[24]

The creation of units in Samoa posed a unique problem. It required legislation extending JROTC eligibility, previously restricted to US citizens, to US nationals. Residents of American Samoa and the nearby Swains Island were the only people who fell into this category. Congress passed the enabling law, PL 95–358, in September 1978, opening the way for units in the Pacific.[25]

GEOGRAPHICAL FOOTPRINT

During this period, the migration of the program's geographical center continued its southward track. Demand drove this migration. While southern schools flooded the Pentagon with applications, few schools in the Northeast or Northern Plains submitted requests. In 1971, the air force reported that schools in only two of the eleven states without units had submitted applications for new units.[26]

This skewed distribution pattern also reflected state laws and policies. Many southern states did not require the JROTC instructors to have teaching certificates or baccalaureate degrees; many also excused instructors from regular hiring or retention procedures. In the North, educational and certification standards for instructors were higher and more strictly enforced. In Wisconsin, authorities required all military faculty to possess bachelor's degrees and teaching credentials. Attempts to circumvent these requirements usually met with failure.[27]

In North Central states like Montana, Wyoming, and the Dakotas, geography impeded JROTC growth. The population densities in these states were extremely low, and schools serving rural populations were small and widely dispersed. High schools with enrollments under one hundred were numerous. In 1970, enrollment topped the hundred mark in only 122 of North Dakota's 263 high schools. The story was the same in adjacent states, resulting in many schools being unable to meet the enrollment minimum.[28]

ADVENT OF THE AVF

Despite Robert S. McNamara's attempts to make the JROTC responsive to defense needs, little headway was made in this regard until the early 1970s. It was only when draft calls dwindled that the services made systematic attempts to mesh the JROTC closely with recruiting.[29] The "advent of the Modern Volunteer Army," the ROTC director of the Continental Army Command (CONARC) said, had "placed a new dimension on JROTC." Now, it attracted a "considerable amount of interest" because it could help the army reach "the goal of a zero draft." The JROTC instructors were told to "increase the interface between JROTC and SROTC" and emphasize opportunities in the army.[30] The air force looked at the program as "a valuable route by which the Air Force [could] gain high quality accessions." Project Volunteer, a study predicting that the end of conscription would entail a steep drop in the number and quality of enlistees, had highlighted the "need to give more emphasis to Junior ROTC."[31] An army survey (1970) highlighted the value of the JROTC to manpower procurement. It found that the JROTC graduates were overrepresented in the army, accounting for 6.5 percent of enlistees, 15.5 percent of officers, 10 percent of West Point cadets, and 33 percent of ROTC four-year scholarship winners, and had disproportionately high retention rates.[32]

In September 1971, the army announced it was no longer operating the JROTC "with minimum . . . expense." During the draft, it did not see the necessity of generously funding programs that helped recruiting. Now, with the prodding of Project Volunteers' recommendation for an expanded recruiting program, it did. The army gave each junior unit additional money "to help recruitment and to publicize the Modern Volunteer Army." Overall, the program's budget climbed from $6 million in fiscal year 1970 to $7.7 million in fiscal year 1972, while funding for advertising and publicity rose tenfold. These outlays were paltry by Pentagon standards, but for the JROTC, they were a sizable sum.[33]

The army altered recruiting policies and introduced new incentives to entice cadets to enlist. Beginning in 1971, cadets could enlist in the advanced grades of E-2 to E-4, depending on the length of their participation, instructor recommendations, and enlistment test scores. The army also broadened the JROTC access to the Military Academy. Formerly limited to military honor schools, it opened special ROTC nominations to the academy to all qualified cadets.[34]

The navy and air force also adopted advanced promotion incentives and offered more four-year ROTC scholarships to cadets. *Dedicated* air force scholarships to junior cadets rose by over 40 percent between 1972 and 1973.[35] In addition, the air force introduced Armed Services Vocational Aptitude Battery (ASVAB) testing in high schools (1974) and sent air force nurses and Women's Air Force (WAF) recruiters into units, targeting women for enlistment.[36]

The DOD also sought to raise the congressionally fixed unit ceiling from 1,200 to 1,800.[37] It wanted to eliminate the physical examination as an enrollment prerequisite and, if this was not practical, have the government pay for the exam. As it was, many students in the JROTC's "natural constituency"—students from poor neighborhoods—were effectively barred from the JROTC because they could not afford the physical.[38]

Withal, the DOD urged Congress to sanction the enrollment of resident immigrants, lower the minimum unit enrollment threshold from one hundred to fifty, and fund summer camps. Opening the JROTC to immigrants was considered particularly important. Units in schools serving large immigrant populations found it difficult to attract enough US citizens to meet the minimum enrollment standard. Resident immigrants often outnumbered citizens in these schools but could not be counted for enrollment. Neither could they be issued uniforms, even though many were lawful permanent residents and eligible to enlist. It was unfortunate, instructors complained, that legally admitted immigrants had to be turned away. Hundreds of good prospects were being lost as a result.[39]The lowering of the enrollment minimum would make it easier to penetrate sparsely populated areas in the North Central region, giving units there a better chance of meeting congressional viability standards. Paying for cadets to attend summer camp would supposedly boost enrollment and motivate more cadets to enlist.[40] None of these proposals received immediate congressional approval. Some gestated for years before being enacted. Still, they testified to the new importance the DOD attached to the JROTC.

SHORTAGE OF AFRICAN AMERICAN OFFICERS

The services employed the JROTC to attack one of their most pressing problems—the shortage of African American (AA) officers. The drive for Black officers was both an attempt to alleviate a general shortage of lieutenants and part of a federal push for equal opportunity. Civil rights organizations pressured the DOD to recruit more Black officers. They expected the DOD, as the nation's largest employer, to set the example for the rest of society. Observers saw political, social, and military dangers stemming from the dearth of AA officers. This imbalance might cast doubt on the government's resolve to maintain a democratic, multicultural society at home and support democracy and pluralism abroad. It could also have negative operational consequences, by lowering morale and threatening unit cohesion. Without a critical mass of junior officers with whom they could relate, Black enlisted men and women might leave the service.[41]

An ambitious, if short-lived, scheme for recruiting Black officers through the JROTC was introduced in 1971. In that year, the army reserved one four-year ROTC scholarship for each JROTC-affiliated high school in a "disadvantaged poverty area." Applicants for this program only had to meet minimum standards to receive an award.[42]

CONARC officials objected to the scheme because it would reduce the number of scholarships available to the high school population at large. In effect, it reserved one-seventh of all four-year scholarships for a group of students who made up less than 1 percent of male seniors. From the CONARC perspective, the scheme was unfair and counterproductive since it would probably lead to a lowering of scholarship standards.[43]

The chair of the House Armed Service Committee (HASC) vigorously denounced this initiative, characterizing it as discriminatory. Faced with such criticism, the army "temporarily" shelved the special program in May 1971. It was never revived.[44]

This setback notwithstanding, the army's drive to recruit more AA officers achieved some success. The number of JROTC graduates enrolling in the SROTC at historically Black colleges and universities (HBCUs) climbed steeply after 1970, rising from 232 in 1970 to 409 in 1979. This was significant since HBCU graduates accounted for more than 70 percent of Black officer accessions at the time.[45]

Four factors contributed to this increase. First, the number of AA students enrolled in college more than doubled during the 1970s. This rise coincided with the opening of the JROTC to Black people in the South. Second, between 1965 and 1974, the army added seven Black colleges to the thirteen already in the ROTC institutional base.[46] Third, the resources expended on officer recruiting grew substantially.[47] Finally, the army lowered ROTC admission standards to revive officer production. In 1971, it abandoned the ROTC qualifying (RQ) test—a mental screening mechanism used since the Korean War. The Cadet Evaluation Battery (CEB), more of an attitude or personality assessment tool than a mental ability test, replaced the RQ test, making it easier for academically challenged cadets to qualify for the senior program. The lowering of testing standards was a boon to enrollment in the less competitive HBCUs, where a disproportionately large number of JROTC graduates matriculated.[48]

The JROTC's success in AA officer recruiting transcended HBCUs. The program's surging input into college programs was enabled by a 20 percent increase in the Army ROTC institutional base between 1965 and 1973. A disproportionately large number of new units were in marginally selective, predominantly majority southern colleges. The JROTC graduates flocked to these less competitive schools, where their chances of acceptance were high. This, too, enhanced AA officer output.[49]

RECRUITING PROBLEMS

The services approached enlisted recruiting more carefully. They feared that excessive aggressiveness would alienate school officials and impede enlistment efforts. That fear was justified. As draft calls dwindled after 1970, recruiters began to visit high schools more frequently and in larger numbers. Their methods were often blunt and unsophisticated and tended to turn off students, teachers, and principals. By 1971, many educators had become so distraught over their techniques that they barred recruiters from their schools. ROTC officials, upset with the Recruiting Command's aggressive tactics, demanded that recruiters tone down their campaign because of its detrimental effects on the JROTC's standing in schools and communities.[50]

The JROTC instructors were semipermanent fixtures in schools. They strove to maintain good relations with principals, faculty, and local supporters. Instructors "assiduously avoided" giving the impression that they were recruiters for fear of compromising their position. Recruiters, with no organic connections with high schools, had no such qualms. Their principal fear was missing their recruiting targets. Preserving good relations with high schools was a secondary concern for them.[51]

The services are not monolithic organizations but vast and complex bureaucracies composed of competing interest groups that harbor distinct and often conflicting agendas. In the early 1970s, the interests of recruiters often clashed with those of ROTC instructors, inducing the latter to repudiate the methods of the former. To the outside observer, the ill-coordinated actions and mixed messages coming out of this internecine bickering smacked of duplicity. Actually, they were more reflective of conflicted bureaucracies pursuing divergent goals.

Recruiting through the JROTC became more complicated with the advent of the AVF, as the public's understanding of citizenship began to change. In the era of the draft, citizenship and military service were closely linked in the public mind. When conscription ended, the relationship between citizenship and military service became "less obvious" and the task of projecting the JROTC as a citizenship program more difficult. It was particularly difficult in the 1970s, a decade in which distrust of the government was strong and the public stature of the military was low.[52]

CITIZENSHIP TRAINING

While recruiting assumed greater importance, it did not become the top priority, at least not immediately. There were goals that overshadowed recruiting. The JROTC's reputed capacity for teaching citizenship, patriotism, and respect for authority had great salience among political leaders searching for ways to ease social tensions.[53]

The JROTC's role as an agent of civic socialization had received little official emphasis in the 1960s, with McNamara at the helm. This began to change in the late 1960s as citizenship training came back into vogue. Indeed, producing responsible citizens became a national imperative.

The JROTC was now seen as a cure for the "ills of a permissive society" and a bastion of traditional values in a society racked by tumult and rebellion. Other students might be led astray by the blandishments of agitators or swept along by the spirit of the times, but the JROTC cadets maintained a steady course. They shunned violence and excess and, amid their disheveled and unhygienic classmates, maintained "a neat haircut, clean fingernails, polished shoes, shining brass"—outward manifestations of the orderliness and attention to detail they imbibed through the JROTC.[54] Their loyalty and equilibrium stood out in an age defined by flag burnings and antigovernment protests.

DOMESTIC ACTION

The JROTC's role as an instrument to promote good citizenship was placed on full display with the launch of the federal government's Domestic Action Program (DAP). Intent on allaying social tensions, the administration pressured the DOD to "use defense resources to aid in alleviating social ills and increasing opportunities for the disadvantaged."[55] It wanted the services to devote as much attention to "solving the problems on the home-front" as they did to "preparing for combat," with "every military installation" becoming involved in this campaign to build "a better society." The president set up an organization, the Domestic Action Council, to coordinate this effort.[56,57] Army medical and engineer units became particularly active in this effort because of their expertise and equipment. Medical specialists held clinics and conducted medical screenings, while engineer units took part in community construction projects. Units of all types conducted programs for disadvantaged youths.[58]

The new emphasis on domestic action affected the JROTC. The army encouraged instructors and cadets to demonstrate their civic-mindedness. Brigadier General Wilfred W.K. Smith wanted the JROTC to "lead the way" in "improving the ecology, assisting underprivileged youths, [and] otherwise demonstrating interest in civic action and human betterment programs."[59]

Both senior and junior units joined in this domestic action campaign. Cadets took part in charitable and public service endeavors, purchasing toys for nurseries, preparing Thanksgiving meals for poor families, holding immunization campaigns for preschool children, and leading fundraising drives for the March of Dimes. The JROTC units had always done this, but they did so now as part of a broader national strategy.[60]

The DAP made the JROTC cadets not only the providers of service but the recipients as well. A primary thrust of the DAP, launched in 1969, centered on disadvantaged youth living in urban areas.[61] Federal authorities hoped to use the DAP to boost "total national security" by diffusing social tension in inner cities. Reducing injustice, ending discrimination, and eliminating deprivation were vital to this effort.[62]

Administration critics likened the DAP to a pacification program. There was some truth in this analogy. Federal officials employed the vocabulary of counterinsurgency to describe the DAP and looked to the military's experience in Vietnam as a model for action. The Blue Ribbon Defense Panel, a body chartered by President Nixon to conduct a holistic review of the DOD, recommended (July 1, 1970) that a study be made about how successful techniques used by US forces in Vietnam to regenerate communities could be applied to working with minority and other disadvantaged groups in the United States, especially in central cities and depressed rural areas.[63]

Inherent in the DAP was the idea that a military regimen had remarkable curative powers for inner-city youth. This idea was powerfully expressed in the famous report of Daniel Patrick Moynihan, the assistant secretary of labor. In *The Negro Family* (or the Moynihan Report), Moynihan asserted that there was a "special quality about military service for Negro men." The armed forces, he wrote, were, given "the strains of the disorganized and matrifocal family life in which so many Negro youth come of age," a striking and "desperately needed change." They offered a "world away from women, a world run by strong men of unquestioned authority," in which "discipline, if harsh, [was] nonetheless orderly and predictable" and in which "rewards, if limited, [were] granted on the basis of performance." Military regimentation offered an alternative to their volatile existence.[64]

The DAP sponsored summer employment projects, visits to military installations, athletic programs, and summer camps. The camps removed young people (ages ten to twenty-one) from ghettos during the volatile and violent summer months, gave lectures on patriotism and citizenship, and provided training in basic military skills. Hundreds of military bases hosted DAP activities, in which millions of young people took part. Participation grew from 225,000 in 1969 to 2.7 million in 1971.[65]

Another facet of the DAP was the JROTC. The Blue Ribbon Defense Panel lauded the program for giving young people "a chance to make up for the opportunities many of them missed because they [came] from broken homes, and [had] not had the advantage of parental attention, training, leadership, and discipline."[66] Cadet training could turn marginalized students into productive citizens and equip them with workplace skills.

The composition of the JROTC and location of its units made it an ideal instrument of social and economic uplift. More than one-fifth of its units were in "disadvantaged poverty areas." The expansion of the late 1960s and early 1970s had bolstered the JROTC presence in southern and midwestern cities like Atlanta, Memphis, Dallas, Fort Worth, Chicago, and Gary and resulted in an explosion of Black enrollment in inner-city schools.[67]

While the DOD encouraged urban schools to host the JROTC units, encouragement was usually not necessary. Most schools that fell within the DAP's purview already had a strong interest in the program and needed no prodding by the Pentagon. Indeed, the zeal evidenced by minority-dominated schools disheartened the JROTC's opponents. One activist complained of the strong support the program enjoyed in Black and Chicano high schools. The JROTC cadets, he explained, received many benefits, including "free clothing, status, and the possibility of a full college scholarship." Financial assistance for college was especially important "in an era of increased college costs and dwindling scholarship programs." A Chicano activist noted how many Catholic high schools in the Southwest appeared "only too eager" to host a unit.[68]

Another attractive feature of the JROTC was its purported ability to bring order to and combat violence in urban schools. In Philadelphia, scores of young people had died from gang-related activities in the early 1970s. Concerned citizens wanted to introduce the JROTC into area schools to solve the "gang problem."[69]

In New York, educators, led by the Conference of Large City Boards of Education, lobbied to have the JROTC introduced into the public schools of the state.[70] The executive secretary of the conference, Eugene Samter, urged Governor Nelson Rockefeller to sanction military instruction during regular school hours. Such training, he said, would satisfy the "need and desire of many young people for a more orderly, organized, and purposeful lifestyle." Such a lifestyle was urgently needed given the "social confusion in our large cities." Principals in southern cities credited the JROTC with suppressing the unrest that often accompanied desegregation. The program's stabilizing presence along with the DOD's reputation as an equal opportunity employer purportedly worked to reduce tension and unrest on school campuses.[71]

PUBLIC OUTREACH

After the draft ended, public outreach was another traditional role that regained its vitality. The military's standing with the public was at low ebb. In fact, it had never been lower since the advent of scientific opinion sampling. In a speech delivered in late 1971, a former chief of staff of the army, General Matthew Ridgway, declared, "Never before in my lifetime has the Army's public image suffered so many grievous blows and fallen to such low esteem."[72] The secretary of defense, Melvin Laird, echoed Ridgway. He deplored the "abusive defamation of the military that circulates in many quarters of our society." He considered such contumely dangerous to national security.[73]

The JROTC could help salvage the reputation of the military. Instructors and cadets told the military's story to the American public and created "favorable attitudes and impressions towards the services." One navy spokesman told the *Washington Post* that the program "exhibits the Navy to the public eye." Another asserted that the Navy JROTC connected the navy to "Main Street, USA."[74]

The JROTC instructors were key players in this effort. They were the services' goodwill ambassadors. Their charge was to "influenc[e] the public mind" by being active members of the faculty, joining civic organizations, and talking to youth groups. One instructor described his routine: "Kiwanis club on Wednesday, speaking to the Sons and Daughters of 'I Will Arise' on Friday, and cooperating with the Campfire Girls in their project on Rifle Marksmanship."[75] Reaching out to the public was a critical task at a time when the DOD was attempting to make the AVF work.

MANAGEMENT

While the management arrangements of the air force and navy remained stable, those of the army underwent a major overhaul. This overhaul was part of the larger Steadfast Reorganization that occurred in the wake of Vietnam. Before July 1973, CONARC's commanding general was responsible for the army's entire system of education and individual training. He directed a large, diverse organization of which the ROTC was only a small part. Beneath CONARC, the commanding generals of the four continental US armies constituted the next level of the management chain. Those commanders, too, headed large, diverse organizations. Their ability to focus on the ROTC was limited.[76]

This decentralized management apparatus suffered from layering deficiencies and an excessive span of supervision. The magnitude of the problem was illustrated in the First Army area, where one officer supervised fifty-seven junior units in addition to ninety-seven senior ones.[77] Another flaw was the slow response to correspondence because of processing delays at intermediate levels. There was no clear chain for administration. It often took weeks for routine communications to worm their way down this Byzantine administrative structure to the individual unit.[78]

The army created a Deputy Chief of Staff for ROTC (DCSROTC) at the new Training and Doctrine Command (TRADOC) headquarters to rectify the problems. A general officer headed the DCSROTC. Four regional headquarters dedicated exclusively to ROTC management formed the intermediate level of command. Below the regions were area directors, who were part of the region staff. The new structure brought a reduced span of control, a functionally aligned management chain, and general officers dedicated exclusively to the ROTC.[79]

Nevertheless, the reorganization did not significantly benefit the JROTC, which remained what the historian Russell Weigley called an "inveterate" organization—a dispersed and heterogeneous organization that defied centralized direction.[80] Each of the ROTC's four regional headquarters retained a semiautonomous status. Each headquarters was larger than the DCSROTC staff at TRADOC. And like the DCSROTC staff, each region had a brigadier general as its chief. Regions were consequently inclined to chart their own course.

The lack of a separate JROTC staff further impeded management. The prime focus of every staff section was the senior program. Neglect of the JROTC was the inevitable result. The "constant, watchful attention" necessary to ensure compliance with policy and adherence to standards was absent.[81]

Air force and navy programs were not free of management issues. Since their headquarter staffs were sparsely manned, those services, too, struggled to enforce policies and suffered from a variety of administrative deficiencies.[82] Still, the problems faced by the smaller and more centralized air force and navy programs were less acute than the army's. They had a cohesiveness that the army lacked.[83]

END OF DÉTENTE

In the mid-1970s, US-Soviet relations began to sour. Soviet adventurism in the Global South aroused American mistrust. Soviet moves in Angola, Yemen, and the Horn of Africa contrasted with the Kremlin's cautious behavior earlier in the decade and led Zbigniew Brzeziński, President Jimmy Carter's national security adviser, to declare that the détente was at an end.[84]

The late 1970s saw the services reach their post-Vietnam nadir. This was the period of the "Hollow Army," a label used to describe the army's fragile condition. Personnel and equipment shortages degraded readiness while drug abuse sapped the vitality of the force.[85] The budget limitations imposed by Congress and the DOD lowered the quality of life for service members and degraded training programs, many of which were eliminated, consolidated, shortened, or offered less frequently.[86]

The recruiting environment was terrible. Initially, the AVF, buoyed by adequate funding and an abundance of volunteers, had flourished. But an upturn in the domestic economy, the erosion of military pay, and the termination of the Vietnam-era GI Bill led to serious manpower problems in the late 1970s. The drop in the unemployment rate was perhaps the biggest blow to recruiting. With civilian jobs plentiful, the services found themselves turning to young men and women who scored in the lower mental categories of the armed services vocational aptitude battery (ASVAB) to fill their ranks.[87]

Enlistment and retention rates sagged between 1976 and 1979. All services felt the pinch, but the army suffered the most. It failed to reach its strength goals in any of these years. Officer recruiting emerged as a severe problem in the army. In 1976, the Pentagon announced that the army would have to double the ROTC's annual output of lieutenants by fiscal year 1980 to meet mobilization needs.[88]

AUSTERITY

The pressure to slash spending grew in the aftermath of the Vietnam War. The services responded by reducing troop strength, pruning management layers, and making greater use of the reserve components (RC).[89] The ROTC felt the effects of these cuts. The DCSROTC staff at TRADOC headquarters lost more than 25 percent of its personnel allotment in fiscal year 1974.[90]

The drive to pare service budgets accelerated after 1975. The JROTC saw its travel budget substantially reduced. Staff visits and annual inspections had to be postponed or eliminated. With less frequent instructor-management interaction, the services' control over units weakened, regulatory compliance became more problematic, and program quality suffered. As one official explained, "The real key to quality in our program rests on just how much we know about our units from actually observing their operation."[91] Funding limitations also bedeviled training. Courses and extracurricular activities were eliminated, consolidated, or abbreviated to stay within budgetary restrictions. Curriculum development funds dried up, trips to military installations were canceled, and camps were shortened or curtailed. Many units had to tap into nontraditional sources of funding or increase their fundraising activities to sustain themselves.[92]

ATTEMPT AT ELIMINATION

Early in the Carter presidency, there was an attempt made to sever the JROTC from the DOD either by abolishing the program or by shifting responsibility for it to another federal agency. In January 1976, the OMB, as part of its Seventy Issues initiative, announced that the JROTC would be studied "in the context of its contributions to defense manpower requirements." Shortly thereafter, a bill was introduced in the House calling for the program's elimination. The bill evoked a fierce reaction and was easily defeated.[93]

The Association of Military Schools and Colleges of the United States (AMSCUS) took an active role in defeating the elimination attempt, bombarding Congress and the Pentagon with letters of protest.[94] It enlisted the support of Senator Strom Thurmond to fight "any effort to eliminate or transfer . . . jurisdiction for the JROTC program."[95] Thurmond sent a letter to the president, informing him that the proposed OMB study was merely a "straw man" that ignored the true value of the JROTC. The JROTC's primary goal did not involve recruiting or military training. Its principal thrust was to develop in young people the qualities of leadership, self-discipline, and good citizenship. He reminded Carter of the overwhelming support the program enjoyed in Congress and among the public.[96] Faced with such stiff opposition, the administration abandoned its plans for program dismemberment and shifted its efforts to harnessing the JROTC to defense priorities.

The administration ordered studies to examine program outcomes. The DOD formed a tri-service committee to undertake this task. It gave the committee a broad mandate. In addition to exploring the JROTC's recruiting value, it was tasked with investigating its "secondary" objectives: the purpose of the JROTC, as perceived by Congress and the DOD, and the program's staffing, enrollment, and cost.[97]

Out of the 1976 OMB directive came two major reports. One, completed by the DOD in October 1976, reached essentially the same conclusions drawn by a second and more comprehensive air force study, released in 1977. This latter study investigated the origins of the program, its history, its recruiting record, its social and military benefits, and its manifold purposes, as well as its staffing and costs. Because of its breadth and similarity to the DOD study, only it will be dealt with here.[98]

The junior program's influence on accessions was the principal concern of the OMB, so the air force study group addressed this concern first. The group reached its conclusions through a convoluted process, cobbling together various DOD reports from the early 1970s and, from these documents, reaching some conclusions. The group found that (1) "somewhere in the neighborhood" of 40 percent of cadets intended to enter military service after graduation; (2) the JROTC could be expected to furnish between 1 and 2 percent of air force enlistees in any given year; and (3) as the JROTC expanded, that percentage would rise.[99]

The report warned that the JROTC's contribution to accessions could not be "definitely determined." There was limited information available about the JROTC graduates. Some of their data was taken from the Air Force JROTC accessions reports, which were discontinued after the 1970–1971 school year. The elimination of this instrument took way the one semireliable means the air force had to gauge the program as a source of accessions. Even if those reports had been continued, however, no cause-and-effect relationships could have been established.[100]

The investigation of the JROTC goals highlighted both the ambiguity and inconsistency that had traditionally surrounded these areas. It began by noting that recruiting was a secondary goal. The military cast of a junior unit was more a method than an objective. The primary purpose of the JROTC was to help high school students become "better-adjusted, better-informed, more highly motivated space-age citizens." In any case, the joint nature of the program—it was staffed by military instructors but managed by school officials—necessarily restricted the program's recruiting function. Moreover, teaching good citizenship did not exclude military training. In fact, providing military training and teaching good citizenship were highly compatible endeavors, military values being "wholly consistent with values inherent in the responsibilities of citizens."[101]

The Air Force admitted that, although it was not the prime objective, recruiting was one purpose of the program: "With the zero-draft and all-volunteer armed force, the AFJROTC program fulfills a vital role in attracting young men and women to seek out a career in the Air Force." Even in units where recruiting was not overt, "favorable attitudes" toward military service were cultivated.[102]

The study attached great importance to public outreach. It found American youths' ignorance of national security affairs to be disturbing. The AVF would fail without the understanding of the public. The Air Force JROTC filled a crucial need by acting as a link between the public and the military. It produced citizens with a basic knowledge of security objectives and a recognition of the need for strong armed forces.[103]

The air force admitted that multiple goals led to uncertainty and confusion. Even its Advisory Panel on ROTC, made up of sympathetic educators, believed that the program's goals needed better articulation. As things stood, the simultaneous pursuit of so many disparate goals and objectives bred distrust and suspicion.[104]

The JROTC's goals were shaped by multiple inputs. The interests of local schools and communities, state governments, the military services, Congress, the administration, and a host of minor actors all had to be considered. And since priorities changed as the international situation, economic circumstances, and domestic priorities changed, goals tended to be broadly construed and frequently revised. These shifts were often interpreted as indecision, confusion, or duplicity on the part of the services.[105]

The study found that a large gap existed between instructors' perceptions of student motivations and actual student motivations. Instructors ranked enrollment motivations as follows: (1) interest in aviation (47 percent); (2) drill and uniforms (32 percent); (3) other reasons (11 percent); (4) enlistment (6 percent); and (5) SROTC (4 percent). Cadets ranked their reasons in the following order: (1) enlistment (50 percent); (2) interest in aviation (30 percent); (3) easy courses (13 percent); and (4) drill and uniforms (7 percent). Particularly striking were the differing values placed on enlistment. With students, it was the principal motivator; with instructors, it was a minor one.[106]

Also discussed were the benefits of the JROTC. The program improved student behavior, integrity, and self-discipline; provided career counseling and vocational training; assisted recruiting; offered scholarships and service academy appointments; hosted extracurricular activities; gave leadership training; and enhanced military-civil articulation.[107] The program's shortcomings were also noted. One weakness was curricular redundancy. Most training was repeated in basic training and the SROTC. In addition, the

JROTC was an inefficient officer producer. It drew principally from schools with large non-college-bound student populations. Even in schools with high college attendance, it attracted less-capable students. The incompatibility of the JROTC's curriculum with the educational goals of high schools was another deficiency. The report alleged that there were no public education objectives that related to military drill. Nor did the curriculum teach leadership. Quite the opposite; it taught followership. Conformity and obedience seemed paramount.[108]

The appropriateness of the JROTC citizenship education was questioned. Such instruction belonged "in a free-wheeling civics class and not in a strictly regimented military studies class." The air force admitted that the oft-repeated charge that the JROTC was a "soft sell" recruiting program had some basis in fact. The Air Force JROTC's final objective, which was to "motivate students for career in aerospace and the United States Air Force," confirmed this.[109]

The air force study thus conceded that many charges against the program had firm foundations and urged that these charges be addressed. Nevertheless, the overall impression left by this detailed report was a favorable one. The authors lauded the many benefits the JROTC brought to schools, the air force, and the nation, and warned of the dangers that would attend eliminating, reducing, or shifting the responsibility for the program to another federal agency.

The report found that the services were similar with respect to unit staffing. The air force, for example, had an average of 2.13 instructors per unit, with each school normally having one officer and one noncommissioned officer (NCO). Lieutenant colonels constituted 70 percent of the aerospace education instructors (AEIs). The remainder was evenly divided between colonels and majors.[110]

Usually, retired officers taught aerospace education while NCOs (assistant aerospace education instructors (AAEI)) taught leadership and oversaw training. All AEIs had baccalaureate degrees, 48 percent had master's degrees, and 1 percent had PhDs. One-third of AEIs had formal teaching experience, either in civilian or military schools. More than half of all AAEIs had completed some college work, 18 percent had baccalaureate degrees, 3 percent had master's degrees, and 0.3 percent had PhDs. About 38 percent had formal teaching experience, mostly in the air force school system. The average age of instructors was 50.25 (45.7 at the time of employment).[111]

The relationship between the JROTC staff and local school authorities was found to be quite good. Cooperation between principals and JROTC staff was viewed as good to excellent by 88 percent of instructors. Only 5 percent characterized principals as indifferent.[112]

The amount of time instructors spent performing additional duties was another matter of interest. The air force resented having its instructors diverted from their primary responsibilities, but, at the same time, it wanted them to appear as team players. A survey found that instructor use varied widely, with 37 percent of instructors performing additional duties daily, 32 percent occasionally, and 25 percent never.[113]

While similar in many areas, the air force program differed from those of the other services in certain key respects. The educational levels and teaching experience of army and Marine Corps instructors did not stack up well against their air force counterparts. Ground forces' instructors lagged far behind in terms of education and teaching experience. The cost of the program also varied across the services. The average cost per cadet ranged from $104 in the army to $218 in the Marine Corps. This pattern had been consistent since the integration of all the services into the program in the mid-1960s.[114]

JROTC DECLINE

After a decade of uneven growth, the JROTC enrollment began to decline in 1975. Officials attributed this drop-off principally to the shrinking high school cohort. Between 1975 and 1979, the number of fourteen-to-seventeen-year-olds enrolled in secondary schools fell 4.4 percent, while enrollment in the JROTC dropped 4 percent.[115] Funding constraints, personnel reductions, and resource shortages also contributed to the decline. Tight budgets inhibited visits to military installations, marksmanship competitions, drill meets, and social functions. Declining advertising budgets reduced program visibility, and diminishing administrative support lowered unit performance. Instructors became frustrated because these cutbacks occurred without the services adjusting expectations or requirements.[116]

To arrest the fall, the DOD made another attempt to extend the institutional base at mid-decade. Defense leaders had repeatedly petitioned Congress to raise the unit ceiling since David Packard's request for more units in 1971. These efforts finally bore fruit in July 1976 when President Gerald Ford signed PL 94–361, raising the unit ceiling from 1,200 to 1,600.[117]

The boon to JROTC enrollment that many anticipated, however, didn't materialize. The "austere budget situation" shipwrecked the expansion. Between 1975 and 1978, the JROTC registered a net gain of only six units. Congress, worried that growth would create a bevy of small, inefficient units, had refused to appropriate the funds necessary to propel meaningful growth.[118]

SMALL UNITS

The proliferation of small, uneconomical units was a problem that had plagued the JROTC for decades. The demise of the compulsory JROTC and the creation of hundreds of new units combined to cut average unit size almost in half between 1967 and 1975. Regulations prescribed that the services should place struggling units on probation or terminate them. They hesitated to do this, however. Instead, they tried to resuscitate underachieving units by giving them additional time and resources to reach the enrollment minimum.[119]

To help floundering units, the services provided various types of assistance, including marketing, advertising, and administrative support. They also relied on cross enrollment, which brought in additional students from neighboring schools. It was an expensive expedient since it required more resources and involved considerable transportation costs.[120]

These efforts to bolster unit viability met with limited success. The army was the least successful, as evidenced by the 9 percent drop in its average unit size between 1975 and 1980. The air force and the navy achieved better results. Still, at the end of the decade, unit viability continued to be a problem affecting all services.[121]

Traditionally, the services allowed new units a grace period of three years to reach one hundred cadets. This policy permitted orderly growth, in consonance with the annual intake of students into high school. But it also was very inefficient. In the 1972–1973 school year, thirty-six of the forty-nine new Navy JROTC units did not meet the statutory standard. Congress upbraided the services for creating units without considering enrollment criteria. It then ordered the services not to establish any new programs until all deficient ones were closed. Although the services could have used their own money to expand, they chose not to do so. Funds were in short supply, and the JROTC remained near the bottom of service priorities.[122]

MILITARY SCHOOLS

In the 1970s, the fortunes of the private military academies continued to decline, forcing some to take extraordinary measures to survive. Scores of them partnered with state and county agencies to remediate troubled students. Juvenile courts and welfare agencies assigned youths to military institutes, which were paid between $400 and $700 a month for each student. Agencies justified this expense by explaining that it cost a comparable sum ($548 per month) to support a youth in foster care. For many institutes, accepting wards of the state was an existential matter. Since their heyday in the 1950s, the popularity of these schools had fallen markedly. Between the late 1950s and the mid-1970s, two-thirds of them disappeared. Academy presidents could not be too selective if they hoped to save their institutions.[123]

Critics saw the enrollment of troubled students as a mixed blessing. The practice further damaged the reputation of academies, which already bore the stigma of being havens for refractory adolescents. On the other hand, some saw the practice as a boon for the students and schools. It afforded opportunities to troubled adolescents previously available only to children of the affluent. Educators approved because it removed troublemakers from local schools.[124]

TRAINING

With the resurgence of the Soviet threat in the late 1970s, the JROTC training took on a more military bent. The services turned away from the liberal policies and progressive pedagogical methods introduced in the Vietnam era. Still beset by educational critics and a determined albeit weakening anti-JROTC movement, however, they proceeded gingerly.

General William DePuy had introduced the back-to-basics approach to training in the army school system when he was appointed TRADOC's first commander in July 1973. Under DePuy, the focus turned back to building tactical and technical proficiency. The academically flavored courses of the type popular in the late 1960s were scaled back or eliminated. At the Engineer School, lieutenants now read manuals on the operation of a bulldozer rather than military classics like Sun Tzu. DePuy wanted to do the same in the high school and college ROTC programs. Lingering antimilitary sentiment combined with doubts about the aptness of tactical training in schools to inhibit the implementation of Dupuy's agenda.[125]

Steven Selden and Alan Feldman from the University of Pennsylvania's Graduate School of Education provided perhaps the most widely read contemporary critique of the JROTC. In their report, they scored the curriculum for its internal inconsistencies, disingenuous statements, and incompatibility with secondary education while denouncing the noncritical attitude that permeated the program. Cadets were explicitly admonished to avoid "faultfinding and criticism." They characterized the military history course as superficial and sterile. Its apparent aim was to indoctrinate students in military values rather than educating them about important issues of war and peace. Marksmanship training was not only dangerous but inappropriate. Far from solving the problem of gang violence in American cities, the JROTC made it more lethal.[126]

One widely publicized contretemps involving the JROTC occurred in April 1975. Someone had alerted the *National Enquirer* of the following passage in the JROTC text for sophomores:

> The trench knife and bayonet are excellent weapons. . . . The blunt end of a hand ax can be used to stun an enemy; the cutting edge is employed to kill. A machete can also be used for cutting and stabbing. . . . Clubs, blackjacks, sticks, and pistol butts are used chiefly to stun; however, a hard blow on the temple or base of the neck may kill. A blackjack is improvised by filling a sock with wet sand. Another effective weapon, the garotte, may be made by fastening a wood handle to each end of an 18-inch length of wire.[127]

The *Enquirer*'s staff asked the army if this "helpful information for 15-year-old[s]" appeared in the JROTC text. The army admitted that it did and then ordered instructors to delete the offensive passage immediately. But the damage had already been done. The excerpt from the manual made it into several national publications, including the *Nation* and the *Washington Post*.[128] After the incident, the army expunged explicit references to tactics and weapons from the curriculum.[129]

While opposition to tactical training pushed the services to de-emphasize the program's martial aspects, countervailing forces drove the JROTC in the opposite direction. A worsening international environment, recruiting deficits, and a growing fiscal crisis drove the services to revamp the JROTC to address current defense needs.

The OMB memorandum ordering the study of the JROTC included a directive to evaluate the program's cost-effectiveness. This spurred the services to experiment with nontraditional training schemes. The army crafted the most controversial one. Put forward by Major General James Cochran III, the First ROTC Region commander, it called for the JROTC to become part of the army's basic training establishment. The internal debate inspired by this proposal highlights the pressures and intellectual crosscurrents that buffeted the program in the late 1970s.[130]

Cochran set out to link the JROTC more closely with the active army, the RC, and the SROTC. He had two objectives in mind. First, he wanted to transform the JROTC into a more effective accessions device. Placing junior cadets in close contact with active duty and reserve soldiers, he believed, would serve that purpose. Second, he wanted to turn summer camp into the equivalent of basic combat training. According to his plan, high school students who completed this enhanced version of summer training would be sent directly to line units upon joining the RC, saving the army millions in training costs. The proposal was "close hold"—that is, it was not to be discussed outside of command channels. A public revelation of these proposals, it was feared, would cause a "misunderstanding" to arise about the JROTC's purpose.[131]

Skills taught in basic training were already included in the JROTC curriculum. With a "slight adjustment" of that curriculum, a cadet could be trained to the requisite standard. The proposed training had three facets: (1) an on-campus phase taught by the JROTC instructors, (2) a cooperative phase taught by nearby RC units, and (3) a summer phase conducted by active or RC instructors. At summer camp, cadets would receive leadership training, observe firepower demonstrations, participate in field exercises, and learn military skills that could not be trained on campus—like the operation of machine guns, light antitank weapons, and claymore mines. A test of this concept, involving four hundred cadets, took place at Fort Bragg in June 1977. It was a "resounding success." Cadets received "excellent training," and, more importantly, many subsequently enlisted.[132]

Nevertheless, TRADOC rejected Cochran's model. While the scheme might help recruiting and reduce training costs, Major General Charles Rogers, TRADOC's ROTC director, observed, "I am deeply concerned about the possible adverse impact such training may have on the overall JROTC program." First, the proposed scheme would yield few soldiers. Funding limitations would permit only a small fraction of cadets to attend camp. Second, the plan did not provide for a period of socialization and adjustment to military life, both crucial facets of basic training. Third, the initiative would elicit criticism from the civilian sector. "We continuously tell school administrators, counselors, parents and students that the purpose of the JROTC program is not to recruit students for the military," one officer explained. While recruiting might be a by-product of JROTC participation, there was an understanding that "no active recruiting [took] place." Schools might drop the program if the army conducted "blatant" recruiting.[133] Finally, the plan would violate the spirit of public law and call into question the program's legitimacy. If the new model's purpose was to change the character of the JROTC from citizenship development to recruiting, then it should be rejected.[134] Compromising the JROTC's basic civic orientation would be a betrayal of public trust.

During this period, the services had to incorporate women into their training programs. In general, they did not regulate such training very closely. Other than a few directives forbidding female participation in combat-related training, the army allowed instructors to train women as they saw fit. The navy took a similar approach, generally limiting itself to offering advice. That advice was not always particularly helpful. It advised instructors, for example, that girls could be helpful with office work but were "too fragile" to handle a Springfield rifle during drill. The navy did not prohibit their participation in drill, however. Some units conducted separate classes and formed separate marching units for women, while others trained and drilled on an integrated basis.[135]

The air force and Marine Corps were on the two ends of the policy spectrum with respect to gender roles. The former was, of the four services, the most progressive, while the Marine Corps was the most traditional. In 1972, the Marines began offering "young ladies" instruction in "poise, hearing, speech, how to wear a uniform, how to apply makeup, [and] instruction in formal ceremonies such as receptions, teas, etc." One critic likened this to "charm" training for flight attendants.[136]

RECRUITING CRISIS

At the end of the decade, a severe recruiting crisis induced the services to transform their programs into more effective accessions instruments. This was clearly seen in the Air Force JROTC. In February 1977, the air force told instructors that they were "currently working in the toughest recruiting environment since the inception of the all-volunteer force."[137] It directed them to link up cadets with local recruiters and forge closer relationships with recruiting offices. Still, Air Force ROTC headquarters insisted that the program's purpose had not changed. Instructors should leave active recruiting to recruiters and shield cadets from undue recruiting pressure.[138]

As the recruiting crisis worsened, the air force revised its policy and frankly told instructors that it "need[ed] help to recruit." In September 1978, it introduced the Air Force Recruiter Assistance Program, which formalized the cooperation between the recruiting service and the JROTC. Instructors began submitting referral cards on cadets interested in military service. In November, Air Force ROTC headquarters completed its policy about-face and started insisting that the JROTC *was*, in fact, a recruiting program. It sent a message to instructors declaring:

> We do not agree that the JROTC program was not designed by Congress . . . as a recruiting device . . . let's be realistic—whether you call it "recruiting" or not, the very nature of the program dictates that it does have a recruiting effect. As our boss once stated, "Though a school board may say they are 'against recruiting,' they 'prostituted' themselves the moment they accepted the JROTC program." We've talked to a lot of folks (parents, principals, and teachers) and most don't seem to get hung up on "recruiting." It's done (and accepted) in almost every part of our society. . . . The cold hard facts right now are that the all-volunteer force concept is not working as well as desired. It looks like the Air Force may miss its enlisted recruiting goal for the first time, so the AFJROTC (along with every other Air Force agency) will be asked to help. We just can't see that it's asking too much of anyone to request your support in this area. It's not as if you're doing these young folks an injustice through subterfuge—rather you're probably doing them a great favor by getting them interested in the Services.[139]

To boost recruiting, the air force in January 1979 sweetened enlistment incentives for JROTC graduates by bringing its accelerated promotion policy online with those of the army and navy. In the past, the air force had lost cadets to other services because of the "extra stripe" their competitors offered. It had refrained from acting earlier because it feared the move would result in lowering quality. By 1979, that was no longer a concern.[140]

In the 1970s, the JROTC rebounded from a period of stagnation. The abatement of antimilitary sentiment, the extension of the JROTC overseas, the growing participation of minorities, and the conversion to a four-year format added students and schools to the JROTC. But it was the admission of women that provided the most powerful spur. Without women, enrollment would have continued to fall.

The JROTC underwent significant changes in the 1970s. Women and minorities, excluded in the past, now constituted a large and growing part of enrollment. The program also had a different order of priorities. With the approach of the AVF, recruiting assumed greater prominence.

Still, recruiting was only one of the JROTC's objectives. As the services disengaged from Vietnam, shrank in size, and transitioned to an all-volunteer format, the junior program's role in public outreach grew. Staying connected with the American people was essential in an era in which few citizens experienced military service firsthand. Citizenship training also remained an area of emphasis. Inculcating patriotism and discipline in adolescents seemed a compelling mission in an age of political turmoil and social unrest. The JROTC was viewed as especially useful in inner cities, where its putative ability to promote order and reduce violence made it a popular educational alternative. It played a key part in Nixon's Civic Action Program, designed to mollify urban unrest.

At mid-decade, the international and domestic situations changed. Détente began to break down, the employment picture brightened, recruiting became problematic, and budgetary stringency intensified. The JROTC felt the fiscal pinch. Funding for advertising, travel, camps, activities, and training dried up, and headquarters scaled back their inspection and visitation programs.

Recruiting through the JROTC took on a renewed urgency after 1977. Plagued by recruiting shortfalls, the services looked to the junior program to help with accessions. As the JROTC entered the 1980s, it faced a new set of challenges. Its response to these challenges will be taken up in the next chapter.

8

JROTC in the Reagan Era, 1980–1985

In the early 1980s, a crisis in Soviet-American relations, a shrinking youth cohort, reserve manpower shortfalls, a new military doctrine, and an educational crisis conditioned the environment in which policy was charted.

After the Soviet invasion of Afghanistan in December 1979, détente, already unraveling, gave way to the Second Cold War. Congress, alarmed by Soviet aggressiveness, revitalized the military by raising military pay, buying new equipment, and replenishing depleted supplies. The buildup that ensued was, in budgetary terms, the largest in the post–World War II era.

The atmosphere for this military renaissance was propitious. After 1980, the propensity for military service soared, reflecting a more confident national mood and growing unemployment. Both enlisted and officer recruiting improved. Nevertheless, the services still faced serious manpower problems. The most critical was the manpower deficit plaguing the reserve components (RC), which remained several hundred thousand below mobilization needs.[1] Moreover, while short-term recruiting forecasts were auspicious, the long-term outlook appeared bleak. Officials worried about the effect of a shrinking youth cohort on recruiting. The seventeen-to-twenty-one age group peaked in 1978 and then began to decline. Relief could not be expected until the mid-1990s, when the second-wave baby boom generation would begin to affect recruiting.[2]

The early 1980s saw the unveiling of a new military doctrine, AirLand Battle, which stressed technology to offset Soviet advantages in people and equipment. Western forces could defeat numerically superior Warsaw Pact armies with the skillful application of new weapons. To be effective, however, the new weapons required a more intelligent and technologically sophisticated soldiery to operate them. The recruiting record of the late 1970s did not augur well in this regard. In fiscal year 1980, more than half of the army recruits fell into Category IV, the lowest scoring mental category on the Armed Forces Qualification Test (AFQT) eligible to enlist. Observers linked recruiting difficulties with the erosion of educational standards. One indicator of this erosion was falling SAT scores. Between 1963 and 1980, verbal scores fell by fifty points and math scores by forty. This portended trouble for an increasingly high-tech army.[3]

In August 1981, the Ronald Reagan administration created the National Commission on Excellence in Education. The commission's mandate was to examine the quality of education in the United States. Its report *A Nation at Risk* (1983) starkly delineated deficiencies in the educational system. It included an ominous warning: "The educational foundations of our society are presently being eroded by a rising tide of mediocrity that threatens our very future as a Nation and a people." Alarmed, state governments began prescribing more rigorous academic standards for high schools.[4]

The state of science and mathematics education aroused concern. The shortage of minorities and women in these fields was particularly troubling. Stanford professor Paul Hurd warned, "We are raising a new generation of Americans that is scientifically and technologically illiterate."[5] Congress reacted to this crisis by passing PL 96–516 (1981), which incentivized youth in "socially and economically disadvantaged groups" to pursue science, technology, engineering, and mathematics (STEM) studies.[6]

JROTC EXPANSION

The Carter-Reagan military buildup entailed an expansion of both the JROTC and Senior ROTC (SROTC). PL 96–413 (1976) was the legislative basis for the expansion. It authorized a ceiling of 1,600 units.[7] To help small schools in sparsely populated states in the Northern Plains and Midwest, Congress passed PL 96–342 (1980). This law lowered the minimum unit size from one hundred cadets to 10 percent of a school's total enrollment. Lawmakers were keen to extend the JROTC into impoverished rural areas where program benefits would be appreciated and propensity for service was high. By 1985, 157 schools had qualified for units under this law.[8]

The services differed in their approach to expansion. The army proceeded hastily and haphazardly. It created units before they received their full complement of instructors or supplies. The army was in such a hurry to begin that it failed to clearly articulate the purpose or parameters of expansion. Underlying this haste was the fear that funds earmarked for the program had to be spent quickly or they would be siphoned off to address more urgent priorities.[9]

The other services expanded in a more measured manner. While the army expanded with a bare-bones budget and limited staffing, the navy and air force delayed growth until all necessary resources were available. In the end, several hundred army units were short at least one instructor.[10]

The program expanded where expansion was easiest—in the inner city and poor rural areas. Regionally, the Southeast experienced the biggest gains. Training and Doctrine Command (TRADOC) had enjoined region commanders to concentrate on the twenty-eight states where the JROTC had the smallest presence. However, in the army's hurry to expand, managers felt they could ill afford to spend time coaxing reluctant school administrators to apply for units. Thus, states below the Mason-Dixon Line received more than their fair share of units.[11]

During the expansion of the early 1980s, the JROTC unit strength rose by 30 percent, while enrollment grew by 25 percent (see appendix B). Growth was cut short by budget shortfalls, which resulted in the Department of Defense (DOD) missing its 1,600-unit target by 8 percent. The air force and navy proved more reluctant than the army to shift funds from other areas to keep the expansion on track. Thus, the army attained 96 percent of its goal, while the other services settled for 85 percent.[12]

Contrasting unit selection criteria illumines the services' different expectations for the JROTC. The air force linked its criteria to recruiting goals. Since it had comparatively high intellectual standards for enlistment, it placed considerable weight on academic factors. Its academic-quality criteria included SAT and ACT scores, National Merit Scholarships, college-bound students, and the availability of advanced mathematics, science, foreign languages, and English courses. Forty out of 105 points in its unit evaluation system related to academic quality.[13]

Academic credit was another selection criterion. The air force held that the type of credit awarded had "a direct bearing on the enrollment and success of a unit" and pressed schools to grant core credit for JROTC courses. Educational reform initiatives had limited electives, so many students *had* to earn core credit to enroll in the JROTC. The air force tried to increase its intake of minority students pursuing STEM degrees, by giving special consideration to schools hosting a chapter of the National Action Council for Minorities in Engineering.[14]

The army had very different selection metrics. Noticeably absent from its criteria were factors related to academic attainment. The strength of school and community support stood at the top of the army's criteria list.[15] The army expected schools to hold up the JROTC as a "desirable instructional activity." Only then could a "sound basis for cooperation" exist.[16] Material support was also important. Through experience, the army had learned that the amount of aid provided to a unit depended on the attitude of the school board and the generosity of organizations like the Veterans of Foreign Wars (VFW) and the American Legion.[17] Where the JROTC received strong support, units were vibrant. Where such support was minimal, units struggled.

The services competed to position units in low-demand areas. Because of their more systematic methods of selection and the geographic distribution of their installations, the air force and the navy fared relatively well in this competition, achieving a more balanced, if still imperfect, distribution of units than the army.

All services, except the Marine Corps, acknowledged the equitable distribution of units as a desirable objective. The Marine Corps found it too troublesome and uneconomical to adopt as a goal. In northern states, interest in the JROTC was low. Few schools applied for units. Moreover, finding retired officers and noncommissioned officers (NCOs) willing to live in these states was difficult. The dearth of large military bases made the cost of living for retirees very high.[18]

DEMOGRAPHICS

By the 1980s, the JROTC's demographic profile had diverged sharply from that of the general high school population. Cadets were more likely than other students to have parents who were veterans, come from low-income families, belong to single-parent homes, and identify as a minority. The perception that the JROTC was a poor kids' program had a basis in fact.[19]

The ethnic balance of the JROTC continued to shift as minorities increased their already large presence. By the mid-1980s, only 47 percent of army enrollment was white, down from 58 percent a decade earlier. This compared to 75 percent in the general population and 68 percent in public schools (K–12).[20] Educational reform may have affected the ethnic balance by discouraging the JROTC participation among college-bound students, a disproportionate share of whom were white. The services also played an important part by prioritizing the establishment of units in minority high schools.[21] The popularity of military service among minorities was another factor. While Black propensity for service was declining, it was still three times higher than white propensity. Moreover, the JROTC retained its appeal to Black educators in cash-starved inner-city schools. It brought order and resources to schools plagued by disappointing educational outcomes, declining government assistance, and increasing classroom violence. Most significant of all, perhaps, military service in Black high schools did not carry the stigma it did in many white institutions.

Minority representation in the navy and air force programs, while growing, remained lower than in the army's. One study found that 63 percent of graduating seniors in the air force and navy programs were white, which is not surprising given their enlistment standards. The STEM orientation of the navy and air force curricula may also have played a part by discouraging many STEM-averse minority students from joining.[22]

RECRUITING

Recruiting pressure in the early 1980s brought changes to the program. In the army, the JROTC began cooperating with the US Army Recruiting Command (USAREC) to become a key part "of the total army recruiting effort." This meant forging closer ties with recruiters.[23] It also entailed curricular changes. More class hours were devoted to military career fields, and marksmanship training was changed from a mandatory to an optional activity. Rifle marksmanship was a sensitive issue because more and more states were barring weapons training in public schools. This enrollment barrier disappeared in September 1982 when marksmanship became an optional activity.[24]

Army leaders wanted high-quality enlistees—recruits with the mental acumen and technological savvy—to maintain and operate the new weapons entering the arsenal. The pattern of unit growth did not support the army's desires. The expansion had more firmly anchored the JROTC in less academically oriented schools—schools where students generally lacked the skills needed to meet the demands of a high-tech force.[25] Few scholars or student leaders joined. One principal called cadets "gray students"—students who left no mark on the school and were soon forgotten after graduation.[26]

Other forces reduced the pool of high-quality applicants. The education reform movement was one. The drive to raise educational standards took off in 1983, when a flood of reports decrying the state of public schools came out.[27] Educational officials reacted by adopting higher graduation standards (forty states), overhauling their systems of testing, raising the number of hours students spent in the classroom (twenty-seven states), raising teaching certification requirements (thirty-five states), and adding STEM, English, and other core requirements to curricula. These measures drove students to devote more time to studying and discouraged the college-bound from joining the JROTC.[28] Stricter attendance standards likewise hurt enrollment. Fewer excusable absences forced units to alter training schedules. Parades and inspections, if not eliminated, had to take place before or after school, making the program less convenient.[29]

Most worrisome of all, the program's contribution to officer and enlisted recruiting plummeted between 1980 and 1986. The Army JROTC's input into the SROTC and the enlisted ranks nose-dived by over a third. The program's concentration in "less academically oriented" institutions and the army's concomitant adoption of more rigorous enlistment criteria contributed to this.

Recruit quality had become a major issue in the late 1970s as the services, facing severe recruiting shortfalls, sacrificed quality for quantity. In 1980, over half of the army's enlistment cohort scored in the Category IV range on the AFQT. After 1980, an economic downturn combined with military pay raises gradually improved recruiting. In the army, the percentage of Category IV recruits dropped from 52 percent in 1980 to less than 4 percent in 1986, while the portion of recruits in Categories I–IIIa rose from 8 to almost 70 percent.[30] This rise in quality did not bode well for recruiting in the JROTC, whose cadets clustered in the lower ranges of the AFQT. The influx of high-quality recruits squeezed out lower-scoring applicants. A similar dynamic was at work in the SROTC, where the number of JROTC graduates entering the program plunged.[31]

The air force outpaced the army in recruiting through the JROTC. The number of Army JROTC enlistments dropped, while the number of Air Force JROTC enlistments increased slightly. The air force had more allure than the other services. It was modern, high-tech, and glamorous. Moreover, the Air Force JROTC was less of an inner-city program. In an era of high accessions standards, the Air Force JROTC cadets were more likely than army cadets to qualify for enlistment.

Army officials ascribed the air force's success to the linking of its program to accessions goals. Through its curriculum and unit selection procedures, the air force structured its JROTC to attract high-quality students. The air force's management structure was another factor. Although the air force and navy programs were smaller than army's, their management structures were larger and more centralized. At the national level, they maintained management cells whose sole responsibility was JROTC supervision. No such cell existed at TRADOC headquarters.[32]

Because of its decentralized structure, the Army JROTC's orientation varied from area to area. The emphasis placed on recruiting, the type of recruiting accentuated, the training offered, and the activities pursued were place dependent. This variability was evident at the regional level, where each headquarters put its distinctive stamp on the program. In some regions, the JROTC resembled a paramilitary organization, in which drill and military skills were curricular staples and recruiting was openly conducted. In others, the JROTC was a citizenship program, in which overtly military aspects of the program were downplayed and recruiting was conducted discreetly or eschewed entirely.[33]

The environment shaped the character of the program in each region. The Fourth Region headquarters considered the JROTC to be a citizenship program. Communities on the Pacific coast had a more progressive orientation than communities in the nation's heartland. They were also less inclined to regard military service as a badge of distinction and more likely to object to recruiting in schools. By adopting the theme of citizenship, the Fourth Region hoped to avoid contention, placate school officials and community leaders, and pave the way for the JROTC's acceptance.[34]

Both the Second and Third Region headquarters, on the other hand, viewed the JROTC as a recruiting instrument. The former focused on enlisted recruiting and the latter on officer recruiting. Recruiting did not carry negative connotations in the heartland, where the Second and Third Regions were based. In fact, schools in many southern and midwestern states welcomed recruiters, viewing them as purveyors of desirable occupational options. Recruiting there was often openly conducted.[35]

The conflicting conceptions of the JROTC coexisting within the army management chain were cast in bold relief by a controversy over enrollment eligibility. In some areas, the JROTC accepted physically and mentally disabled students along with noncitizens. Some objected to enrolling students who were ineligible to enlist. Accepting them reflected a perspective left over from an era in which the services attempted to increase the program's social utility. By the early 1980s, the issue of social relevance was no longer as pressing. Faced with reserve officer shortages and recruiting problems, the services could not afford to squander resources on students who couldn't serve. Moreover, the practice of enrolling noncitizen and disabled students was illegal. Title X of the US Code stipulated that only physically fit US citizens were eligible to enroll. The JROTC managers had to stop this patently illicit practice.[36]

Other service leaders championed a more inclusive enrollment policy. Proceeding from the premise that the JROTC was a citizenship program, they saw no reason to exclude disabled or noncitizen students from the rolls. In fact, citizenship training seemed especially appropriate for foreign-born youth. Through such training, these students could be assimilated into the societal mainstream and be made productive citizens.[37]

The claim that letting the militarily unqualified enroll in the JROTC violated federal law drew a sharp retort. Some schools *required* the JROTC to accept such students. The practice was in consonance with federal and state policy, which prohibited discrimination in education. Rigid adherence to Title X would alienate school officials, lower the program's community standing, and make the army appear unenlightened.[38]

In the end, the services chose the inclusive approach. Banning disabled or noncitizen students was deemed inconsistent with the JROTC's purpose. While enlistments were desirable outcomes, recruitment was not the primary objective. Instead of banning disabled students, some suggested, the services should try to change federal law to authorize their enrollment.[39]

Another point of contention was the requirement for an equitable geographic distribution of units among states. Many considered this requirement to be counterproductive. New units should be created not for distributional equity but for expected returns. Pouring resources into areas where military service was unpopular was nonsensical.[40]

This argument drew sharp rebuttals. Achieving broad geographical representation, some insisted, was more important than boosting enlistment. The military should not draw from only certain areas of the country. It needed to reflect the entire nation, and this included achieving balance among geographic regions as well as among different ethnic groups. In the end, the advocates of geographic equity won out, at least on the policy level.[41]

MILITARY TRAINING

The discordant views about the JROTC's purpose were again underscored by a squabble that erupted in the training arena. As things stood, some Army JROTC units assiduously avoided tactical training, while others embraced it. Units in the latter category stirred the ire of the Army ROTC chief, Major General Robert A. Sullivan. "At the risk of dampening enthusiasm," Sullivan told region commanders in September 1982, "I must caution you not to expand JROTC instruction into areas which are not within the congressional intent of program objectives." Tactics were not within the program's writ and should not be taught to cadets. It was "imperative" that units adhere to the "spirit and letter" of the law.[42]

This rebuke did not leave an enduring impression. Tactical training continued. The steady turnover of personnel, sparse staffing, the heterogeneity of the institutional base, and the program's geographic dispersion frustrated efforts to enforce policy.[43] At the unit level, too, the army's control was limited. Policies violating local tradition or entailing substantial changes in unit routine often foundered. They could not survive contact with the local environment. The expectations of cadets, parents, principals, and teachers set the parameters within which units operated.

Although Sullivan discouraged hardcore tactical training, he encouraged the teaching of "soft" military skills required of military science (MS) Is and MS IIs—freshmen and sophomores—in the SROTC. He sought to continue the effort launched in the late 1970s, which aimed at extracting more military value out of the JROTC without turning it into an overt vehicle for preinduction military training.[44]

Two of those "soft" skills—oral and written communications—were major problems for officer aspirants. The inability of lieutenants to express themselves in speech and writing had been extensively documented by the Army Research Institute (ARI) and found to have contributed significantly to the high failure rates at branch Officer Basic Course(s) (OBC) in the early 1980s. To rectify this problem, the army introduced the Enhanced Skills Training Program (ESTP) at selected historically Black colleges and universities (HBCUs). The ESTP's purpose was to equip officer aspirants with the basic academic competencies necessary for success. The JROTC's emphasis on communication skills aligned closely with this effort.[45]

The army also essayed to strengthen citizenship instruction. While citizenship had long been listed as the program's principal focus, formal classes on this subject were nil. To remedy this shortfall, new classes like Profiles of Heroes and Community Service were inserted into the curriculum.[46] These classes, however, were not new; they were repackaged versions of old ones. Nevertheless, they did underline the army's renewed emphasis on citizenship studies.[47]

The new classes served two additional purposes. One was recruiting. Courses like Profiles of Heroes were designed to inspire cadets to enlist. A second purpose was to solidify the JROTC's position in the school and community. The Community Service course focused on what had become a vital part of the high school experience. By the 1980s, community service had become a graduation requirement in many schools.[48]

IMPEDIMENTS TO EXPANSION

Untoward effects attended JROTC growth in the early 1980s. The army experienced a further weakening of its ability to control its far-flung units. The expansion overwhelmed regional headquarters. The First Region saw its unit total rise by a third, from 225 to 298. The region commander, Brigadier General Curtis F. Hoglan, found this growth disconcerting. In his 1984 annual assessment, he noted that a "year ago, [he] cautioned that [they] were close to the straw breaking the camel's back. [They were] there now in First Region." Hoglan had to treat the JROTC with "benign neglect" because of the priority attached to the SROTC.[49]

Manpower shortfalls began to plague the program. While the unit base expanded, instructor authorizations remained constant. By 1985, the program was 20 percent under its instructor needs. The situation was more dire than the 20 percent deficit indicated. The JROTC staff were frequently diverted from their prime duties to support the college program.[50]

Resource and funding constraints stressed the JROTC management. A shortage of travel funds prevented regional staffs from making annual inspections. The regions resorted to expedients to offset limitations. Some turned to the SROTC instructors for help. This imposed a burden on the SROTC cadre, who reaped little benefit from these inspections. Other regions engaged officers and NCOs from the RC to relieve the burden. This expedient, too, proved a less-than-ideal option. Reservists preferred to devote their time to matters directly connected to their primary mission.[51]

In this period of scarce resources, new units in the army suffered the most since no provision had been made for start-up costs. They struggled to buy basic supply items. The failure or inability of many schools to provide equipment and facilities made the problem worse.[52] Advertising money was likewise in short supply. This shortage "severely hampered" efforts to boost enrollment and create new units. Often, local media coverage was the only publicity units could arrange. The lack of advertising money made the JROTC, one officer noted, one of the "least publicized programs" of the military.[53]

In this austere environment, old complaints took on new life. Two effective stimulants to enrollment were visits to military installations and attendance at summer camp, neither of which was subsidized by the services. Cadets and instructors had to pay their own way. This "severely limited" attendance at these events and supposedly hurt recruiting.[54]

The curriculum was another victim of the budget crunch. A lack of money inhibited curricular revisions and the updating of texts. Films and posters increasingly featured cadets in outdated uniforms. "Cost-effective" workbooks supposed to obviate textual inconsistencies only added to the confusion. The use of such materials placed the JROTC at a competitive disadvantage with respect to other academic departments.[55]

The JROTC's budgetary woes exacerbated the situation. Managers complained that funding deficits combined with more stringent academic standards and a declining high school population to create a "difficult operating environment." Established units struggled to sustain enrollment, while new ones strained to reach the enrollment minimum. Most units lost ground; the average unit size fell from 169 in 1980 to 156 in 1986. This 10 percent decline was steeper than the drop in the US high school–age population or the enrollment decrease in JROTC-affiliated schools. Instructors had to recruit more aggressively to keep afloat.[56]

The passage of the Balanced Budget and Emergency Deficit Control Act (the Gramm-Rudman-Hollings Act) in 1985 occasioned another round of belt-tightening. This act delayed the creation of new units, froze instructor hiring, and cut deeper into supply and travel budgets. The legislation worried managers who saw the program's vigor bound up with frequent contact between the chain of command and the instructor force. Regular interface between headquarters and field elements fostered standardization, the enforcement of standards, and high unit morale. The absence of such interaction generated turmoil and instructor misconduct.[57] By late 1984, money and personnel were in such short supply that the army had to truncate the expansion, calling a halt to unit growth at the 865 mark instead of the 896 limit allowed by law.

OPPOSITION TO THE JROTC

The expansion elicited a reaction from the JROTC's opponents. Ideological objections to the program did not resonate loudly in the early 1980s, however. With the military enjoying high public esteem and patriotism once again in fashion, expressions of antimilitary sentiment rang hollow.[58] Campaigns to derail the creation of new units usually highlighted practical issues instead of moral ones.[59] One anti-JROTC activist explained why his group eschewed ideological arguments: "We did not need to assume additional burdens of trying to get the school board to reject Reagan's foreign policy or militarism in general." To have done so would have cut off potential allies and erected barriers to his agenda. His group would surely have lost if the JROTC debate became a conflict between peace and patriotism.[60]

Local squabbles usually revolved around concrete issues. The JROTC supporters argued that a unit was an inexpensive way to acquire more teachers, more courses, and more activities. The program gave schools two instructors for the price of one, proffered non-college-bound students an occupational alternative, and provided scholarships to students going to college. The JROTC was, in addition, an invaluable disciplinary tool. In an era when violence and crime in public schools was endemic, the JROTC's reputation for bringing order to the classroom had an obvious attraction.[61]

The JROTC's detractors refuted these claims. The financial advantages associated with a unit were largely illusory, they argued. Hidden costs, in fact, made the JROTC a drain on schools. These cost factors included classrooms, storage areas, drill and marksmanship facilities, desks, computers, and administrative support. Moreover, the JROTC courses were of doubtful academic value. Money could be better spent on hiring teachers who taught subjects with real academic merit. Critics also complained that the JROTC instructors were exempt from state certification standards. Many even lacked bachelor's degrees.[62]

Hosting a unit entailed a diminution of local autonomy. While schools made the hiring decision, they had to select from slates of candidates provided by the services. To compile their lists, the services used criteria—such as appearance and bearing—that bore little relation to academic qualifications.

In addition, the school had little control over the curriculum. Adopting the prescribed curriculum was a prerequisite for getting a unit.[63]

The educational objectives pursued by the services were ambiguous and difficult to evaluate. For example, the army listed good citizenship as its principal objective, but it did not define the term, offered little relevant instruction, and did not measure its effectiveness in developing good citizenship.[64] The ambiguity of its educational objectives suggested that the JROTC was a front to disguise covert agendas like recruiting.

Occasionally, opponents garnered enough support to stop the launch of new units. They reportedly blocked the creation of units in Lacey, Washington, and Saginaw, Michigan (1985), and prevented the start of a public military academy in Cincinnati (1983).[65] But such cases were rare. In most places, the JROTC supporters easily triumphed over weak opposition. Although most principals believed that the JROTC was a recruiting instrument, one scholar found, it did not lessen their support. The "powerful influence of the military" and the prevailing "economic climate" frustrated the plans of the program's foes.[66]

INTERNAL ARMY STRIFE: THE ARMY STUDY

In the early 1980s, the program garnered much attention from the Pentagon. Despite an uptick in recruiting, the army was still beset with personnel problems stemming from a shrinking youth cohort and reserve manpower shortfalls. Some complained that the JROTC was off track and did not contribute to the army's core mission. Army leaders became so concerned that they launched a comprehensive study of the JROTC. General John A. Wickham, the chief of staff of the army (CSA), chartered a group to conduct the study. The group's findings thoroughly impressed Wickham and led him, in November 1985, to ask Congress to raise the army's unit cap from 896 to 1,791.[67]

Wickham had given that group a broad charter—to make the JROTC more supportive of defense priorities. This involved weighing the pros and cons of JROTC expansion, assessing the program's overall value, and, somewhat paradoxically, exploring the merit of dismembering the program. Its extensive and diffuse writ reflected the disparate conceptions of the JROTC that uneasily coexisted among army leaders.[68]

The group began its investigation in January 1985. Over the next ten months, it made numerous visits to units, consulted TRADOC headquarters, and spoke with the other services. It crafted one of the most thorough reports on the ROTC ever compiled. The report painted an unflattering and candid picture of the JROTC. It described an organization in chaos. Regulations were out of date, regions operated autonomously, interservice coordination was poor, and liaison with accrediting organizations was weak.[69] The study group's final report (1986) is useful for several reasons. First, it highlights the practical issues with which the services were dealing in the early 1980s. Second, it documents the internal struggle within the services about what the JROTC's purpose(s) should be.

In its final report, the group concluded that the closely intertwined problems of faulty organization, bare-bones staffing, and insufficient funding accounted for many of the program's troubles. There was no single office within TRADOC headquarters devoted exclusively to JROTC management and thus no influential advocate to protect the program's interests. Responsibility was diffused throughout the staff. This anomalous structure saved manpower but made coordination between headquarters and other organizations difficult in the extreme. In practice, this meant that management fell upon staff officers of junior rank. One full-time civilian educational specialist was finally added to the ROTC's training division in 1982. But one low-ranking civilian was manifestly inadequate for such a large program.[70]

The group compared army staffing with that of the other services and found the former wanting. The navy and air force, with smaller programs, maintained larger staffs. This allegedly reflected not only their culture but their more operationally grounded expectations for the program.[71]

A lack of command attention also bedeviled management. The SROTC dominated the attention of the staff. Over time, this led to a "tradition of continuous neglect." The TRADOC staff lacked even a "basic" understanding of the program. Management problems were exacerbated by a lack of data. Key information was not being collected. Managers did not have enlistment data for graduates, college attendance rates by school, academic credit for JROTC courses, or the educational credentials of instructors. Such information was necessary to make informed decisions.[72]

ROTC regional headquarters were likewise beset with staffing difficulties. During the recent expansion, three of the four regions cut their JROTC staffs. Moreover, each region organized its JROTC staff differently. Some had a separate JROTC cell, while others did not. These variations obstructed communications between elements of the management chain and impeded data collection.[73]

The study group also found that the JROTC needed a "comprehensive" mission statement that precisely limned and prioritized its principal goals. Although public law, DOD policy, and army regulations enumerated goals and objectives, there was no succinct statement of the "overall goal" toward which these separate and conflicting objectives led. Indeed, the Congress, the DOD, the army, TRADOC, and the four ROTC regions all listed different objectives. This sowed confusion in the field and in the chain of command.[74]

The group castigated the army's refusal to integrate the JROTC into its "manpower acquisition system." Regulations specifically stated that units were not enlistment or officer-producing programs. This statement, the study group wrote, was confusing, unnecessary, and counterproductive since it prevented the program's inclusion in recruiting and marketing plans. Recruiting had to be listed in any future mission statement.[75]

The JROTC was not positioned to attract the best students. In the mid-1980s, the average high school had a college attendance rate of 50 percent. Two-thirds of JROTC high schools fell below this mark. A survey of Albuquerque, New Mexico, schools found that cadet grade point averages (GPAs) were well below average, and 15 percent of cadets were in nongifted special education programs.[76]

This quality issue was bound up with the JROTC's "image problem." Outside the army, the program was seen as the domain of low-achieving students and disadvantaged schools. Within the army, it was viewed as a social program and a distraction from more important tasks. It existed only because Congress had forced it on the services. The shoddy appearance of cadets likewise hurt the program's public image. Cadets were issued fatigues but not boots. When a unit stood in formation, observers saw a motley collection of would-be soldiers wearing a wide assortment of footwear. Such a scene presented a "disturbing" picture.[77]

According to the study group, a curriculum revamping was sorely needed. As it was, over 30 percent of the program of instruction (POI) was devoted to drill. Instruction should feature subjects signaling academic credibility, like science and math. The army should learn from the other services. Not only were the air force and the navy in more "academically oriented" schools but their curricula were more rigorous and better designed to stimulate interest in STEM. The army's learning outcomes did not even address academics. The other services were consequently in a better position to attract high-quality, technologically literate recruits.[78]

The JROTC, the study group charged, adopted a reactive approach to curriculum revision. The air force laid out the revision process in considerable detail, while the army made changes only when deficiencies surfaced. Written guidance was absent. Revisions took place in an academic vacuum. No outside experts participated. Nor was the curriculum aligned with civilian educational standards. Curriculum development seemed driven by immediate and disparate stimuli. A disjointed POI was the inevitable result.[79]

The lackluster quality of instructors frustrated attempts to implement a more rigorous curriculum. Instructor selection standards were low and instructor management procedures unsystematic. The army did not advertise open positions and, in two regions, did not interview applicants. Hiring decisions rested not on educational criteria but on factors such as personal appearance and military bearing. The hiring process was "catch as catch can" and did nothing to counteract the notion that the JROTC was run by substandard retirees.[80]

The study group's final report warned that the JROTC, if it continued its existing course, would remain a social program, capable of teaching citizenship but unable to help the army achieve its recruiting goals. The group offered some suggestions. One was that the JROTC's institutional midpoint be brought closer to the national norm. If the average high school had a 50 percent college attendance rate, then the average unit should have a 50 percent college attendance rate. Schools with high go-to-college rates had to be brought in. The study group advised that TRADOC cooperate with USAREC to identify the "right" high schools. The First and Second Regions had already linked up with the Recruiting Command and achieved "excellent" results.[81]

Another recommendation was to reorient the curriculum to gain more academic credit in general science and social studies. This would entail devoting 89 of the 108 hours of annual instruction to academic subjects. An improved POI would attract better students, gain core academic credit, and prepare cadets for college. In addition, the group proposed that one hundred hours of science and math be added to the curriculum to foster an appreciation of the "technical requirements of the modern age." These hundred hours were to be added to the 108 already in the POI.[82]

To raise faculty quality, an instructor recruiting plan should be developed—a plan that would stress educational attainment. It would require annual performance appraisals and a probationary period for new instructors. These two provisions would weed out substandard performers.[83]

An enlarged summer program was another item in the study group's blueprint. The army should raise the annual camp attendance from five thousand to twenty thousand cadets. Camps should be revamped to prepare cadets for leadership positions during the school year. Not all cadets should be groomed for leadership, however. Of the twenty thousand who attended summer training, only five thousand would be sent to a special camp of "near OCS [Officer Candidate School] quality."[84]

Recruiting loomed large in the study group's plans. The group wanted TRADOC to take a more overt role in recruiting. Steps had already been taken in this direction. The JROTC, for example, had been included in the army's Officer Accessions Plan for FY 1987–1991. Still, more needed to be done. Instead of approaching the matter obliquely, managers should assign definite goals for officer and enlisted recruiting, as Maxwell Taylor had done in the 1950s.[85]

Perhaps the group's most controversial recommendation was the Total Army Sponsorship Program. The goal of this program was to integrate the JROTC fully into the army's manpower acquisition system. This involved upgrading preinduction training, connecting instructors and cadets more closely with the army, and linking the JROTC to active and reserve units. Soldiers would visit high schools, attend school events, and train junior cadets. All this would be done subtly to preclude the JROTC appearing as a recruiting tool.[86]

The study group briefed its findings to TRADOC in January 1986. In the briefing, it endorsed Wickham's expansion plan, appealed for a curriculum overhaul, and urged the army to be more generous in supporting the program. Only if army leaders evidenced greater zeal for the JROTC could the tradition of neglect that had grown up around the program ever be broken.

INTERNAL ARMY STRIFE: TRADOC'S REBUTTAL

While the CSA's group was conducting its study, a TRADOC task force undertook a parallel evaluation. Earlier, General Wickham had directed General William Richardson, the TRADOC commander, to draft a plan for an "organizationally streamlined" and "administratively efficient" program "capable of fulfilling its statutory purpose" and meeting the expectations of Congress and the DOD. The Junior ROTC Improvement Program (JRIP) was the result.[87]

The JRIP mirrored, in many respects, the study group's report. Both documents recommended expanding summer camps, refining the curriculum, bolstering staffing, streamlining administration, upgrading data collection, and raising instructor selection standards. Within these areas of agreement, however, there were sharp differences of emphasis. While both bodies worried about instructor selection standards, the JRIP task force showed more concern about appearance, age, and physical condition than academic prowess. Many instructors, it was pointed out, were overweight and physically unfit, sported long hair and untrimmed mustaches, and wore ill-fitting uniforms and gaudy jewelry. Many were septuagenarians, even though the mandatory retirement age was sixty-five.[88]

The academic background of instructors was a concern of both groups. The TRADOC group, however, identified the dearth of teaching certificates as the principal problem. The lack of credentials led civilian teachers to view their military colleagues as inexperienced laypeople. Certificates would raise the status of instructors and lessen the likelihood of the JROTC being dismissed as an extracurricular activity. Perhaps the task force was inspired by the example of the air force, more than half of whose officer-instructors had teaching certificates.[89]

The expansion policy crafted by Richardson's task force was much less ambitious than the one adopted by the Pentagon group. The former proposed an expansion of only thirty-five units. The new units were to be in states where the JROTC was underrepresented, not in states where enlistment propensity was high. The JRIP developers regarded the CSA's goal of 1,791 units as too grand, even counterproductive. Growth of this magnitude would further skew unit distribution since demand for units was stronger in states that were already oversubscribed. Funding worries also affected their thinking. Experience suggested that the army would have to take money away from other programs to pay for the expansion.[90]

Both groups agreed that data collection had to be improved. As things were, JROTC managers made decisions with only fragmentary information at their disposal. But while the CSA's minions focused on what data should be collected, Richardson's people concentrated on the instruments of data collection. Only automation, they believed, could ensure the timely availability of data.[91]

The need for more regular funding was another shared conviction. The army's parsimony had debilitating consequences. The assistance given to the

JROTC varied from post to post and was subject to sudden change. Units sometimes arrived at a post only to learn that the promised aid was unavailable. Such incidents ruined training and lowered morale.[92]

Staffing was another area of general agreement. But while Wickham's group focused on national and regional staffing, the JRIP's authors concentrated on the school district level. An officer known as the Director of Army Instruction (DAI) had traditionally managed unit clusters in large urban areas. He dealt with issues that affected all units in a district. There were seventy DAIs in the mid-1980s. These officers, however, were not funded by the army or the school district. They had to be "taken out of hide." Hence, seventy units were short at least one instructor. The JRIP urged the army to recognize these positions and pay the salaries of the DAIs.[93]

The JRIP's critique of the curriculum differed from that of the study group; it did not call for an overhaul of course content or a more academic orientation. True, the task force found the POI to be repetitious, boring, and outdated, an affront to high achievers. But, unlike the study group, the task force rejected the idea of adding one hundred hours of high-tech instruction to the curriculum or revising courses to gain academic credit. It merely wanted the army to upgrade texts to make them more relevant and interesting. As it was, the motley collection of field manuals and official publications that served as texts reflected poorly on the program. The task force wanted new lesson plans, workbooks, and instructor manuals. The intent was not to change the program's focus but to make course offerings more engaging.[94]

Thus, despite their shared belief that the JROTC needed reform, the study group and task force entertained different conceptions of the program. The former saw the JROTC as a seedbed of officers and enlisted soldiers for the army and sought to integrate it into the army's recruiting and education systems. It held up the navy and air force programs as exemplars. The study group saw no conflict between citizenship and recruiting. As one member commented, "Citizenship training and recruiting are not diametrically opposed concepts, and good programs that provide good citizenship training naturally help recruiting." The TRADOC group, on the other hand, wanted to avoid activities that implied "blatant" recruiting. More closely connected with the field than Wickham's group, the task force was more sensitive to local sentiment and the pitfalls of overt recruiting. It viewed recruiting and citizenship training as diametrically opposed activities. Anyone who insisted that the two were mutually supportive was being disingenuous.[95]

When the task force submitted the JRIP to General Richardson for his approval, it contained few of the Wickham group's core proposals. The task force decisively rejected the Total Army Sponsorship Program, the heart of the Wickham plan; it compromised the program's citizenship emphasis and could become a public relations disaster. Parents, schools, and communities could "easily misinterpret the program as an effort to recruit and militarize children." The sponsorship program would be an "uncontrollable management nightmare." Active and reserve units were not familiar with the JROTC and would have to be trained on how to interact with high school units. Managing such a program would require a huge staff, which the army was unlikely to provide.[96]

The recommendations to target schools with high college attendance rates and to use USAREC to select new units were also rejected. Again, the recruiting implications of these proposals sparked concern. PL 88–647 mandated a "fair and equitable distribution" of units by state, not by recruiting potential.

Not all the CSA's suggestions were rejected. Some were merely postponed. The idea of creating a separate JROTC staff was adopted in December 1987. Other suggestions were accepted immediately, such as the proposal calling for a new mission statement. Much discussion occurred before this statement was agreed upon, however. In January 1985, TRADOC proposed a mission statement that placed citizenship at the forefront of the JROTC's charter. That statement read: "To develop informed and responsible citizens and to provide an understanding of the U.S. Army in support of national objectives." The CSA's group rejected this version because it did not encompass its expectations of the program, nor did it give expression to the "quest for academic credibility." The study group's proposed statement included the following objectives: acquaint students with the technical requirements of the modern age, promote an understanding of the basic elements of national security, and develop an interest in the military services as a possible career.[97]

Wickham weighed in with a statement of his own that listed program objectives in what he considered to be the appropriate order: develop informed and responsible citizens, aid the growth of leadership potential, strengthen character through teaching service values, acquaint cadets with the technology of a modern military force, promote an understanding of the historical role of citizen-soldiers, and create an interest in military service as a career.[98] The CSA's mission statement was officially adopted but soon quietly set aside.

The TRADOC task force also had some of its recommendations rejected. Its proposal to require instructors to earn teaching certificates was dismissed by the TRADOC's ROTC chief as counterproductive. One officer described the idea as a "classic example of a self-inflicted fatal wound" that could "spell the eventual doom of the JROTC program." Few army officers and NCOs had teaching certificates. To expect an NCO to have both a degree and a teaching certificate was "absolutely absurd." Retirees would resign if they had to obtain state certification. In any case, a teaching certificate was "totally worthless" for someone teaching JROTC, since teaching was not the essence of the program. It was only one of an instructor's many responsibilities, and by no means was it the most important. Moreover, a degree requirement might cause attrition. If instructors earned degrees, they would leave the program and accept regular teaching positions. Regular faculty had shorter hours and received higher pay.[99]

In the end, it was the plan of the TRADOC task force, shorn of its more controversial provisions, that was accepted as the basis for the curricular revamping. This final version of the JRIP aimed to improve cadet appearance and discipline, introduce a computerized management information system, recognize the DAI, enlarge summer camps, and develop better instructional materials.[100]

Despite its inclusion in the JRIP, the expansion of summer camps did not occur. The DOD's comptroller ruled that funding camps was illegal. The law stipulated that the services were restricted to providing texts, equipment, and uniforms to units. The costs of summer training could not be covered. The legal argument masked a more fundamental objection to summer camps. The DOD did not want to squander money on an enterprise that promised few concrete returns. The comptroller declared it "highly questionable" that the DOD derived any benefit from the JROTC. Funds would be better spent on programs directly benefiting the services. The proposal to fund the DAI also ran aground. Again, defense officials objected to spending money on a position with no defense-related purpose.[101]

The final version of the JRIP fell well short of the CSA study group's expectations. It did not make the JROTC more supportive of recruiting, link the program closely with the operational army, inject more academic rigor into JROTC courses, or provide for high-tech instruction for cadets. Some perceived it as a victory for the status quo—as a victory of "marching" over "mathematics."

To others, however, the JRIP was a significant achievement. It provided for stricter instructor selection standards, streamlined administration, upgraded instruction, and, most importantly from the TRADOC perspective, preserved the program's traditional focus on citizenship training. By preserving that traditional focus, the JRIP's authors believed they had saved the army from embarrassment.

As part of the DOD's rejuvenation in the early 1980s, the services launched an expansion of the JROTC. The army's expansion proceeded in a precipitous and desultory manner. The haste stemmed from a desire to effect the expansion before funding dried up. The air force and navy adopted more systematic and measured expansion strategies.

At mid-decade, concerns about a declining high school–age and college-age population and the need for high-quality recruits again spurred interest in the JROTC. The CSA convened a study group to examine the program and recommend ways to make it responsive to operational requirements. The group called for the JROTC to be reconfigured to become part of the recruiting effort and a more efficient provider of preinduction military training.

A TRADOC task force conducted a parallel examination of the program. It, too, advocated reform—but reform at the margins. The task force wanted to improve the curriculum rather than fundamentally change the program's direction. In its plan, the JRIP, there was no hint of drawing back from the inner city or increasing academic rigor. Nor was there an emphasis on high-tech instruction—an area that had figured so prominently in the plans of the study group. The adoption of the JRIP disappointed many defense leaders. From their perspective, this decision meant that the JROTC would remain a social program, geared toward inner cities and mediocre students, incapable of addressing the operational needs of a modern, high-tech army.

9

JROTC at the End of the Cold War, 1986–1992

In the late 1980s, the tension between the United States and the Soviet Union abated. Glasnost, perestroika (1985), and the Reykjavik Summit (1986) attested to the new spirit in international relations. Cries for a peace dividend grew as the Soviet threat dissipated. A more benign international environment combined with rising worries about the huge federal deficit to restrain defense spending. The services suffered recurring bouts of fiscal belt-tightening as Congress looked for ways to economize.[1]

The new realities triggered a drop in defense manpower. Between 1985 and 1992, the size of the military plunged drastically. The sharpest drops occurred after the fall of the Berlin Wall. The annual intake of enlisted recruits for the active forces sank by 43 percent. Officer requirements also slumped, with the army slashing its ROTC officer-recruiting mission by nearly 50 percent.[2]

Congress prodded the Pentagon to expedite the drawdown. The Department of Defense (DOD) resisted these cuts, contending that it could not absorb them without damaging morale and degrading readiness. Congress agreed to slow the pace of cuts but insisted that reductions must occur. Accordingly, in fiscal year 1987, the services began incentivizing junior officers to voluntarily resign and ordering involuntary releases for several hundred colonels and lieutenant colonels.[3]

As international tension subsided, the DOD's focus became more diffuse. Pressed to show relevance, the department assumed a larger role in domestic affairs. Of the many domestic concerns vying for attention, none touched the JROTC more than the failings of public education. In the mid-1980s, a flood of reports on the nation's floundering schools ignited a wave of reform. This literature described school systems afflicted by drug abuse, crime, violence, disorder, and ineffective teachers.[4]

Anxiety about US economic competitiveness and social stability spurred educational reform. Particularly alarming was the academic performance gap between minority and Caucasian students. Although that gap had narrowed since 1970, minority youth continued to trail majority students on tests of math and reading proficiency.[5]

President George H. W. Bush's Education Summit (September 1989)—attended by many of the nation's governors—was a milestone in the educational reform effort. The governors elaborated six national education goals to be met by the year 2000. Four had special relevance for the JROTC: goal 2, by 2000, increase the high school graduation rate to 90 percent and reduce the gap in graduation rates between minority and majority students; goal 3, by 2000, ensure that students in grades four, eight, and twelve demonstrate competency in challenging subjects like English, math, and science; are prepared for responsible citizenship and productive employment; and perform community service; goal 4, by 2000, make US students first in the world in science and math achievement; and goal 6, by 2000, ensure schools are drug- and violence-free, have a disciplined environment supportive of learning, and offer drug and alcohol prevention programs.[6]

ARMY REORGANIZATION

Among the services, the army experienced the most organizational tumult in the late 1980s. Its ROTC struggled with a number of unique problems. To alleviate these difficulties, in 1986 army leaders created a separate ROTC command, named the US Army Cadet Command (USACC). Its purpose was to reduce the autonomy of regional chiefs, consolidate authority in a single commander, and enhance policy enforcement. Both General William Richardson and the new USACC commander, Major General Robert Wagner, were ardent exponents of the idea.[7]

The Training and Doctrine Command (TRADOC) commander wanted a staff large enough to control the program's far-flung detachments. He saw program quality closely bound up with the degree of supervision that could be exercised over units. To establish the new command, Richardson acted unilaterally. This annoyed authorities in Washington who wanted to hold down costs and reduce "overhead."[8]

A separate ROTC command was not a novel idea. The concept had been percolating through defense channels for decades. A 1964 army study concluded that bringing the ROTC under "uniform, authoritative control" was necessary for efficient management. A Marine Corps study (1973) observed that command status brought greater "visibility," direct access to senior leaders, and more clout in obtaining resources.[9] The creation of the USACC gave the ROTC a discrete management structure devoted exclusively to protecting ROTC interests and a staff large enough to control the program.

The JROTC did not benefit as much as the SROTC from the new command. Upon activation in April 1986, Cadet Command still had not created a dedicated JROTC management cell.[10] It was not until December 1987 that a separate high school division appeared. Even then, it consisted of just five people. Only gradually would the division evolve into a full-fledged directorate.[11]

STASIS

As already noted, the army had considered expanding its JROTC in 1985. That expansion did not occur. In fact, unit strength declined, dropping from 865 units in 1986 to 853 in 1991. The unit totals of the other services flatlined, with the air force, navy, and Marine Corps recording net gains of five, seven, and two units respectively, leaving their program totals well below legislative limits (see appendix B).[12]

The program's base remained static despite pressure from Congress and the public. Congress members and community leaders inundated the services with requests for new units. One army official described this pressure as "constant" and "intense."[13] Senator Strom Thurmond submitted a request for an impoverished school district in his state.[14] The army rejected Thurmond's appeal, citing lack of funds.[15] The air force rejected an application request from a school in Georgia congressman J. Roy Rowland's district. "We would certainly enjoy" establishing a unit there, an officer told Rowland, but there was not enough money. The air force had ninety-eight schools on the waiting list, and the congressman's school was number 72. There were only two openings that year, and the competition for those two vacancies was intense. In any case, public law required that units be equitably distributed throughout the nation. Georgia already had ten more than its proportional share.[16]

Within the army, opposition to expansion centered in Cadet Command. There, leaders feared that the program's enlargement would further skew the geographic balance of the JROTC.[17] Funding was another concern. Richardson told the chief of staff of the army (CSA) that expansion was inadvisable given the funding restrictions imposed by the Gramm-Rudman-Hollings Balanced Budget Act. The army had to fix what it had before adding more units.[18]

Both Richardson and Wagner worried that expansion would weaken the SROTC. Neither man wanted to hobble the recent reforms made in the senior program by diverting resources to the JROTC.[19] Wagner insisted that the JROTC must not be allowed to interfere with "commissioning the future leaders of the U.S. Army" and vowed, "I will not establish any new Junior ROTC units unless ordered to do so. . . . Improvements for the Junior Program financed at any expense to the Senior Program are unacceptable."[20] He resented the intense lobbying by influential politicians and railed against "political establishments." Wagner ordered his staff to document all attempts to apply such pressure. Fending off federal legislators was a difficult undertaking, requiring the expenditure of large stores of political capital.[21]

The USACC commander vented his anger against expansion during a visit to the First Region headquarters in March 1986. The region staff began its briefing with an overview of the JROTC. Wagner abruptly stopped the presentation and told the region commander that he did not want to waste time on a program that did not produce lieutenants. Wagner asked why resources were being expended on a program that was largely composed of "lumps."[22] He wanted athletes and scholars. Not only would they be better candidates for commissioning, but they would create a more flattering image of the program.

The reluctance of the services to expand their programs opened the way for the Coast Guard's entry into the JROTC. Coast Guard officials opened their service's first unit in Miami-Dade County, Florida, in 1989. With this step, the Coast Guard hoped to increase "interest in . . . career opportunities among minority high [school] students." At the time, minorities composed less than 3 percent of its enlisted force and less than 2 percent of its officer corps.[23]

IMPEDIMENTS TO GROWTH

The program's contraction in the late 1980s was attributable to more than unsupportive leadership. Budget stringency was a more critical factor. In the half decade after 1985, the JROTC budget shrank by more than 5 percent. This led to a moratorium on the creation of new units in 1988. This moratorium, in effect for two years, prevented the replacement of units lost through normal attrition.[24] Moreover, funding decrements exacerbated instructor shortages. By October 1988, the Army JROTC had fallen 173 instructors below requirements. This shortage, in turn, depressed enrollment. Encumbered with more responsibilities, instructors found less time to recruit. Cutbacks also left less money to buy uniforms, awards, and instructional materials. Student enthusiasm and instructor morale inevitably waned.[25] One disgruntled senior army instructor (SAI) complained that he and his colleagues felt like "the bastard child at a family reunion." They were ignored until someone wanted information.[26]

Educational reform reportedly contributed to the stagnation. More exacting graduation requirements and new college preparatory curricula made the JROTC less attractive to college-bound students. A Director of the Army Instruction (DAI) in Georgia complained that the state legislature had passed a bill called Quality Basic Education (QBE), which spurred a proliferation of new, more demanding college preparatory tracks. These tracks left no time for electives like the JROTC. They also affected the program's socioeconomic balance. Many units that drew students from white, middle-class areas had severe enrollment issues. The DAI urged restraint in closing units, especially in his district, where the QBE was still in the "shakedown" period.[27]

With tightening academic standards, the issue of academic credit for the JROTC again took center stage. The services implored school officials to award more core credit. Elective credit was helpful, but only core credit would suffice. Without it, the program would struggle to attract college bound students and attain the socioeconomic balance it sought.[28]

The downward trend in enrollment also reflected the continuing decline of the fourteen-to-seventeen-year-old age group, which fell by over 7 percent between 1986 and 1990. True, JROTC enrollment declined less than the overall age cohort; the program's school penetration rate actually rose.[29] But this was little comfort to defense leaders who were searching for ways to improve accessions.

The widespread use of cross enrollment may have prevented unit viability problems from becoming worse. But it did this at the expense of economy and efficiency.[30] The scope of the cross-enrollment "problem" was extensive. In May 1987, the army's four region headquarters reported that there were 122 cross-enrolled schools participating in the JROTC.[31] An egregious example of cross enrollment occurred at Cypress Lake High School (Florida) in

1988. Cyprus Lake entered into cross-enrollment agreements with multiple outlying institutions. Instructors maintained these "mini programs" while enrollment at the host school tanked. This was a classic case of shoring up a faltering unit through cross enrollment.[32]

Besides propping up inefficient units, cross enrollment served two other questionable ends. First, principals used it to circumvent DOD policy. When schools were denied a unit, they would resubmit their applications under the cross-enrollment label. This gambit allowed schools to evade the statutory requirement for a "fair and equitable distribution" of units among states. Another use of cross enrollment was to gain more instructors. This practice violated regulations, was unfair, and gave short-staffed units "legitimate grounds for crying 'Foul.'"[33]

In August 1976, the DOD announced that although federal law did not prohibit the practice, cross enrollment was tantamount to the creation of extra units. It was permissible only when it became impractical for a student enrolled in a host school to continue to attend courses at that school. One such situation was where court-ordered desegregation resulted in a school district realignment, in which students formerly enrolled in the JROTC at one school had been assigned to a new school without a unit.[34]

The DOD opposed the practice because of its cost. Cross enrollment entailed increased transportation costs, more outlays for instructors' salaries, and higher unit operating expenses. A TRADOC regulation prohibited the practice unless the unit secured an exception to policy.[35] Proscriptions against cross enrollment, however, had little effect. School administrators and JROTC instructors ignored DOD guidance and pressed ahead, undeterred by edicts from above.[36]

The inability of the services to suppress cross enrollment can be attributed to two main factors. First, local pressure often proved more powerful than DOD policy. Instructors found it difficult to resist the entreaties of school officials and community leaders. Second, especially in the army's case, an inveterate command system obstructed policy enforcement. Higher headquarters were not even aware of many cross-enrollment agreements.

DECLINE

Between 1990 and 1992, the JROTC went from stagnation to decline. Participation levels fell by 7 percent. Moreover, the JROTC experienced a relative as well as absolute decline. After rising from 11.47 to 11.68 percent between 1986 and 1990, the program's participation rate fell to 11.08 percent by 1993. The JROTC's popularity seemed to be eroding.[37]

The ongoing decline of the high school cohort helped explain this. So did media coverage of the Persian Gulf War, which depicted service in the armed forces as difficult, harsh, and lethal. The post–Cold War demobilization was another cause. The DOD's annual intake of new recruits sank sharply after the fall of the Berlin Wall as the services' need for manpower fell. With opportunities in the military drying up, the JROTC lost some of its appeal.[38]

The continuing budget squeeze added to the JROTC's troubles. It compelled the services to cut back on summer training and other activities.[39] The Army Reserve, which furnished drill sergeants and equipment to camps, likewise faced budget cuts and had to scale back its assistance.[40]

The reduction of US forces in Europe was another factor. As US forces withdrew from Germany, DOD Dependents Schools closed or lost enrollment, precipitating a fall in both enrollment and unit strength. Between 1989 and 1992, the Army JROTC lost four of its nineteen units and 45 percent of its enrollment.[41] These declines were only partially offset by the creation of units in Korea and Japan.[42]

RECRUITING

The JROTC's input into accessions continued to decline after 1985, hitting a post-Vietnam nadir in 1987. This occurred while army recruiting flourished. Recruiting was so good, in fact, that the service raised its minimum mental test standards for enlistment. But what was good for the active-duty force was not good for the JROTC. With the higher standards, fewer JROTC cadets qualified for enlistment or commissioning.[43]

The JROTC scholarship application rate in the Army JROTC was disappointing. In the 1985–1986 school year, only 14 percent of four-year-scholarship applicants had been cadets. This translated into a unit submission rate of only 1.78. The win rate of JROTC scholarship applicants was also low. Only 275 of the 1,574 Army JROTC applicants won an award. This low success rate was in part due to the lack of extracurricular participation among the JROTC applicants. Relatively few listed any additional extracurricular activities on their applications. From this, analysts concluded that students who took part in the JROTC did so at the expense of other activities. This finding was in accord with other studies indicating that most cadets were marginal students who were not fully engaged in their schools.[44] While the percentage of JROTC graduates entering the services declined, the percentage of graduating cadets indicating an intention to join the military rose substantially. This suggested that the drop in JROTC accessions was a matter not of propensity but of inability to meet enlistment standards.

The recruiting environment soured after 1987. The next year, the reserve component (RC) missed their recruiting goals, while the active force met its mission by lowering recruit quality. The SROTC, too, floundered. It approved more waivers and drew more heavily from colleges with lower admission standards. The accessions downturn resulted from an improving economy, a rising employment rate, a shrinking manpower pool of seventeen-to-twenty-one-year-olds, a widening disparity between military and civilian pay, an erosion of in-service education benefits, and fiscal stringency.[45]

As accessions faltered, the services ratcheted up their recruiting efforts.[46] They made recruiting visits to schools with increasing frequency. The president of one military institute told of a visit from a hectoring colonel from Cadet Command, who pressed him for more enlistments. The president informed the colonel that his institution had an enviable academic reputation, and he would not sanction enlisted recruiting among his students. The colonel departed in high dudgeon.[47]

While the push for accessions at the more selective military schools had little success, program-wide the situation appeared much better after 1987. What was bad for the army benefited the JROTC, or at least JROTC graduates who wanted to enlist. The JROTC's input into the enlisted force and the SROTC rose substantially. The gains achieved in officer recruiting were particularly noteworthy. The program's contribution to the SROTC rose by 79 percent between 1987 and 1988.[48]

Several factors propelled this upswing. Access into the SROTC advanced course became easier. More students received advanced placement credit for the JROTC than in the past. The Army SROTC had traditionally turned to lateral entry programs like Basic Camp and the JROTC when the recruiting environment deteriorated. Students from these programs generally scored lower on standardized tests and earned lower grades than the cadet population at large. This time was no different. Lower selection standards paved the way for increased JROTC input.

A change in the ROTC scholarship system may have helped. The federal drive for economy resulted in a cap being placed on the value of Army ROTC scholarships. Previously, scholarship recipients received full tuition and fees. Beginning in 1988, the army capped scholarships at 80 percent of tuition. As a result, the ROTC scholarship lost much of its appeal, especially for the brightest students who went to selective colleges. The slack was taken up by inexpensive, less-selective state-supported institutions, where tuition, room, and board were less burdensome. And it was in these minimally selective state-supported institutions that the JROTC graduates clustered.[49]

The JROTC's input into the enlisted force also rose. Again, declining accessions standards help explain this. The upturn in JROTC input coincided with an increase in new recruits classified in Armed Forces Qualification Test (AFQT) Categories IIIb and IV, the lowest-scoring categories eligible for enlistment. Most JROTC graduates scored in these ranges.

THE SOCIAL IMPERATIVE

The army continued to revise its junior program along the lines laid out in the Junior ROTC Improvement Plan (JRIP).[50] It also reinvigorated its efforts to raise graduation rates, renewed its emphasis on citizenship training, and emphasized technological education and the boosting of cadet self-confidence. This package of initiatives was given the codename Operation Young Citizen.[51]

While this initiative seemed like standard fare, it turned out to be a milestone. It signaled the growing importance of the societal imperative for the JROTC. As public anxiety about domestic ills grew, the DOD came under increasing pressure to use its people and resources to address social issues. The JROTC's emphasis on raising the graduation rates of minority students addressed a top national concern. The development of self-confidence, a long-standing objective of the JROTC, took on new meaning. It was now seen as key to preparing minorities for collegiate success. Black students from poor urban neighborhoods or rural areas were at a disadvantage when thrust into an integrated college environment. They often experienced adjustment problems, due in no small part to a lack of confidence.[52]

Acquainting cadets with technology was an objective that aimed to encourage the pursuit of high-tech degrees by minorities and women, who were underrepresented in science, technology, engineering, and mathematics (STEM) fields. Typical of defense STEM initiatives was one launched by the army and navy in the National Capital Area in 1986. Operating under the aegis of the DOD's Science and Engineering Apprenticeship Program (SEAP), it provided eight-week apprenticeships to high school students in federal laboratories. The Science, Technology, and Research Students (STARS) program had a similar thrust but was geared toward younger audiences. It offered seventh and eighth graders in DC public schools a three-day immersion course to pique interest in science careers. The services later inserted STEM modules into their JROTC curricula.[53]

The army added twelve hours of technology awareness instruction to the program of instruction (POI); the air force and navy already had STEM-oriented curricula. This additional army instruction encouraged cadets to take math and science in high school and Science, Math, and Engineering (SME) subjects in college. Courses offered by the Army JROTC were nontechnical in nature. They included Technology's Effects of Society, the History and Components of the Computer, and Ethical Problems Related to Technology.[54]

The Army's Cadet Challenge was another initiative that addressed societal concerns. It was originally conceived as a comprehensive health and physical fitness program reminiscent of the one Edgar Z. Steever had introduced in Wyoming's public schools in 1915. It included an instructional component that stressed the importance of diet for good health and gave advice about what types of foods should be consumed or avoided. This aspect of Cadet Challenge served a purpose that was salient in many of the JROTC's poorer schools.[55]

Drug abuse prevention was a key part of the revision. Many reports like *Building Our Workforce* and *A Nation at Risk* warned that the nation's educational problems could not be solved until drug abuse among high school students was brought under control. Accordingly, the services inserted drug abuse prevention into the curriculum at each grade level.[56]

While raising graduation rates, promoting STEM study, developing self-confidence in potential enlistees and officer candidates, teaching nutrition and health, and encouraging students to remain drug free had obvious military utility, the DOD's embrace of these objectives was not merely instrumental. It was another example of the services fulfilling their domestic obligations.[57]

OPERATION CAPITAL

No single initiative was more reflective of the JROTC's new social orientation than Operation Capital. In it, one could discern the emerging defense priorities that would guide the JROTC over the next decade. Launched in August 1989, this program targeted "high-risk and minority youth" in inner cities. Although the thrust of Operation Capital was not new, it took on a new aspect in the late 1980s as the DOD adjusted to new domestic and international conditions.

As with similar projects in the past, there was no unanimity among defense leaders about Operation Capital's value. Some senior officers regarded this initiative as tangential to the military's primary mission. At the same time, there was a growing realization within the Pentagon that unless the services performed socially useful functions, defense claims on resources and public support might erode.[58]

The army's embrace of Operation Capital reflected this awareness. Resources and visibility would accrue to organizations seen as fulfilling domestic priorities. One such priority was the war on drugs. The first drug czar, William Bennett, injected new vigor into the antidrug effort in 1989, bringing the problem of substance abuse into the national spotlight.[59] Drug abuse was only one problem paralyzing urban schools. Popular media brimmed with horror stories about schools afflicted with gang violence, teenage pregnancies, spiraling dropout rates, crumbling infrastructure, barebones budgets, robbery, rape, arson, and assault. The intense media coverage of these problems struck the JROTC managers, who recognized the opening this created for the program. An article appearing in the February 1, 1988, edition of *Time* magazine made a deep impression on the army. That article described problems facing urban schools and featured a photograph of the principal of a "virtually all-black" magnet school in Atlanta surrounded by a JROTC honor guard. To army officials, the message in this photograph was powerful. The army's JROTC director contacted William Bennett's office to ensure that the secretary had seen the photograph.[60]

Bennett's successor as secretary of education was Lauro Cavazos. The new secretary's writ encompassed increasing educational opportunities for minorities, raising graduation rates, boosting student competency in difficult subjects, and making schools free from drugs, violence, and disorder. Operation Capital addressed all of these goals.[61]

Operation Capital began as a partnership between the army and the Washington, DC, school system. The operation initially involved 874 cadets in eight high schools. Washington was chosen as the site because of the media attention given to the city's problems. These problems included a high homicide rate, a skyrocketing number of drug arrests, and some of the lowest high school graduation rates in the nation. The location also ensured ready access to government leaders, whose support was vital.[62]

The operation's unit selection criteria reflected the army's resolve to help schools that had urgent needs but whose problems stood a reasonable chance of successful remediation. The selection criteria were (1) large, minority populations, (2) clear drug or dropout problems, (3) the support of school officials, (4) excellent community relations, and (5) motivated managers and experienced instructors.[63] To assist, the army assigned an officer to the staff of the DC school system. It was his responsibility to evaluate each unit, determine its strengths and weaknesses, and formulate a plan to help it address its weaknesses.[64]

The operation sought to maximize student participation in the JROTC. This effort involved securing the active cooperation of school administrators in boosting enrollment and recruiting successful people to tell cadets about the importance of completing high school and avoiding drug use. The army used drill competition and a weeklong summer camp to teach teamwork and build self-esteem.[65] It also encouraged involvement in community support programs to instill a service ethos in cadets. None of this was new, but the context was. Not since the Domestic Action Program of the early 1970s had the inner-city emphasis of the JROTC been so strong.[66]

ROTC leaders envisaged a role for Operation Capital that extended beyond the boundaries of the District of Columbia. Initially, they aimed to extend the operation to thirty-four additional cities. Later, they discussed implanting Operation Capital in every inner-city high school in the country. These ambitious schemes never materialized, but the program was exported to nine additional cities and 115 schools by 1991. Baltimore, Detroit, Chicago, Shreveport, Dallas, Denver, El Paso, Honolulu, and San Diego were the participating cities.[67]

The army claimed that Operation Capital was a huge success. It cited increased enrollment as proof. Between 1988 and 1989, the percentage of DC public school students enrolled in the JROTC rose from 7.6 to 9.7 percent. Public schools in six of the nine other cities also registered gains, with schools in Chicago and Shreveport leading the way.[68] The JROTC graduation rates also climbed in six cities, with cadets completing high school at rates considerably above those of fellow students.[69] The army's community service program was another bright point. It enjoyed great success in the DC area, where service projects were warmly embraced by school officials and local communities.[70]

The luster of Operation Capital was somewhat dimmed by the decline in the graduation rate in DC. That rate fell by 7 percent between 1990 and 1991, making the performance of JROTC cadets only marginally better than that of the general student body. Other initiatives that were part of the operation also achieved lackluster results. Generally, activities that were not part of the JROTC's traditional repertoire struggled to take root.[71]

From the army's perspective, Operation Capital's real value could not be apprehended through quantitative measurements. To be sure, numbers were important for external consumption and for the benefit of higher headquarters, where statistical gauges were the currency of business. But for ROTC leaders, numbers were less meaningful than firsthand observations from the field. Managers formed their opinions by talking to cadets, instructors, teachers, principals, and city officials. And from these sources, they received the message that Operation Capital was a useful program that had many admirers and a wide base of support.

AWARENESS PRESENTATION TEAMS

In 1990, the air force initiated a project with the same general purpose as Operation Capital. The project's aim was to dissuade students from engaging in a range of destructive behaviors. The air force, viewing its JROTC as an "oasis of success" amid urban turmoil, decided to share its success throughout the K–12 world. Its tools were Awareness Presentation Teams (APT). These teams, composed of cadets, visited elementary and middle schools to help younger students "overcome the problems facing young people." The APT goals included conducting drug-education programs and improving the lives of "less fortunate students" through summer leadership programs. The APTs set up cadets as role models, who by their example and presentations would deter drug use and other pathologies among younger students.[72]

The air force targeted schools in states in which the JROTC was underrepresented. The program quickly became an item of great interest to senior air force leaders. In fact, by November 1992, it was the only item concerning the Air Force JROTC routinely briefed to them. Because the APT program's focus was on younger students, the air force used the number of APT presentations delivered as its gauge of effectiveness. As of February 1, 1992, APTs had made presentations to more than twenty-five thousand students. The air force was pleased with these results.[73]

OPPOSITION TO THE SOCIAL IMPERATIVE

Not everyone within the JROTC community was enthusiastic about the direction the program was taking. The revision of the army curriculum to address "timely and current social concerns relevant to our nation's inner cities" did not resonate in institutions whose students harbored higher aspirations than completing high school or enlisting in the military. To this audience, the JROTC's makeover represented a degradation of academic quality.[74]

Resistance to the JROTC's new direction crystallized in 1986 at the annual meeting of the Association of Military Schools and Colleges of the United States (AMSCUS). At that meeting, it was announced that the army would introduce a new JROTC curriculum. This announcement sparked "considerable" concern among attendees. The president-elect of AMSCUS and president of Culver Military Academy, Ralph N. Manuel, objected that the new POI was "too vocationally oriented" and "not challenging enough academically." That curriculum had little to offer to schools like Culver, where most students were college-bound. Many Culver graduates, in fact, attended selective civilian universities or service academies. If they entered the service, they did so as officers. The new POI was ill-suited for students of this caliber. For them, exhortations to steer clear of drugs and fast-food restaurants and stay in high school had little value.[75]

Manuel asked the army to allow Culver to design a curriculum for upper-end military schools. The army assented. Drawing from syllabi from the service academies, the Culver staff drew up a curriculum, which it presented to the army in September 1987. By that time, however, the army had experienced a change of heart. In the summer of 1988, it withdrew its endorsement of the Culver plan. All schools, it directed, would now follow the prescribed program.[76]

The army's difficulties with Culver and similar schools stemmed not from curricular concerns but from low enlistment rates among their graduates. The army's need for enlistees was urgent, so the army was not in the mood to compromise. To Culver's historian, this was proof that the army saw his school as a way to fill its noncommissioned officer (NCO) ranks.[77]

At its 1988 annual meeting, AMCSUS asked the army to show more flexibility regarding the curriculum. But the army refused to relent. The "Culver administration," the school's historian wrote, "found itself in the untenable position of being required to teach an inferior program which denigrated the intelligence of its college-bound cadets." Accordingly, Culver ended its seventy-three-year relationship with the ROTC in 1989.[78]

Culver's president complained that ROTC leaders would not recognize the difference between college preparatory and turnaround schools. Schools of the latter type catered to troubled and underachieving youth who had languished in the public school system. Military institutes offered them a second chance. Manuel charged that the army was unable to envision another paradigm for a military school, attempting instead to stuff Culver into a mold for which it was unsuited.[79]

Culver's exit from the program symbolized the DOD's turn toward disadvantaged communities. To be sure, the program had been moving in that direction for years. But the severing of ties between the army and Culver, one of the most prestigious military institutes, was symbolic. It delineated the issues contending for the soul of the program in stark terms. Other selective institutes, it is true, remained in the program. But their association was often an uneasy one. Their disquietude would grow in the early 1990s as the post–Cold War demobilization began and the drive to make the JROTC more responsive to the needs of the disadvantaged accelerated.

ELIMINATION ATTEMPT

While the pressure to employ the military in socially constructive ways grew, a consensus among senior defense leaders about appropriate missions for the armed forces had not yet congealed. One group of officials wanted to keep the military focused on defense against foreign threats and resisted the domestic employment of the military. This opposition manifested itself in mid-1989 when the DOD abruptly cut off the JROTC funding. While the services quickly restored funding, they did so at reduced levels.[80]

This foray against the program was minor compared to a more serious attack later that autumn. This latter attempt to shutter the program grew out of Project Quicksilver, a defense plan to reduce the military to a size commensurate with the realities of the post–Cold War world. That plan called for dramatic cuts in personnel and the abolition of organizations that did not perform core functions. The JROTC was an obvious target. Only military institutes were to be spared.

The army vigorously opposed this incursion against the program and dragged out all the traditional justifications for its continuation. It pointed to the JROTC's domestic benefits—such as higher graduation rates and reduced adolescent drug abuse—and underlined the program's contribution to recruiting.[81] ROTC leaders also stressed the JROTC's public outreach value. In some places, JROTC instructors and cadets formed the only visible link between the services and the American public. With the impending post–Cold War demobilization, outreach seemed more important than ever.[82]

More prosaic arguments were advanced to save the program. First, the JROTC's elimination would yield only meager savings—only $33 million and one hundred personnel. These paltry savings would not be worth the social costs incurred. Second, the program's elimination would unleash a storm of protest. ROTC leaders reminded the Pentagon of what had happened when Robert S. McNamara attempted to abolish the JROTC in the mid-1960s. If the JROTC was dissolved, a similar outburst could be expected.[83]

Before the Pentagon could effect its plan, news of the proposed move leaked into the public domain and produced the predicted reaction. Letters denouncing the proposed action soon bombarded Congress, the president, and the DOD. The Army Advisory Panel, a group of prominent educators who advised the army on educational policy, added its protest to the scores of others directed at Washington. The panel strongly condemned the dissolution, contending that JROTC instructors served as "excellent, solid role models for disadvantaged children, especially those living below the poverty level from single-parent families."[84]

Representative Floyd Spence of Kentucky was one of the most vociferous congressional critics of the move. He vowed to one distraught colonel that he would use his influence to stop the elimination. He wrote to Secretary of Defense Richard Cheney, demanding that he reconsider his position.[85] When Senator John Glenn learned of the move, he contacted Christopher Jehn, the assistant secretary of defense (force management and personnel), and insisted that his department rescind the decision. Jehn assured Glenn that he would act to ensure the JROTC's continuance.[86]

By mid-February 1990, the DOD realized it had made a serious miscalculation. It then attempted to undo the damage. One senior defense official admitted that it was a "dumb" move. The idea had "slipped through the cracks and never should have been approved." His department was "trying to find a way to get it fixed." If this could not be done internally, defense officials would have to go to Congress with their "tails between [their] legs" and ask for help in rectifying the mistake.[87]

The reasons cited to explain the Pentagon's about-face were manifold. The assistant secretary of the army (manpower and reserve affairs), G. Kim Wincup, offered the following rationale: "In view of the visibility of the program, its potential in assisting in the war on drugs, and the growing congressional concern, I believe [a] re-evaluation of the elimination proposal is warranted." One Senate staffer cited the program's recruiting value. "Junior ROTC," he asserted, "is a cheap recruiting device. If we wanted to cut money, we would cut the recruiting budget before eliminating Junior ROTC."[88]

In the end, the pressure brought to bear by the program's defenders compelled the Pentagon to retreat. The DOD's director of education and officer procurement policy (D/EOPP) told Senator Sam Nunn on March 13, 1990, that the Pentagon had no plan to eliminate the program. The JROTC was a statutory program and "would require a legislative amendment . . . to be terminated."[89]

The attempted dismantling of the JROTC produced great turmoil in the field. Instructors upbraided defense leaders for attempting such a ploy. They felt disgusted and betrayed. Their protests flowed into congressional offices and service headquarters. Air force officials characterized the situation as a "firestorm." During the first week of February 1990 alone, they received more than 175 telephone calls from agitated instructors. Many of these retirees found it incomprehensible that the DOD could even consider such a step, given the accolades it had bestowed on the program in the past. They also resented the underhanded way in which the Pentagon tried to effect the elimination. Plans were drawn up without consulting the field. Indeed, instructors were not informed that anything was afoot. The deep rift between the services and instructors that grew out of this episode took years to disappear.[90]

After 1986, both enrollment and unit strength flagged. Funding shortfalls, a declining student population, and weak support in the Pentagon accounted for much of this downslide. The decline during the Gulf War stemmed from fears about the risks of military service, talk about defense downsizing, and increasing fiscal stringency.

The JROTC's contribution to enlisted recruiting rose in the late 1980s, when the recruiting environment took a turn for the worse. In this new environment, the services had to accept more Category IIIb and IV enlistees to meet accessions targets. The decline in recruit quality opened the way for more JROTC graduates to enter the military. A similar dynamic was at work in officer recruiting, where lowered accessions standards opened the way for more JROTC participation.

The JROTC's focus turned toward at-risk students and disadvantaged communities. In part, this reflected federal priorities. As the Soviet threat waned, domestic problems achieved greater saliency. Adolescent drug abuse, violence in schools, and low high school graduation rates among minorities became matters of intense national concern.

The services revised their curricula to address federal priorities. Modules on technology, drug abuse prevention, proper diet, exercise, test-taking techniques, and time management were added to the class schedule. More stress was also placed on community service projects, which were seen as preparing students to be loyal members of a participatory democracy.

10

JROTC in the Post–Cold War Era, 1992–1996

After the Cold War, the defense budget accelerated its downward slide, dropping by 17 percent between fiscal years 1991 and 1996. At the same time, troop strength nose-dived, with the Department of Defense (DOD) losing about 25 percent of its active duty and 20 percent of its Reserve Component (RC) strength. Unit deactivations and base closings accompanied these reductions. The SROTC lost a sizable portion of its institutional base. The army alone saw its ROTC unit strength fall from 415 in fiscal year 1990 to 270 in fiscal year 1996.[1]

To accomplish manpower cuts, the DOD lowered recruiting goals, raised accession standards, offered special separation incentives, and invoked involuntary release measures. To ease the transition to civilian life for discharged service members, the DOD launched employment programs like New Careers in Education, which helped former service members become teachers.[2]

With the emergence of a new international order, the nation shifted its gaze from foreign threats to domestic issues. One of the most pressing of these was the plight of disadvantaged youth. Programs like the army's Operation Capital and the air force's Awareness Presentation Teams (APT) program now proliferated. By 1996, the government had in place 131 programs to help "at-risk and delinquent" young people.[3]

The dim employment prospects for marginalized youth aroused concern. A growing underclass of poorly educated and unskilled workers, it was feared, would have dire social consequences. Better education seemed to be the answer, but many public schools were in no condition to improve outcomes. Reports told of an educational system in turmoil with dropout rates surging and basic academic skills among high school graduates deteriorating. Some warned of an impending crisis in the workforce.

America 2000, the name given to the George H. W. Bush administration's educational reform agenda, had employment preparation as a major goal. President Bush and his secretary of education, Lamar Alexander, unveiled the initiative in April 1991. The effort entailed creating better schools through parental choice, national testing, alternative teacher certification, the establishment of job-related skill standards, and municipal "report cards" to measure progress.[4]

The Secretary of Labor's Commission on Achieving Necessary Skills (SCANS) was formed to identify the most essential work skills. Its report (1991) bewailed the lagging productivity of American workers, the low cognitive skill levels of high school graduates, and the meager results achieved by previous educational reform efforts. It identified what students must know and do to secure meaningful employment. These job prerequisites included basic literacy and numeracy skills and personal qualities like diligence and reliability.[5]

JROTC EXPANSION

In the emerging post–Cold War world, the ambiguity that had surrounded the JROTC's purpose faded. National leaders now showered money and attention on a program that could address multiple needs. Bolstered by this support, the JROTC embarked on an expansion that, in absolute terms, was the largest in its history (see appendix B).

President Bush set the azimuth for the JROTC's growth in a speech at Lincoln Technical Institute in Union, New Jersey, on August 24, 1992. In that speech, Bush announced that he was doubling the size of the JROTC, which he described as "a great program that boosts high school completion rates, reduces drug use, . . . and gets kids firmly on the right track." The expansion was part of the Youth Skills Initiative, a program to prepare non-college-bound youth for the workplace. According to Bush, foreign economic competition, the proliferation of complex technologies, and a dynamic labor market necessitated such initiatives.[6] The Youth Skills Initiative had multiple components, which included a Youth Training Corps (YTC), focused on vocational training and the JROTC. The YTC and the JROTC had the additional benefit of offering employment options for recently discharged veterans.[7]

In fiscal year 1993, the National Defense Authorization Act (NDAA) raised the JROTC unit ceiling from 1,600 to 3,500—600 above the number cited in the president's speech—and fixed the expansion's focus on impoverished urban areas.[8] It soon became apparent, however, that the goal set by Congress was too ambitious. Fiscal constraints, school budget shortages, and "stringent educational requirements" forced a tempering of government aspirations. So, too, according to General Colin Powell, did staffing problems. Finding instructors willing to serve in inner-city schools proved more problematic than expected. Retirees shunned inner cities because of the lack of nearby military bases and the dangerous conditions that prevailed.[9] Thus, by the time the expansion began in May 1992, the DOD had settled on a more modest goal of 2,900 units. Even so, the expansion entailed the addition of 1,421 units to the 1,479 then in existence.[10]

DRIVERS OF EXPANSION

The expansion rode on a wave of congressional and public support. One of the most influential voices advocating a greater domestic role for the military was Senator Sam Nunn of Georgia, chair of the Senate Armed Services Committee (SASC). Nunn introduced a bill to increase military involvement in projects addressing critical domestic needs. Employing military capabilities to solve internal troubles, he wrote, would both serve the nation and help the DOD shore up its shaky budgetary position. There was great uncertainty about the size and composition of the forces that would be needed in the future. New and legitimate missions might not halt the drawdown but would limit its severity.[11]

The April 1992 riots in Los Angeles made a deep impression on Nunn. The disturbances, he noted, were reminders that the nation faced "severe domestic challenges . . . daunting as any potential foreign threat." The Soviet danger may have vanished, but the United States was "still battling . . . drugs, poverty, urban decay, lack of self-esteem, unemployment, and racism." The military could not solve all these problems but could help assuage them. Its capabilities should be leveraged to tackle issues like deteriorating infrastructure, the lack of role models for disadvantaged teens, limited educational opportunities for the underprivileged, and the serious health and nutrition problems facing children.[12]

Nunn enumerated military capabilities that could remediate domestic problems. At the top of his list was the provision of role models. According to the senator, the "hard-working, disciplined men and women" of the armed forces "can serve as a very powerful force among our young people—especially where family structures are weakened by poverty, drugs, and crime." Why not use these role models to elevate inner-city and rural youth "who may never have had a father in their own home."[13]

Just as salient was the JROTC's capacity as an enabler of learning. Educators attested to the program's ability to create a stable, safe environment in which students could pursue their studies without fear or distraction. They claimed that the program fostered order in the classroom, reduced misbehavior, deterred drug abuse, and alleviated other difficulties that made it difficult for students to learn.[14]

Colin Powell focused the DOD's attention on the JROTC and became the principal uniformed champion of the program's interests. Powell even diverted funds from other programs to ensure the expansion went forward. The chairman characterized the program as a "social bargain" and the "best opportunity for the Department of Defense to make a positive impact on the Nation's youth." He, too, was moved by the Los Angeles riots. Events in that city, he wrote, propelled the plight of inner-city youth into the national consciousness. Stories of children engaging in gang violence and running drug rings "attest to the devastating impact that a lack of self-discipline, dearth of positive role models, and severe peer pressure can have on society." The JROTC, with its "well-trained and highly motivated role models" and emphasis on responsible citizenship, would dissuade adolescents from engaging in the type of behavior witnessed in Los Angeles.[15]

Another impetus for expansion was a fear of the military's diminishing societal visibility. The post–Cold War drawdown, with its personnel reductions, base closings, and ROTC unit closures, had lowered the military's public profile. As channels of civil-military interaction narrowed, public support for the military would likely erode. The services might shrink to the point of "social irrelevance."[16] Public outreach thus became of paramount importance. And the JROTC seemed an excellent way, as the sociologist Charles Moskos observed, to "maximize the number of young people . . . who pass through a military experience."[17]

At the same time, the federal government wanted to provide employment for recently retired personnel. In May 1992, the army formed a task force to explore ways retirees could be used to burnish the military's image in local communities. In August, Robert Silverman, the assistant secretary of the army (manpower and reserve affairs), asked the DOD to create JROTC instructor positions in the Los Angeles area for some of the thirteen thousand veterans who were then in the army's New Careers in Education database. Silverman knew that only a handful of jobs were available but hoped that opening these positions would serve as a precedent and facilitate the employment of veterans in other locales. His action signaled the army's intent to make the JROTC an important component of its jobs program.[18]

Powell released his expansion plan in the spring of 1992. That plan called for the phased growth of the JROTC over three years, beginning in 1992. It would bring the JROTC's unit total to 2,900 by 1995.[19] The DOD listed increasing the JROTC presence in needy high schools as a prime goal. Accordingly, the 1993 NDAA authorized special financial assistance to disadvantaged institutions, granting them five years of special aid to defray the cost of instructor salaries. This aid was critical because school budget shortages were the prime obstacle to new program beginnings. The DOD also noted that there were no units in Montana and only one each in Vermont, South Dakota, and Oregon. Five states—Delaware, Iowa, Maine, New Hampshire, and North Dakota—had only two units. The department wanted to address this maldistribution.[20]

The DOD left the detailed planning to the services. True to its tradition, the army got off the mark first. In mid-October 1992, the army contacted the ninety-five schools on its waiting list and offered them a unit. A similar offer was made to cross-enrolled schools. The army's plan had ambitious objectives; it wanted to plant a unit in every state, in every US city with a population above 150,000, and in the nation's hundred largest school systems. It also aimed to redress the program's regional imbalance. The army placed particular emphasis on the Northern Plains and Northeast, which in the past had proved impermeable to the program—the former because of geography and the latter because of the prevailing political culture.[21]

The other services found the DOD's original expansion timeline too condensed and took a more deliberate approach to expansion. Their goals were broadly like the army's. Their objectives included fortifying their presence in disadvantaged schools as well as rectifying the skewed distribution of units. As with the army, their presence was weakest in the Northeast and Northern Plains.[22]

To manage the expanded institutional base, the services needed larger staffs. The army added twenty civilian employees to its staff, a fourfold increase, and received official recognition of the Director of Army Instruction (DAI) position. The air force, navy, and Marine Corps likewise bolstered their management staffs—the air force by 170 percent.[23]

The staffing moves were significant, given the intensifying push within the DOD to trim the workforce. Within the department, every position was scrutinized; most organizations lost people in the process. The growth of JROTC staffs was indicative of the strong backing given to the program by defense leaders. While its managerial apparatus remained small relative to its size and reach, it was more robust than it had been for decades, perhaps more robust than ever.

In the mid-1990s, the DOD abandoned its original expansion target. Growth had entailed huge outlays of money that the DOD had not anticipated. Moreover, after 1992, fiscal stringency, modernization efforts, and an accelerating pace of deployments placed additional stress on the defense budget. Managers scrutinized expenditures to achieve savings. The army's budgetary position was particularly fragile. It absorbed a big blow at the end of 1995 when US forces became involved in a massive operation in the Balkans—Operation Joint Endeavor. The army had to take money from its operating accounts to pay for this operation.[24]

In the end, the DOD had to stop short of its 2,900-unit goal and extend its expansion timeline. Unit strength peaked in 1996 at 2,588 units. This represented a shortfall of about 11 percent, with the army accounting for the entire shortfall.[25] Perhaps the retirement of Colin Powell in September 1994 contributed to the derailing. With Powell's exit, the JROTC lost a powerful advocate. Still, it is doubtful if even Powell's presence could have significantly affected the outcome.

The other services attained their expansion goals. To be sure, they did not escape the fiscal pinch. They eliminated certain activities and curtailed others.[26] Even so, the other services fared better than the army. Several reasons help explain this. First, the other services were not as stressed by budget cuts. Funding for advanced weapons has historically been less prone to reductions than financing to sustain troop strength. The air and sea services were also less involved in contingency operations and deployed less frequently. Second, the air force and navy had been alive to the dangers of overextension from the start and trimmed back their original targets accordingly. As in the 1980s, the navy and air force resisted growth without the requisite resources on hand.

Even with its struggles, the expansion significantly extended the military's reach into the nation's educational system. In the four years after 1992, enrollment grew by almost 81 percent and the program's unit base by 75 percent. In 1992, JROTC units were in 4 percent of American high schools and enrolled fourteen of every thousand students. By 1996, they were in 7.5 percent of high schools and enrolled eighteen of every thousand students. At the same time, units became more robust; the average annual expenditure per cadet rose from $241 to $505 over the course of the expansion.[27]

The services made headway in extending the program into underrepresented regions and states. By 1995, every state had a unit. Progress also occurred on the regional level. New England, the region most resistant to the JROTC, experienced the largest *relative* gains, with the Northern Plains coming in a respectable second. Overseas units also fared well, with their number more than doubling. Most surprising was the army's entry into northeastern cities, one of its longtime objectives. Its creation of units in Buffalo and New York City marked its entrance into New York's public school system.[28]

Nevertheless, the overall distribution of army units remained skewed. The five states recording the greatest *absolute* unit gains were all in the South, already the most overrepresented region. Florida (fifty), North Carolina (forty), Virginia (thirty-seven), Texas (thirty-five), and South Carolina (thirty-three) were the biggest winners. These five states accounted for 40 percent of the expansion nationwide.[29] The JROTC's core thus remained fixed in a swath of states that stretched along the nation's southeastern quadrant.

The army's priorities contained built-in contradictions that stifled efforts to correct the program's regional imbalance. Giving precedence to cross-enrolled schools and schools on the waiting list worked to preserve the distributional status quo. Even without contradictory priorities, however, it is doubtful that unit distribution could have been substantially altered. The JROTC was simply more popular in the South than in other regions.

While the services did not substantially change the regional balance, they did enlarge their presence in inner cities and disadvantaged rural areas. The 1993 NDAA poured $9 million of additional funding into 324 "needy" schools. The army had the largest number of these schools (187), followed by the navy (81), air force (49), and Marine Corps (7). Before 1992, the services were in 409 inner-city schools representing 28 percent of units. Roughly half of the new units, or 515, were in inner cities. Thus, by 1996, 924 units, or 36 percent of all units, were in the inner city. Texas (124) now had the largest number of such units, followed by California (96), Florida (65), Georgia (51), and Maryland (42).[30]

DEMOGRAPHY OF EXPANSION

Minority representation in the JROTC burgeoned during the expansion. By 1996, 60 percent of enrollment consisted of minority students, up from about 50 percent a decade earlier. Minority enrollment in the JROTC was twice that of public high schools in general, which stood at 35 percent at the time. The army still maintained the largest minority enrollment, but its lead over the other services had dwindled.[31]

Locational factors may help explain the army's continuing lead in minority representation. Military posts were a magnet for the JROTC units. This gave the army an advantage because its installations were clustered in the South, the region with the highest military propensity and the largest African American population. While 70 percent of army personnel lived in southern posts, only 55 percent of navy and air force members did. Curricular differences may also have played a role. The technical orientation of the air force and navy programs repelled many minority students.

Female participation in the JROTC also continued to grow. Between 1990 and 1997, the female representation in the Army JROTC climbed from 39 to 44 percent. The other services saw similar gains. The connection between increasing female enrollment and the expansion, however, is difficult to gauge. Female enrollment, after all, had been steadily growing since 1972, when the program was first opened to women.

African American women had a strong affinity for military service and contributed greatly to growing female and minority enrollment. In the mid-1990s, Black women accounted for over 40 percent of enlisted women and almost 20 percent of female commissioned officers in the army. While Black men were underrepresented in the officer corps, African American women were overrepresented. The large number of Black women entering the JROTC was not surprising. In her dissertation about the JROTC in Virginia public schools, Rachelle Perusse offered a profile of a student most likely to be referred to the JROTC by school counselors. That student was "a physically able African American female with a GPA (grade point average) between 2.0 and 3.5 who attend[ed] school on a regular basis and [was] interested in entering the military upon graduation."[32]

A Center for Strategic and International Studies (CSIS) study of Chicago schools found that Black and Hispanic women enrolled in the program at a disproportionately high rate. The opposite was true of Black and Hispanic men, who recoiled at JROTC regulations governing personal grooming and dress. Minority women found much to like in the JROTC. A unit gave them counseling, mentorship, and a chance to lead, which was reflected in the large number of women who held top leadership positions. Nationwide, more than two-thirds of battalion commanders, the highest-ranking cadets, in the Army JROTC were women. An article in the March 4, 1996, edition of the *Los Angeles Times* noted the large number of women and recently arrived immigrants who participated in the JROTC. At Belmont High School, four of the seven top cadet officers were women; the commander was a woman who had recently arrived from Guatemala.[33]

All this suggests that minority women viewed the JROTC in much the same way they did the military—as a place that allowed them to develop their potential. Some had a very different perspective on the matter. They saw minority women's affinity for the military as a reflection of existing societal inequalities. Lack of opportunities elsewhere channeled minority women along paths that more affluent youths tended to avoid.[34]

CAREER ACADEMIES

One initiative launched in the early 1990s to improve the employment prospects of at-risk youths was the JROTC Career Academies Program. This program was a joint venture between the DOD and the Department of Education (DOE) intended to conjoin the training and discipline of the JROTC with the school-within-a-school model used to help low-performing students in traditional high schools.

The career academy concept originated in Philadelphia in 1969 in response to civic disorder. Its focus was on providing entry-level jobs for public school graduates. The idea caught fire in the 1990s as the nation focused on educational reform and the problems of disenfranchised youths. Over the decade, the number of academies rose fifteenfold. Congress, in the School-to-Work Opportunities Act of 1994, identified career academies as a preferred approach to vocational education.[35]

The JROTC Career Academies Program preceded the School-to-Work Opportunities Act by several years. The White House announced the program on May 28, 1992. A press release declared that the DOD and DOE would work with school districts, "particularly urban districts with at-risk students," to create career academies that offered enhanced technical training in conjunction with the JROTC. By the 1994–1995 school year, thirty-eight high schools hosted the JROTC Career Academies. The next year, the army opened another five partnership academies, which were affiliated with Cities-in-Schools Inc. and had one nonuniformed instructor instead of the normal five or ten.[36]

The JROTC Career Academies flourished. By 2000, academies were operating in thirty-three cities and twenty-three states, with an enrollment of 3,800 cadets. In some programs, the occupational focus was military service; teachers informed students of enlistment options and taught military values. Others had a technical focus. Typical of this latter type was the JROTC Academy of Information Technology in Beaumont High School (BHS) in Saint Louis. Beaumont served an area plagued with violence, gangs, and drugs. Thirty-three percent of the households in the area earned less than $12,000 per year, 74 percent received public assistance, and about 87 percent had children who received free or reduced lunches. African American people constituted 99 percent of BHS's 1,300 students, one-third of whom were enrolled in special education, which was the largest instructional unit at BHS.[37]

The JROTC Career Academies blueprint had the following elements: the structure of a school within a school, block scheduling, an integrated vocational and academic curriculum, a low student-to-teacher ratio, a business partnership, common teacher planning, and the incorporation of JROTC staff and curriculum into the academy program. Cadets could choose among a range of occupational fields such as masonry, carpentry, electronics, computer technology, health, and aviation. Participants took discrete course sequences offered in morning and afternoon blocks from instructors who taught solely within the academy. These instructors remained with cadets throughout their high school experience. Small classes facilitated frequent student-faculty interaction. Academy supporters claimed that this created a sense of stability and belonging absent in traditional high schools. The most important aspect of the career academy model, according to federal officials, was the "integration of the vocational technical program with core academic subjects" in a way that allowed "students to see the importance and relevance of their academic subjects to possible future careers." The JROTC curriculum supposedly strengthened the career academy model by integrating academic and vocational instruction with leadership skills.[38]

To their advocates, the JROTC Career Academies were devices for coping with challenges facing the services, school systems, and employers. They aligned with three educational reform initiatives: school restructuring, dropout reduction, and school-to-work transition. The highly structured academies kept at-risk students in school by providing a nurturing environment, developing vocational skills, and forming good workplace attitudes.[39]

As educational reform grew in saliency, school-to-work programs became more popular among educators, who saw them as effective means to address employer complaints about undereducated high school graduates entering the workforce. At the same time, Congress was searching for ways to cushion the effects of military downsizing on communities and enable an orderly transition to the post–Cold War economy. The Pentagon sought to find employment openings for veterans who had been thrust into the job market while the public anticipated a peace dividend that could fund social programs and other domestic needs. The JROTC Career Academies responded to all these challenges.[40]

The JROTC Career Academies, however, had mixed success in adhering to the career academy model. Structural changes proved easier to effect than instructional changes, which tended to be time-consuming and expensive. The creation of schools within schools, the introduction of block scheduling, and the establishment of business advisory boards usually occurred quite quickly. On the other hand, the identification of an occupational focus; the integration of academic, vocational, and military instruction; and meaningful input from business partnerships came more slowly, if at all. Budgetary pressures, the lack of military retirees with teaching certificates, personnel turbulence, and state testing mandates also impeded strict adherence to the model.[41]

Nevertheless, academies produced positive outcomes. Attendance rates increased by 10 to 20 percent. Grades and graduation rates also rose, albeit less sharply. Explanations for these results varied. Some attributed success to the vocational component of the curriculum. Others emphasized the contributions of teachers who maintained a close watch over their charges. RAND stressed the value of the nurturing environment that pervaded the academies.[42]

Army observers gave a more restrained endorsement of the academies. While acknowledging the impressive results attained in some schools, they noted that academies were less successful in others. The degree of success achieved was dependent on, inter alia, the vitality of the partnership formed with the business sponsor. In many cases, this partnership remained weak or nonexistent. Moreover, researchers who evaluated career academies floundered in a sea of confounding variables. It was difficult to determine causation in a program whose boundaries were so fluid and amorphous.[43]

CORRECTIONAL FACILITIES

The planting of JROTC units in juvenile correctional facilities was another experiment launched in the 1990s. Civilian-run disciplinary centers had been a part of the educational landscape since the nineteenth century. In the modern era, they reached their peak of popularity in the 1990s, just as the JROTC began its expansion. Their luster gradually wore off, however. Their outcomes were not as enduring as once believed.

The JROTC's involvement with correctional facilities was limited. The army was the only service to participate, and it partnered with only three correctional centers: Birchwood High School in West Columbia, South Carolina (1993), John H. Smyth High School in Hanover, Virginia (1996), and Okeechobee Juvenile Justice Center in Okeechobee, Florida (2000). Nevertheless, these units had symbolic significance. They exemplified the JROTC's ideal of preparing disadvantaged and troubled youths to function in the adult world.

The units had differing degrees of success. The army judged the unit at Birchwood to have been very effective. It attributed that accomplishment, in part, to strong support from the state government. The governor's attendance at the unit's activation ceremony on October 1, 1993, symbolized this support. Birchwood was an accredited high school that adopted the standard JROTC curriculum. Its program was highly structured. Discipline was enforced through a merit and demerit system. Cadets' days were regulated from the time they woke up at 5:30 a.m. until they went to bed at 9:30 p.m. Cadets wore uniforms seven days a week. Their conduct was monitored continuously. A typical day consisted of early morning physical training, drill, six hours of academic classes, and homework in the evening.

Cadets averaged an eight-month stay at Birchwood. Upon their release, they had a Birchwood-appointed liaison officer to ease their transition back into their communities. They also took part in a Mentor at the Gate program, designed to steer discharged cadets away from dysfunctional relationships and activities. The overall student recidivism rate was 73 percent but among Birchwood's JROTC cadets it was only 2 percent.[44]

Smyth's setup was similar to Birchwood's. Like Birchwood, Smyth adopted the standard JROTC course. Cadets wore uniforms throughout the week, followed a highly structured routine, and experienced continuous monitoring. Cadets remained longer at Smyth than at Birchwood—eighteen to twenty-four months rather than eight. Smyth, too, had a program to ease the students' transition back to school. It diverged from Birchwood in that it required all cadets to enroll in the JROTC.[45]

The cadet recidivism rate at Smyth was low—15.6 percent in fiscal year 2004—although not as low as Birchwood's. The compulsory nature of its program helps explain this. So does Smyth's admission policy, which was not as selective as Birchwood's. Unlike the latter, it took in many students who had committed serious offenses. Nevertheless, state authorities allowed cadets to participate in public events outside the center; it was the only correctional facility in the state accorded this privilege.[46]

Officials at Smyth and Birchwood ascribed much of their success to the JROTC program. Wearing the uniform and belonging to a distinct unit boosted self-esteem. Physical exercise and extracurricular activities provided emotional and physical outlets. Discipline and leadership training engendered respect for authority and teamwork. The curriculum developed patriotism and respect for law and order. Through the mentorship of instructors, cadets picked up values, attitudes, and work habits that prepared them for adulthood.[47]

Additional insight into Smyth's and Birchwood's success can be gained by comparing it to an unsuccessful experiment. The Okeechobee Juvenile Detention Center was a privately operated, state-supported institution that was part of the public school system. The army approved Okeechobee's request for a National Defense Cadet Corps (NDCC) unit in January 1999. The center received a JROTC unit the following year. The unit's existence, however, was short-lived. By 2003, it had been closed.[48]

The army attributed the failure to several things. First, the student body was not amenable to remediation. Unlike Smyth and Birchwood, the center took in students with acute behavioral problems. Second, the turbulence at Okeechobee was greater. Students rotated through Okeechobee at a rapid rate, leaving little time for instructors and the program to work their effects. Finally, the unit did not operate in a regular high school environment. The center had the unmistakable flavor of a prison, whereas Smyth and Birchwood had a more benign air about them.[49]

STEM INITIATIVES

Guiding students to pursue science, technology, engineering, and mathematics (STEM) disciplines was another priority in the expansion. Since 1945, the federal government had pushed science and math education. The proliferation of nuclear arsenals and the Soviet launch of Sputnik in 1957 intensified that push. Congress passed the National Defense Education Act (NDEA) in 1958, unleashing a flood of federal funds for programs that promoted science and engineering education.[50] The STEM emphasis resonated with the services, which were struggling to attract people capable of being trained to repair and operate advanced weapons systems.[51] In 1996, the Army Science Board (ASB) published a study titled *The Science and Engineering Requirements for Military Officers and Civilian Personnel in the High-Tech Army of Today and Tomorrow*, which focused attention on the army's shrinking supply of technologically literate soldiers. The ASB suggested several ways to increase this supply. The JROTC was one of them.[52]

The army partnered with the National Science Center (NSC) to improve science and math education in schools. In August 1992, General Gordon Sullivan, the chief of staff of the army (CSA), endorsed the center's outreach program and directed the army's NSC task force to explore ways to enlarge it. That fall, the army started a pilot project with two components: the Preview Discovery Center (PDC) and the educational outreach program, both of which aligned with the America 2000 strategy. The goal of these ventures was to make American students "first in the world in mathematics and science achievement."[53]

The PDC hosted exhibits that encouraged young people to study math and applied science. Of more immediate import to the army, however, were the educational outreach programs. These programs included a science-by-mail program, interactive satellite teleconferencing programs, summer and special workshops, and a Mobile Discovery Center van.[54]

The CSA's pilot program inserted mathematics and science workshops into summer camps and the JROTC curriculum. Every camp, except those overseas, now included the NSC's math and science modules. The pilot aimed to motivate more than educate. Most instruction was of the hands-on, interactive variety. The math and science modules featured short problem-solving and simulation exercises such as the construction of a flashlight using single series and single parallel circuits, the building of a telegraph key, and the transmission of a message in Morse code.[55]

CURRICULAR REVISION

Curriculum revision continued during the expansion. Its focus was on inner-city schools. This meant making the program of instruction more socially relevant. A comparison of the 1990 and 1993 versions of the army's curriculum demonstrates how one service attempted to do this.[56]

In the new version, the army deleted most objectives aimed at recruiting or the acquisition of basic military skills. In their stead, it substituted subjects that addressed the needs of urban schools: life management skills, goal setting, conflict resolution, daily planning, and personal finance. Accelerated learning and Winning Colors, a personality assessment tool that helped cadets identify behavioral strengths and weaknesses and clarify career plans, were also part of the package. Finally, the army aligned its curriculum with the America 2000 strategy, building lessons on communication skills, cultural diversity, technology, nutrition, government, the environment, geography, and career preparation.[57]

Summer camps flourished after the army began funding them in 1992. Attendance rose from eight thousand to nineteen thousand over three years. The army distanced camps from military training by banning tactical and weapons training while encouraging adventure and leadership training. The idea was to bring JROTC camps closer to summer camps conducted in the civilian world. Outward Bound was the model. That program taught survival skills and fostered teamwork, perseverance, and leadership.[58]

As schools came under more pressure to improve performance, they experimented with outcome-based education, faculty development programs, alternative scheduling models, and instructional technology. The JROTC got caught up in these efforts. It was especially keen on instructional technology. The services imported interactive video technology into classrooms and made more use of computer-assisted instruction. Technology-enhanced instruction made classes more fun for students and less burdensome for instructors.[59]

The JROTC also began to sync its classes with block scheduling, permitting longer classes and a deeper exploration of subject matter. The traditional fifty-minute period, many educators believed, was too short to accommodate teaching strategies like cooperative learning, laboratory experiments, and long-term group projects. To enable cadets to remain enrolled during skipped semesters, the services introduced programmed texts.[60]

The services continued their push for academic credit during the expansion. They bolstered the academic content of the curriculum and accelerated instructor certification. These efforts paid dividends in states like Florida, North Carolina, and Hawaii, which granted credit to cadets for physical education, health, government, civics, history, and, in the case of the air force and navy, science. The precedents established in these states, it was hoped, might prove useful in negotiations with others. This hope proved illusory. To be sure, awarding equivalency credit for physical education remained a common practice. But beyond that, the results were modest. By the mid-1990s, less than a third of the states granted academic credit for the JROTC.[61]

The air force and army blamed higher educational standards and the decentralized educational system for the problem. "There is no answer [to the problem] that will work for all states," one air force official noted. "Individual states and school districts are not in concert with their approach to credits." Another complicating factor was instructor aversion to challenging subject matter. Difficult courses repelled students. While some critics judged the reading level of JROTC texts to be too low, instructors thought it was too high. They preferred activities over classroom work; instead of having cadets read about environmental issues, they conducted field trips to landfills and treatment plants so cadets could observe environmental science in action.[62]

There was ambivalence about the academic portion of the curriculum. On the one hand, instructors wanted core academic credit for JROTC classes. On the other, they wanted to make instruction fun and exciting. But it was difficult to combine academic rigor with entertainment in one course. When attempts were made to achieve that combination, the result was often a course that fell short in both areas.[63]

Moreover, many instructors were ill-equipped to teach academic courses. Roughly half of the noncommissioned officers (NCOs) in the army program, for example, did not have baccalaureate degrees. An even larger percentage lacked state teaching certification. Earning teaching credentials took time, and many instructors did not have that time. They performed a host of duties unrelated to academic instruction in areas like administration, counseling, advising, and coaching. The ground forces suffered more than the sea and air forces. Retired naval and air force officers were more likely to have STEM-related degrees than their army and marine counterparts, making it easier for the former to gain academic credit for their courses.

CONTINUITY

Despite efforts to reconfigure the program, the daily routine of the average unit remained relatively stable. The historian William Reese noted that despite the mountain of educational reform literature and the work of several generations of professional educationalists, life in the classroom changed very slowly. Time-honored practices and traditions endured.[64]

The same was true for the JROTC. The services continued to see the program's principal value not in the subjects it offered but in the values it instilled, the attitudes it developed, and the attributes it formed. And cadets learned these things by belonging to an organization that gave them confidence, a feeling of accomplishment, and a sense of structure in their lives.[65]

Thus, traditional activities continued their predominance. Community service projects remained a JROTC mainstay. Cadets continued to raise money for charities, assist with blood drives, visit homes for the elderly, and usher at civic events. In the 1990s, these activities became more salient as schools incorporated community service into their curricula. Drill and leadership training also retained their centrality, giving cadets a chance to lead and work as a member of a team.[66]

The JROTC often encountered difficulties when it ventured away from its traditional focus and embraced core academic subjects. History was a particular problem because the services were wont to combine history with heritage and try to both educate and inspire. Combining these two disparate and often conflicting goals did not always translate well in an academic setting.

OPPOSITION

Attacks on the JROTC intensified during the expansion. The core of anti-JROTC opposition consisted of an eclectic assortment of groups, including the American Friends Service Committee (AFSC), Committee for Conscientious Objection, Center for Defense Information, Veterans for Peace, War Registers League, Gay and Lesbian Alliance Against Defamation (GLAAD), and the Project on Youth and Nonmilitary Opportunities (Project YANO).

These actors waged campaigns to block the creation of new units and close existing ones. They furnished kits, press releases, training sessions, and other assistance to like-minded citizens.[67]

The release of a report titled "Making Soldiers in the Public Schools: An Analysis of the JROTC Curriculum" in April 1995 revitalized the anti-JROTC movement. The report, published by the AFSC, was the work of Catherine Lutz and Leslie Barnett, both associated with the University of North Carolina, Chapel Hill. Its message was that the JROTC did far more to obstruct than promote learning. While conceding the altruistic motives of many instructors, the authors argued that pressure on the DOD to defend its budget, provide employment to veterans, and recruit overrode purer motives. Like the report of Steven Selden and Alan Feldman in the mid-1970s, the report of Lutz and Barnett encapsulated the arguments used to counter the program's growth in the mid-1990s.[68]

Schools with JROTC, they asserted, suffered because the costs of the program outweighed its benefits. While schools received aid, they incurred substantial obligations. Schools had to provide facilities and pay for utilities and salaries, diverting resources away from more pressing needs. The effects of maintaining a unit were especially pernicious in poor schools, where budgets were stretched to the breaking point.[69]

The services filled the curriculum with subjects of little academic merit. Drill consumed more time than any other activity. Other activities of doubtful academic value included battlefield tours, military base visits, and parades. Lutz and Barnett excoriated the JROTC history module for being biased, jingoistic, racist, and shallow. Citizenship instruction, they charged, conflated democracy and patriotism with military service. Textbooks were written at a low reading level, and the messages conveyed were uncomplicated, even simplistic. Leadership training communicated authoritarian values. Rather than teaching leadership as understood by most civilians, it stressed conformity and obedience to authority.[70]

Low selection standards for instructors were another issue. Applicants had to be certified by the military, which placed as much weight on military criteria as it did on educational attainment. The authors also lamented the surrender of autonomy that came with a unit. Schools had to select instructors from an approved list of candidates and accept a military curriculum. In addition, there were few female instructors, although women made up over 40 percent of enrollment.[71]

Claims of success were inflated and unproven. There was no evidence that the JROTC produced better Americans. Indeed, the services did not even define what producing better Americans meant. Neither was there proof that the JROTC reduced drug abuse, raised attendance, boosted graduation rates, or improved grade point averages. The attrition rate was so high that it confounded meaningful analysis, in any case. Finally, they blasted the services for concealing the JROTC's role in recruiting. It was difficult to distinguish between recruiting and the program's stated goal of creating favorable attitudes toward careers in the armed forces. The two seemed identical.[72]

The report of Lutz and Barnett did not cover all the bases of criticism. GLAAD excoriated the program because it denied civil rights to gays and lesbians and brought homophobic bigotry into high schools. Project YANO charged that the JROTC was antilabor, noting how the program undermined the collective bargaining power of public school teachers.[73]

The barbs of critics sometimes had palpable effects. The critique of Lutz and Barnett led to the revision of the army's history text. Usually, however, the criticism worked in more subtle ways. It seeded the environment in which discussions about the JROTC occurred and reinforced the dissociation between citizenship and military service.

Opposition also came from influential people in Congress and the DOD who objected to military involvement in social programs. To these observers, subsidizing the JROTC only diverted time and resources away from more pressing priorities. Robert Dornan, a conservative Republican congressman from California, questioned the wisdom of doubling the size of the JROTC at a time when drastic cuts were being made in the defense budget. Funds earmarked for the program could be better spent upgrading operational readiness or modernizing the nation's aging arsenal. The SASC inserted into the 1996 NDAA a provision slashing the JROTC budget by 10 percent. The Air Force Association denounced the reductions, warning that the air force alone would have to close eighty-three units and exclude nine hundred students if the cuts were allowed to stand. It took the intervention of Senator Sam Nunn and the Joint Chiefs of Staff to restore the funding.[74]

Some officers criticized the program because it smacked of "tin soldiering." High school students wearing chrome helmets, carrying demilitarized rifles, and executing intricate drill movements on the gymnasium floor made a mockery of the military profession. Furthermore, the training was useless from a military standpoint. One retired army general scored the program for its emphasis on drill and display. The backbone of the JROTC, he asserted, was "training right out of 1895; rifles, trinket-laden uniforms, drill and ceremonies, plus a modicum of physical fitness." He wanted to "raise cadet sights above winning drill competitions to computer-aided skill acquisition."[75]

Defense officials also questioned the program's worth. The JROTC gave the army only 255 more recruits, representing an 8 percent increase, in the 1995–1996 school year than it had in 1991–1992, even though JROTC enrollment had increased by 62 percent and the number of graduating seniors by 16 percent. Neither did the program's contribution to officer recruiting keep pace with the expansion. JROTC input into the Army SROTC advanced course rose by only 12 percent.

Lost or ignored in this discussion of outcomes was a factor that contributed to these lackluster recruiting results: the sensitivity of JROTC enlistment rates to changes in recruit quality metrics. In the early 1990s, enlistment standards were high. At the same time, large numbers of at-risk students flowed into the JROTC. Many had academic, medical, or legal problems that barred them from military service. One can readily see that simple correlations of enlistment rates with JROTC enrollment gains were not very helpful—at least not as a measure of motivation to enlist.[76]

JROTC proponents refuted their detractors and continued to tout the program as an antidote to the ills afflicting high schools. In the early 1990s, it was the JROTC's supposed effects on the minds and characters of disadvantaged youth that supporters emphasized. The program steered inner-city youth away from guns and violence and imparted to them a sense of purpose, hope, and accomplishment. The JROTC purportedly became a surrogate family for students who were wards of the state or who lived in a household without a male role model. Educators heralded the disciplinary value of the JROTC. It was useful for the rehabilitation of refractory students and as a cure for delinquency and behavioral disorders. Supporters continued to emphasize its success in guiding cadets toward military service. Despite the enlistment drop-off in the early 1990s, cadets remained four or five times more likely than their contemporaries to enter military service.[77]

In its battle with critics, the JROTC enjoyed one huge advantage: it was the only program of its type with the reach and resources to address the problems facing the nation's educational system. It had no viable organizational competitors.

After the Gulf War, the push to align the size, structure, and missions of the armed forces with new post–Cold War realities gathered momentum. In this environment, the JROTC assumed a renewed importance. It seemed well suited to addressing urgent internal problems and demonstrating the military's relevance in the new age. With the backing of Congress and the administration, the program embarked on an expansion. In absolute terms, it was the largest in JROTC history. Between 1992 and 1996, the DOD created more than 1,400 units and saw enrollment rise by over 160,000 cadets. In the expansion, the DOD targeted at-risk students living in disadvantaged communities.

Later in the decade, euphoria over democracy's triumph over totalitarianism gave way to a more somber assessment of the international scene. Pressure on the defense budget and growing recruiting deficits placed an increasing strain on the services. By the end of the decade, the all-volunteer force was experiencing a crisis. Once again, the JROTC had to adjust its priorities to accommodate new conditions and new demands. This will be dealt with in the final chapter.

11

JROTC Enters the Twenty-First Century

In the late 1990s, Congress continued its efforts to reduce the deficit and harvest a peace dividend. Lawmakers sparingly doled out money for defense. The Department of Defense (DOD) budget contracted by 14 percent between fiscal years 1997 and 1999.[1] During this time, the armed forces experienced acute recruiting shortfalls. The army suffered the most. By 1999, it was falling ten thousand short of its goal. The quality of new recruits also deteriorated. With jobs plentiful in a resurgent economy, the services struggled to fill their ranks with capable people. Between 1992 and 2000, the proportion of new army recruits with a "high quality" classification fell from 78 to 52 percent.[2]

These recruiting woes stemmed from the post–Cold War drawdown, a robust civilian economy, competition from higher education, a dearth of recruiting resources, and attitudinal and demographic changes. The size of the recruiting pool was significantly smaller in 1999 than it had been a decade earlier, because of declining fertility rates in the 1970s. The propensity to serve also plummeted. With the economy booming, military service seemed less attractive. Congress became alarmed about recruiting deficits. Its anxiety peaked in fiscal year 1999 when recruiting shortages seemingly spiraled out of control. Congress reacted by approving more generous enlistment incentives, granting sizable pay raises, and enlarging the JROTC.[3]

THE JROTC UNDER SIEGE

After 1995, government support for the JROTC weakened. In a 1997 report, the Government Accountability Office (GAO) condemned the DOD's underwriting of the JROTC. It characterized the JROTC as a social program with little military value and recommended its discontinuance. The services' commitment to the JROTC also waned. The Army Cadet Command (USACC) came under congressional scrutiny in the spring of 1999 when the House Armed Service Committee (HASC) received "anecdotal information" indicating that units were being "under-resourced." Instructors had to buy classroom equipment with personal funds, and cadets were not issued uniforms. In May 1999, Senator Ernest Hollings disclosed that he was "receiving reports from students, educators, and parents from all across South Carolina" telling him that cuts to JROTC funding were "adversely affecting" the program. Hollings pointedly asked the service chiefs what was happening.[4]

The navy denied there was anything amiss. Its 1998 JROTC budget was only 2 percent below that of 1997. Naval officials admitted, though, that maintaining funding at its existing level brought problems. Because of the expansion of the early 1990s, the portion of the budget spent on instructor salaries had risen from 54 percent to 85 percent. Since salaries were set by law, the navy looked to areas such as uniforms and staffing to reduce costs. When asked by a Senate committee if the JROTC could be expanded, the navy replied that it could not. The demand was there, but the cost would be exorbitant. Growth could only occur at the expense of other national security imperatives.[5]

EXPANSION

Nevertheless, the recruiting crisis at the end of the decade resulted in new importance being attached to the JROTC. An expansion of the junior program was a key element of the multifaceted congressional reaction to the crisis. The congressional plan for the JROTC called for the phased growth of the program to the statutory limit of 3,500 units between 2000 and 2006.[6]

After the expansion was underway, an impatient Congress pushed for accelerated progress. It urged the defense secretary to beat the 2006 deadline and revise the service distribution scheme. Growth should not be sidetracked by service-imposed limits; units should be allocated on the basis of the service's eagerness to expand. Congress also pushed to raise the statutory unit cap above 3,500. Both Donald Rumsfeld and his deputy, Paul Wolfowitz, gave Congress their support. Accordingly, the 2002 National Defense Authorization Act (NDAA) abolished the 3,500-unit ceiling and cleared the way for greater and faster growth.[7]

Congress, now struggling to support the manpower requirements of the global war on terror (GWOT), exerted more pressure on the services to expand in the 2007 NDAA. It directed the DOD to determine if legislative changes since 1976 permitted a more extensive use of cross enrollment. The DOD did not like the cross-enrollment expedient but grudgingly took the hint.[8]

The impetus for growth came from several sources. The recruiting crisis of the late 1990s, of course, was the most powerful stimulus. All three services missed their recruiting goals in 1999. One facet of this crisis was flagging minority officer recruiting. In 2000, Hispanic people constituted less than 3 percent of military officers but 13 percent of the U.S. population as a whole. Shortfalls in African American officers were less severe but still worrisome. The services' repeated attempts to recruit more Black officers over the last three decades had achieved limited success.[9]

A growing civilian-military divide also fueled the expansion. In the 1990s, pundits complained that civil-military relations were deteriorating. The society was becoming increasingly estranged from the military. Few among the nation's political elites had firsthand military experience, and the percentage of veterans in the general population was at a historic low. The closure of military installations and the concentration of forces in a few megabases within the United States added to the isolation. This retreat into isolated enclaves created a garrison mentality.[10] In this environment, public outreach took on increased importance, and, once again, the government looked to the JROTC for help.[11]

To others, the JROTC appeared as a way to advance national educational objectives. Supporters billed the program as the centerpiece of the DOD's "commitment to America's Promise for Youth," an outgrowth of the Presidents' Summit for America's Future (1997) that had the avowed aim of building "the mind and character of every child, from every background."[12] Senator Strom Thurmond believed that the educational benefits of the program were so pronounced that it should be "spread . . . to every corner of the Nation."[13]

Public anxiety about disorder and violence in public schools was also a spur to growth. Incidents like the one at Columbine High School (Colorado) suggested that public schools were dangerous places, racked by crime and violence. Although the frequency of such incidents decreased between 1992 and 1999, public toleration of such behavior declined more sharply.[14]

Finally, public demand fueled growth. In 2002, almost halfway into the expansion, the waiting list for new units still registered seven hundred schools. The DOD's problem was not enlarging the JROTC but managing its growth.[15] The DOD's management of the list had elicited recrimination. The Senate Armed Services Committee (SASC) charged that the department lacked coherent policies for selecting schools from the waiting list. When asked, defense officials admitted as much. The SASC pushed Rumsfeld to make the unit selection process more transparent.[16]

Senator Thurmond had been sharply critical of the DOD's initial coolness toward growth. At one congressional hearing, he informed David Chu, the assistant secretary of defense (ASD) for manpower, that schools had been on the waiting list for a decade but were no closer to obtaining a unit. It was unconscionable that some schools remained on a list for years while others attained units in a few months. Chu, however, remained focused on attaining "geographical equity." Giving schools in overrepresented states priority would penalize schools in underrepresented states. The only way to promote geographical diversity while paring down waiting lists was to conduct another expansion. But Chu opposed this option; the JROTC was already "prudently funded and properly scoped" to attain defense goals. In the end, Congress overrode DOD objections. It removed the 3,500-unit unit cap and kept up the pressure to extend the program to all schools that wanted it, regardless of location.[17]

While the expansion of the early twenty-first century did not achieve greater geographical equity, it brought a more equitable distribution of units among the services. By 2006, units were spread among the services in the approximate proportions specified by law, with the army having slightly less than half of all units and the navy and air force each having about a quarter. Now, unit ratios aligned closely with service troop strengths. The *enrollment* distribution, though, remained skewed. The army still enrolled 56 percent of all cadets in 2006, down only 4 percent from 1990.[18]

The expansion did not proceed smoothly. School budget shortfalls and the No Child Left Behind (NCLB) Act forced unit disestablishments and disrupted the opening of new units. To keep the expansion on track, more units had to be added than anticipated. The army, for example, had to create ninety-four new units in fiscal year 2005 instead of the projected forty-five, to meet the expansion timeline.[19]

The bare-bones management structures complicated growth. During the 1990s, the services had shed administrative staff to reduce costs and save manpower. The navy led the way, cutting its JROTC management apparatus by 50 percent. These cuts caused span-of-control issues, leaving the services struggling to control more units with depleted staffs.[20]

The Army JROTC underwent a significant change when it was placed under the newly created Army Accessions Command (USAAC) in 2002. The USAAC oversaw the recruiting and initial entry training of the army's officers and enlisted soldiers.[21] The ROTC command viewed this "extra" layer of command with skepticism since it inhibited the USACC's direct access to the Pentagon and damaged the army's image on college and high school campuses. As its name suggests, the USAAC was primarily about recruiting, which made many educators skittish.[22]

PUBLIC MILITARY INSTITUTES

One of the most publicized developments in the new century was the emergence of military institutes in public schools. While private military institutes had been part of the JROTC since 1916, military institutes in public schools were a more recent phenomenon. To gain institute status, schools had to offer a four-year course of military training, organize their student bodies into cadet corps, enroll all students in the JROTC, and adopt military standards of conduct and dress.[23]

The first public school to acquire institute status was the Franklin Military School in Richmond. Formed as an alternative high school within the Richmond public school system, it opened in September 1980. The navy established two public institutes in 1981—one in Saint Louis and the other in Sandy Hook, New Jersey. Seventeen years elapsed before the army set up a fourth institute in Kenosha, Wisconsin (1998).[24]

It was the introduction of the military institutes in the Chicago Public School (CPS) system that focused national attention on this educational model. The city of Chicago, to improve the academic performance of students from low-income, minority neighborhoods, created the Chicago Military Academy–Bronzeville in 1999.[25] The CPS model quickly caught on and spread across Chicago and to other cities. Eight more cities had established institutes by 2007. In Oakland, the California National Guard joined with the city administration to found the Oakland Military Institute in 2001.[26]

In both Chicago and Oakland, the mayors—Richard Daley and Jerry Brown—played leading roles in creating the institutes. The product of a Jesuit high school, Brown believed that a controlled, disciplined environment was key to success in inner-city schools. In a military academy, he remarked, "Everywhere you look, you're reminded of what you're supposed to do." When you come from a community with "dope dealers on the corners and a low rate of college attendance, you need something with a strong focus."[27]

In Chicago, a prime objective was preparing students for postsecondary education.[28] Within a few years of adopting the military institute model, Chicago authorities began reporting rising student achievement levels and graduation rates. The chief executive of the CPS, Arne Duncan, reported that in the 2007–2008 school year, the graduation rate in Chicago's institutes exceeded the district average by a substantial margin: 94 versus 84 percent. In Philadelphia, eleventh-grade cadets at the Elverson Military Academy achieved even more remarkable results. Seventy percent of Elverson's students attained the basic level on the state's math test, compared to 41 percent for the district. On the reading test, the spread was 88 percent to 58 percent.[29]

The outcomes were not always as clear-cut as officials claimed, however. The studies underlying these claims had restricted the field of tabulation to institutes that enjoyed stable management. It was unclear if success was due more to the continuity of management or to the adoption of the military model. Other instances of success were attributable to selectivity. Chicago institutes, for example, accepted only one in ten applicants.[30]

Not all institutes were located in the inner city or focused on disadvantaged students. The navy's Delaware Military Academy (DMA) accepted applicants from across the state. Its student body was 18 percent African American, 2 percent Hispanic, and 80 percent Caucasian (2009). The DMA was geared toward good students who wanted to learn in a structured, disciplined environment. At the Sarasota Military Academy (SMA), students spanned the socioeconomic spectrum. About 10 percent received partly or wholly subsidized lunches. The student body, although predominantly Caucasian, was more diverse than Sarasota County as a whole. The academy reported remarkable testing results. Ninety percent of its students passed the state math test (FCAT); only Florida's school for the gifted attained better results.

Nevertheless, the SMA and DMA were the exceptions that proved the rule. The demand for military institutes was the greatest in distressed areas, and it was there that the military model reportedly had its most beneficial effects.[31] Jeffrey Mirel asserted that city leaders adopted radical reforms like military institutes because "the problems in urban schools [were] so severe and [had] gone on so long."[32] They simply saw no alternative.

NDCC RESURGENCE

In the expansion of the new century, the National Defense Cadet Corps (NDCC) experienced a resurgence. After 1964, the program began a sharp decline. By 1987, it was on the brink of extinction. Only two units, with a combined enrollment of 240 cadets, remained. It began to revive in 2000. By 2007, there were twenty-five units—all army—with 3,750 cadets. Most schools created NDCC units with the expectation of someday gaining JROTC status.[33]

The most ambitious scheme to establish NDCC programs occurred in Georgia. Governor Sonny Montgomery jump-started NDCC growth by authorizing special funds for each of the state's thirteen congressional districts. He chose the army's program because of its willingness to locate in poor rural areas. The other services were not so inclined.[34]

MIDDLE SCHOOLS

One controversial development in the new century was the growth of military involvement in elementary and middle schools. To be sure, this was not a new development. For decades, the JROTC units had interacted with middle and elementary schools. These initiatives, however, were local and drew no support from the services.[35]

In 2000, the relationship between the JROTC and middle and elementary schools became more formal. The army partnered with Junior Achievement to create the Junior Achievement National Military Role Model Program (JANMRMP). In this program, cadets from the SROTC and JROTC entered middle and elementary schools to teach life skills and warn against drug use. The DOD saw the JANMRMP as a way to "reconnect America with its military." A project of greater scope was the Adopt-a-School Program, introduced by the army in 2005. Under this program, units started mentorship programs in middle and elementary schools, teaching life skills and citizenship.[36]

Cities also sponsored middle school units. By February 2008, Baltimore, Chicago, Dallas, Houston, Fort Worth, Clear Creek (Texas), Lancaster (Texas), Tulsa, Wichita, Atlanta, Columbus (Georgia), Richmond, Jacksonville, and Miami had independent middle school programs. There were undoubtedly others, but, since middle school units were not officially recognized, they escaped federal notice.[37]

Chicago led the way. It had eighteen middle school units by 2006. Wichita also built a strong program. By May 2007, it had eleven middle school units with a combined enrollment of 1,400 cadets. The Wichita Middle School Leadership Program employed certified teachers as instructors and offered a curriculum like the JROTC's.[38] It had a strong extracurricular component. Cadets participated in drill competitions, leadership camps, academic tournaments, and community service projects. Principals claimed that the program reduced disciplinary problems, raised attendance rates, and fostered order in the classroom. Some middle schools gave up teacher allocations to start a military unit.[39]

Fort Worth founded the Junior Cadet Corps (JCC). The JCC began with six middle schools and 600 students in 2002; it grew to eleven schools and 1,300 students by 2007. Its purpose was to curb gang activity, reduce the dropout rate, and improve student behavior.[40] The Dallas–Fort Worth area soon became a focal point for middle school military training. The first annual National Middle School Instructors' Conference took place there in January 2008. Instructors from Chicago, Wichita, Dallas, Fort Worth, Houston, Clear Creek, and Lancaster attended. The conference promoted the standardization of middle school units across the country and began a campaign to secure the DOD's official recognition of their programs.[41]

CURRICULAR REVISIONS

In early 2000, the army began a major curricular redesign. The constant curricular tweaks over the last decade had created a patchwork and outdated curriculum.[42] To rationalize its program, the army organized its offerings by academic subject instead of by LET (class) levels. Modules included Leadership, Life Management, Wellness, Geography, Citizenship, and American History. This move signaled a growing recognition of the importance of academics to the program. For decades, academic offerings had been a type of smokescreen—a device to allow the military to get its foot into the classroom door. Pressure generated by school reform now forced a reconsideration of this perspective.

The army hoped that, with its revision, it could receive core credit for courses in civics and social studies. This hope proved illusory. The NCLB Act

(2001) restricted the teaching of core subjects to credentialed teachers. The army then returned its focus to noncore subjects. But educators resisted this effort also, fearing that they might be displaced by the JROTC instructors. In the end, little changed as far as credit was concerned.[43]

The navy and air force had an advantage over the army in the pursuit of credit. Both offered more courses oriented toward science, technology, engineering, and mathematics (STEM) and employed more qualified instructors. In 2008, 77 percent of air force instructors, for example, had baccalaureate or associate degrees; 98 percent of its officers had at least a master's degree. Not surprisingly, the air force and navy received more academic credit than the other services for their courses.[44]

Nevertheless, efforts at curriculum revision did bring some benefits. Most importantly, they facilitated regional accreditation. By mid-decade, all programs had been accredited. The Marine Corps was the first to attain accreditation in the early winter of 2005. It was followed by the army in June 2005, the air force in September 2005, and the navy in December 2006. The NCLB Act made such accreditation key to the JROTC's continued viability.[45]

The JROTC's renewed emphasis on STEM education was part of a wider national campaign to produce scientifically and technologically literate young people for the workforce.[46] As the pace of globalization was accelerating, the country's STEM educational base was deteriorating.[47] The report of the Hart-Rudman Commission (2001) identified the deterioration of STEM education as the "gravest threat to . . . national security." The America Competes Act (2007), designed to produce STEM-trained talent for industry, attacked this problem by increasing federal investment in STEM education programs at the National Science Foundation and in the Department of Education (DOE).[48]

The military also needed STEM talent. The shortage of STEM-trained specialists for the operational forces and defense laboratories kept growing. The army found it difficult to address its deficits because of competing fiscal priorities, most notably the GWOT. In fact, the army temporarily ceased its support of the National Science Center (NSC) and eliminated math and science modules in the JROTC.[49]

The army's interest in STEM revived in late 2006, when its Engineer Branch began complaining about shortages of certified engineers. It had been compelled to commission criminal justice and humanities majors, people who were manifestly unfit to take on the more complex jobs of the Engineer Branch. As a result, the Army JROTC reestablished links with the NSC and entered a partnership with the Hispanic Engineer National Achievement

Awards Corporation (HENAAC, 2008), an organization of Hispanic STEM professionals. It also incorporated *America's Army*—a video game developed by the Army's Office of Economic Manpower and Analysis to stimulate interest in STEM—into its curriculum.[50]

The centerpiece of the air force's STEM effort was the Aerospace and Technology Honors Camp (2002). Aerospace firms, air force bases, and SROTC-affiliated colleges hosted these camps, which were open to rising juniors and sophomores.[51] The navy held Science and Technology Camps. It partnered with Embry-Riddle Aeronautical University in Daytona Beach and the University of San Diego in this effort. Cadets took computer science and engineering classes, participated in robotics competitions, and took part in a variety of other hands-on activities.[52]

CAREER AND TECHNICAL EDUCATION

In the new century, the JROTC became more involved in career and technical education (CTE). Since the publication of *A Nation at Risk* in 1983, workforce readiness had been a focus of educational-policy discussions. Employers sought workers who were equal to the demands of the emerging global, knowledge-based economy. A growing number of states began categorizing the JROTC as part of the CTE track. By 2009, thirteen states had done so. This presented the program with both opportunities and difficulties.[53]

On the negative side, CTE retained the stigma associated with vocational education. It had long been considered the domain of students unsuited for college. It also clashed with the NCLB Act, which was focused on raising academic standards and preparing students for college.[54] Many JROTC instructors found the CTE bureaucratically burdensome. In Tennessee, retired colonel Thomas McConnell, Director of Army Instruction (DAI) for the Clarksville–Montgomery County Schools, considered state rules regulating CTE to be stifling. He questioned CTE's value to JROTC. "I am just not sure," McConnell wrote, "I would want to wade into that marsh [i.e., CTE] unless some great benefit would accrue, and I can't think of a single benefit to the program that overrides or exceeds what we get as an academic elective course of instruction."[55]

Despite these negative perceptions, CTE did garner considerable support among educators. Its proponents saw it as an educational option that offered multiple and tiered pathways for secondary education. They argued that, contrary to popular belief, CTE and academic achievement were not mutually exclusive.[56] Retired lieutenant colonel Nicolle Wheeler, the DAI in Fulton County, noted that CTE included many subjects at many levels. Fields as diverse as culinary arts, information technology, and leadership could fall within its purview. Programs could be tailored to students who joined the workforce, attended two-year institutions, or pursued a bachelor's degree. In Georgia, the JROTC thrived as a CTE pathway. Cadets received academic credit, and instructors found certification easy. The CTE designation permitted the JROTC to join the state's CTE organization, which upheld JROTC interests in matters concerning policy and personnel.[57]

STIFF ACADEMIC REQUIREMENTS

Despite strong congressional and public backing, the JROTC suffered from enrollment anomalies in the early 2000s. Florida and California had the biggest problems, but every state was affected to some degree.[58]

The services attributed their enrollment issues to several factors. One was the GWOT. Media coverage associated military service with hardship, injury, and death. Students and their parents wanted none of it. Stiffer academic requirements were also a factor. The NCLB Act originally focused on grades three through eight, but mandatory testing gradually extended to higher grades. This trend accelerated after January 2005 when President George W. Bush, in his State of the Union address, promoted the extension of high-stakes testing to high schools. From 2001 to 2008, the number of states requiring an exit examination for graduation rose more than fourfold.[59]

During this time, states prescribed stricter academic standards and aligned graduation requirements with skills demanded by colleges and employers. Mississippi mandated that ninth graders complete four years of English, math, science, and social studies to receive a diploma. Oklahoma followed the lead of Arkansas and Indiana in requiring all students to take a college-bound curriculum unless their parents requested a waiver. Fewer students could enroll in elective programs like the JROTC because of elevated graduation requirements. Some states made students who failed state exams ineligible for elective or extracurricular programs.[60]

The situation prompted yet another push for academic credit. Some progress was made, but most states were not supportive. California, concerned with the epidemic of obesity among adolescents, raised physical education (PE) standards. At the same time, the state board of education ruled that the JROTC did not prepare students to meet PE requirements. Both the secretary of defense and the chief of naval operations asked Governor Arnold Schwarzenegger to intervene on behalf of the program. The governor expressed support but could do little to help.[61]

Even some federal agencies were unsupportive of the JROTC's quest for credit. Despite entreaties from the DOD, the DOE refused to sanction academic credit for the Marine Corps PE and wellness courses. The DOD Dependents Schools granted a mere 1.5 credits for JROTC courses in life skills and career education.[62]

Staffing shortages likewise hurt enrollment. In 2009, eighty-eight army units had only one instructor. Enticing retirees to apply for positions in inner-city and isolated rural schools remained difficult. Many schools had bare-bones budgets and could not offer adequate compensation to military faculty. Others were in locales with few amenities or were distant from military bases.[63]

Staffing quality was an issue. Under NCLB standards, teachers of core subjects had to meet the highly qualified licensure criteria. Although subjects such as PE, health, and JROTC were not held to the highly qualified standard, many schools treated them as if they were. The problem of unqualified instructors was widespread. In 2009, the Office of Management and Budget found that there were three thousand noncommissioned officers (NCOs) instructors who were not fully qualified. Many lacked baccalaureate degrees and were barred from teaching.[64]

Not all services were equally affected. The air force was in the best shape. Most of its instructors had degrees. The navy ranked second, with about 40 percent of its NCO instructors being college graduates. The Marine Corps was in the worst shape. Frequent deployments prevented most marine NCOs from entering baccalaureate programs.[65]

The services allegedly aggravated the problem with their blasé approach to instructor hiring. The army did not have a systematic process to recruit faculty. Little use was made of professional journals, social networking websites, or army transition courses. Moreover, the army made no systematic effort to enlist the support of state attorneys general, the Reserve Officers' Association, the American Legion, and other organizations with ties to former service members.[66]

BUDGET PROBLEMS

Budget shortfalls held down enrollment and unit growth. While Congress directed a JROTC expansion in the 2007 NDAA, it did not authorize the necessary funds. One service even had its JROTC budget cut by 15 percent. The air force attributed these difficulties to Program Budget Decisions 720 and 707, which shunted JROTC funds into projects of greater operational value. The slashing of state and local educational budgets hurt the JROTC as much as federal cutbacks did. Units held fundraising events and scrounged for supplies to keep afloat.[67] Financially floundering schools attempted to survive by funding their units at minimal levels or by cutting back on JROTC staff. Others closed their units.[68]

The JROTC's fiscal woes worsened in 2008 when the Great Recession delivered a body blow to the economy. Foreclosures, falling home prices, and high unemployment rates afflicted most communities. The housing crisis had a devastating impact on the JROTC because many school budgets depended on property tax revenue. In fact, more than 50 percent of school districts depended on property taxes for at least a quarter of their annual budget. High unemployment aggravated the effects of the housing meltdown. Unemployment eroded the local tax base and forced parents of school-age children to leave their communities in search of jobs.[69]

The economic collapse made state aid to education problematic. Florida, California, Nevada, and Arizona suffered acutely from the downturn. In Florida, where state funds constituted 41 percent of public school budgets, the state suffered a $5 billion educational underage. The crisis compelled schools to take extraordinary measures. Schools slashed K–12 teaching positions, furloughed teachers, reduced salaries, adopted four-day school weeks, cut periods from the school day, and eliminated sports teams, after-school activities, and summer school.[70]

The JROTC shared in the budgetary misery. Some schools eliminated one of their two JROTC instructors or shared instructors with other high schools. Others cut the JROTC transportation budget, which led to the cancellation of various competitions. One school dropped block scheduling and erased an entire semester of the JROTC.[71] The demands of the NCLB Act interacted with the nation's economic problems and the continuing US involvement in Southwest Asia to make the job of the JROTC instructor an exceedingly difficult one.

ANTI-JROTC AGITATION

Anti-JROTC protests continued during this time of turmoil. The disturbance that drew the most publicity occurred in San Francisco. The city hosted seven units—six army and one navy—with a collective enrollment of over one thousand cadets. Surprisingly, given the city's political climate, the program was popular. It had maintained above-average enrollment since 1966, when the city received its first unit. A cardinal reason for this success was the granting of equivalency credit for PE. Although California adopted more stringent PE requirements after NCLB, the decision to allow credit substitution remained with local school boards, most of which continued to grant credit. But in 2006, the San Francisco School Board, in response to a threatened lawsuit, held an emergency meeting to vote on whether to continue its substitution policy. After a tie vote, the board scheduled another meeting at a time when JROTC supporters would be absent. At the second meeting, the board rescinded its substitution policy. This led to a precipitous drop in enrollment.[72]

The school board wasn't finished. It attempted to eliminate the program. On November 14, 2006, the board voted to drop the JROTC and replace it with a comparable nonmilitary program. The vote was not in response to protests by educators or students. In fact, the principals of all seven schools strongly supported the JROTC, as did most teachers and students. Instead, the vote reflected the sentiments of a majority of school board members. These members argued that, although the JROTC allowed lesbian, gay, bisexual, and transgender (LGBT) students to participate, it was nonetheless discriminatory. They saw it as part of a military establishment that recruited students for an unpopular war and enforced the unfair Don't Ask, Don't Tell DOD policy. After the vote, Mark Sanchez, an openly gay board member, told the *Bay Area Reporter* that he objected to "the military's anti-LGBT . . . hiring practices, which is absolutely what they do in terms of hiring their instructors." His colleague on the board, Eric Mar, supported him, declaring, "It's clear with the military, if you're gay and out, you don't get the same opportunities." The American Civil Liberties Union (ACLU) and the American Friends Service Committee backed the board, arguing that military programs were not appropriate for public schools.[73]

The board's decision drew an angry reaction. In the US House of Representatives, Senator James Inhofe called the school board's decision "arrogant, mean-spirited, [and] absolutely foolish" and asserted that it reflected "a gangrenous, antimilitary bigotry." The *San Francisco Chronicle* rejected charges that the program was biased and poorly managed. According to the *Chronicle*, far from being discriminatory, the program was highly inclusive. The athletic and disabled; college-bound and barely graduating; gay and straight; white, Black, and brown students were all welcome.[74]

A group called the Friends of JROTC spearheaded a campaign to reinstate the program and restore credit. It touted the program as a model of inclusion and heralded its life-skills training program while it rejected accusations that the JROTC was a recruiting tool, noting that only two cadets from the city's units had enlisted in 2007.[75]

These JROTC activists enlisted the support of luminaries like Senator Dianne Feinstein, Attorney General Jerry Brown, and the former San Francisco mayor Willie Brown to place a measure reestablishing the JROTC on the ballot. The measure, Proposition V, passed with a 55 percent majority.[76]

Despite the outcome, the school board bottled up the resolution. After a five-month wait, state assemblywoman Fiona Ma finally came forward with a proposal to reinstate the JROTC in San Francisco schools and grant participants PE credit. Lawmakers, she declared, could not allow "renegade school board members to play games with the lives of our high schoolers." Ma warned that the JROTC's elimination would compel students to find other ways to satisfy PE requirements, which in turn would require more state dollars. Reinstating the JROTC would keep federal dollars in San Francisco schools, provide students with more choices, and save San Francisco thousands of dollars.[77]

On May 12, 2009, the city's board of education voted to restore the JROTC. The school board's vote was taken amid a tumultuous gathering of two hundred supporters and opponents of the program. At one point, the board president had to clear the room to restore order. The vote to restore the program met with an emotional outburst by JROTC backers.[78]

The program's rebirth was due to pro-JROTC activism, a turnover in school board membership, and the absence of a suitable replacement program. The school board's ideological approach to the issue probably didn't help its case. Anti-JROTC campaigns generally enjoy more success when they follow a more prosaic strategy, focusing on specific, local issues.[79]

CHILD SOLDIERS

Defense officials had to battle accusations that the US military was recruiting child soldiers. The issue had gained saliency with the publication of the UN

Child Soldiers Global Report in June 2001. The report surveyed the recruitment laws and practices of 180 countries around the world. It charged that military recruiters in the United States harassed young people and subjected girls to sexual harassment. It was extremely critical of military training programs in US schools, especially the Young Marines and the JROTC. The JROTC, the report alleged, promoted violence and targeted minorities and the poor for enlistment.[80]

The ACLU reinforced the UN report. It quoted an army regulation stating that the JROTC "should create favorable attitudes and impressions . . . toward careers in the Armed Forces" and an army policy memorandum directing the JROTC to help the US Army Recruiting Command. It condemned the targeting of underage children, charging that the DOD collected information on sixteen-year-olds, marketed military service to thirteen-year-olds through *America's Army*, and sanctioned the enrollment of children as young as eleven in middle school units.[81]

The involuntary placement of students in the JROTC also aroused the ACLU's ire. In Los Angeles, "high school administrators were enrolling reluctant students in JROTC as an alternative to overcrowded gym classes." In Buffalo, someone had enrolled the entire freshman class at Hutchinson Central Technical High School in the JROTC. Hutchinson's assistant principal told one parent that her daughter could not drop the program; she would be punished if she did. Three military academies in Chicago followed the same protocol.[82]

The ACLU found the existence of elementary and middle school units very disturbing. In these units, eleven-year-olds drilled with wooden rifles, studied military history, visited military bases, and wore uniforms once a week. These middle school units were virtual replicas of JROTC programs.[83] The charges upset congresspeople and defense officials, who, although doubting the report would hurt recruiting, feared that it would require extensive public relations work to explain why the Child Soldiers Protocol was not applicable to the JROTC and similar youth programs.

ANOTHER EXPANSION

One expansion hardly ended before another began. In 2009, the JROTC stood on the threshold of another round of growth. In its markup of the 2009 NDAA, the HASC told the services to enlarge the JROTC to four thousand units by 2012. Yet once again, the stated intent was to achieve a more equitable geographical distribution of programs and strengthen the JROTC's presence in poor areas. As this legislation wound its way toward passage, fiscal reality and the exploding costs of the Iraq and Afghanistan wars tempered congressional ambitions. In its final form, the NDAA both lowered the unit goal to 3,700 units and extended the expansion timeline until 2020.[84]

Recruiting again factored into the expansion decision. Before the passage of the 2009 NDAA, Congress expressed concern about the quality of new recruits. Military-age youth suffered from behavioral disorders, poor physical fitness, and a lack of self-discipline—flaws that narrowed the recruiting pool and complicated training. Indeed, because of various physical, legal, medical, mental, and psychological irregularities, only 27 percent of military-age people were even qualified to enlist. The severity of these issues, it was hoped, could be alleviated through the JROTC.[85]

The ground forces had reached a recruiting nadir between fiscal years 2005 and 2007. To obtain enough recruits, they lowered quality standards and showered incentives on new recruits. The army's situation was the direst. In desperation, it raised its intake of high school dropouts and Armed Forces Qualification Test (AFQT) Category IV recruits and increased enlistment waivers. The army even began accepting felons. By 2008, recruiting showed signs of improvement. Rising unemployment rates, the improved security situation in Iraq, military pay increases, and lower recruiting goals drove this upswing. Nonetheless, the army recognized that its recruiting base was fragile; quality markers still fell below historic norms. The army resolved to enlarge its intake of high-quality applicants to ensure that there was enough skilled manpower available to prosecute the wars in Southwest Asia.[86]

The transition from the Bush to the Barack Obama administration did not dim the enthusiasm for expansion. The services remained focused on attracting a capable and diverse pool of candidates. Particularly worrisome to the DOD was the continuing lack of minority representation in officer training programs and certain combat and high-tech enlisted specialties.[87] The JROTC's demographic makeup promised to redress ethnic and gender imbalances within the force. Minorities constituted a majority in each program, ranging from a high of 66 percent in the Army JROTC to a low of 54 percent in the Navy JROTC (2010). Women, too, were well represented, ranging from a high of 45 percent in the Army JROTC to a low of 30 percent in the Air Force JROTC.[88]

MILITARY LEADERSHIP DIVERSITY COMMITTEE

To address minority officer shortfalls, Congress established the Military Leadership Diversity Commission (MLDC) in September 2008. The Congressional Black Caucus had been pressing defense leaders to increase diversity among senior officers. "Just as our military looks like America, so too must our general officers," said House Majority Whip James E. Clyburn (D-South Carolina). "A military that is proportionally representative of all races, cultures and ethnicities increases the readiness and efficiency of our fighting forces."[89]

The creation of the MLDC was the latest in a series of initiatives to boost minority participation in officer programs. At the turn of the century, the army had introduced the Hispanic Access Initiative (HAI), which targeted colleges with high concentrations of Hispanic students. Later, in 2004, it convened the Committee on Diversity and Advancement in the Army (CODA) to study ways to make commissioning programs more accessible to minorities. The MLDC's writ was wider than that of the HAI or CODA. It encompassed all services, was more comprehensive, and, most importantly, was congressionally empowered.[90]

The MLDC assessed "the ability of current recruitment and retention practices to attract and maintain a diverse pool of qualified individuals in . . . pre-commissioning officer development programs." It noted that the DOD already sponsored a dozen K–12 programs focused on increasing the number of youths qualified for military service, attracting underrepresented demographic groups to the military, and raising awareness of military career opportunities among students too young to enlist. The commission was especially keen to tackle military disqualification factors among middle and high school students. This involved expanding the program's reach in middle and high schools.[91]

EDUCATIONAL INITIATIVES: TROUBLED SCHOOLS, DROPOUT PREVENTION, STEM

Another force driving growth was the JROTC's perceived efficacy in regenerating troubled schools. One Obama administration official labeled the reclamation of underachieving schools the nation's number one (educational) weakness and greatest need. School turnaround, he said, should entail investments at the state, district, and school levels. National nonprofit groups like City Year, Boys and Girls Clubs, and the JROTC should be enlisted in turnaround efforts because of their ability to project support nationwide.[92]

The JROTC's reputation as an effective dropout prevention program raised its stock as a school turnaround agent. Secretary of Education Arne Duncan commended Chicago's military career academies for their success in improving graduation rates, promoting college attendance, and facilitating the college application process for disadvantaged students. Chicago's academies were, he opined, a perfect supplement to Obama's College for All initiative.[93]

The JROTC's alignment with high-profile educational initiatives likewise helped the cause of expansion. Congressional and military leaders saw the easily malleable JROTC program as a convenient and inexpensive way to bolster regional studies. The services had already incorporated language, regional, and cultural learning in their education systems;[94] the JROTC only needed to be integrated into this effort.[95]

The motive for stressing regional studies went beyond military concerns. As one publication explained, "Technology is obliterating geographic boundaries and time zones." People needed "a deeper understanding of the thinking, motivations, and actions of different cultures, countries and regions." This deeper understanding would, in turn, foster "tolerance, and acceptance of ethical, religious, and personal differences." Increasingly, employers regarded foreign languages and regional geography as the new basics for the workplace.[96]

The JROTC's embrace of STEM education likewise enhanced its social capital. Like area studies, STEM initiatives furthered both military and wider national goals. The *2010 National Security Strategy* and the DOD's *Education and Outreach Strategic Plan for 2010–2014* articulated STEM's criticality in making the United States more competitive in the global marketplace. American universities were facing growing challenges in maintaining the nation's STEM lead. Other nations were catching up. Russia, a nation with half the population of the United States, was producing an equal number of engineers. The United States had to keep ahead of the competitive curve.[97]

The federal government launched scores of initiatives to support its STEM strategy.[98] In all, there were over 130 DOD programs designed to promote K–12 STEM education. The JROTC not only had an organic STEM component but supplemented other K–12 programs by publicizing and supporting them.[99]

The JROTC's participation in the campaign to combat the obesity epidemic also bolstered its perceived social value. The American Public Health Association projected that obesity would add hundreds of billions to the nation's annual health-care costs and account for more than a fifth of health-care spending. It would also take away millions of productive hours from a workforce pressed by heightened competition in a globalizing economy.[100] The obesity crisis was already inhibiting recruiting. Mission Readiness, an organization of retired senior officers, warned Congress in 2010 that nine million seventeen-to-twenty-four-year-olds, or 27 percent of young adults, were too fat for military service. Obesity among children and young adults had tripled between 1980 and 2010 and threatened national security. To make matters worse, the obesity rates were the highest in the most prolific recruiting states.[101]

The number of applicants rejected for obesity rose sharply after the mid-1990s. Seventy percent of candidates failed their enlistment because of being overweight between 1995 and 2008. This made obesity the leading medical cause for rejection. When weight problems were combined with educational deficits, criminal records, and other disqualifiers, the ineligibility rate rose to nearly three-quarters.[102]

Congress attacked the obesity epidemic in 2013, when it enjoined the DOD to disseminate information on healthy body weight and the risks of obesity throughout the force.[103] Accordingly, the JROTC bolstered its health, wellness, and fitness programs, emphasizing healthy diets and good sleep hygiene. Again, these topics were not new in the JROTC, but they became more salient.

JOBS FOR VETERANS

Job creation for veterans was another force strengthening sentiment for expansion. The military began to draw down in 2009. This presented a challenge for the DOD because the Great Recession of 2008 had created high unemployment among veterans, particularly post-9/11 veterans. Joblessness among male veterans ages eighteen to twenty-four stood at almost 22 percent in 2010. Unemployment also posed a fiscal threat to the defense department. In 2011, the army alone was spending more than $500 million per year on unemployment compensation.[104]

The Obama administration formed a DOD–Veterans Affairs (VA) Task Force to investigate the issue while Congress in the 2009 NDAA created more jobs for discharged officers and NCOs. Congress was especially worried about job opportunities for disabled soldiers, known as wounded warriors. Congress expected the JROTC to hire some of these veterans.[105]

MECHANICS OF EXPANSION

The DOD crafted unit selection criteria to implant new units in areas best situated to enable the services to "make a difference." Criteria included Title I eligibility; indicators of need (local unemployment rates, illiteracy rates among adults, graduation rates, Recognized American School Counselor Association (ASCA) Model Program (RAMP)scores); the availability of postsecondary education; core academic credit; school financial solvency; school facilities; and the fair and equitable distribution of units. Title I and "indicators of need" together accounted for 40 percent of a school's score.

The JROTC expansion that was directed in the 2009 NDAA did not materialize as planned. It slowed in 2011 and came to a halt in 2013. The budget crisis was the principal obstacle. Pressure to slow the expansion started to build when President Obama signed the Budget Control Act (BCA) in August 2011. This act eventually led to a sharp reduction in defense spending.[106]

The cuts caused a delay of the expansion. For a time, Congress remained committed to the goal of reaching 3,700 units by 2020. But fiscal difficulties soon forced Congress to change its tune. In June 2012, the SASC lowered the expansion target, told the services to keep the JROTC within funding limitations, and admitted that its mandate to create 250 new units by 2020 was unrealistic. Now, the DOD had to lower its sights and establish not less than 3,000 but not more than 3,700 units by September 2020. This, in effect, sanctioned a contraction of the JROTC base.[107] At the same time, the SASC praised the navy's move to substitute inexpensive NDCC units for inefficient JROTC programs.[108]

Sequestration made the sustainment of the JROTC base problematic. The services even considered cutting units, reducing instructor training, and postponing curriculum development. The air force told an especially dismal story. The 2013 NDAA had provided enough money for it to maintain 870 units. Sequestration placed this level in danger and even threatened the air force's ability to pay instructor salaries, which absorbed 93 percent of JROTC funds.[109] While the DOD's worst fears were not realized, the department had to give up any hope of a meaningful expansion.

PROJECT PASS

In March 2009, the USAAC, the National Association of State Boards of Education (NASBE), and the DOE formed a partnership to improve student performance in at-risk schools. The intent of this partnership, dubbed Project PASS (Partnership for All Student Success), was to improve high school graduation rates in areas where dropout rates were extremely high.[110] The controversial part of the PASS was the age of its objects. The program targeted middle schools connected with underperforming high schools. To rescue at-risk students from failure, it was believed necessary to intervene while they were still in middle school. “Students who drop out,” Brenda Welburn, NASBE’s executive director, explained, “have usually already made that decision in middle school and are just waiting until they’re old enough.”[111]

Under PASS, schools with a high proportion of at-risk students were to receive a comprehensive middle school to high school transition program, extra help to meet state standards, and additional funds. The USAAC was to provide funds and other assistance. NASBE’s tasks included coordinating the efforts of the USAAC and the DOE, facilitating state and city participation in a pilot program, and developing metrics to evaluate the PASS Pilot.[112]

The army, aware of the hostility the initiative would excite, stressed that PASS was not the JROTC in middle schools. Rather, it was a NASBE initiative that used army educational models to improve graduation rates. Officials had abandoned the original name for the program, JROTC Plus, because of the implications it carried. Nevertheless, the PASS used the same programs that made the JROTC “so successful.”[113]

Planning for the PASS Pilot began in November 2009. Six states, all located in the South or Midwest, competed to participate. The PASS soon ran into complications. Funding was the biggest issue. There was no DOE financial support for the PASS Pilot. Moreover, in the original project design, some costs were identified as belonging to the army but were not included in the JROTC budget. Because of this oversight, the pilot launch date was postponed to January 2011. The impediments convinced the NASBE that the field of participating schools was too large. The pilot would have to be trimmed back.[114]

A meeting in March 2010 brought more bad news. The participants reported that no progress had been made in identifying funding sources. Moreover, coordinating the project was turning into an imbroglio. The circumstances in each district were so different that it made planning convoluted. Planning proceeded, but the funding problem cast a pall over the project.[115]

While planning was underway, the Junior Leadership Corps (JLC) emerged as an adjunct to the PASS. The JLC grew out of the older Adopt-a-School Program. Both targeted middle schools. The JLC had a curriculum modeled after that of the JROTC. It taught healthy lifestyle choices, goal setting, effective relationships, and active community involvement. And, like the PASS, it focused on dropout prevention. It was lumped together with the PASS since the two initiatives had similar goals.[116]

On March 11, 2011, Secretary of Education Arne Duncan and the chief of staff of the army (CSA), General George Casey, officially launched Project PASS and the JLC in a ceremony at North Middle School in Radcliffe, Kentucky. It was one of five schools taking part in the pilot.[117] Shortly after the ceremony, though, the PASS project became unhinged. While the House passed a bill (H.R. 5136) enabling the project, that bill never became law. There were two cardinal reasons for the demise of PASS. The most obvious was a deteriorating fiscal situation. The army abruptly cut the program's budget when the costs became clear. Moreover, defense officials worried that the army had overstepped its bounds in funding PASS. There was, some claimed, no legislative sanction for the army to support such a venture. Doing so represented a misallocation of funds. The program's final weeks were thus mired in controversy.[118]

A negative public reaction contributed to the project's dismantlement. Introducing military programs into middle schools was bound to raise concerns. Parents, along with peace and religious organizations, objected to the militarization of thirteen-year-olds. Even parents who countenanced the JROTC in high schools balked at creating military programs in the seventh grade. Similar protests had forced the closing of the Army Experience Center in Philadelphia in 2010. That experiment also had targeted students as young as thirteen.[119] From the army's perspective, the demise of PASS was not a total loss. The JLC survived the storm, albeit at a level below that originally envisaged.

JROTC STUDY

In January 2014, the CSA, General Ray Odierno, directed Training and Doctrine Command (TRADOC) to conduct a JROTC study. He wanted to gauge how closely the JROTC aligned with army priorities. The study had four parts: (1) assess JROTC effectiveness from the army's standpoint; (2) delineate the forces affecting JROTC policy; (3) provide a demographic snapshot of the program; and (4) summarize major issues that had faced the JROTC since 2006.[120]

The study concluded that the JROTC was, on balance, "successful." The high value communities placed on the JROTC, long unit waiting lists, strong congressional support, and widespread public approval all attested to the program's effectiveness and popularity. So did the program's high graduation, cocurricular participation, and enlistment rates.

The army generally met its goal of establishing units in locales where they could have the greatest impact. Most of its units, 90 percent, were in Title I or Title I–eligible schools. A disproportionately large number of programs were in inner-city schools where grade point averages (GPAs) and graduation rates fell below the national average and where indiscipline and dropout rates exceeded the national mean.[121]

Still, the study found, the JROTC did have its shortcomings. It had not achieved geographic diversity. Units were not proportionately distributed among the states. Rather, they were concentrated in states with high propensities for military service. Nor did the JROTC have an adequate presence in "underrepresented growth areas." These were areas that had a "talented and diverse population" but did not produce many recruits; they included cities like Los Angeles, New York, Houston, Chicago, San Francisco, and Dallas–Fort Worth. In Texas, about 75 percent of the population resided in the Dallas–Fort Worth and Houston areas, but only thirty-six of its two hundred JROTC units were situated in these cities.[122]

Funding constrained the growth and quality of the JROTC. The money problem went beyond the size of the budget; it also involved the unpredictable nature of the funding. The BCA and the heavy reliance on continuing budget resolutions made the money flow problematic. Planning in such an unstable fiscal environment was difficult. Funding irregularities combined with legal and regulatory strictures to block the hiring of instructors, degrade the quality of the cadet experience, and stunt the growth of the program.[123]

Responding to congressional concerns about the program, the RAND Corporation followed the army report with its own study (2016). It found that the JROTC had been more effective in achieving certain kinds of balance than in others. The JROTC was well represented in public schools with large minority populations, in schools serving poor areas, and in the Southeast. On the other hand, the program was underrepresented in isolated, rural communities and in about two-thirds of the states. To achieve a more equitable balance, RAND advised examining the problem of instructor availability.[124]

RECENT DEVELOPMENTS

The JROTC experienced a shock in 2022 when a *New York Times* investigation was made public. This investigation revealed that in the past five years, thirty-three JROTC instructors had been criminally charged with sexual misconduct involving students, a rate that was "far higher than the rate of civilian high school teachers."[125] Congress subsequently started its own investigation, which found that, over the same five-year period, there had been sixty allegations of sexual misconduct by instructors, of which fifty-eight were substantiated.[126] The congressional inquiry found that an inadequate screening of instructor applicants and inadequate oversight by the DOD were behind these crimes. The services, with their limited staffs, couldn't inspect units on a regular basis. Some units went for years without a formal visit from their higher headquarters.[127] The Pentagon scrambled to set up checks and procedures to prevent this type of abuse from reoccurring.

After a period of relative stasis, sentiment for expansion revived in 2018. In that year, Senator Roger Wicker introduced a bill to authorize the expansion of JROTC presence "in low-income, rural, and underserved areas of the United States." The legislation provided that, starting in fiscal year 2019, the services could establish up to one hundred units in targeted areas. Congress labeled the bill the JROTC Opportunities for Transformation Change Act or JROTC ACT. The bill made it less expensive for small schools to staff units by permitting NCOs with bachelor's degrees to fill senior army instructor positions, reducing the minimum staffing requirement to a single instructor, and paying instructors on ten-month rather than twelve-month contracts.[128] The JROTC Act also improved management by finally standardizing data collection across the services.[129]

In August 2020, Congress, in a dramatic move, urged the secretary of defense to double the size of the JROTC. It set a target of six thousand units, which was to be achieved by September 30, 2031.[130] This move was inspired by the recommendations of the National Committee on Military, National, and Public Service, which wanted to harness the JROTC to improve recruiting, attack the obesity epidemic, teach workplace skills, narrow the civil-military divide, reinvigorate civic education, and promote STEM study, workforce preparation, financial literacy, physical fitness, and public outreach.[131] The proposed expansion, however, has not materialized. Congress and the DOD were concerned about the costs and hesitated to proceed before the requisite resources were in hand.[132]

Domestic turmoil and the military recruiting crisis of the early 2020s were perhaps the prime movers in this so far unrealized push for expansion. The services have faced huge accessions deficits in the early 2020s. According to many observers, this recruiting crisis has been the most serious in the history of the all-volunteer force. Once again, many looked to the JROTC as a possible solution to the problem. In testimony before the HASC in 2021, General James McConville, the CSA, noted that the JROTC was in 10 percent of high schools but that 49 percent of the young men and women who enlisted in the army came not necessarily from the program itself but from schools that hosted a JROTC unit. There was, he concluded, great value in exposing students to the military, even if that exposure was oblique.[133]

At the time of this writing (January 2025), JROTC strength stands at about 3,500 units and a little over 538,000 cadets. The program's unit and enrollment levels have fluctuated little over the last decade. Potential for growth remains, however. Section 551 of the 2024 NDAA left room for expansion when it set program parameters between 3,400 and 4,000 units. This enabled the services to schedule the addition of fifteen more units before the end of FY 2025. It is notable that the 2024 NDAA removed the requirement for the "fair and equitable distribution" of units across the country. How or whether this will affect the JROTC is not yet apparent.[134]

Several recent legislative changes could affect the JROTC. PL 116–92 sanctioned the enrollment of homeschooled students in the JROTC and opened the way for eighth graders to enroll if they are colocated with ninth to twelfth graders. The same law "authorized" JROTC instruction in STEM fields. While STEM activities have been part of the program for some time, this legislation reflected a renewed appreciation for the JROTC as an "accessible, high ROI/low-cost opportunity" to prepare the future defense workforce in areas such as computing, cybersecurity, defense technologies, and artificial intelligence (AI).[135]

Two developments are reflective of this new STEM emphasis. One is the entry of the newest service, the Space Force (est. December 2019), into the

JROTC program with the conversion of ten Air Force JROTC detachments into Space Force JROTC units in fiscal year 2022. The second was the conversion of nine Army JROTC programs into cyber units in the fall of 2022 and, at roughly the same time, the incorporation of a STEM component into the JROTC Cadet Leadership Challenge. These latter were internal moves, but they did signify the direction the program was heading.[136]

The JROTC has been an important part of the military establishment's articulation with society since its inception. Its multiple goals have frequently been adjusted or reshuffled to accommodate changing circumstances and defense priorities. These changes have generated confusion and suspicion and opened the program to frequent attack. Many have questioned the JROTC's claims of success and the propriety of its objectives. The program's lofty but ill-defined goals defy precise measurement and assessment. The attempts of its supporters to "prove" the JROTC's efficacy have been hampered by the nature of evidence they can adduce. The available data on JROTC outcomes can establish correlation but not causation. Thus, its effectiveness as an instrument of citizenship education, recruiting, or any of the scores of other roles it has played cannot be quantifiably or definitively determined.

The JROTC has been assailed by critics from both the Left and the Right. The former view it as militaristic, oppressive, racist, misogynistic, jingoistic, and intellectually stifling. The latter consider it inefficient, ineffective, and tangential to the military's primary purpose of defending the country. The most serious threats to the JROTC's existence have come from within the DOD, from where high-ranking officials, in efforts to achieve budgetary savings, have launched multiple attacks against the program.

Nevertheless, the JROTC has enjoyed wide acclaim and popularity throughout its history. The long lists of schools seeking units and its army of congressional backers attest to the value that the public and its leaders have attached to this program. So, too, does the strong public reaction to attempts at shuttering the program as the strong public outcry against Robert S. McNamara's efforts in the early 1960s to abolish the program powerfully illustrate. McNamara, like many officials after him, met an unbreachable wall of resistance.

Both critics and proponents of the JROTC tend to miss the intimate connection between the program and the nation's long tradition of domestic military engagement. The military's involvement in civil projects began in the early republic and continues to this day. Until the eve of World War II, in fact, the military's domestic roles were arguably more salient than its military ones. The JROTC, then, should not be viewed as an abnormality but as an extension of a long-established custom.

A brief glance at the program's origins can tell us much about the program's variegated nature. The JROTC was born at a time when the world's most powerful nations were either at war or preparing for war. War Department leaders viewed it as a means to facilitate mobilization while avoiding the dangers of militarism. At the same time, there were other, and some might argue more powerful, forces at work in the program's creation. We have seen how in the nineteenth century, educators used school-based military training to pursue multiple extramilitary objectives. These goals remained relevant in the 1910s as the nation not only readied itself for war but adjusted to a rapidly growing, industrializing, and urbanizing society. Educationalists hoped to use high school military training to develop workplace skills, assuage labor problems, promote social tranquility, produce good citizens, and pursue other objectives. Prioritizing these many pressing goals proved very difficult. Each goal had a legion of influential proponents who could bring considerable pressure on its behalf. A certain ambiguity of purpose arose from this multiplicity of objectives, an ambiguity that imbued the JROTC with a protean nature, enabling it to shift its focus according to external conditions and address multiple policy imperatives, social and military.

An understanding of the JROTC's development as an arm of the military has more than academic interest. It can also be useful to military leaders, civilian policymakers, educators, and various other stakeholders who must chart the way ahead for the program. A study of the JROTC's military history cannot provide lessons, of course, but it can enrich the context in which interested parties think about the JROTC. Without historical perspective, people are more likely to consider the ROTC in the context of immediate issues and through narrow lenses. If this book does nothing else, I hope it will stimulate a more informed and nuanced discussion of a program that has for more than a century been an important link between the military and the society it serves.

Acknowledgments

I would like to acknowledge and express my appreciation to my colleagues, friends, and associates who provided valuable assistance to me in preparing and researching this book over the course of many years. I owe a huge debt of gratitude to Joseph S. Craig, the director of the Book Program for the Association of the US Army (AUSA) and a member of that organization's National Security Studies Staff. His advice regarding the writing and organization of the manuscript was invaluable. He read multiple iterations of the manuscript and provided detailed comments and suggestions for improvements. Joseph Craig introduced me to Natalie Clausen O'Neal, the senior acquisitions editor at the University Press of Kentucky. She was extremely supportive of my project, provided valuable guidance about the preparation of my manuscript, and shepherded me through the publishing process. She and her entire team were great to work with and made the experience enjoyable.

William A. Taylor, a professor of history at Angelo State University and peer reviewer for this book, provided crucial advice on the revision of the manuscript. His direction added depth to the book and significantly improved the final product. E. Casey Wardynski, a former assistant secretary of the army (Manpower and Reserve Affairs) and director of the army's Office of Economic and Manpower Analysis (OEMA), provided counsel and vital insights, not only into the JROTC but into the functioning of the Defense Department as a whole. His successors at OEMA, David Lyle, Carl Wojtaszek, and Mark Crow, contributed immeasurably to my understanding of the JROTC and, more broadly, the way the army works.

Leo J. Daugherty, a colleague and friend, repeatedly encouraged me to write this book and provided a plethora of documents from the US Army Cadet Command and US Army Accession Command Archives. He also supplied invaluable information about the workings of the command. A host of other Cadet Command leaders, both past and present, were also key in creating this book. Leon McMullen, deputy director of the JROTC Directorate; James Wood, chief of operations and training for JROTC; and Donna Rice, director of JROTC Education, gave their knowledge, time, and extremely helpful assistance in constructing this book. Joseph O'Donnell, Cadet Command's deputy chief of staff; Bert Huggins, Cadet Command's chief of research and diversity; Gary Tatro, Cadet Command data analyst; and former Cadet Command commanders Major General (retired) Robert Wagner, Walter Arnold, James Lyle, W. Montague Winfield, Arthur Bartell, Peggy Combs, and Christopher Hughes all added immensely to my understanding of the ROTC, both the junior and senior divisions.

I received critically important aid from the staff of the US Army Heritage and Education Center (AHEC). The historians, archivists, information specialists, and staff at the center lent exceptional archival support, guided me through a surfeit of primary source documents, and led me through a maze of subject files. They even allowed me access to research materials before the archives opened to the public. In particular, I would like to thank Richard Sommers, Arthur Bergeron, James A. Knechtmann, Richard L. Baker, Stephen M. Bye, Jessica J. Sheets, Joanne B. Lamm, Shannon S. Schwaller, Rodney Foytik, Thomas E. Buffenbarger, Steven Semmel, Riley Johnson, Melissa Wilford, Bill Rotella, Duane Miller, Guy Nasuti, Monica Followell, David Dias, Christopher Morin, and Gary L. Johnson for their expert guidance and assistance, as well as Clifton P. Hyatt, Marlea Leljedal, Lori Wheeler, and Lisa Newman for their help in the acquisition and transmission of documents, books, and other research materials.

The Archives and Library Staff at the US Military Academy aided me in multiple ways. Suzanne Christoff, associate director for strategic initiatives; Mark Danley, special formats cataloging librarian; Celeste Evans, archives and special collections research support librarian; Sharon Gillespie, information services technician; Susan Lintelmann, archives and special collections research support librarian; Alicia Mauldin-Ware, archivist; Elaine McConnell, monographic cataloging librarian; Laura Mosher, cadet engagement librarian; and Susie Sizemore, information services technician, were particularly helpful. They provided crucial research assistance, fielded numerous inquiries, located and acquired rare books through interlibrary loan, opened extensive library resources to me, and provided invaluable archival support, steering me to a host of primary sources.

The staff at the Archives and Special Collections at Tulane University provided crucial research guidance and helped me locate obscure documents that were not only hard to locate but key to my research efforts. At the Louisiana State University Archives, the staff afforded excellent archival help, greatly aiding my research efforts and skillfully conducting subject searches that produced precise detail on particular topics. The librarians and archivists at Clemson University's Special Collections and Archives guided me through a labyrinth of collections and pointed me toward areas that directly addressed my research agenda. The librarians and staff at Air University Library at Maxwell Air Force Base were remarkably accommodating and helpful. They steered me through numerous publications and documents that were key to my research and went out of their way to ensure I located what I needed.

My wife, perhaps, deserves the most thanks. She provided research assistance, a prodigious amount of typing, and enduring support. It is to her that I dedicate this book.

Appendix A

JROTC
Enrollment and Unit Strength
1919–1966

School Year	Number of Units	Enrollment
1919–1920	50	45,139
1920–1921	57	46,538
1921–1922	106	37,225
1922–1923	100	37,346
1923–1924	99	40,324
1924–1925	101	42,190
1925–1926	100	38,225
1926–1927	100	38,148
1927–1928	100	39,978
1928–1929	100	40,521
1929–1930	103	41,334
1930–1931	106	41,637
1931–1932	105	40,556
1932–1933	103	39,466
1933–1934	103	38,728
1934–1935	104	40,479
1935–1936	105	41,053
1936–1937	140	53,202
1937–1938	142	57,777
1938–1939	140	61,791
1939–1940	139	65,282

(continued)

(*continued*)

School Year	Number of Units	Enrollment
1940–1941	139	68,895
1942–1949	139	72,151 (avg)
1950–1951	139	57,750
1951–1952	138	61,280
1952–1953	n.d.	66,670
1953–1954	n.d.	66,694
1954–1955	n.d.	59,876
1955–1956	n.d.	59,343
1956–1957	n.d.	59,138
1957–1958	n.d.	60,197
1958–1959	n.d.	60,567
1959–1960	n.d.	59,825
1961–1962	295	60,766
1962–1963	295	n.d.
1963–1964	294	n.d.
1964–1965	293	73,745
1965–1966	287	96,366

n.d. = no data.

Appendix B

JROTC
Unit Strength
1966–2024, Selected Years

Year	Army	Navy	Air Force	Marine Corps
1966–1967	400	16	20	2
1967–1968	476	39	65	n.d.
1968–1969	519	55	112	n.d.
1969–1970	562	78	144	n.d.
1970–1971	585	97	160	16
1971–1972	595	127	194	24
1972–1973	628	185	235	30
1973–1974	646	219	275	n.d.
1974–1975	648	219	266	n.d.
1975–1976	650	219	275	n.d.
1976–1977	643	219	276	n.d.
1977–1978	642	214	275	n.d.
1978–1979	645	209	274	n.d.
1979–1980	664	206	278	n.d.
1980–1981	666	233	285	60
1981–1982	699	233	285	n.d.
1982–1983	711	233	286	n.d.
1983–1984	760	233	286	n.d.
1984–1985	818	233	286	n.d.
1985–1986	863	233	286	n.d.
1986–1987	865	241	296	n.d.
1987–1988	864	241	306	n.d.

(continued)

(*continued*)

Year	Army	Navy	Air Force	Marine Corps
1988–1989	865	237	316	n.d.
1989–1990	865	232	316	80
1990–1991	853	229	316	80
1991–1992	856	228	315	103
1992–1993	856	226	320	110
1993–1994	1142	318	426	136
1994–1995	1242	359	506	174
1995–1996	1357	397	586	174
1996–1997	1362	435	609	174
1997–1998	1368	435	609	178
1998–1999	1370	434	609	210
1999–2000	1370	490	669	220
2000–2001	1420	562	697	223
2001–2002	1465	582	744	222
2002–2003	1510	623	744	265
2003–2004	1530	624	744	285
2004–2005	1563	624	746	n.d.
2005–2006	1555	619	794	260
2006–2007	1653	619	794	260
2007–2008	1645	624	794	n.d.
2008–2009	1665	613	869	222
2009–2010	1688	639	884	n.d.
2010–2011	1688	642	884	260
2011–2012	1688	n.d.	867	n.d.
2012–2013	1688	n.d.	879	n.d.
2013–2014	1731	n.d.	864	n.d.
2014–2015	1709	n.d.	872	n.d.
2015–2016	1701	573	878	236
2016–2017	1709	583	869	251
2017–2018	1709	583	n.d.	n.d.
2018–2019	1704	583	n.d.	n.d.
2019–2020	1704	583	920	271
2020–2021	1702	583	885	255
2021–2022	1727	643	875	256
2022–2023	1729	658	848	254
2023–2024	1734	658	853	252

n.d. = no data.

Notes

1. ANTECEDENTS

1. Donald Downs and Ilia Murtazashvili, *Arms and the University* (New York: Cambridge University Press, 2012), 80–81.

2. Jennifer Mittelstadt, *The Rise of the Military Welfare State* (Cambridge, MA: Harvard University Press, 2015), 74.

3. Robert Wooster, *The United States Army and the Making of America: From Confederation to Empire, 1775–1903* (Lawrence, KS: University of Kansas Press of Nebraska, 2021).

4. Brian Linn, *Real Soldiering: The US Army in the Aftermath of War, 1815–1980* (Lawrence: University Press of Kansas, 2023); Michael Neiberg, *Making Citizen-Soldiers: ROTC and the Ideology of American Military Service* (Cambridge, MA: Harvard University Press, 2001).

5. Jason Warren, "Liberty Paradox," in *Drawdown* (New York: NYU Press, 2016), 57; J. Bartlett, ed., *Records of the Colony of Rhode Island and Providence Plantations* (New York: Adamant Media, 2005), 2:53, 114, 172, 539.

6. Lester Webb, "The Origins of Military Schools in the US Founded in the 19th Century" (PhD diss., UNC–Chapel Hill, 1958), 1.

7. Ibid., 216.

8. William Ellis, *History of Norwich University, 1819–98* (Concord, NH: Rumford, 1898), 1:67.

9. Neiberg, *Making Citizen-Soldiers*, 18–19; Dean Baker, "The Partridge Connection" (PhD diss., UNC–Chapel Hill, 1986), 40.

10. Baker, "Partridge Connection," 155.

11. Donald Parkerson and Jo Ann Parkerson, *Transitions in American Education* (New York: Rutledge Falmer, 2001), 129.

12. Alvan Hadley, "The Association of Military Colleges and Schools of the US (AMCSUS) and the Struggle for the Survival of Military Preparatory Schools in America" (PhD diss., University of Kentucky, 1999), 236; Gene Lyons and John Masland, *Education and Military Leadership* (Princeton, NJ: Princeton University Press, 1959), 142.

13. *Military Training in High Schools of the US, ROTC* (Washington, DC: CMEF, 1939), 3 (hereafter cited as *MTIUSHS*).

14. Theodore R. Sizer, *The Age of the Academies* (New York: Teachers College, Columbia University, 1964), 122.

15. James Morrison, *The Best School in the World, 1833–1866* (Kent, OH: Kent State University Press, 1986), 106; Walter Kolesnick, *Mental Discipline in Higher Education* (Madison: University of Wisconsin Press, 1958), 6–11; Bruce Allardice, "West Points of the Confederacy," *Civil War History* 43, no. 4 (1997): 310; Neiberg, *Making Citizen-Soldiers*, 15.

16. Henry Barnard, *Military Schools and Courses of Instruction in the Science and Art of War in France, Prussia, Austria, Russia, Sweden, Switzerland, Sardinia, England, and the United States* (New York: E. Steiger, 1872), 876; Allardice, "West Points of the Confederacy," 310.

17. Baker, "Partridge Connection," 140; Allardice, "West Points of the Confederacy," 310.

18. Webb, "Origins of Military Schools," 29; Arthur Ekirch, *The Civilian and the Military* (Colorado Springs, CO: Ralph Myles, 1972), 63; Cong. Chronicles, 64th Cong. (1916), V53, Pt7, 5944.

19. Webb, "Origins of Military Schools," 43, 62.

20. Francis Smith, *The Regulations of Military Institutions Applied to the Conduct of Common Schools* (New York: Wiley, 1849), 19–23, 30.

21. Ibid.; Webb, "Origins of Military Schools," 63; Allardice, "West Points of the Confederacy," 310.

22. Joseph F. Kett, *Rites of Passage: Adolescence in America, 1790 to the Present* (New York: Basic Books, 1977), 40; David MacLeod, *Building Character in the American Boy* (Madison: University of Wisconsin Press, 1983), 86; Marcus Cunliffe, *Soldiers and Civilians* (Aldershot: Gregg Revivals, 1993), 226.

23. Edward Mulineux, "Physical and Military Exercises in Public Schools," *American Journal of Education (AJE)*, June 1862, 513; John Hope Franklin, *The Militant South, 1800–1861* (Urbana: University of Illinois Press, 1856), 133; "Military Schools and Education," *AJE*, March 1862, 314; Allardice, "West Points of the Confederacy," 310.

24. *Cong. Globe*, 37th Cong., 2d Sess., 164 (1861–1862).

25. Ibid., 879–880; *MTIUSHS*, 2–3.

26. Kett, *Rites of Passage*, 40.

27. "Military Drill in Schools," *Christian Examiner*, March 1864, 239, 376; *MTIUSHS*, 3.

28. E. Dwight, "A Plan for Military Education in Massachusetts," *AJE*, December 1863, 689.

29. Margaret M. Gearheart, "Military Instruction in Civilian Institutions of Learning, 1862–1914" (master's thesis, University of Iowa, 1928), 136.

30. "Eagleswood Military Academy," *AJE*, September 1863, 471; Mulineux, "Physical and Military Exercises," 524.

31. Robert Kemble, *The Image of the Army Officer in America* (Westport, CT: Greenwood, 1973), 68.

32. *MTIUSHS*, 3, 11.

33. MFR, COL Bacherach, A/C, ROTC Liaison Group, October 14, 1948, subject: ROTC Units in the DC HSs, RG319, CAR, box 80, folder 3, National Archives, College Park, MD (hereafter cited as NACP).

34. Garrett Drummond, "Military Training in the Secondary Schools of America," *Infantry Journal* 31, no. 2 (1927): 611; *MTIUSHS*, 4; Charles Bradley, Principal, Manual Training High School, to Aaron Grove, SPT/Denver Schools, July 22, 1897; Edward Krug, *The Shaping of the American High School* (New York: Harper and Row, 1964), 193; *War Department Annual Report (WDAR), 1894* (Washington, DC: War Department, 1894), 841; *Manual for the HS Cadet Corps of Washington, D.C.* (1917), 3–5.

35. David Tyack, *Turning Points in American Educational History* (Waltham, MA: Blaisdell, 1967), 353.

36. Hadley, "Association of Military Colleges and Schools," 53–57; Michael Pearlman, *To Make Democracy Safe for America* (Urbana: University of Illinois Press, 1984), 15, 99–100.

37. Clifford Putney, "Muscular Christianity," in *The Encyclopedia of Informal Education*, accessed December 31, 2024, https://www.ined.org/christianeducation/muscular_christianity.htm.

38. Parkerson and Parkerson, *Transitions in American Education*, 134–35.

39. MacLeod, *Building Character*, 45.

40. Robert Matson, "Joseph Wood Hill: Civilian Soldier in Education and Politics," *Oregon Historical Quarterly* 90, no. 1 (Spring 1989): 14–15.

41. Ibid.; Brooks Kleber to Jamestown High School, n.d., Training and Doctrine Command Archives (TA).

42. *Congressional Record* (*CR*), 46th Cong., 2d Sess. (1879–1880), V10, 390; 51st Cong., 1st Sess. (1889–1890), V21, 6975; 54th Cong., 1st Sess. (1895–1896), V28, 583; 55th Cong., 2d Sess. (1897–1898), V31, 1524; Gearhart, *Military Instruction*, 14.

43. *WDAR, 1897*, 1:145.

44. *WDAR, 1894*, 1:184; *1897*, 1:219; *1895*, 1:188; *1896*, 1:194.

45. Gearhart, *Military Instruction*, 71, 78–81.

46. *WDAR, 1894*, 1:184; *1897*, 1:23, 64.

47. Gearhart, *Military Instruction*, 116.

48. Walter Millis, *The Martial Spirit* (New York: Literary Guild of America, 1931), 35.

49. MacLeod, *Building Character*, 83, 116.

50. Ibid.; "Military Instruction in Schools," *Army and Navy Journal* (*A&NJ*), June 19, 1909, 1181.

51. Gearhart, *Military Instruction*, 118.

52. Benjamin Harrison, "Military Instruction in Schools and Colleges," *Century* 47 (January 1894): 368–69.

53. Mary Dearing, *Veterans in Politics* (Baton Rouge: LSU Press, 1952), 472, 476–77.

54. Ibid., 478.

55. Millis, *Martial Spirit*, 35; MacLeod, *Building Character*, 83.

56. MacLeod, *Building Character*, 87.

57. Ibid., 88, 90, 92.

58. Thomas Lawlor and George Wingate, *Military Instruction in the Public Schools* (New York: GAR, 1895), 30.

59. Cunliffe, *Soldiers and Civilians*, 43.

60. Drummond, "Military Training," 611; *MTIUSHS*, 4; "Playing with Fire," *Dial*, May 16, 1896, 293.

61. Dearing, *Veterans in Politics*, 478.

62. Lawlor and Wingate, *Military Instruction*, 14.

63. Ibid.

64. Seth Kershner, Scott Harding, and Charles Howlett, *Breaking the War Habit* (Athens: University of Georgia Press, 2022), 9. In 1895, the New York State Legislature passed a law authorizing military training in schools, but it was vetoed by the governor.

65. *Educational Review*, May 1895, 525.

66. Gearhart, *Military Instruction*, 119.

67. Lawlor and Wingate, *Military Instruction*, 35.

68. Dearing, *Veterans in Politics*, 478–79.

69. *Report of the Commissioner of Education for the Year 1898–99* (Washington, DC: GPO, 1900), 1:479.

70. *CR*, 53d Cong., 3rd Sess. (1894–1895), V27, 477, 1259, 1589–90; Gearhart, *Military Instruction*, 15, 16, 122.

71. *CR*, 54th Cong., 1st Sess. (1895–1896), V28, 238–39; 55th Cong., 1st Sess. (1897), V30, 48; editorial, *Harper's Weekly* 40 (1896): 243; "Playing with Fire," 293.

72. "Playing with Fire," 293.

73. *CR*, 56th Cong., 2nd Sess. (1900–1901), V24, 49, 849; *WDAR, IG to the Secretary of War, 1902*, 385–86; Gearhart, *Military Instruction*, 8–19.

74. "Military Training in Schools," *A&NJ*, September 4, 1915, 6.

75. Leon Green, "Military Training in the Schools of Sumter, S.C.," *American Review of Reviews*, November 1915, 52; Marvin Kreidberg, *History of Military Mobilization in the US Army, 1775–1945* (Westport, CT: Greenwood, 1975), 210; National Center for Education Statistics, table 3, http://nces.ed.gov/programs/digest/d96/D967.org.asp; MacLeod, *Building Character*, 92.

76. *MTIUSHS*, 837.

77. *CR*, 62nd Cong., 1st Sess. (1911), V47, 1619.

78. Brooks Kleber to General French, April 30, 1980, TA.

79. BG L. R. Gignilliat, "Students and the National Defense," *World Tomorrow*, October 1926, 152, 167.

80. L. Halliburton, "A Brief History of Military Training at Fork Union Military Academy," *Sabre*, March 11, 1971, 3.

81. Ira Reeves, *Military Education in the United States* (Burlington, VT: Free Press, 1914), 25.

82. Allan R. Millett and Peter Maslowski, *For the Common Defense* (New York: Free Press, 1994), 310–14.

83. MacLeod, *Building Character*, 192; Allan Millett, *Military Professionalism and Officership in America* (Columbus, OH: Mershon Center, 1977), 17.

84. MacLeod, *Building Character*, 179; Rose Hayden-Smith, *Soldiers of the Soil: A Historical Review of the United States Spring Garden Army*, Center for Youth Development, UCCE (Winter 2006).

85. Gignilliat, "Students and the National Defense," 11; Kershner, Harding, and Howlett, *Breaking the War Habit*, 15.

86. NJ Commission on Military Training and Instruction in High Schools, *Report to the Legislature, 1917* (Trenton: MacCrellish & Quigley, 1917); MA Report of the Special Commission on Military Education and Reserve, December 1915, 28–29.

87. Jonathon Zimmerman, "Storm over the Schoolhouse: Exploring Popular Influences upon the American Curriculum, 1890–1941," *Teachers College Record*, Spring 1999, 609; Report of Committee 6 to Committee 1, *The Effect of Anti-war Societies on the ROTC*, October 9, 1925, AWC CA, 1925–1926, G-1 Course, file 926-2.1, US Army Heritage and Education Center (AHEC) Archives.

88. E. Z. Steever, "The Wyoming Plan of Military Training for the Schools," *School Review* 25, no. 3 (1917): 145; "Citizenship Training," *A&NJ*, September 25, 1915, 99;

Charles Johnston, "Discussion and Correspondence-Military Training in American High Schools," *School and Society*, February 19, 1916, 278–81.

89. Steever, "Wyoming Plan," 145; George Creel, "Wyoming's Answer to Militarism," *Everybody's Magazine* February 1916, 150–55; Air Force JROTC Junior Program Directorate (AFJROTCJPD), *AFJROTC Study*, Air University, Maxwell AFB, AL, 5/31/1977, 136 & C1–2 thru C-4.

90. Steever, "Wyoming Plan," 146.

91. Garrett Gatzemeyer, *Bodies for Battle: US Army Physical Culture and Systematic Training, 1885–1957* (Lawrence: University Press of Kansas, 2021), 2–6.

92. Steever, "Wyoming Plan," 145; Ping Ling, "Military Training in the Public Schools," *Pedagogical Review* (1918): 259–61; Creel, "Wyoming's Answer to Militarism," 150–55.

93. *AFJROTC Study*, 7, C2–5, C2–7.

94. *WDAR, 1916*, 1:42.

95. Creel, "Wyoming's Answer to Militarism," 150–155. Morris Janowitz and Stephen Westbrook, eds., *The Political Education of Soldiers* (Beverly Hills, CA: Sage, 1983), 253.

96. Lewis Todd, *Wartime Relations of the Federal Government and the Public Schools, 1917–1918* (New York: Arno & NYT, 1971), 101.

97. Ibid., 102.

98. Drummond, "Military Training," 611; Steever, "Wyoming Plan," 43; E. Z. Steever and J. L. Frink, *The Cadet Manual: Official Handbook for High School Volunteers of the United States* (Philadelphia: Lippincott, 1918), xii.

99. MacLeod, *Building Character*, 179.

100. Todd, *Wartime Relations*, 108; "Camp Steever Is Turning Out Real Fighters," *National Service*, August 1918, 48–50.

101. Walter Millis, ed., *American Military Thought* (Indianapolis: Bobbs-Merrill, 1966), 273.

102. *WDAR, 1912*, 1:99.

103. Lee Harford, *A Comprehensive History of the JROTC, 1818–1993* (Fort Monroe, VA: United States Army Cadet Command, 1993), 23; *WDAR, 1913*, 1:19; *1915*, 1:159; *1916*, 1:38; John Clifford, *The Citizen Soldiers: The Plattsburg Training Camp Movement, 1913–1920* (Lexington: University Press of Kentucky, 1972), 52–53.

104. Charles Taylor, "Underage Military Training," *National Service*, August 1917, 187–88; "MTCA Notes," *National Service*, February 1918, 84–86; Pearlman, *To Make Democracy Safe*, 99, 102–104; E. Harburg, "Work of the MTCA and Its Accomplishments at Camp Steever," *National Service*, October 1918, 176–79; "Making Army Officers at Plattsburg," *National Service*, June 1917, 62; "Report of the Secretary of the MTCA," *National Service*, January 1918, 443.

105. Army Service Forces (ASF), *History of Military Training: ROTC and 55c (NDA) Schools, 1939–1945*, October 5, 1945, 7, 8.

106. Leonard Wood, *Our Military History* (Chicago: Reilly & Britton, 1916), 201. See William Woolley, *Creating a Modern Army: Citizen-Soldiers and the American Way of War, 1919–1939* (Lawrence: University Press of Kansas, 2022), 13–14.

107. Wood, *Our Military History*, 199–204.

108. Ibid., 200.

109. "An Army of the People," *National Service*, February 1917, 34; Oswald Villard, *Universal Military Training* (New York: CMT, 1918), 6–7; William A. Taylor, *Every Citizen a Soldier: The Campaign for Military Training after World War II* (College Station: Texas A&M University Press, 2014), 14.

110. Leonard Wood, "The Plattsburgh Idea," *National Service*, February 1917, 12–13.

111. S. Rep. 452 (1916); *WDAR, 1916*, 1:171; Woolley, *Creating a Modern Army*, 21.

112. *WDAR, 1913*, 1:14.

113. Ibid., 1:34–35.

114. NDA 1916, Section 40.

115. Ibid.

116. General staff (GS), War Department (WD), *Statement of a Proper Military Policy for the United States* (Washington, DC: GPO, 1915).

117. GS, WD, War College Div., *Study on Educational Institutions Giving Military Training as a Source of Officers for a National Army*, WCD 9053–121, November 1915; *The Standardization of Methods of Military Instruction at Schools and Colleges in the United States*, WCD 9089–8, November 1915; supplement to *The Statement of a Proper Military Policy for the United States*; "Plan for Military Training in Public Schools of US," *Report of the CSA to Secretary of War* (Washington, DC: GPO, 1917), 5–8.

118. *MTIUSHS*, 4.

119. Todd, *Wartime Relations*, 108–109.

120. Ibid., 110.

121. *WDAR, 1920*, 1:260; *1919*, 1:21.

2. JROTC IN THE AFTERMATH OF WAR, 1918–1929

1. Richard Stewart, ed., *American Military History* (Washington, DC: USACMH, 2005), 2:53–55; "Editorial Comment," *National Service w/International Military Digest*, April 1918, 197.

2. SECWAR to the President, April 21, 1922, RG165, WD(G-3), 1919–1925, box 8, entry 228, NACP.

3. Woolley, *Creating a Modern Army*, 43; I. B. Holley, *General John M. Palmer, Citizen Soldiers, and the Army of a Democracy* (Westport, CT: Greenwood, 1982), 478.

4. Oliver Spaulding, *The US Army in War and Peace* (New York: G. P. Putnam's Sons, 1937), 460.

5. Woolley, *Creating a Modern Army*, 30; Millett and Maslowski, *For the Common Defense*, 384–86.

6. Woolley, *Creating a Modern Army*, 74, 112.

7. Harford, *A Comprehensive History of the JROTC*, 3; *WDAR, 1922*, 1:186; *1923*, 1:136; *1924*, 1:141.

8. *WDAR, 1922*, 1:186; *1923*, 1:136; *1924*, 1:141.

9. Robert Klein, *An American Century: The History of Massanutten Military Academy* (Woodstock, VA: Massanutten Military Academy, 2001), 56, 92–93.

10. Zimmerman, "Storm over the Schoolhouse," 609.

11. *WDAR, 1920*, 1:209.

12. L. P. D. Warren, *A History of Officer Procurement and the Development of the Officer Corps* (Washington, DC: USACMH, 1948), 194.

13. Memo for COS, June 9, 1937, subject: Selection of Honor Military Schools 1937; RG407, WD, 1926–1939, box 39, NACP.

14. MG H. Ely to TAG, February 27, 1930, subject: Honor Military Schools, RG407, WD, 1926–1939, box 49, NACP.

15. Army Service Forces (ASF), *History of Military Training: ROTC and the 55c Schools, 1939–1945*, October 5, 1945, 21; *WDAR, 1918*, 1:21–22; *1919*, 1:320–22; *1920*, 1:206.

16. H.R. Rep. No. 631 (1928).

17. ASF, *History of Military Training*, 23.

18. Dean Rusk, T7P, oral history, 57–58, Dean Rusk Collection (DRC), Richard B. Russell Library for Political Research and Studies, UGA (RBRLPRS); Chief of Infantry to ACS, G-3, June 5, 1936, subject: Inspector of Infantry, JROTC Units (Second Corps Area), RG407, AG, box 37, NACP.

19. Memo to CG, Third Army, October 11, 1939, subject: Ages of ROTC students, RG407, AG, box 37, NACP.

20. BG George Tyner, memo, ACS, FOR COS, June 5, 1937, subject: Reclassification of Certain Class MJ (ROTC) Institutions, RG407, box 61; Report of Inspector of Infantry, JROTC Units (2d Corps Area), RG407, box 37, NACP.

21. Woolley, *Creating a Modern Army*, 76–77.

22. *WDAR, 1919*, 1:21–22.

23. James Heuer, *Springboard for Leaders* (Rockford, IL: The Rockford Board of Education, 1963), 10.

24. *WDAR, 1922*, 1:186.

25. BG John Hughes, ACS FOR CSA, memo, January 8, 1936, subject: Proportion of Junior to Senior ROTC Units, RG407, AG, box 68, NACP (hereafter cited as Hughes, Proportion).

26. *WDAR, 1920*, 1:209; *1922*, 1:185; *1930*, 1:152.

27. *WDAR, 1919*, 1:21–22; *1920*, 1:8; *1924*, 1:11.

28. *WDAR, 1922*, 1:227; *1926*, 1:45; *1928*, 1:13–14.

29. Hughes, Proportion; LTC Edmund Bullis, "The Organization, Training and Mission of the ORC-ROTC-CMTC" (lecture, AWC, October 22, 1926), AHEC (hereafter cited as Bullis, Lecture); MAJ Robert Daniels, Supp. 3 to Rept. of Comm. 2, October 19, 1932, subject: ROTC, AHEC (hereafter cited as Daniels, ROTC); BG L. R. Gignilliat, "Students and the National Defense," *World Tomorrow*, October 1926, 148.

30. Daniels, ROTC; Heuer, *Springboard for Leaders*, 16; Supp. Military History, Joplin HS, Joplin, MO, SY 1925–1926; *WDAR, 1927*, 1:1; *1928*, 1:1.

31. Garrett Drumond, "Military Training in the Secondary Schools," *Infantry Journal*, December 1927, 614.

32. Heuer, *Springboard for Leaders*, 13–14.

33. "Military Training in Cleveland," *School Review*, March 1926, 165; "Universal Military Training in Cleveland High Schools," *World's Work*, March 1921, 584; "Editors Comment on Pacifistic Efforts to Abolish Military Training," *Army and Navy Journal* (*A&NJ*), February 20, 1926, 1.

34. Reinhold Neibuhr, "The Threat of the R.O.T.C.," *World Tomorrow*, October 1926, 154–56; Roswell Barnes, *Militarizing Our Youth* (New York: CME, 1927), 3–4.

35. "Military Training and American Schools and Colleges," *School and Society*, December 1925, 777.

36. Laura Lloyd, "The Welsh-Frazier Bill and the Nye-Kvale Bill" (PhD diss., University of Maryland, 1990), 57; Daniel Barthell, "The Committee on Militarism in Education, 1925–1940" (PhD diss., University of Illinois, 1972), 100–105.

37. Ekirch, *The Civilian and the Military*, 231; "Nye-Kvale Bill Limiting Federal Support of the R.O.T.C.," *PMS&T*, May 1936, 2.

38. "WD Statement on Personnel Requirements for the ROTC," *PMS&T*, May 1937, 7.

39. *WDAR, 1935*, 1:13.

40. Woolley, *Creating a Modern Army*, 35.

41. *Sp. Rept. of SECWAR to the President, Conference on Training for Citizenship and National Defense, 1922* (Washington, DC: GPO, 1923), 18.

42. Synopsis of Conference Proceedings, March 12–13, 1920, Between SPTs of Public Schools, Officers on ROTC Duty at Department HQs, and HS Units and WD Officers, RG165, WD/G-3, 1920–1921, box 2, entry 228, NACP.

43. Ibid.

44. C. R. Mann, Chairman, to D/WPD, April 1, 1920, subject: ROTC in Secondary Schools, RG165, WD, box 1, entry 228, NACP.

45. Ibid.

46. WPD/GS, Spec. Reg. 44, *ROTC, Authorization, Establishment, Administration, Training* (Washington, DC: GPO, 1921), 1 (hereafter cited as SR 44).

47. Ibid., 2.

48. Ralph Talbot, "Military Credits for JROTC Graduates upon Entry to Senior Units," *PMS&T*, October 1937, 1; SR 44, 21.

49. LTC R. Hill, "Development of the ORC-ROTC-CMTC, and Desirable Modifications in Present Policies" (lecture, AWC, October 16, 1933), 15, AHEC (hereafter cited as Hill, Lecture).

50. Daniels, ROTC.

51. SR 44, 26.

52. *AR of Superintendent, USMA* (West Point, NY: USMA PO, 1939), 3.

53. *WDAR, 1922*, 1:141; *1925*, 1:15.

54. *WDAR, 1921*, 1:57; *1929*, 1:79; *1939*, 1:46.

55. Hill, Lecture.

56. *WDAR, 1921*, 1:22.

57. Army Regulation (AR) 150-5, *Enlisted Reserve Corps (ERC)* (Washington, DC: War Department, September 30, 1931), 3; *WDAR, 1921*, 1:22; *1922*, 1:142.

58. "Training for War," *New Republic*, December 16, 1925, 101; Woolley, *Creating a Modern Army*, 78.

59. *WDAR, 1920*, 1:208.

60. "The Uplift Hits the Army," *American Mercury*, June 1925, 136–41.

61. Winthrop Lane, *Military Training in Schools and Colleges of the US* (New York: Garland, 1971), 5.

62. Diane Ravitch, *The Troubled Crusade: American Education, 1945–1980* (New York: Basic Books, 1983), 91.

63. Derek Heater, *A Brief History of Citizenship* (New York: NYU Press, 2004), 131.

64. *Contribution of Military Training to Public Education* (Washington, DC: CME, 1938), 3 (hereafter cited as MT in Education).

65. William Edwards, "JROTC in Public Schools," *Infantry Journal*, October 1924, 413.

66. MT in Education, 1–7.

67. John Erskine, *Universal Training for National Defense* (Madison, WI: CME, 1940), 7; Mrs. Henry Doyle, "Cadet Training: Guarantee for Democracy," in *Adjutant* (Washington, DC: HS Cadets, 1940), 23.

68. "Value of Civilian Cooperation," *A&NJ*, May 27, 1922, 5.

69. Bullis, Lecture; "Value of Civilian Cooperation," *A&NJ*, May 1922, 5.

70. "ROTC: JROTC Division," *A&NJ*, June 10, 1922, 5; Willard Nash, *A Study of the Stated Aims and Purposes of the Departments of Military Science and Tactics and Physical Education in the Land-Grant Colleges of the US* (New York: Teachers College, Columbia University, 1934), 104.

71. TAG, WD, *The Educational System of the US Army* (Washington, DC: GPO, 1920), 31.

72. *WDAR, 1921*, 2:141.

73. Ibid.

74. Rept., Sub-Comm. 6 to Comm. 1, "The Effect of Anti-war Societies on the ROTC," 1926–1927, AHEC; J. J. Fulmer, memo for D/G-1, AWC, December 20, 1924, subject: Anti-war Societies, AHEC (hereafter cited as Fulmer, Memo).

75. Supp. 5, Rept. of Comm. 8, Course, AWC, 1924–1925, December 20, 1924, subject: Interests of the G-1 Division in Anti-war Societies, AHEC; Fulmer, Memo.

76. Orvel Johnson, *Military Education in Our Schools and Colleges* (Washington, DC: ROTC AUS, 1932), 57–58, 61–62; MAJ Martin Wise, Supp. 4 to Rept. of Comm. 8, AWC, 1924–1925, December 20, 1924, subject: Radical Societies: Industrial and Political, AHEC; J. J. Fulmer, Supp. 1 to Rept. of Comm. 8, Course, AWC, 1924–1925, G-1, December 20, 1924, subject: Professional Anti-war Propagandists, AHEC.

77. *Program of Instruction (POI), JROTC* (Washington, DC: War Department, January 24, 1933), 4.

78. Lane, *Military Training*, 4.

79. US, *Citizenship Training Manual No. 1* (Washington, DC: GPO, 1921), 1–12.

80. Elvid Hunt, "Officer Influence in High Schools," *Infantry Journal*, November 1922, 507; "Are the Schools Being Militarized?," *Literary Digest*, December 26, 1925, 23, Lane, *Military Training*, 27.

81. COL Curtis Green, Supp. 3 to Rept. of Comm. 8, Course, AWC, 1924–1925, G-1, December 20, 1924, subject: Educational Efforts of Anti-war Societies, AHEC.

82. Ekirch, *Civilian and the Military*, 224.

83. Woolley, *Creating a Modern Army*, 99.

84. Edwards, "JROTC in Public Schools," 413.

85. Hunt, "Officer Influence in High Schools," 507–508.

86. F. L. Beals, *Camp Roosevelt* (Menasha, WI: George Banta, 1921), 41–43.

87. Ibid., 43.

88. Proceedings of Regional ROTC Conference, Fort McPherson, GA, October 28–30, 1937, CME, 22.

89. Ibid.

90. "Facilities Essential for the Establishment of JROTC Units," *PMS&T*, March 1938, 6.

91. Doyle, "Cadet Training," 23.

92. Parkerson and Parkerson, *Transitions in American Education*, 155.

93. William Bagley, *Classroom Management* (New York: MacMillan, 1913), 35.

94. Ibid., 38.

95. Ibid., 34–40, 96–97, 262–66; Parkerson and Parkerson, *Transitions in American Education*, 156–57.

96. Emily Elmore, "Squads for Discipline," *American Physical Education Review*, January 1923, 25–26.

97. Ibid., 26.

3. DEPRESSION AND WAR, 1930–1945

1. John Brown, *Kevlar Legions* (Washington, DC: USACMH, 2011), 480.

2. John Killigrew, *The Impact of the Great Depression on the Army* (New York: Garland, 1979), I-17.

3. Ibid., iv, III-4.

4. Ibid., I-17/18, II-2/3, II-5.

5. Ibid., II-6/14.

6. Ibid., II-19/21.

7. Ibid., II-27.

8. Ibid., V-22–28; Kershner, Harding, and Howlett, *Breaking the War Habit*, 46.

9. Killigrew, *Impact of the Great Depression*, V-7–11.

10. Ibid., V-14.

11. *WDAR, 1933*, 1:7–9, 33; *1934*, 1:52–53, 95; Arthur Leary, *The Role of the U.S. Army in Nation Building* (Carlisle, PA: USAWC, 1970), 13; Killigrew, *Impact of the Great Depression*, X-15, 16, X III-4; TAG to ACS/G-3, April 2, 1934, subject: ROTC Camp Attendance, RG407, WD/AG, 1926–1939, box 73, NACP.

12. *WDAR, 1933*, 1:7–9, 44; *1934*, 1:52–53, 95; CG/4Corps to TAG, July 14, 1932, subject: Report of Corps Area CDR's 1932 ROTC Inspections, RG407, WD, 1926–1939, box 64, NACP.

13. Report, Third Army JROTC Advisory Council Meeting, n.d., Tab D, "History of the JROTC Program"; Civilian Military Education Fund, *Military Training in High Schools of the United States: R.O.T.C.* (Washington, DC: Civilian Military Education Fund, 1936), 10; *Special Military History*, Joplin HS, Joplin, MO, SY 1925–1926; *WDAR, 1933*, 1:7–9.

14. Duncan Major, A/COS, memo, May 26, 1933, subject: ROTC Policy, RG407, 1926–1939, box 74, NACP.

15. Gerald Brennan, "Military's Peacetime Role: Implications of the CCC Experience" (master's thesis, Fort Leavenworth, KS, USACGSC, 1971), 52.

16. Killigrew, *Impact of the Great Depression*, IX-13–16.

17. Ibid., IX-17/18.

18. *Military Training in HS of the US, ROTC*, 10.

19. Rept. of Inspection, Porterville Union HS/JC, CA, 55c unit, March 17, 1932, RG407, AG, 1926–1939, SEC 1, box 44, NACP.

20. GEN Malin Craig to BG W. K. Naylor, December 21, 1935, RG407, AG, 1926–1939, ROTC, box 65, NACP.

21. *WDAR, 1935*, 1:47, 49, 64–65; *1936*, 1:32–33; *1937*, 1:9–10.

22. E. Gruber, C/TB, G-3, "Address on the Cause and Cure of War," March 3, 1937, 2, Nat'l. Comm. on the Cause and Cure of War Collected Records, Swarthmore Peace

Collection (hereafter cited as Gruber, Cure); *WDR, 1935*, 1:47–50; *1936*, 1:36, 91; "Nye-Kvale Bill Limiting Federal Support of the ROTC," *PMS&T*, May 1936, 2; BG John Hughes, ACOS for CSA, memo, January 8, 1936, subject: Proportion of Junior to Senior ROTC Units, RG407, AG, 1926–1939, SEC 2, box 68, NACP (hereafter cited as Hughes, JROTC Units).

23. Memo, A/COS FOR TAG, September 11, 1935, subject: New JROTC Units, RG407, AG, 1926–1939, SEC 2, box 68, NACP.

24. MG R. M. Beck, A/COS, for TAG, December 29, 1938, subject: ROTC Units in NJ, RG407, AG, 1926–1939, SEC 2, box 58, NACP.

25. Rept. of Annual Inspection (RAI), 1932, 55c NDA School—Florida MA, Jacksonville, RG407, AG, SEC 1, box 44, NACP.

26. RAI, February 17, 1932, 55c NDA School, Amarillo HS, RG407, AG, SEC 1, box 44, NACP; Robert Collins to TAG, June 26, 1931, subject: ROTC Inspections, RG407, AG, SEC 1, box 46, NACP; Hughes, JROTC Units.

27. RAI, 1932, 55c NDA, Jamaica HS; RAI, 55c NDA School, Sacramento HS, May 20, 1932, RG407, SEC 1, box 44, NACP; Charles Sharpe, President, Carbondale Ministerial Association, to WD, July 9, 1936, RG407, SEC 2, box 71, NACP; Secretary of AAUW, resolution, July 9, 1936, subject: Opposition to ROTC in HS, RG407, SEC 1, box 44, NACP.

28. Hughes for COS, memo, December 31, 1935, subject: New ROTC Units, RG407, SEC 2, box 68, NACP.

29. Ibid.

30. COL H. R. Richmond to CG/4Corps, December 20, 1937, subject: Spec/Inspection, Pearl River JC, Poplarville, MS, RG407, SEC 2, box 37, NACP.

31. COL Gordon Catts, Extract Report of ROTC Unit at Pearl River JC, Poplarville, MS, February 6, 1936, RG407, box 61, NACP.

32. MAJ George Hadd, A/AG, HQ2Corps, Governors Island, NY, to TAG, October 25, 1935, RG407, box 70, NACP.

33. MG George Moseley to MG E. T. Conley, TAG, May 24, 1937, RG407, box 61, NACP; Moseley to TAG, January 27, 1937, subject: Establishment of a Junior Unit of the ROTC, RG407, box 72, NACP.

34. HQ-7Corps to PMS&T, St. Joseph HS, MO, June 20, 1939, subject: ROTC Training in Bartlett HS, RG407, box 35, NACP; T. E. Dale to CG/7Corps, June 22, 1939, RG407, box 49, NACP.

35. BG R. E. Beck, ACOS, to TAG, July 5, 1938, subject: JROTC Units (Hawaii), RG407, box 60, NACP.

36. *WDAR, 1936*, 1:32; *1937*, 1:8, 30, 32; "WD Appropriates $1,000,000 for New Units of the ROTC in Schools and Colleges," *New Republic*, June 19, 1935, 151; "ROTC Gains," *Survey Graphic*, November 1935, 337; Kreidberg, *History of Military Mobilization*, 379, 452; "Senate Rescinds Action on ROTC Instructors: New Units Eliminated—Advanced Course Increase Allowed," *PMS&T*, May 1939, 1–2; "ROTC Funds for Pay of Cadets at West Point," *PMS&T*, May 1939, 2; "WD Statement on Personnel Requirements for the R.O.T.C.," *PMS&T*, May 1937, 7–8; *WDAR, 1940*, 1:61.

37. MAJ Olsen, AAG/2Corps to TAG, May 9, 1936, RG407, AG, 1926–1939, ROTC, box 72, NACP; GEN Malin Craig to BG W. K. Naylor, December 21, 1935, RG407, box 65, NACP.

38. George Tyner, ACOS, to COS, May 28, 1937, subject: Discontinuance of JROTC Units in 4th Corps, RG407, box 61, NACP.

39. L. John Shuman, AG, to TAG, July 31, 1937, subject: Establishment of New ROTC Units, RG407, box 7; MAJ Daniels AAG to TAG, July 20, 1936, RG407, box 64, NACP.

40. *Military Training in HS of the US*, 3; "Largest ROTC Unit," *PMS&T*, October 1937, 3; Gruber, Cure, 3.

41. MG E. T. Conley, TAG, to Fritz Lanham, HR, March 4, 1936, RG407, box 70, NACP; Memo, COL George Tyner, ACOS, FOR COS, August 13, 1936, subject: Establishment of JROTC Unit at North Fulton HS, Atlanta, RG407, box 65, NACP; TAG to CG/9Corps, June 24, 1937, subject: Expansion of JROTC Unit, RG407, box 34, NACP.

42. John Shurman, AGD, to TAG, July 31, 1937, subject: Establishment of New ROTC Units, RG407, box 60, NACP.

43. Franklin, *The Militant South*, 43.

44. Cunliffe, *Soldiers and Civilians*, 23.

45. Peter Karsten, "Armed Progressives," in *The Military in America*, ed. Peter Karsten, 2nd ed. (New York: Free Press, 1986), 261.

46. *JROTC Manual, 1935* (Washington, DC: GPO, 1935), 7.

47. Revision of 1928 POI for Junior Units (CS), January 24, 1933, RG407, AG, 1926–1939, box 35, NACP (hereafter cited as Revision, POI); Fork Union MA, *The Skirmisher* (Fork Union, VA: Fork Union Military Academy, 1937), 99.

48. Revision, POI.

49. Ibid.

50. COL H. H. Tebbets to PMS&Ts, Fourth Corps, June 18, 1930, subject: Instructional Methods, RG407, box 44, NACP.

51. H. D. Mitchell to TAG, July 14, 1930, subject: Formal AI, 55c Schools, ROTC, RG407, box 49, NACP.

52. MAJ H. P. Banks to TAG, May 26, 1930, subject: Inspection Reports of JROTC Unit, RG407, box 44/37/49, NACP; Revision, POI.

53. Ibid.

54. F. L. Beals, *Camp Roosevelt: Its History and Development* (Menasha, WI: George Banta, 1921), 8; Klein, *An American Century*, 56–57.

55. CPT J. E. Harriman, for Asst. Comdt., AWC, October 12, 1938, subject: Refresher Course for NCOs DEML (ROTC), AHEC.

56. Killigrew, *Impact of the Great Depression*, IX-6, 10, 12.

57. Joel Springer, *The Sorting Machine: National Educational Policy Since 1945* (New York: McKay, 1976), 28; Parkerson and Parkerson, *Transitions in American Education*, 207.

58. Proceedings of the Regional ROTC Conference, Fort McPherson, GA, October 28–30, 1937, CMEF, 9.

59. Jonathon Zimmerman, "Storm over the Schoolhouse: Exploring Popular Influences upon the American Curriculum, 1890–1941," *Teachers College Record*, Spring 1999, 612.

60. Killigrew, *Impact of the Great Depression*, IX-6, 12.

61. Ibid., XIV-17, 29.

62. Ibid., 30.

63. Chief of Infantry for Asst. COS, G-3, October 3, 1934, subject: ROI, ROTC, 1Corps, RG407, AG, 1926–1939, ROTC, box 41, NACP.

64. Ronald Schaffer, "The War Department's Defense of ROTC, 1920–1940," *Wisconsin Magazine of History* 53, no. 2 (Winter, 1969–1970): 110–12; Zimmerman, "Storm over the Schoolhouse," 623n33.

65. Orientation for ROTC Duty: A Compilation of the Experiences of Military Instructors at Educational Institutions, Civilian Military Education Fund, Washington DC, 1934, RG407, box 72, NACP.

66. Schaffer, "War Department's Defense," 114.

67. Army Service Forces (ASF), *History of Military Training: A History of the Reserve Officers' Training Corps and the 55c (NDA) Schools, 1939–1945* (Washington, DC: War Department, October 1945), 84, 85, 97.

68. Ibid., 99.

69. Ibid., 84–85, 97.

70. Ibid.

71. Ibid., 97.

72. Klein, *American Century*, 14; ASF, *History of Military Training*, 84, 93.

73. Arthur Coumbe, Lee Harford, and Paul Kotakis, *The U.S. Army Cadet Command: The First 10 Years* (Stillwater, OK: New Forums, 1996), 8, 21.

74. James Hewes, *From Root to McNamara* (Washington, DC: USACMH, 1983), 67–90.

75. ASF, *History of Military Training*, 34.

76. Ibid.

77. Ibid.

78. Ibid.

79. Memo, Exec. for Reserve and ROTC Affairs, for Special Planning Division, OCSA, April 5, 1944, subject: Post-war Planning—ROTC, RG407, AG, 1926–1939, box 39, NACP.

80. Ibid.; *High School Victory Corps: Hearing on S. 875, Before the Committee on Education/Labor*, 78th Cong. 14 (1943).

81. American Legion, *Military Training in High and Preparatory Schools*, n.d., OPR, RG A0002, range Z, box 37, LSU Archives (LSUA).

82. Dept. of Educ. LA, Cir-2257, re: HS Military Drill, n.d., OPR, RG A0002; "How the Louisiana Plan Started," OPR, RG A0002, range Z, box 37, LSUA.

83. American Legion, *What the Training Does* (n.d.); *Military Training in High and Preparatory Schools*, n.d., OPR, RG A0002, box 37, LSUA.

84. Richard Ugland, "Education for Victory," *History of Education Quarterly* 19, no. 4 (Winter 1979): 435–37.

85. *High School Victory Corps*, 14.

86. Ibid.

87. Ibid.

88. US War Department, *History of Military Training* (Washington, DC: WD Hist. Div., 1944–1946), 1–5.

89. Ugland, "Education for Victory," 439.

90. Ibid., 442.

91. *High School Victory Corps*, 14.

4. FROM TRUMAN TO KENNEDY, 1945–1963

1. Maurice Matloff, *American Military History* (Washington, DC: USACMH, 1969), 200.

2. Eliot Cohen, *Citizens and Soldiers* (Ithaca, NY: Cornell University Press, 1985), 56–58.

3. Ravitch, *The Troubled Crusade*.

4. Report, *Statistics Branch, GS/WD, ROTC Enrollment, SY 1939/1940* (Washington, DC: War Department, 1940), I:B-70; *ROTC Enrollment Report (ER), SY 1950–1951* (Washington, DC: Department of the Army, 1951).

5. GEN Omar Bradley, CSA, memo, March 27, 1947, subject: Draft: Postwar ROTC, box 79 (hereafter cited as Bradley, Postwar); CSGOT, MG H. R. Bule, AD/O&T, to CAR-ROTC, August 17, 1948, subject: Proposed Change to Memo 145-10-32 (Establishment of JROTC Units), box 80; BG Wendell Westover, ERROTCA, to LTC William Sherman, Eau Claire SHS, WI, February 26, 1948, box 3, RG319, CAR/GC, 1948–1954, NACP.

6. Eliot Cohen, *Making Do with Less* (Carlisle, PA: USAWC, SSI, 1995), 4; Dennis Ippolito, *Federal Budget Policy and Defense Strategy* (Carlisle, PA: USAWC, SSI, 1996), 3.

7. Tami Biddle, "Shield and Sword," in *The Long War*, ed. Andrew Bacevich (New York: Columbia University Press, 2007), 141.

8. Ibid.

9. *Expansion of the ROTC: Hearing before the Senate Armed Services Committee*, 80th Cong. 8 (1947); E. V. Weichel, Supt. Moultrie PS, to Richard Russell, May 1, 1951, RBRC, RBRLPRS, UGA; Bradley, Postwar.

10. BG Wendell Westover, ER-ROTCA, to Senator Spessard Holland, July 16, 1948, RG319, CAR/54, box 3, NACP; Frederick Hayden, C/ROTC Div, for GEN Lindeman, February 24, 1955, subject: Study of Junior Division ROTC, RG319, CAR/54, box 35, NACP (hereafter cited as Hayden, Study).

11. W. A. Bass, Supt., Nashville CPS, to CG, Third Army, July 24, 1952, RG316, CAR/54, box 7, NACP.

12. Bernd Baetcke, *The ROTC* (Ft. Leavenworth, KS: USAWC, 1951), 4; DOD/CCC, *Reserve Forces for National Security: Report to the Secretary of Defense* (Gray Committee Report) (Washington, DC: GPO, 1948), 4–6.

13. MFR, LTC C. O. Buckland, ROTC Div\ERROTCA, February 28, 1952, subject: Conference Re: Review of the ROTC, RG319, CAR/54, box 81, NACP.

14. MFR, LTC Charles Buckland, ROTC Div/ERROTCA, July 17, 1951, subject: Telephone Call from LTC R. Johnson (Tacoma), RG319, CAR/54, box 81, NACP; Briefing, RES/ERROTCA, to LTG Maxwell Taylor, September 4, 1951, subject: ROTC, RG319, CAR/54, box 82 (hereafter cited as Taylor, ROTC); COL Joe Ross, C/MCD, to CSA, October 30, 1951, subject: ROTC—Review of ROTC, RG319, CAR, 1954, box 81, NACP (hereafter cited as Ross, Review).

15. MFR, COL David Gibbs, A/SoGS, December 19, 1951, subject: Review of the ROTC, RG319, CAR/54, box 81, NACP (hereafter cited as Gibbs, Review).

16. CGOT, BG D. Ogden, AD/O&T, to ARROTC, July 16, 1949, subject: Proposed Rescission of AR 145-10, May 28, 1931, RG319, CAR/54, box 79, NACP.

17. Taylor, ROTC.

18. Ibid.

19. Taylor, *Military Service and American Democracy*, 33–41; Rodger Venzke, *Confidence in Battle, Inspiration in Peace* (Washington, DC: U.S. Army Chief of Chaplains, 1977), 37.

20. Richard Hutchinson, *The Churches and the Chaplaincy* (Atlanta: John Knox, 1975), 147.

21. Anne Loveland, "From Morale Builders to Moral Advocates," in *The Sword of the Lord*, ed. Doris Bergen (South Bend, IN: Notre Dame Press, 2004), 234.

22. "4 U.S. Clergymen Urge Haste on Aid," *New York Times*, October 5, 1947, 2.

23. Venzke, *Confidence in Battle*, 57.

24. MAJ James Burleson, ROTC/LO, to CO/NY Military District, October 3, 1951; Burleson to COL Thomas Joyce, C/IL Military District, October 15, 1951, RG319, CAR/54, box 81, NACP.

25. COL Frederick Haydon, C/ROTC Division, for GEN Lindeman, February 24, 1955, subject: Study, Junior Division ROTC, RG319, CAR, 1955, box 35, NACP; Taylor, ROTC.

26. Overton Brook, "We Can Have Army Enlisted Reserves," *Reserve Officer*, January 1950, 5.

27. COL George Butler, DC/ARROTC, to D/OT, May 11, 1949, subject: Proposed Change to Memo 145-10-32, RG319, CAR, 1954, box 79, NACP; GEN Maxwell Taylor, CSA, memo, February 27, 1957, subject: AR and ROTC, FY 1958, RG319, RA/CoR, 1957, box 1, NACP.

28. DA, *ATP 145-4, POI for CS ROTC*, February 21, 1950 (hereafter cited as ATP, CS).

29. HQ/CA Military District to CG/6Army, July 10, 1950, subject: Proposed Revision of ROTC, RG319, CAR, 1948–1954, box 79, NACP; Gibbs, Review; RES-ROTC, Ralph Hansen, XO, ARROTCA, to DCSPER, October 17, 1956, subject: JROTC, RG319, CAR, 1956, box 48, NACP (hereafter cited as Hansen, JROTC).

30. Ross, Review; RES, LTC Bachorash, CARROTC, for DCS/OA, September 17, 1951, subject: Army ROTC, RG319, CAR, 1954, box 81, NACP.

31. Ross, Review; GSGOT, MG Cleft Andrus, DO&T, for Karl Bendetsen, September 2, 1949, subject: ROTC Trainer Personnel, RG319, CAR, 1948–1954, box 79, NACP (hereafter cited as Andrus, JDIV); CSGOT, memo, September 26, 1949, subject: The Educational Program for the ROTC, RG319, CAR, 1948–1954, box 79, NACP.

32. Biddle, "Shield and Sword," 14.

33. COL Hayden, ROTC/CARROTC, Concept of Study: Application of a Modified Form of "Operation Teammate" to Instructor Personnel in ROTC, May 27, 1955, RG319, CAR, 1955, box 38, NACP (hereafter cited as Operation Teammate); Change 2 to Army Regulation (AR) 145-350, *Reserve Officers' Training Corps, Organization and Training of Units* (Washington, DC: Department of the Army, March 18, 1954), 3.

34. *ROTC Enrollment Report (ER), FY 1953–1954* (Washington, DC: Department of the Army, 1954), 1–15; *ROTC Enrollment Report (ER), FY 1954–1955* (Washington DC: Department of the Army, 1955), 10–17.

35. Hayden, Study; LTC Long to CARROTC, February 7, 1955, subject: Requests for Additional JROTC Units, RG319, CAR, 1955, box 36, NACP.

36. MG Philip Lindeman, ARROTCA, to AC&RC, COS, ASA (MP&RF), July 16, 1957, subject: AA Personnel Support for ROTC and AR, RG319, RO/CoR, 1957, box 2, NACP; MG Ralph Palladino, Chief, USARROTC, to AC & RC, November 29, 1957,

subject: Review of the ROTC, RG319, RO/CoR, 1957, box 3, NACP (hereafter cited as Palladino, ROTC).

37. Taylor, ROTC.

38. MG John Klein, TAG, to CARROTC/DCSOPS/DCSPER, June 6, 1956, subject: Establishment of JROTC Units in Savannah, RG319, CAR, 1956, box 48, NACP (hereafter cited as Klein, Savannah).

39. LTC Miller to TAG, April 3, 1955, subject: Reallocations to Provide Additional ROTC Instruction, Dallas HS, RG319, CAR, 1955, box 38, NACP.

40. LTC Miller to CARROTC/ACoS, May 11, 1955, subject: Reallocations for Additional ROTC Instruction, Dallas HS RG319, CAR, 1955, box 38, NACP.

41. John Nonnett, A/XO, to D/OT, August 19, 1949, subject: Proposed Rescission of AR 145–10 (1931), RG319, CAR, 1948–1954, box 79, NACP; BG D. Ogdan, AD/O&T, to CARROTC, August 16, 1949, subject: Proposed Rescission of AR 145–10 (1931), RG319, CAR, 1955, box 35, NACP.

42. DA, Evaluation of Possible Savings in FY 1964 Programs, September 28, 1962, RG319, RAS/OCR/CG, 1962, box 8, NACP; Senator Richard Russell to MG Miles Reber, June 9, 1953, RBRC, RBRL, UGAL (hereafter cited as Russell, Reber).

43. Russell, Reber; Taylor, ROTC.

44. Hayden, Study; Charles Stevenson to A. C. Smith, CG/5Army, June 12, 1952, RG319, CAR, 1948–1954, box 7, NACP.

45. The Educational Program for the ROTC: RG 319, Records of the Army Staff, Records of the Office of the Chief of Reserves, Correspondence 1957, 320.2–322, box 2 (hereafter cited as Ed., Program]; LTC Kilday, ROTCD/ARROTCA, study, July 16, 1957, subject: AA Personnel Support for the ROTC, RG319, RAS/RO/CoR, 1957, box 2, NACP (hereafter cited as Kilday, ROTC); Klein, Savannah.

46. Hansen, JROTC; Hayden, Study.

47. Operation Teammate.

48. Palladino, ROTC.

49. *ROTC Enrollment Report (ER), FY 1955–1956* (Washington, DC: Department of the Army, 1956), n.p. to *ROTC Enrollment Report (ER), 1959–1960* (Washington, DC: Department of the Army, 1960), n.p.

50. Info Paper, Non-expansion Policy for the ROTC, n.d., RG319, CR, 1957, box 1, NACP.

51. COL Homer Case, C/Manpower Control Division, G-1, to G-3, May 4, 1950, subject: Admission of JCMI Graduates to OCS, RG319, CAR, 948–1954, box 79, NACP.

52. MG Edward Witsell, TAG, memo, October 11, 1950, subject: Consolidation of MI & MS Institutions into the Same Classification, RG319, CAR, 1948–1954, box 80, NACP (hereafter cited as Witsell, Memo).

53. COL Hayden, ROTC/CARROTC, January 6, 1955, Study: MS in the 55c Program, RG319, CAR, 1955, box 39, NACP; Palladino, ROTC.

54. Witsell, Memo; COL Frederick Hayden, C/ROTCD, for GEN Lindeman, November 8, 1955, subject: POI and Training for MS Div Units, RG319, CAR, 1955, box 36, NACP (hereafter cited as Hayden, POI).

55. Taylor, ROTC; Ross, Review.

56. DF, COL R. Cato, AD/O&T/ODCSOPS, to CARROTC, July 18, 1957, subject: Active Army Personnel Support for the ROTC, RG319, ROCoR, GC, 1957, 320.2–322, box 2, NACP (hereafter cited as Cato, Support).

57. Hayden, POI; Palladino, ROTC; Cato, Support.

58. Kilday, ROTC.

59. *ER, FY 1955–1956.*

60. COL Frederick Hayden, ROTCD/EARROTC, for GEN Lindeman, June 29, 1956, subject: Study: Support of 55c NOA, RG319, CAR, 1956, box 48, NACP (hereafter cited as 55c, Study); Senator Richard Russell to Herbert Dunlap, Prof., McCallie School, July 23, 1953, RBRL, UGAL (hereafter cited as Russell, Letter).

61. R. Stewart, *American Military History,* 2:262.

62. RPB, *Study on Procurement of Reserve Officers from All Sources* (Washington, DC: GPO, 1955), 2; DOD, *AR-FY 1956* (Washington, DC: GPO, 1957), 12; CONARC/G-3/SMEP, *FY 1955, 7/1/1954–12/31/1954* (Washington, DC: CONARC, n.d.), 14–15, TA.

63. CONARC/G-3/SMEP, *FY 1955, 1/1/1955–6/30/1955* (Washington, DC: CONARC, 1955), 17, TA.

64. Joseph Rockis, *AGF Demobilization Studies: Role of the ORC and the ROTC in AGF, September 1, 1945–March 10, 1948* (Washington, DC: Army Historical Section, March 18, 1949), 39; Office, Chief of Army Field Forces (AFF), *Annual History, 1948* (Fort Monroe, VA: AFF, 1948), 3.

65. S. Rep. No. 83–673, vol. 1 (1953); LTC G. M. Bacharach, C/ROTCD/CARROTC, for COL Butler, September 14, 1950, subject: 55c NDA Military Schools Problems & Possible Solutions, RG319, CAR, 1948–1954, box 80, NACP; Russell, Letter; 55c, Study.

66. CONARC, *Reserve Component Division, G-3, Summary of Major Events & Problems, January 1, 1955–June 30, 1955* (Fort Monroe, VA: CONARC, 1955), 3, TA (hereafter cited as SMEP, 1955); 55c, Study.

67. 55c, Study.

68. SMEP, 1955.

69. Hansen, JROTC.

70. SMEP, 1955.

71. BG Lauren Williams, C/MD, to ACoS/G-3, January 15, 1953, subject: Army Organization for ROTC, RG319, CAR, 1948–1954, box 83, NACP; Baetcke, *ROTC,* 5.

72. COL George E. Butler, *Summary Sheet/Staff Study by ACoS, G-3, on Army Org for ROTC Program,* July 7, 1952.

73. Ibid.; Earl Johnson, ASA (M&RF), for CSA, December 12, 1951, subject: Review of ROTC, RG319, CAR, 1948–1954, box 81, NACP.

74. Hayden, POI; ATP, CS, 2; George Rankin, "The Administration of the Army ROTC Units" (master's thesis, Syracuse University, 1949), 29.

75. SMEP, 1955, 4, 6; *ROTC Enrollment Report (ER), SY 1964–1965* (Washington, DC: Department of the Army, 1965), n.p..

76. Michael Stewart, "Raising a Pragmatic Army" (PhD diss., University of Kansas, 2010), 146.

77. ATP, CS, 3.

78. Troy Shelby, XO, to CLL, September 22, 1955, subject: Summer Field Training of JROTC Cadets of Byrd and Fair Park HS, Shreveport, LA, RG319, CAR, 1955, box 37, NACP.

79. Hadley, "Association of Military Colleges and Schools," 87.

80. A. Osden, C/O&TD, ACS/G-3, to TAG, October 2, 1950, subject: Consolidation of Class MI/MS Institutions into the Same Classification, RG319, CAR, 1948–1954, box 80, NACP.

81. Bacharach for Butler, 24; ATP, CS, 1962:6.

82. ATP, CS, 1955, 1957.

83. Glen Nelson, XO/CARROTC, to DCSOPS/DCSPER, June 13, 1956, subject: Establishment of JROTC Units in Savannah, RG319, CAR, 1956, box 48, NACP; GEN Maxwell Taylor, CSA, memo, February 27, 1957, subject: Army Reserve and ROTC, FY 1958, Change Order 1, RG319, RO/CoR, 1957, box 1, NACP.

5. MCNAMARA AND THE MODERN JROTC, 1963–1964

1. Russell Weigley, *History of the US Army* (Bloomington: Indiana University Press, 1984), 596–97.

2. Ibid.

3. US Department of Defense, "Robert S. McNamara," SECDEF Biographies, accessed December 10, 2024, https://history.defense.gov/Multimedia/Biographies/Article-View/Article/571271/robert-s-mcnamara.

4. Ibid.

5. H.R. Rep. No. 925 (1963) (hereafter cited as ROTC, 925); Christopher Bogden, "The Perceived Value of JROTC" (PhD diss., Harvard University, 1984), 17–18; Mary Pardue, "ROTC Program to Get Study," *Fort Worth Star-Telegram*, February 8, 1963, 2; "Drastic Cutback in ROTC Program to Be Proposed," *Fort Worth Star-Telegram*, January 6, 1963, 4; "McNamara Aims at Reduced Cost," *Dallas Morning News*, January 6, 1963, 5.

6. Thelma Slayden, "Junior ROTC Helps High School Boys as Soldiers and Patriotic Citizens," *Officer*, May 1969, 13; "ROTC Bill at a Crucial Point," *Officer*, September 1964, 5; Craig Karpel, "The Teenie Militarists," *Ramparts*, August 1968, 44.

7. *ROTC Program: Hearings pursuant to H.R. 4427 & H.R. 4444, Before Subcommittee 3 of the House Armed Service Committee*, 88th Cong. 6386 (1963) (hereafter cited as SC3, HASC).

8. Ibid., 6391.

9. Ibid., 6427.

10. Ibid., 6504–505, 6509–11, 6440–41; Slayden, "Junior ROTC Helps," 14; Karpel, "The Teenie Militarists," 44.

11. SC3, HASC, 6385–6387.

12. Herman Talmadge, "Reports from Washington," April 3, 1963, RBRLPL, UGAL.

13. Ibid.

14. ROTC, 925; Bogden, "Perceived Value of JROTC," 20; "Special Committee Studies Junior ROTC Program," *Air Force Times*, May 15, 1963, 23; AFROTC Jr. Plans Dir., *AFJROTC Study* (Maxwell AFB, AL: Air University, 1977), 14.

15. "ROTC Expansion," *CQ Almanac*, 1964, https://library.cqpress.com/cqalmanac/document.php?id=cqal64-1304926.

16. ROTC, 925; SC3, HASC, 6386; Ad Hoc Committee for JROTC, report, April 30–June 7, 1963, subject: Future Ops. of the Junior Division ROTC and NDCC, Tulane University Archives (hereafter cited as FOJD).

17. FOJD, 10.

18. William Taylor, *Junior Reserve Officers' Training Corps: Contributions to America's Communities* (Washington, DC: CSIS, 1999), 41–42.

19. "Anti-segregation Issue Kills House ROTC Bill," in *CQ Almanac*, 19th ed. (Washington, DC: *Congressional Quarterly*, 1964), 441, http://library.cqpress.com/cqalmanac/cqal63-1317489.

20. FOJD, 24–25.

21. Ibid., 25–2.

22. Ibid., 26.

23. Ibid., 27.

24. Ibid., 5–23.

25. Ibid., 9–2.

26. *ROTC Program*: Hearing Before the House Armed Services Committee, 88th Cong. 33 (1963), 6424.

27. FOJD, 28.

28. Ibid., 25, 5–23-A.

29. Ibid., app. 15.

30. Ibid., 24, 9–4.

31. *ROTC Program*: HASC, 33 (1963), 6447.

32. FOJD, 9–1/3.

33. Ibid., 15–16, 9–2.

34. Ibid., 15, 26, 9–2.

35. H.R. Rep. No. 917, at 15 (1963).

36. FOJD, 9–3.

37. Ibid., 17–20.

38. Ibid., 20.

39. Ibid., 21.

40. Ibid.

41. Ibid.

42. Ibid.

43. SC3, HASC, 6539.

44. FOJD, 21.

45. Ibid.

46. Ibid.

47. Ibid., 6–1.

48. Ibid.

49. Ibid.

50. Ibid.

51. Ibid.

52. Ibid.

53. Ibid., 5–27-A.

54. Ibid.

55. Ibid, 15–23.

56. Ibid.

57. Ibid.

58. Ibid.

59. Ibid.

60. Ibid.

61. Ibid.
62. Ibid.
63. Ibid.
64. Ibid., 15–16, 25, 9–1.
65. Ibid.
66. H.R. Rep. No. 917 (1963).
67. FOJD, 25.
68. Ibid.
69. Ibid., 16–1/2.
70. Ibid., 7–15.
71. Ibid., 7–16.
72. Ibid.
73. Ibid.
74. Ibid.
75. *Hearing on H.R. 9124: ROTC Vitalization Act of 1964, Before the Senate Armed Services Committee*, 88th Cong. 58 (1964).
76. FOJD, 7–16.
77. Ibid., 5–28-A.
78. Ibid., 7–16.
79. Ibid.
80. Ibid.
81. Ibid., 28.
82. Ibid., 28.
83. Ibid.
84. Ibid.
85. Ibid., 5–22-A.
86. Ibid., 5–28-A, 6–1.
87. Ibid., 28.
88. Ibid., 7–4, 9–1.
89. Ibid.
90. Ibid.
91. Ibid.

6. JROTC EXPANSION DURING THE VIETNAM WAR, 1964–1973

1. William A. Taylor, *Military Service and American Democracy: From World War II to the Iraq and Afghanistan Wars* (Lawrence, KS: University of Kansas Press, 2019), 107; Jennifer Mittelstadt, *The Rise of the Military Welfare State* (Cambridge, MA: Harvard University Press, 2015), 75–76; Bernard Roster, *I Want You: The Evolution of the All-Volunteer Force* (Santa Monica, CA: RAND, 2006), 135. As they did the JROTC, many critics characterized Project 100,000 as a "social experiment," part of Johnson's Great Society program.

2. Cyrus Vance, Dep. SECDEF, to Richard Russell, Chm. SASC, July 2, 1964, in S. Rep. No. 1514 (1964); Memo for President, Wilfred Rommel, Acting AD, Leg. Ref., BOB, October 8, 1964, subject: Enrolled Bill HR9124—ROTC Vitalization Act, in S. Rep. No. 1514 (1964) (hereafter cited as Rommel, ROTCVA); William Cohen, A/S, HEW, to Kermit

Gordon, Dir, BOB, October 2, 1964, in S. Rep. No. 1514 (1964); "Special Committee Studies JROTC Program," *Air Force Times* (*AFT*), May 15, 1963, 23:14.

3. SC3, HASC, 6517.

4. H.R. Rep. No. 925, at 31 (1963); "Debacle in the First House Test Blocks ROTC Reforms for Year," *Officer*, January 1964, 5.

5. "Briefly noted," *CCCO New Notes*, September 10, 1964; Richard Malishchak, *Military Training for 14-Year-Olds* (Philadelphia: United Church Press, 1973), 8–9.

6. *88th Congressional Record* (*CR*), (1964), V114/P12, 22978–22981.

7. *88th CR*, (1964), V123/PT14, 18765; AFJROTC Prog. Dir., *AFJROTC Study* (Maxwell AFB: Air University, 1977), 132 (hereafter cited as AFJROTCS).

8. *88th CR*, (1964), V110/PT11, 14636, 14686.

9. F. Edward Hebert, *Last of the Titans*, with John McMillan (Lafayette: Center for LA Studies, University of SWLA, 1976), 27.

10. Rommel, ROTCVA.

11. "The Hebert Plan," *Officer*, XL, November 1964, 2.

12. Rommel, ROTCVA, chap. 102, SEC 2031.

13. Ibid.; Bogden, "Perceived Value of JROTC," 21; "Army Junior ROTC Program," March 17, 1964, Mil. Asst. A (MMA), SF, box 9, folder 2, Strom Thurmond Collection (STC), SC, Clemson University Library (CUL).

14. Robert McNamara, Memo for President, October 3, 1964, LBJ Archives (LBJA).

15. Myer Feldman, Memo for President, October 13, 1964, subject: HR9124—Changes in ROTC, LBJA.

16. "Johnson Hits Expansion of JROTC," *AFT*, October 28, 1964, 25:10.

17. *The Code of Federal Regulations of the USA, Part III, ROTC Programs for Secondary Educational Institutions* (Washington, DC: GPO, 1966), 138–39; DOD Dir. 1215.13, October 31, 1965, 1–7 (hereafter cited as DODD, 1215.13).

18. ROTC/NDCC Dir., CONARC, *Fact Sheet (FS)* (Fort Monroe, VA: USCONARC, 1970), subject: The Army JROTC; ROTC Man. 145-4-1, *JROTC Manual*, September 1967, 1:23; ATP145-10, *POI Junior Division ROTC & NDCC*, December 30, 1966, 2–4; CONARC, Rept. of 5th JROTC/NDCC Cong., September 5–8, 1967, 153 (hereafter cited as Rept., 5JROTC/NDCC); D. S. Capozzalo, "NJROTC: Profile and Practice," *US Naval Institute Proceedings* (*USNIP*), July 1975, 98.

19. DODD, 1215.13, 3; White House, Press Release, "Statement by the President," October 14, 1964, LBJA.

20. DODD, 1205.13, 5; *AR145-10* (n.p.: HQDA, 1966), 8; HQ/CONARC, *History of the Junior ROTC* (Fort Monroe, VA: USCONARC, 1966).

21. "Briefly Noted," *CCCO News and Notes*, October 11, 1959, 3.

22. CONARC, "History."

23. Ralph Williams, "The Junior NROTC," *USNIP*, June 1969, 136; R. R. Panzer, "JROTC: A Synopsis," *Marine Corps Gazette* (*MCG*), June 1969, 13.

24. CONARC, Msg 51907, Subject: Staffing for Army ROTC Jr. Div., February 1, 1966; "Slots Open for Retirees," *Army ROTC Newsletter (AROTCN)*, July 9, 1967, 5.

25. Rept., 5JROTC/NDCC, 154.

26. DOD, *AR-FY1966* (Washington, DC: GPO, 1967), 181–82; Rept., 5JROTC/NDCC, 4, 27.

27. "CONARC to Run Jr. ROTC," *AROTCN*, April 6, 1967, 4; Rept., 5JROTC/NDCC, 27.

28. Rept., 5JROTC/NDCC, 4, 15.

29. Ibid.; *Enrollment Report (ER), Army ROTC* (Washington, DC: Department of the Army, 1964–1974), 45–59 (hereafter cited as *ER, AROTC*).

30. ROTC, 925.

31. Malishchak, *Military Training for 14-Year-Olds*, 15.

32. Rept., 5JROTC/NDCC, 27; *ER, AROTC, SY 1965–66 & 1966–67*; Reserve Officers' Training Corps Vitalization Act of 1964—An Act to Amend Title 10, "United States Code, to Vitalize the Reserve Officers' Training Corps programs of the Army, Navy, and Air Force, and for Other Purposes, Public Law 88-647," *U.S. Statutes at Large* LXXVIII (1964), 1063–64; *ER, TRADOC, FY 1973*, 45–59.

33. COL Shaffer, AG, CONARC, to CG, CONUSA/Alaska/Pacific/SOUTHCOM, May 13, 1968, subject: Cross-Enrollment in JROTC, TA.

34. Ibid.

35. Joel Springer, *The Sorting Machine* (New York: McKay, 1976), 123.

36. Ibid.

37. Ravitch, *Troubled Crusade*, 233–34.

38. Springer, *Sorting Machine*, 227, 230, 256.

39. TRADOC, *History of the JROTC* (Fort Monroe, VA: TRADOC, n.d.).

40. Ravitch, *Troubled Crusade*, 152.

41. Ibid.

42. *ER, AJROTC, FY 1964–1972* (Washington, DC: Department of the Army, 1964–1972).

43. Melvin Ecke, *From Ivy Street to the Kennedy Center* (Atlanta: Atlanta Board of Education, 1972), 109, 129.

44. Ibid., 321.

45. Ira Jarrell, Supt., APS, TAG, letter, February 26, 1952, RG319, CAR, 1948–1954, box 6, NACP.

46. Ecke, *From Ivy Street*, 321, 370.

47. Ibid., 370–76.

48. *ER, AJROTC, FY1965–1968* (Washington, DC: Department of the Army, 1974); Andrew Coulson, *Market Education* (New York: Transaction, 1999), 275.

49. Rept., 4AJROTC/NDCC, 5; *ER, AJROTC, SY 1973–1974* (Fort Monroe: TRADOC, 1974), 45–59.

50. Ken Berry, "Parcel Working to Ban ROTC in High Schools," *Arizona Republic*, September 1, 1973), 8; *AFJROTC Bulletin* (*AFJROTCB*), October 1973, 7.

51. William Boyer, "Junior ROTC: Militarism in the Schools," *Phi Delta Kappan*, November 1964, 119.

52. Derrick Shearer, "The Brass Image," *Nation*, April 20, 1975, 161–62.

53. Gayle Koontz and Ted Koontz, "New Front in the Battle with Militarism," *Mennonite*, June 19, 1973, 400; Steve Gulick, "JROTC: 'Solving' a Gang Problem," *CCCO News Notes*, Fall 1974, 7.

54. Thomas Conrad, Glenn Sheehan, and Stephen M. Gulick, "Junior ROTC—Expanding," *Counter-Pentagon* 2, no. 1 (February 1975): 5.

55. Boyer, "Junior ROTC," 119–20; Koontz and Koontz, "New Front in the Battle with Militarism," 400.

56. An Act Revising the Education Law and the Statutes Relating to the State Library and the State Museum and Continuing the Department of Higher Education and the State Department of Education and Establishing a New Title to Be Known as Title 18A, Education, of the New Jersey Statutes, The New Jersey Statutes, Chapter 271, P.L. 1967 & Title 18A: 35-11, eff. January 11, 1968, 388; LTC Kennedy, U.S. Air Force, Presentation Delivered at the Fourth Annual CONARC Junior ROTC/NDCC Conference, Fort Monroe, VA (August 1971), 47 (hereafter cited as Kennedy, Presentation); Koontz and Koontz, "New Front in the Battle with Militarism," 400; Report of the 10th Annual CONARC ROTC Conference, Fort Monroe, VA (August 1972), 61, 214; Joseph V. Spitler, *Army ROTC: How to Revitalize the Program* (Carlisle, PA: Army War College, 1971), 56; Robert K. Musil, "Militarism in Education," *Nation*, April 5, 1975, 402; "Briefly Noted," *CCCO News Notes*, 1973, 6; "JROTC—KO'd Twice," *Counter-Pentagon*, n.d., 1.

57. Journal of the Senate of the State of New York, 194th Session, Senate No. 425A, an Act to Amend the Education Law, in Relation to Military Instruction in the Public Schools during School Hours, January 6, 1971, 290; Letter, Leon E. Giuffred, New York State Senator, to Honorable Michael Whiteman, Counsel to the Governor, re: S-1399, A-30,0001, n.d.; Memorandum, Robert D. Stone, State Education Department, to Counsel to the Governor, June 1, 1973, subject: S.1399 (Assembly Reprint 30,0001).

58. Martin Sexton, "ROTC Cadet Corps Flourishing," *MCG*, October 1972, 50; Thomas Murphy, "High School Howgozit: The NJROTC Comes of Age," *USNIP*, September 1973, 109.

59. Rept., 4AJROTC/NDCCC, 1973, 5, 69–71, 121, 135; "Junior ROTC Grows," *AFT*, April 22, 1970, 30:14.

60. Larry Watson, "NJROTC Diary," *USNIP*, July 1971, 45.

61. Ibid.; CONARC, "History."

62. Rept., 4AJROTC/NDCC, 135, 137.

63. Ibid.

64. Kennedy, Presentation, 46; COL Posey Starkey, Rept., 4AJROTC/NDCC, 119.

65. Kennedy, Presentation, 135; *ER, AJROTC, FY 1964–1965* (Washington, DC: Department of the Army, 1965), 52–57; *ER, AJROTC, FY 1975–1976* (Fort Monroe, VA:TRADOC, 1976), 48–55.

66. James MacGregor, "Trimming the Ranks: Many Military Secondary Schools Battle for Life," *Wall Street Journal*, January 8, 1969, 34.

67. Richard Davies, "A History of Military Schools in the U.S." (PhD diss., University of Indiana, 1978), 76.

68. Ibid.

69. Morris Janowitz, *The Professional Soldier* (New York: Free Press, 1974), 46.

70. Arthur Coumbe and Lee Harford, *U.S. Army Cadet Command: The 10 Year History* (Fort Monroe, VA: USACC, 1996), 203.; Rept., 4AJROTC/NDCC, 5; Malishchak, *Military Training for 14-Year-Olds*, 10.

71. Susan Filson, "DC Pupils to Be Told They Needn't Take Cadet Training," *Washington Post*, March 20, 1967, B-1.

72. Ibid., B-3.

73. Ibid., B-1.

74. Ibid.

75. Watson, "NJROTC Diary," 47; *AFJROTCB*, March 1971, 2; December 1976, 2; *AFJROTC Newsletter* (*AFJROTCN*), December 1977, 3; February 1978, 5.

76. "Junior Instructional Materials Support," *AROTCN*, October–November 1967, 4; Rept., 5th AJROTC/NDCC Conference, July 1967, 168–69.

77. CONARC, *Annual History Review, FY 1970* (Fort Monroe, VA: CONARC, 1970), 255–56; CONARC, *Annual History Review, FY 1971* (Fort Monroe, VA: CONARC, 1971), 2.

78. Malishchak, *Military Training for 14-Year-Olds*, 15; *AFJROTCB*, March 1971, 2.

79. Rept., 4AJROTC/NDCC, 108; *AFJROTCB*, January 1971, 3.

80. *AFJROTCB*, March 1971, 3; Rept., 4AJROTC/NDCC, 108; Msg, CONARC, June 22, 1966, subject: ROTC Curriculum Revision; COL Sidney Gritz, AG, CONARC, memo, August 2, 1966, subject: Curriculum for JROTC, Class MI Units, TA.

81. Rept., 4AJROTC/NDCC, 108.

82. USCONARC, DCS for Individual Training, Junior Division POI, *Army ROTC Junior Green Book* (Fort Monroe, VA: CONARC, October 1970).

83. Ibid.

84. Ibid.

85. *AFJROTCB*, November 1966, 3; September 1973, 8.

86. COL Thomas Lamb, Rept., 4AJROTC/NDCC, 18.

87. "Junior ROTC," *Commanders Digest*, January 23, 1975, 10 (hereafter cited as "JROTC," *CD*).

88. Ibid., 6; Malishchak, *Military Training for 14-Year-Olds*, 22.

89. Capozzalo, "NJROTC," 98.

90. Samuel P. Huntington, *The Soldier and the State: The Theory and Politics of Civil-Military Relations* (New York: Vintage Books, 1964), 261. In recognition of the diverse functions the army has performed, Samuel Huntington bestowed the epithet of the nation's "obedient handyman" on it.

91. "JROTC," *CD*, 3, 11; Malishchak, *Military Training for 14-Year-Olds*, 16.

92. *AFJROTCB*, January 1966, 6; May 1972, 3.

93. *AFJROTC Bulletin*, May 1972, 3.

94. "JROTC," *CD*, 3.

95. Sexton, "ROTC Cadet Corps Flourishing," 51.

96. Rept., 4AJROTC/NDCC, 108; *AFJROTCB*, April 1971, 7; October 1971, 12–14; November 1973, 1; Capozzalo, "NJROTC," 99.

97. Williams, "Junior NROTC," 137; Ken Allen, "Junior ROTC Trains Leaders," *Airman*, November 1969, 26; *AFJROTCB*, September 1971, 1; October 1973, 7; J. McCarthy, "ROTC Offers Advantages, Too," *Arizona Republic*, September 10, 1973, 5.

7. THE ADVENT OF THE AVF, 1973–1980

1. David Coleman, "US Military Personnel, 1954–2014," History in Pieces, accessed July 7, 2016, https://historyinpieces.com/research/us-military-personnel-1954-2014.

2. Russell Weigley, *History of the U.S. Army* (Bloomington: Indiana University Press, 1984), 596–97.

3. Gus Lee and Geoffrey Parker, *Ending the Draft* (Ft. Belvoir, VA: HRRO, 1977), 167–68.

4. DA, *Modern Volunteer Army Experiment, 1971* (Arlington, VA: ARI, 1979), 2–8.

5. Raymond Garthoff, *Detente and Confrontation* (Washington, DC: Brookings Institution, 1985), 468, 478.

6. Ibid., 478.

7. Frederick Brown, "The Army and Society," *Military Review*, January 2, 1997, 14; Edward Glick, *Soldiers, Sailors and Society* (Pacific Palisades, CA: Goodyear, 1971), 10; David Bobrow, "Bread, Guns and Uncle Sam," in *New Civil-Military Relations*, ed. John P. Lovell and Philip S. Kronenberg (New Brunswick, NJ: Transaction Books, 1974), 301; D. F. Fleming, "Will Militarism Destroy the United States," in *The Military in American Society* ed. Martin Hickman (Beverly Hills, CA; Glencoe, 1971), 19; Morris Janowitz, "The Decline of the Mass Army," *Military Review*, February 1972, 11.

8. Assistant Secretary of Defense, Public Affairs (ASD, PA), "Melvin Laird, SECDEF, Annual Convention of the Overseas writers Association," *news release* (Washington, DC: OSD, October 22, 1967).

9. Hal Howes to Sen. Strom Thurmond, September 11, 1974, MMA, SF, box 9, folder II, STC/CUL (hereafter cited as Howes, Thurmond); "AFJROTC Program at 165 High Schools," February 6, 1970, MMA, SF, box 9, folder II, STC/CUL.

10. Howes, Thurmond.

11. Louis Lefkowitz, AG, memo for Governor, June 13, 1973, re: Senate 1399, Ass. Reprint, 30,0001.

12. PL 93–165; *AFJROTCB*, January 17, 1974, 1.

13. Delores Battle, "Women in the Defense Establishment," in *Defense Manpower Commission Staff Studies*, vol. 4 (Washington, DC: DOD, 1976), 5–6.

14. Jeanne Holm, *Women in the Military* (Novato, CA: Presidio, 1982), 186, 264; "Girls at Morse High School March to Different Drummer," *AROTCN*, November–December 1972, 6; "South 'San' Girl JROTC Unit Shows Smartness," *AROTCN*, March–April 1973, 7; "Women in ROTC," *AROTCN*, November–December 1972, 1A.

15. *ER, AROTC, FY1979–1980* (Fort Monroe, VA: TRADOC, 1979), 51–54; *FY1973–1974* (Fort Monroe, VA: TRADOC, 1974), 45–59; *AFJROTCB*, May 1975, 1.

16. Rept., 4th AJROTC/NDCC Conf. (1971), 108 (hereafter cited as Rept., 4JROTC/NDCC); *AFJROTCB*, July 1967, 2; February 1971, 2; April 1971, 3; May 1971, 3; May 1972, 12; October 1972, 3.

17. Charles Nicholson, Rept., 4AJROTC/NDCC, 137; *AFJROTCB*, February 1973, 1, 7.

18. *AFJROTCB*, May 1975, 1.

19. *AFJROTCB*, February 1978, 4; Beth Bailey, *America's Army: Making the All-Volunteer Force* (Cambridge, MA: Harvard University Press, 2009), 115–16.

20. ER, AROTC, 1964–1980.

21. *AFJROTCB*, February 1972, 8; April 1972, 4.

22. Gerald Leinwood, *Public Education* (New York: Facts on File, 1992), 29.

23. *AFJROTCB*, September 1973, 8.

24. "JROTC in Germany," *Officer*, February 1974, 21.

25. Stu Eisenstadt for the President, September 5, 1978, subject: Enrolled Bill HR 7161/JROTC.

26. Jeremy Mott, "High School Military Training," *CCCO News Notes*, 1973, 4; *Army Times*, October 25, 1972, 3; Rept., 5AROTC/NDCC, September 8, 1967, 154; STAT/LXXVIII, 1964, 1063–64.

27. "Pennsylvanians Counter JROTC," *CCCO News Notes*, Winter 1978, 4.

28. Eric Stroshane, Dir., Pub. Serv., NDS Library, interview, August 22, 2006; NCES, *Statistics of State School Systems, 1965–1966* (Washington, DC: GPO, 1968), 27; Supt. Pub. Instr., *Montana PS Enrollment Data, 1975* (Helena: Supt. Pub. Instr., October 1, 1975).

29. Rept., 4AJROTC/NDCC, 12; "JROTC/NDCC Conferees Propose New Programs," *AROTCN*, July–August 1968, 1; "SAI Conference Held," *AROTCN*, October–November 1968, 1; Weigley, *History of the U.S. Army*, 334.

30. "CONARC Annual Army JROTC Confab Discusses Plans to Strengthen Program," *AROTCN*, September 1971, 10; Rept., 4AJROTC/NDCC, 6; Info Paper, July 7, 1971, MAA, SF, box 9, folder II, STC/CUL.

31. *AFJROTCB*, November 1971, 9.

32. BG T. Tackaberry, DCSPER, DA, presentation, Rept., 4AJROTC/NDCC, 5.

33. William A. Taylor, *The Advent of the All-Volunteer Force: Protecting Free Society* (New York: Routledge, 2023), 176; Rept., 4AJROTC/NDCC, 5; *ER, AJROTC, FY 1970–73* (Fort Monroe, VA: CONARC, 1973).

34. Lee Harford, *A Comprehensive History of the JROTC* (Fort Monroe, VA: USACC, 1992), 12; Rept., 4AJROTC/NDCC, 6, 113; MG A. Smith to CG/CONARC, May 3, 1972, subject: General Officer Visits of JROTC and NDCC HS, TA; ROTCM 145-4-1, *Introduction to Leader Development*, February 1972, 26.

35. *AFJROTCB*, September 1973, 19–20; December 1973, 6.

36. *AFJROTCB*, November 1974, 10; May 1972, 3; December 1971, 7.

37. "JROTC Expansion Sought," *AFT*, July 21, 1971, 31.

38. Rept., 5AJROTC/NDCC, 137.

39. Ibid.

40. "JROTC Programs to be Expanded," *Officer*, March 1973, 22.

41. Clarence Miller, *Procurement and Retention of Black Officers* (Carlisle, PA: USAWC, 1971), 37; Dana Schnidt, "Army Aides Disturbed by Marked Decline in Percentage of Black Officers, Especially in the Lower Ranks," *New York Times*, February 16, 1971, 21; "Army Offers Opportunities for Blacks Gen. Cartwright Tells Hampton Students," *AROTCN*, January–February 1972, 12.

42. Miller, "Procurement and Retention of Black Officers," 37–39.

43. Rept., 5AJROTC/NDCC, 6.

44. MFR, Nicholson, July 28, 1971, subject: Status Report on ROTC Directorate Actions Re: DA Minority Officer Recruitment Study Approved, December 24, 1970; FS, DCSROTC, Mrs. Holliday, April 10, 1978, subject: Financial Need as Criteria for Awarding Army ROTC Scholarships; DA, DCSPER, to CG, CONARC, May 28, 1971, subject: Four-Year Scholarships.

45. *ER, AJROTC, FY 1965–73* (Fort Monroe, VA: CONARC, 1965–1973); *FY 1973–79* (Fort Monroe, VA: TRADOC, 1974–1979).

46. David Webster, Russell Stockard, and James Henson, "Black Student Elite: Enrollment Shifts of High-Achieving, High Socio-economic Status Black Students from Black to White Colleges during the 1970s," *College and University* 56, no. 3 (Spring 1981): 283.

47. BG Wilfred Smith, TRADOC, DCSROTC, interview, June 14, 1997.

48. Sue Mohr and Michael Rumsey, *Cadet Evaluation Battery* (Alexandria, VA: ARI, 1978), 12.

49. *AFJROTCN*, November 1977, 2.

50. Rept. 10AROTC, August 1971, 61, 214.

51. Spitler, *Army ROTC*, 56; "USAREC and ROTC," *AROTCN*, October–December 1970, 4.

52. Malishchak, *Military Training for 14-Year-Olds*, 28.

53. Smith, interview.

54. Rept., 4AJROTC/NDCC, 5; Thelma Slayden, "Good Jobs or OCS Training for Non-college JROTC Boys," *Officer*, June 1969, 24.

55. Melvin Laird, SECDEF (address, National Conference of the Military Chaplains Association, Washington, DC, April 15, 1970).

56. George Corey and Richard Cohen, "Domestic Pacification," *Society*, July–August 1972, 17.

57. Brown, "Army and Society," 8, 13; Diana Leonetta, "And the Pentagon Shall Inherit the Poor? Military Summer Camps," *Fellowship*, July 1973, 5.

58. "Domestic Action Reg," *Officer*, November 1975, 19; "Reserve Units Cited for Community Aid," *Officer*, November 1975, 19; Melvin Laird (address, Saint Leo College, Saint Leo, FL, April 26, 1969); Haynes Johnson and George Wilson, *Army in Anguish* (New York: Pocket Books, 1972), 141–60.

59. "From the DCSROTC," *AROTCN*, September–October 1973, 2.

60. "Underprivileged Children Supported by Army JROTC," *AROTCN*, November–December 1972, 2; "Junior ROTC Cadets of JFK Richmond, Va. Help Navajo Indians," *AROTCN*, July–September 1969, 5; "JROTC Units Assist Needy," *AROTCN*, February–March 1975, 17.

61. Corey and Cohen, "Domestic Pacification," 17.

62. D/SECDEF David Packard (remarks, Meeting of St. Louis Chamber of Commerce, 1970).

63. Blue Ribbon Defense Panel (BRDP), *Report to the President and the Secretary of Defense* (Washington, DC: GPO, 1970), 170.

64. Corey and Cohen, "Domestic Pacification," 18.

65. Ibid.; Leonetta, "And the Pentagon," 5.

66. BRDP, *Report*, 169.

67. *ER, AROTC, FY 1964–1965* (Fort Monroe VA: CONARC, 1965), 34–45; *FY 1973–1974* (Fort Monroe, VA: TRADOC, 1974), 45–59.

68. *Counter-Pentagon*, April 1974, 6; Bob Seeley, "The Ashes of Victory," *CCCO News Notes*, 1973, 2.

69. Steve Gulick, "Militarized America: An Interim Report," *CCCO News Notes*, Summer 1976, 7.

70. Thomas Conrad, Glenn Sheehan, and Stephen M. Gulick, "Junior ROTC—Expanding," *CCCO News Notes*, Summer 1976, 5.

71. Eugene Samter, Ex. Sec., Conference of Large City Boards of Education, to Michael Whiteman, Counsel to Governor, June 7, 1973, Re: A 30000 (S1399).

72. Richard Aliano, "The American Military: A Reappraisal," *Military Review (MR)*, January 1972, 51.

73. SECDEF Melvin Laird, *Statement before HASC on FY 1972–1976 Defense Program and 1972 Defense Budget* (Washington, DC: GPO, 1971), 135.

74. Derek Shearer, "The Brass Image," *Nation*, April 20, 1970, 462; Thomas Murphy, "High School Howgozit: The NJROTC Comes of Age," *US Naval Institute Proceedings* (*USNIP*), September 1973, 107.

75. "Junior Confab Held at USCONARC," *AROTCN*, July–September 1969, 5; Shearer, "Brass Image," 462.

76. TRADOC, 1975 Orientation and Briefing Files (OBF), Briefing for MG McEnery, CDR, Fort Knox, March 1, 1974 (hereafter cited as McEnery, OBF); "Background for Organization for Management of the ROTC and NDCC before Steadfast Reorganization," n.d., 5 (hereafter cited as "Background, Steadfast").

77. Rept., 10AROTC, September 14–15, 1972, 168.

78. "Background, Steadfast."

79. McEnery, OBF; 7; William Calhoun, "Bullish on ROTC," *Army*, May 1974, 36–38; TRADOC, 1974 Bruce Clarke Reference Paper Files, TA; Calhoun, "Bullish on ROTC," 38; Coumbe and Harford, *U.S. Army Cadet Command*, 243.

80. Weigley, *History of the U.S. Army*, 86.

81. Ibid., 91.

82. *AFJROTCB*, September 1973, 2.

83. *AFJROTCB*, May 1971, 2.

84. Kenneth Coffey, "Our Nation's Reserve Forces," in *Professionals on the Front Line*, ed. Eric Friedland, Curtis Gilroy, Roger Little, and W. Sellman (Washington: Brassey's, 1996), 104.

85. ASD (MRA&L), *America's Volunteers*, December 1978, 241, 253; Robert Goldich, "American Society and the Military in the Post–Cold War Era," in *Marching Toward the 21st Century*, ed. Mark Eitelberg and Stephen Mehay (Westport, CT: Greenwood, 1994), 126.

86. DAHSUM, *FY 1978* (Washington, DC: USACMH, 1979), 68; *FY 1975* (Washington, DC: USACMH, 1976), 36.

87. Curtis L. Gilroy and W. S. Selman, "Recruiting and Sustaining a Quality Army: A Review of the Evidence," in *Future Soldiers and the Quality Imperative: The Army 2010 Conference*, ed. Robert L. Phillips and Maxwell R. Thurman (Washington, DC: GPO, 1995), 60; David R. Segal, "Bridging the Gap: Implications for Army Personnel Quality for Contemporary Sociological Research," in Phillips and Thurman, ed., *Future Soldiers and the Quality Imperative* (Washington, DC: GPO, 1995), 312.

88. ASD (MRA&L), *America's Volunteers*, 5; John Brinkerhoff and David Grissmer, "The Reserve Forces in an All-Volunteer Environment," in *The All-Volunteer Force after a Decade*, ed. William Bowman, Roger Little, and Thomas Sicilia (Washington, DC: Pergamon-Brassey's, 1986), 206, 214–15; James Hosek, Richard L. Fernandez, and David W. Grissmer, *Active Enlisted Supply: Prospects and Policy Options* (Santa Monica, CA: RAND, 1984), 192.

89. DAHSUM, *FY 1975*, 5.

90. TRADOC, *Annual Report of Major Activities, FY 1974* (Fort Monroe, VA: TRADOC, 1974), 134–35.

91. Rept., 4AJROTC/NDCCC, 69.

92. "Guam JROTC Rifle Team Raises $24, 070 and Captures USARPAC Commander's Trophy," *AROTCN*, October–November 1975, 8; *AFJROTCB*, December 1975, 1–2;

September 1977, 1; October 1977, 1; March 1978, 14; September 1978, 5; October 1978, 2; January–February 1980, 2.

93. Thurmond to Lanning Risher, Headmaster, June 2, 1976, CMA, box 9, folder: CMA, STC/CUL (hereafter cited as Thurmond, Risher).

94. MG Clifford Drake to Donald Rumsfeld, May 20, 1976; Lanning Risher to Donald Rumsfeld, May 20, 1976, MAA, SF, box 39, folder: CMA, STC/CUL.

95. Thurmond, Risher.

96. Thurmond to the President, June 2, 1976, MMA, SF, box 9, folder: CMA, STC/CUL.

97. Memo, OMB, January 21, 1976, subject: Ref:70 Issues—FY 1977 Budget; AFROTC Jr. Prog. Div., *AFJROTC Study* (Maxwell AFB, AL: Air University, 1977), 6, B4–16; "Description of JROTC Study Called For in President's Issues," April 22, 1976, MMA, SF, box 9, folder: CMA, STC/CUL.

98. AFROTC Jr. Prog. Div., *AFJROTC Study*, 4, 11, 97.

99. Ibid., 42, A7–1, A2–8, A8–2, B4–1, 12/13.

100. Ibid., A8–1, B4–13.

101. Ibid., ix, 18, 26, 50, 51, 134, 137, 138, 139, 141, B4–6, B4–12.

102. Ibid., B4–12.

103. Ibid., 50–51.

104. Ibid., 51.

105. Ibid.

106. Ibid., A2–8, A2–16.

107. Ibid., 39–41, 64–66, 80–81, 95, 121.

108. Ibid., 54, C4–1.

109. Ibid., 56–58.

110. Ibid., 28.

111. Ibid., 29.

112. Ibid., A2–9.

113. Ibid.

114. Ibid., A2–4.

115. T. D. Snyder, A. G. Tan, and C. M. Hoffman, "Chapter 2: Elementary and Secondary Education," in *Digest of Education Statistics 2003* (NCES 2005-025), U.S. Department of Education, National Center for Education Statistics (Washington, DC: GPO, 2005); ER, AJROTC, *FY 1972–80.*

116. *AFJROTCN*, September 1973, 5; September 1977, 2; October 1978, 2.

117. STAT/LXL, 1976, 933; Gulick, "Militarized America," 6; "JROTC Ceiling Raised," *CCCO News Notes*, Winter 1977, 5.

118. Harford, "Comprehensive History of the JROTC," 1.

119. *AFJROTCB*, January 1971, 3.

120. Malishchak, *Military Training for 14-Year-Olds*, 15; *AFJROTCN*, November 1977, 6; September 1978, 28; May 1975, 1.

121. *AFJROTCN*, December 1977, 1.

122. JROTC, "Opposition in Congress," *Counter-Pentagon*, November 1975, 3; D. S. Capozzalo, "NJROTC: Profile and Practice," *USNIP*, October 1975, 97.

123. "Education in Militarism in Education," *Counter-Pentagon*, February 1977, 6.

124. Ibid.

125. COL Lawton for DCSROTC, August 6, 1976, subject: Tactics Instruction in JROTC Curriculum; memo, May 24, 1982, subject: Policy on Teaching Tactics in the JROTC Curriculum, TA.

126. Steven Selden and Alan Feldman, *A Consideration of the Four JROTC Curricula* (Philadelphia: Interfaith Committee on the Draft, 1975), 10–12.

127. Robert Musil, "Operation High School," *Nation*, April 5, 1975, 402.

128. "From the Army," *Counter-Pentagon*, November 1975, 3.

129. Harford, "Comprehensive History of the JROTC," 5; *Program of Instruction—Army JROTC* (Fort Monroe, VA: TRADOC, 1976), 8.

130. MG James Cockran to MG Charles Rogers, October 5, 1977, TA (hereafter cited as Cockran, Rogers).

131. LTC Donald Smith, AG, Fourth Region, memo, December 8, 1977, subject: Interfacing JROTC with the Total Army (hereafter cited as Smith, Interfacing); MG Charles Rogers to CDR, 2-3-4 Regions, November 9, 1977, subject: Interfacing JROTC with the Total Army, TA.

132. Cockran, Rogers.

133. MG Charles Rogers to BG William Barnes, January 16, 1978, subject: Interfacing JROTC with the Total Army, TA.

134. Smith, Interfacing.

135. R. Kennedy, "Navy Blue and Blonde," *USNIP*, September 1973, 50; Mott, "High School Military Training," 4.

136. "First Girls Cadets at Barstow," *MCG*, February 1973, 3.

137. *AFJROTCB*, December 1973, 1; February 1974, 8; February 1977, 4; May 1977, 1–3; September 1978, 4.

138. *AFJROTC*, December 1973, 1; February 1977, 4; May 1977, 1; September 1978, 4.

139. *AFJROTCN*, November 1978, 3.

140. *AFJROTCN*, February 1978, 2; March 1978, 3; September 1978, 1; October 1978, 2; January 1979, 1; September 1979, 1.

8. JROTC IN THE REAGAN ERA, 1980–1985

1. *Toward a Consensus of Military Service: Report of the Atlantic Council's Working Group on Military Service* (New York: Pergamon Press, 1982), 30.

2. Richard Brown, *A Review of the Tri-service Academy and ROTC Scholarship Manpower Requirements* (Carlisle, PA: USAWC, 1984).

3. Andrew Feickert and Stephen Daggett, *A Historical Perspective on "Hollow Forces"* (Washington, DC: CRS, 2012), 9–10.

4. Nat'l Comm. on Excellence in Education, *A Nation at Risk: The Imperative for Educational Reform* (Washington, DC: Nat'l Comm. on Excellence in Education, 1983).

5. Ernest Boyer, *High School* (New York: Harper and Row, 1983), 83.

6. Rosetta Armour-Lightner, *How to Improve Accession Rates and Promotability of Black Officers Commissioned through the AFROTC* (Maxwell AFB, AL: Air War College, 1985), 2–8.

7. COL Albert Barbero to Strom Thurmond, October 5, 1982, MAA, SF, box 9, folder III, STC/CUL.

8. PL 96–342; ER, AJROTC, *FY1985–86* (Fort Monroe, VA: TRADOC, 1986).

9. DA, *ROTC Study Group Report: JROTC, 1916–1985* (Washington, DC: Department of the Army, 1968), 3:2 (hereafter cited as *RSGR*).

10. *RSGR*, 3:2–3.

11. *RSGR*, 2:2; MG John Prillaman, DCSROTC, to Reg. Cdrs, May 3, 1983, subject: JROTC Expansion, TRADOC Archives (TA).

12. CPT John Fedor, D/C Leg. Affairs, Navy, to Thurmond, June 15, 1984, MAA, SF, box 9, folder III, TSC/CUL; Thurmond to Thomas McInville, SPT, Georgetown County SD, June 21, 1984, MAA, SF, box 9, folder III, STSC/CUL; *AFJROTCN*, December 1984, 1.

13. Joseph O'Neil to Thurmond, December 13, 1984; Timothy Titus to Thurmond, December 15, 1986, MAA, SF, box 9, folder III, TSC/CUL.

14. Joseph Nameth to Thurmond, September 16, 1982, MAA, SF, box 9, folder IV, STSC/CUL.

15. AR145–2, *ROTC: Junior Program and NDCC Organization, Operation and Support* (July 1, 1984), 2–1, 2–2; William Roche to Thurmond, February 23, 1982, MAA, SF, box 9, folder IV, STS/CUL.

16. Change 4 to AR 145–2, July 1, 1984, 101.

17. TRADOC, *Semiannual Hist. Rept.* (Washington, DC: TRADOC, 1984), pt. 2, 11 (hereafter cited as TDSHR).

18. Ibid.; MAJ Vandon Jenerette, HQ, Fourth Region, to LTC Larry Robinson, DCSROTC, December 12, 1984, subject: Memo for TRADOC JROTC Seminar 1985, TA.

19. James Harrill, "Attitudes Held by Host Principals Toward Army JROTC in the Third Region," (doctoral diss., University of Northern Colorado, 1984), 12–13; Janet Days and Lee Ang, "An Empirical Examination of the Impact of JROTC Participation on Enlistment, Retention, and Attrition" (master's thesis, NPS, December 2004), 46; Floyd Stephenson, DAI, Muscogee County, Columbus, GA, to CDR/Third Region, September 15, 1989; Briefing, USACC, February 20, 1990, subject: JROTC Ethnic Breakdown, TA.

20. NCES, *The Condition of Education*, Table 4.1: Percentage distribution of public-school students enrolled in kindergarten through 12th grade, by race/ethnicity, Fall 1972–2003, accessed January 2, 2025, http://nces.ed.gov/programs/coe/2005/section1/table.asp?tableID=229.

21. TDSHR, 1983, pt. 2, 7.

22. Huntington, *Soldier and the State*, 53.

23. TDSHR, 1980, pt. 1, 12; 1983, pt. 2, 4.

24. DF, Richard Hoogstaten, TD/TRADOC, February 8, 1983, subject: JROTC/NDCC POI Proposal, TA (hereafter cited as Hoogstaten, POI).

25. *RSGR*, 3:8.

26. Prestina Sanchez-Davis, *A Review of High School ROTC Programs in the Albuquerque PS* (Albuquerque, NM: Board of Education, 1985); *RSGR*, 3:12; Bogden, "Perceived Value of JROTC," 2, 4, 52.

27. CBO, *The Federal Role in Improving Elementary and Secondary Education* (Washington, DC: CBO, 1993), 4–5.

28. COL Victor Fernandez, A/CDR/Third Region, to LTC Robinson, December 27, 1984, subject: JROTC Conference/Workshop for January 7, 1985, TA.

29. COL Donald Andrews, COS/First Region, to CDR/TRADOC, January 3, 1985, subject: JROTC Conference/Workshop, TA.

30. CBO, *Quality Soldiers* (Washington, DC: USACMH, 1987); *Toward a Consensus of Military Service*, 14, 26; *DAHSUM, FY 1986*, 57.

31. MG Daniel French, DCSROTC, to Region/CDRs, April 29, 1981, subject: ROTC Quality Assurance System; BG Donald Connelly, DCSPER, to MG Robert Sullivan, DCS-ROTC, July 5, 1982, TA.

32. *RSGR*, 2:encl. 2–3, C-5.

33. Jenerette to Robinson.

34. Ibid.

35. Ibid.

36. Ibid.

37. Ibid.

38. Ibid.

39. Ibid.; Patrick A. Cross, *A Tradition of Pride, A Reputation of Excellence: The History of the ROTC at Canon City High School* (Canon City, CO: Board of Education, n.d.).

40. COL Richard Elliot, A/DCSROTC/TRADOC, to COL Ambrose Szalwinski, COS/Third Region, May 26, 1981, subject: Recommended Action to Improve JROTC Program, TA.

41. Ibid.

42. MG Sullivan to Region/CDRs, June 2, 1982, subject: JROTC POI, TA.

43. USACC, JROTC Summer Camp: SOP, October 19, 1990, IV: Concept of Training, TA.

44. Hoogstaten, POI; MG Prillaman, DCSROTC, for HQDA/DCSPER, January 6, 1984, subject: JROTC/NDCC POI, TA.

45. Hoogstaten, POI.

46. IP, Mr. Prelewicz, December 29, 1983, subject: JROTC/NDCC POI, TA.

47. Hoogstaten, POI.

48. Ibid.

49. BG Curtis Hoglan to GEN William Richardson, March 8, 1985, subject: Commander's Annual Assessment, 1984, TA.

50. COL Donald Andrews, COS/First Region, to LTC Robinson, January 3, 1985, subject: JROTC Conference/Workshop, TA.

51. Ibid.

52. Ibid.; *RSGR*, 2:4.

53. Andrews to Robinson.

54. Ibid.; *AFJROTCN*, December 1984, 1.

55. Andrews to Robinson; MG Bobby Porter, DMPM, to DCSROTC, February 13, 1984, subject: JROTC/NDCC POI, TA.

56. Andrews to Robinson.

57. MG Prillaman to MG McNair, February 3, 1986, subject: SROTC/JROTC Gramm Rudman Reduction (hereafter cited as SGRR); FS, DCSROTC/RM, February 3, 1986, subject: SGRR, TA.

58. Kershner, Harding, and Howlett, *Breaking the War Habit*, 13, 99–104.

59. Amy Morris, "JROTC in the 1980s," *Counter-Pentagon*, September–November 1980, 2.

60. Glen Anderson, "Community Acts to Oust JROTC from Local High School," *Counter-Pentagon*, September–November, 1980, 2.

61. Bogden, "Perceived Value of JROTC," 111.

62. Ibid.

63. Ibid.

64. Morris, "JROTC in the 1980s," 2.

65. "Public Military High School Struck Down in Cincinnati," *Objector*, October 1983, 4; Phyllis Epting, Joan McCoy, Judy Sarmiento, and Judy Thick, "Reading, Writing, and ROTC," *Nonviolent Activist*, April 1985, 10; Anderson, "Community Acts," 12.

66. Morris, "JROTC in the 1980s," 3; Susan Foster, "Plan to Expand Junior ROTC Program Provokes Debate," *Education Week*, November 3, 1982, 5.

67. *RSGR*, 2:33.

68. Antonio Madrid, DCSROTC, memo, April 10, 1985, subject: General Officer Steering Committee (GOSC), TA.

69. *RSGR*, 2:22.

70. MFR, Margot Moore, TD, January 23, 1986, subject: JRIP Briefing, TA (hereafter cited as Moore, JRIP); *RSGR*, 3:22.

71. *RSGR*, 3:2, 11; Jenerette to Robinson.

72. *RSGR*, 2:21–23.

73. Ibid., 2:12–13, 17, 22.

74. Ibid., 2:15, 17.

75. Ibid., 2:17, 21.

76. Ibid., 2:9.

77. Ibid., 2:8–9, 19, 31.

78. Ibid., 2:27–28.

79. Ibid., 3:27.

80. Ibid., 3:8, 24–25, 27, 33.

81. Ibid., 3:22–23.

82. GEN Richardson to CSA, April 1, 1986, subject: JRIP, TA; *RSGR*, 3:14, 15, 23, 27; Moore, JRIP.

83. Moore, JRIP, 25.

84. Ibid., 30.

85. Ibid., 16.

86. *Study Group Report*, vol. III, 3:20.

87. MSG, MG Prillaman, DCSROTC, to Region Cdrs, November 30, 1984, subject: JROTC Conference and Workshop, TA; MG Prillaman for Region/CDRs, January 13, 1986, subject: JRIP, TA.

88. JRIP, January 14, 1986, annex II.

89. Ibid.

90. Ibid., annex V. See *RSGR*, 3:F-2.

91. JRIP, annex II, app. L.

92. Ibid.

93. Ibid.

94. Ibid.; Hoogstraten, POI.

95. MFR, Jack Ellertson, *RSGR*, August 1, 1985, subject: Trip to Maxwell/AFB, July 18, 1985.

96. Moore, JRIP; Wayne E. Krahn, Training Division, memo, for DCSROTC, February 6, 1986, subject: JROTC Briefing to Secretary of the Army, TA.

97. Memo, November 8, 1985, subject: Mission Statement For JROTC, TAB C to RSGR Recommendation, TA.

98. Ibid.

99. DF, LTC Hawkins, DAI, San Antonio (TX), to CDR/Third Region, December 20, 1985, comments on TRADOC Suppl. 1 to AR 45–2 Draft, TA.

100. Moore, JRIP.

101. Ibid., GEN Richardson to LTG Elton, September 23, 1985, subject: Total Army Sponsorship of JROTC Units, TA.

9. JROTC AT THE END OF THE COLD WAR, 1986–1992

1. Dennis Ippolito, *Federal Budget Policy and Defense Strategy* (Carlisle, PA: SSI, USAWC, 1996), 4–6.

2. "Active Duty Military Personnel, 1940–2011," Infoplease, accessed December 13, 2024, http://www.infoplease.com/ipa/A0004598.html.

3. CBO, *Reducing the Size of the Military Officer Corps* (Washington, DC: CBO, 1988), 5; Dennis Ippolito, *Budget Policy, Deficits, and Defense* (Carlisle, PA: SSI, USAWC, 2005), 13; *DAHSUM-1987* (Washington, DC: USACMH, 1995), 12; *1988* (Washington, DC: USACMH, 1993), 13.

4. CBO, *The Federal Role in Improving Elementary and Secondary Education* (Washington, DC: CBO, 1993).

5. *AFJROTCN*, March 1992, 2.

6. "Goals 20000: The Clinton Education Program," accessed December 13, 2024, https://clinton.presidentiallibraries.us/exhibits/show/education-reform/goals-esea.

7. *RSGR*, 1:i–ii.

8. Ibid., 1:iii.

9. Compt./Army, *A Study of the Organization for Management of the Army ROTC/NDCC Program* (Washington, DC: GPO, 1965), 2.

10. Arthur Coumbe and Lee Harford, *U.S. Army Cadet Command: The Ten-Year History* (Washington, DC: GPO, 1996), 57.

11. Lee Harford, *A Comprehensive History of the Junior ROTC Program* (Fort Monroe, VA: USACC, 1992), 21.

12. LTG Robert Elton, DCSPER, DA, to CDR, TRADOC, January 6, 1986, subject: JRIP, TA (hereafter cited as Elton, JRIP).

13. Donna Marks, IP, September 12, 1990, subject: JROTC Unit Establishment; MFR, CPT John Davenport, April 23, 1990, subject: 1990 JROTC AAR, TA (hereafter cited as Davenport, AAR); TP, USACC, February 3, 1988, subject: HS-OMA Budget for FY 1988 Frozen by TRADOC, TA; Elton, JRIP.

14. Alex Harvin, Maj. Ldr. Emeritus, SC, HoR, to Thurmond, February 23, 1988, MMA, SF, box 9, folder III, STSC, CUL.

15. *ER, AJROTC, FY 1988–1989 through FY 1995–1996* (Fort Monroe, VA: TRADOC, 1989–1996).

16. LTC Stephen Sherwood, Ch./Off. Leg. Liaison, USAF, to Roy Rowland, HoR, April 6, 1989, RBRLPRS, UGAL.

17. MG John Prillaman to CDR/1-2-3–4 Regions, January 14, 1986, subject: JRIP, TA (hereafter cited as Prillaman, JRIP).

18. MFR, LTC Wayne Krahn, March 20, 1986, subject: JROTC (hereafter cited as Krahn JROTC); MG Robert Wagner to GEN Richardson, March 20, 1986, TA (hereafter cited as Richardson, Wagner).

19. GEN William Richardson to CSA, n.d., subject: JRIP, TA.

20. Richardson, Wagner.

21. Krahn, JROTC.

22. Ibid.

23. D/Off. Leg. Aff., Dept. of Navy, for GC/DOD, March 28, 1989, subject: Non D/D 2852, Proposed Legislation, TA.

24. USACC, briefing, August 29, 1989, subject: JROTC Budget Shortfalls, TA.

25. MAJ Shaw, USACC, FS, October 25, 1988, Subject: HS-ROTC Funding, TA.

26. LTC William Simpson, SAI/Saint Joseph HS, Memo, March 1989, for Insp. Off. for the Biennial Command Insp., SAI Comments, TA (hereafter cited as Simpson, Comments).

27. COL (Ret) Floyd Stephenson, DAI/Muscogee SD, to CDR/3-Region, September 15, 1989, TA.

28. Ibid.

29. LTC Bollen, FS, August 16, 1991, subject: JROTC Enrollment; FS, December 2, 1991, subject: JROTC Enrollment Analysis for SY 91–92 (hereafter cited as FS, Analysis); HS-Div, briefing, February 20, 1990, subject: Enrollment Trends, TA.

30. FS, Analysis.

31. MAJ Shaw, HS-Dir., memo, May 26, 1988, subject: Cross-Enrollment (C-E) Requests, TA (hereafter cited as Shaw, Requests); Prillaman, JRIP; COL Thomas Faley for CDR/3-Region, August 2, 1988, subject: Approval of C-E (hereafter cited as Faley, Approval); LTC Howard Gill, C/HS-Div, 4-Region, for CDR/USACC, March 7, 1987, subject: HS ROTC Corrected C-E Schools; LTC William Cook, AG/3-Region, for CDR/USACC, March 7, 1987, subject: C-E Schools; LTC Thomas Musgrave, C/PAT/G3/2-Region, for CDR/USACC, May, 22, 1987, subject: JROTC Cross-Enrolled Schools; COL Kimball, D/HS-ROTC, for CG/USACC, August 31, 1988, subject: C-E Request, TA (hereafter cited as Kimball, C-E Request).

32. COL Thomas Faley to CDR/Third Region, May 7, 1988, subject: C-E Requests, TA; Kimball, C-E Request.

33. Faley, Approval.

34. Carole Fringa, Asst. Gen. Counsel, OSD (Manpower, Health, & Pub. Aff.) for COL Stephen Sutton, OSD (MR&A), August 6, 1976, subject: JROTC-Conduct of Programs in Non-host Schools, TA.

35. Shaw, Requests.

36. COL Robert Cox, C/TD, to CDR/1-2-3-4 Regions, April 17, 1987.

37. *ER, AJROTC, FY 1985–1986 through 1992–1993* (Fort Monroe, VA: TRADOC, 1986–1993).

38. Bollen, FS, February 1, 1993, subject: JROTC Enrollment Analysis, TA (hereafter cited as Bollen, Enrollment).

39. MAJ Piscopo, IP, February 7, 1990, subject: HS-ROTC Travel Funds, TA (hereafter cited as Piscopo, Travel).

40. BG David Allen, COS/First-USA, for CDR/First Region, December 5, 1989, subject: JROTC Summer Camp; COL James Lloyd, COS/1-Region, for COS/1-USA, January 19,

1990, subject: Support for JROTC Summer Camp; COL Ralph Newman, DCST/First Army, For CDR/First Region, February 8, 1990, subject: Support for JROTC Summer Camp, TA.

41. *ER, AJROTC, FY 1989–1990 through FY 1992–1993.*

42. *ER, AJROTC, FY 1986–1987 through FY 1993–1994.*

43. Ibid.

44. Ms. Hornal, USACC, FS, August 29, 1986, subject: JROTC 4-Year Scholarship Winners, TA.

45. *DAHSUM: FY 1988* (Washington, DC: USACMH, 1993), 14.

46. COL Faley for CDR/USAREC, July 6, 1988, subject: JROTC Enlistments; USACC, briefing, November 4, 1988, subject: Disposition of Graduates SY 87/88, TA.

47. Ralph Manuel, Pres., Culver MA, interview with the author, December 13, 2004.

48. Ibid.

49. Coumbe and Harford, *U.S. Army Cadet Command*, 57.

50. COL James Lloyd, *1st-ROTC-Region AR, 1984–1988*, December 11, 1989, C-15, TA.

51. Harford, *Comprehensive History*, 23.

52. LTC Jones, USACC/TD, FS, August 19, 1986, subject: USACC's HBCU TF Issue—Cadet Socialization, TA (hereafter cited as Jones, Socialization); Rosetta Armour-Lightner, "How to Improve Accession Rates and Promotability of Black Officers Commissioned through the AFROTC" (master's thesis, AWC, May 1985), 20–21.

53. Marylin Krupsaw, "1986 Program Report on the Army-Navy Initiative in the National Capital Area in Support of the DoD Science and Engineering Apprenticeship Program for High School Students" (University of the DC, Physics Dept., November 1986), 3–4, 35–36.

54. Ibid.

55. Ibid.

56. Harford, *Comprehensive History*, 4.

57. Jones, Socialization; Armour-Lightner, "How to Improve Accession Rates," 20–21; Roosevelt Greer, "Black Colleges as a Major Source of Black Officers in the Armed Forces" (ICAF, May 1986), 27–28.

58. Coumbe and Harford, *U.S. Army Cadet Command*, 34.

59. Captain Torgler, FS, August 3, 1990, subject: Operation Capital (hereafter cited as Torgler, Capital); CPTs Davenport and Moore, interview by Lee Harford, May 14, 1990, subject: Operation Capital (hereafter cited as Harford, Interview); MG Wagner, CDR/USACC, to CDRs/1-2-3-4 Regions, September 19, 1989, subject: Operation Capital Command Guidance, TA (hereafter cited as Wagner, Guidance).

60. PP, Davenport, January 24, 1990, subject: Operation Capital, TA (hereafter cited as Davenport, OC).

61. Ibid.

62. CPT Davenport, IP, April 26, 1990, subject: Operation Capital Activities, TA (hereafter cited as Davenport, Activities).

63. USACC, briefing, n.d., subject: Rationale for Selection, TA.

64. Davenport, AAR.

65. MOA, MG Robert Wagner, CDR/USACC, and Dr. Andrew Jenkins, SPT/Chief/State School Officer, DC-PS, October 24, 1989, subject: Operation Capital, Annex B-F, TA (hereafter cited as Wagner, Jenkins).

66. COL Andrew Jackson, CDR/Fourth-BDE for DAIs and SAIs, Washington, DC, and Baltimore City Schools, Fourth-BDE/First Region, May 16, 1991, subject: Operations Capital/Charm City Operations Order, TA (hereafter cited as Jackson, Charm).

67. COL Thomas Faley, COS/USACC, memo, August 7, 1989, subject: Operation Capital; PP, USACC, September 6, 1989, subject: Operation Capital; HS-USACC, briefing, n.d., subject: Future Expansion: 34 Cities, TA.

68. *ER, AJROTC, FY 1988–1989.*

69. PP, USACC, September 6, 1989, subject: Operation Capital, TA; Torgler, Capital; Davenport, AAR.

70. Davenport, AAR.

71. Harford, Interview.

72. *AFJROTCN*, November 1990, 1–2; December 1990, 1; January 1991, 3.

73. *AFJROTCN*, December 1992, 1; March 1992, 2.

74. Jackson, Charm.

75. Robert Hartman, "ROTC: Its Place in the History of the Culver Military Academy, 1916–1989," February 2003, 11; Manuel, Interview.

76. Hartman, "ROTC," 12–13.

77. Ibid., 13.

78. Manuel, Interview.

79. Ibid.

80. Coumbe and Harford, *U.S. Army Cadet Command*, 157.

81. USACC, FS, January 23, 1990, subject: JROTC (hereafter cited as FS, USACC); USACC, briefing, n.d., subject: JROTC Scholarship Winner Comparison Data; USACC, briefing, n.d., subject; JROTC Scholarship QEP Winner Comparison, TA.

82. FS, USACC.

83. Piscopo, Travel.

84. TRADOC, *Semi-annual Historical Rept.* (Fort Monroe, VA: TRADOC, 1989), pt. 1, 12, TA.

85. Rep. Floyd Spence to COL John Simms (ret), February 28, 1990; Senator Sam Nunn to John Owen, Pres/North Georgia College, March 28, 1990, TA.

86. Senator John Glenn to John Sims, June 8, 1990; Senator Russell Todd, Pres/Norwich University, February 27, 1990, TA.

87. Rick Maze, "Army Scrambles to Restore JROTC Program," *Army Times*, February 19, 1990, 19; AUSA, "JROTC to Be Fully Funded for FY 1991," *Washington Update*, March 1990, 4.

88. AUSA, "JROTC to Be Fully Funded for FY 1991," 4.

89. LTC Frederick Berry, D/EOPP, to Senator Sam Nunn, March 13, 1990, TA.

90. Piscopo, Travel; *AFJROTCN*, March 1990, 1.

10. JROTC IN THE POST–COLD WAR ERA, 1992–1996

1. *The Budget and Economic Outlook, FY 2002–2011* (Washington, DC: CBO, 2001), 75; *DAHSUM, FY 1992* (Washington, DC: USACMH, 2001), 207; *FY 1995* (Washington, DC: USACMH, 2004), 3; *FY 1996* (Washington, DC: USACMH, 2002), 3.

2. Press Sec./WH, FS, May 28, 1992, subject: Defense Adjustment Assistance; *DAHSUM, FY 1990 & 1991*, 8–12; *FY 1992*, 117, *FY 1996*, 3; 102 Cong. Rec. E2170 (1991);

Emily Feistritzer, *Survey of Military Personnel Interested in Teaching* (Arlington, VA: ARI, 1992), 1.

3. GAO, "At-Risk and Delinquent Youth," RPT-B-260743, March 1996, 2.

4. DoE, *America 2000* (Washington, DC: DOE, 1991).

5. SCANS, *What Work Requires of Schools* (Washington, DC: DOL, 1991), i–viii, 2–3, 21.

6. *DAHSUM, FY 1992*, 60; Gerhard Peters and John T. Woolley, "George Bush, White House Fact Sheet: Youth Skills Initiative," American Presidency Project, August 24, 1992, http://www.presidency.ucsb.edu/ws/index.php?pid=21365.

7. Peters and Woolley, "George Bush."

8. Donna Marks, USACC, FS, May 18, 1992, subject: Response to LTG Dominy on the Potential of JROTC to Maintain Army's Image in Local Communities as It Downsizes, TA (hereafter cited as Marks, Dominy).

9. Colin Powell, CJCS, to SecDef, June 8, 1992, subject: Expansion of the JROTC (hereafter cited as Powell, Expansion).

10. Marks, Dominy; *DAHSUM, FY 1992*, 60; *FY 1994*, 41–42; Andrew Jackson, COS/USACC to CDRs/1/2/4 Regions, November 13, 1992, subject: MOI for the Expansion of the Army JROTC Program, TA (hereafter cited as Jackson, MOI).

11. Sam Nunn, *Domestic Missions for the Armed Forces* (Carlisle, PA: SSI, USAWC, 1993), 7.

12. Ibid.

13. Powell, Expansion; Colin Powell, *My American Journey* (New York: Random House, 1995), 555.

14. Arthur Coumbe, Paul Kotakis, and Anne Gammell, *History of the US Army Cadet Command: Second Ten Years, 1996–2006* (Clearwater, OK: New Forums, 2008), 273.

15. Powell, Expansion; Powell, *My American Journey*, 555; MAJ Tamez, USACC, FS, June 7, 1993, subject: Army JROTC Expansion, TA (hereafter cited as Tamez, Expansion).

16. Don Snider and Miranda Carlton-Carew, eds., *US Civil-Military Relations in Crisis or Transition?* (Washington, DC: CSIS, 1995), 11.

17. Charles Dunlap, "Welcome to the Junta," *Wake Forest Law Review* 29, no. 2 (1994): 367; Stephen Metz et al., *The Future of American Landpower* (Carlisle, PA: SSI/USAWC, 1996), 9.

18. Powell, Expansion; Marks, Dominy; AFROTCJP, notes, 1992, 1; USACC, briefing, March 1994, subject: JROTC Expansion, TA.

19. 102 Cong. Rec. 138 (1992); Keneth K. Peinhardt, *JROTC: Contributions to America's Communities?* (Carlisle, PA: USAWC, 1998), 11–12.

20. USACC, L. Bollen, HSD, for COS, June 2, 1993, subject: TP, MG Arnold—MG Lyle Handover Discussions (hereafter cited as Bollen, Discussions); COL Andrew Jackson, COS, for CDR/1-2-3-4 Regions, December 15, 1993, subject: Indicators for Financial Assistance Based on DA and USACC CDRs Guidance for New and Existing Army JROTC Programs, SY 1994–1995, TA; Jackson, MOI; Tamez, Expansion; Powell, Expansion.

21. Jackson, MOI.

22. Briefing, ATCC-HS, USACC, 15 Oct 1992, subject: Operation Young American, Cdr's Intent; Coumbe and Harford, *U.S. Army Cadet Command*, 278.

23. Bollen, Discussions; *AFJROTCN*, March 1996, 1; MG Wallace Arnold, USACC, for William Clark, PD/ASA-M&RA, October 27, 1992, subject: Temporary Staffing Support

for JROTC Expansion; T. Wilson, AD/MPP, for COL J. Cretella, P&AD/USACC, December 15, 1992, subject: Temporary Staffing for JROTC Expansion; William Clark for Gary Purdum, DCSPER, December 21, 1992, subject: Temporary Staffing Support for JROTC Expansion; COL J. Cretella, PROFS/Note, to CDR/1-2-3-4 Regions, March 12, 1993, subject: NCO Staffing for JROTC Expansion; Ms. McFadden, USACC, FS, January 27, 1993, subject: SROTC/JROTC Retiree Law Changes, TA.

24. *DAHSUM, FY 1996* (Washington, DC: USACMH, 2002), 3.

25. MG James Lyle, USACC, Memo, October 23, 1995, subject: JROTC Expansion Update (SY 96–97); MG James Lyle, USACC, Memo, for CDR/1-2-3-4 Regions, March 8, 1996, subject: JROTC Expansion Guidance; LTC Malone, SAMR, IP, January 15, 1997, subject: JROTC—History of Expansion and Current Status; JROTCD/USACC, FS, December 3, 1996, subject: Army JROTC; JROTCD, Input-USACC-AHS, 1995, TA.

26. *AFJROTCN*, April 1994, 2; June–August 1996, 1; Coumbe and Harford, *U.S. Army Cadet Command*, 278.

27. Peinhardt, *JROTC*, 9.

28. *ER, AJROTC, FY 1992–1993 through 1996–1997*; Taylor, *Every Citizen a Soldier*, 13–14; Peinhardt, *JROTC*, 10.

29. Peinhardt, *JROTC*, 9.

30. CDR Rhonda Syring, OSD/P&R, email, June 9, 2005, subject: Budgets-All Services, 1990–2007.

31. Peinhardt, *JROTC*, 12.

32. Rachelle Perusse, "Perceptions of School Counselors towards JROTC in Virginia Public Schools" (PhD diss., VPI, 1997), 81.

33. Taylor, *Every Citizen a Soldier*, 14; Paul Johnson, "More Students Joining Junior Reserve Officers Training Corps," *Los Angeles Times*, March 4, 1996, B 1–3.

34. Taylor, *Every Citizen a Soldier*, 14.

35. Amanda Biela, "Evaluation of Desired School Outcomes in Chicago JROTC Academies" (master's thesis, University of Chicago, 2002), 37; *The School-to-Work Opportunities Act of 1993*, Pub. L. No. 103-239, Stat. 1361 (1994), Senate, 103C/1S/S1361/SHRG-103-475, September 28 and October 14, 1993 (Washington, DC: GPO, 1994).

36. Lawrence Hanser and Abby Robyn, *Implementing High School JROTC Career Academies* (RAND, 2000), 23; JROTCD/USACC, History of the JROTC Program, SY1997–1998; Office of the Press Secretary, The White House, Fact Sheet, Defense Adjustment Assistance, May 28, 1992.

37. Janet Days and Yee Ang, "An Empirical Examination of the Impact of JROTC Participation on Enlistment, Retention and Attrition" (master's thesis, NPS, 2004), 33; Barry Vanden Berg, HSD/10-Brigade/WR/USACC, interview, April 12, 2007; Walter Wright, SAI/Beaumont HS, IP, n.d., subject: Beaumont HS Demographics, TA.

38. Biela, "Evaluation of Desired School Outcomes," 17; Hanser & Robyn, *Implementing High School JROTC*, 6–7; Career Academies, USACC, internal planning document, n.d., 2; USACC, briefing, September 4, 1996, subject: Career Academies, TA.

39. Los Angeles Unified School District (LA-USD), "JROTC Leadership Development Project" (Concept Paper, LA-USD Committee, July 1992), 3 (hereafter cited as Concept, LA).

40. Robert Silberman, ASA/M&RA, for ASD/FM&P, August 24, 1992, subject: Career Academies; Donna Marks to LTC Bolden, July 15, 1992, subject: Meeting with ASA/M&RA

for Educ&Trng on July 14, 1992, TA; Steven Pearlstein, "Hill Study Urges Programs to Ease Defense Budget Cuts' Impact," *Washington Post*, February 7, 1992, 7; Leslie Gelb, "What Peace Dividend?," *New York Times*, February 21, 1992, 4; Defense, Adjustment.

41. Hanser and Robyn, *Implementing High School JROTC*, 32–33.

42. Marc N. Elliot, Lawrence M. Hanser, and Curtis L. Gilroy, *Evidence of Positive Students Outcomes in JROTC Career Academies* (Santa Monica, CA: RAND, 2001), 14–16.

43. USACC, IP, October 7, 1996, subject: Career Academies.

44. Ibid.

45. Carol Hetler, USACC, IS, April 27, 2009, subject: Army JROTC Units in State Correctional Facilities (hereafter cited as Hetler, Correctional).

46. Ibid.

47. Major Wendell Quash, interview, April 5, 2009.

48. Hetler, Correctional.

49. Donna Rice, USACC, interview with the author, October 19, 2005.

50. Sean Kay, *From Sputnik to Minerva: Education and American National Security* (Washington, DC: NDU, 2009), 2–3; Laura Hamilton, Brian Stecher, and Kun Yuan, *Standards-Based Reform in the United States* (Santa Monica, CA: RAND, 2008), 17; Nat'l Comm. on Excellence in Education, *Nation at Risk*, Washington, DC.

51. Barry Shoop, *Officer Education Reform* (USNWC, 2002), 2–4.

52. Kay, *From Sputnik to Minerva*, 2–3; Hamilton, Stecher, and Yuan, *Standards-Based Reform*, 17; Nat'l Comm. on Excellence in Education, *Nation at Risk*; ASB, 7–8; Shoop, *Officer Education Reform*, 2–4.

53. Lee Harford, *Annual Historical Summary for CY 1992* (Fort Monroe, VA: USACC, 1993), 7; Frederick Rice, *President Bush's Plan to Revitalize America's Schools*, August 18, 1992; http://www.skepticfiles.org/conspire/b34.html.

54. Coumbe and Harford, *U.S. Army Cadet Command*, 282–83.

55. MAJ Tamez, USACC/HSD, FS, January 26, 1993, subject: The NSC and USACC Partnership; USACC, briefing, February 1993, subject: Math and Science Modules; USACC, LTC Glenn Hayes, for CG, October 19, 1995, subject: JROTC Consolidated Summer Camp AAR, SY 94–95; LTC Hayes, HSD/USACC, FS, March 19, 1996, subject: JROTC Program Update (hereafter cited as Hayes, Update).

56. Bollen, Discussions; USACC, Donna Rice to LTC Hayes, January 27, 1995, subject: Plans for Curriculum Development (hereafter cited as Rice, Hayes); *AFJROTCD-Notes, SY1992–1993* (Maxwell, AFB, AL: Air Force JROTC Directorate), 1.

57. Ruben Rivas, *Development of Self Esteem and Learning Skills in Students Participating in the AJROTC* (PhD diss., Loyola University, 1995), 4–5; JROTC, POI; Hayes, Update; Rice, Hayes.

58. MFR, USACC, CPT Harry Green, September 8, 1992, subject: Alternate JROTC Summer Camp AAR; USACC, briefing, October 15, 1992, subject: JROTC Summer Camps; Coumbe and Harford, *U.S. Army Cadet Command*, 285; LTC Glenn Hayes, HSD/USACC, for CDR/1-2-4 Regions, April 6, 1994, subject: Implementation of the JROTC Model Summer Camp; USACC, briefing, April 6, 1994, subject: JROTC Summer Camps; Bollen, Discussions; AFROTCJPD-Notes, SY1992–1993, 1.

59. Carol Freeman and Geoffrey Maruyama, *Primer: Extended-Period Schedules* (Minneapolis, MN: College of Education, University of Minnesota, 1995), 1–2; Bollen, Discussions; Rice, Hayes.

60. G. Hayes, D/HSD, FS, March 19, 1996, subject: JROTC Program Update; Freeman and Maruyama, *Primer*, 1–2.

61. COL Roy Zinser, USACC, memo, November 13, 1995, subject: Curriculum Changes for JROTC; USACC, briefing, April 28, 1997, subject: JROTC Issue.

62. USACC, LTC Hayes for Curriculum Review Board Members, October 20, 1994, subject: Curriculum Review Board Workshop, July 11, 1994.

63. Ibid.

64. William Reese, *America's Public Schools* (Baltimore: Johns Hopkins Press, 2005), 123.

65. Donna Marks, USACC, FS, October 18, 1993, subject: Army JROTC Curriculum; Bollen, Discussions.

66. USACC, briefing, n.d., 1993 Cdrs' Conference, subject: Community Involvement.

67. Taylor, *Every Citizen a Soldier*, 12.

68. Catherine Lutz and Leslie Barnett, "JROTC: Making Soldiers in the Public Schools," *Education Digest*, November 1995, 23; Steven Selden and Alan H. Feldman, *A Consideration of the Four JROTC Curricula: Evaluation and Analysis* (Philadelphia: Interfaith Committee on Draft and Military Information, Spring 1975).

69. Ibid.

70. Ibid., 26.

71. Ibid., 23–29.

72. Ibid.

73. Taylor, *Every Citizen a Soldier*, 7.

74. *AFJROTCN*, November 1956, 1.

75. Paul Gorman, "Preparing the Army for Force XXI," in *Future Soldiers and the Quality Imperative*, ed. R. Phillips and M. Thurman (Fort Knox, KY: USAREC, 1995), 41.

76. USACC, Briefing, March 29, 1994, subject: Disposition of JROTC Graduates (hereafter cited as Disposition, Graduates); USACC, 1995 Tri-service Conference, briefing, March 18, 1995, subject: JROTC Status (hereafter cited as Tri-service Conference).

77. Disposition, Graduates; Tri-service Conference; Janice Laurence and Armando Estrada, eds., *A Comprehensive Study of the JROTC Program* (Monterey, CA: NPS, n.d.); Rivas, *Development of Self Esteem*, 2–3; Hayes, Update; Sandra Bailey et al., *Benefits Analysis of the NJROTC*, NTSC-Orlando (Orlando, FL: NIS, 1992), 5; "Air Guns Battle Real Guns," *American Demographics*, September 1996, 4; Concept, LA.

11. JROTC ENTERS THE TWENTY-FIRST CENTURY

1. *DASUM: FY1999* (Washington, DC: USACMH, 2006), 17; Brown, *Kevlar Legions*, 480.

2. Lawrence Kapp, *Recruiting and Retention in AC Military* (Washington, DC: CRS, 2002), 12.

3. Ibid., 16, 20.

4. GAO, *Addressing the Deficit: Budgetary Implications of Selected GAO Work for Fiscal Year 1998* (Washington, DC: GAO, 1997), 70–71; S. Hrg. 105–776, pt. 1, 1999, 42–43; S. Rept. No. 106–50, 1999, 319.

5. S. Hrg. 106–238, 1999, 44.

6. S. Rep. No. 106–53, 1999, 8; H.R. Rep. No. 106–162, 1999, 349.

7. H.R. Rep. No. 106–644, 2000, 49; H.R. No. 106–616, 2000, 365; 146 Cong. Rec. H8165, 2000; 114 STAT. 1654A–112, 2000; PL106–398 (114, STAT), 2000.

8. H.R. Rep. No. 109–452, 2006, 321; 109 Cong. Rec. H8406, 2006.

9. David Segal, *Social and Cultural Dynamics of American Military Organizations* (Arlington, VA: ARI, 2004), 2; Kenneth Saltman and David Gabbard, eds., *Education as Enforcement* (New York: Routledge Falmer, 2003), 9; Daniel Denning, ASA (M&RA), for SECARMY, n.d., subject: JROTC Program Enhancements; S. Rep. No. 106–50, 1999, 320; 107 Cong. Rec. S1583/2174/2246/2533, S9489 (2001); S. Rep. No. 107–62, 2001, 302.

10. Matthew J. Morgan, "Army Recruiting and the Civil-Military Gap," *Parameters*, Summer 2001, 5; James Kitfield, "Standing Apart," *National Journal*, June 13, 1998, 9; Bobbie Galford, "Bridging the Cultural Communication Gap between America and Its Army," in *Information as Power*, ed. Jeffrey Caton et al. (Carlisle, PA: USAWC, 2009), 62–63, 75.

11. S. Hrg. 106–238, 2000, 40–41.

12. George W. Bush, "The White House," accessed December 15, 2024, https://georgewbush-whitehouse.archives.gov/news/reports/no-child-left-behind.html#:~:text=Taken%20together%2C%20these%20reforms%20express,in%20every%20part%20of%20America.

13. S. Hrg. 106–238, 2000, 770–71; 106 Cong. Rec. S11874/6684/6685 (1999); "Let's Roll!," TF on Protecting Democracy, National Conference of State Legislatures, July 2002; GAO, *School Dropouts*, GAO-02–240, February 2002; S. Hrg. 107–1004, 2002, 138.

14. RAND, *School Violence* (Santa Monica, CA: RAND, 2001), 1; Neil Howe, interview, June 17, 2008; Christopher Robbins, *Expelling Hope* (Albany: SUNY Press, 2008), 35.

15. S. Hrg., 105–776, 1999, 43; S. Hrg. 107–1004, 2002, 138.

16. S. Rep. No. 106–50, 1999, 312–13.

17. 114, STAT.

18. Rose Jordan, A/D, Officer Commissioning Programs OUSD (P&R), to Arthur Coumbe, USACC, February 2, 2009, subject: JROTC Enrollment Numbers.

19. Ibid.

20. United States Army Force Integration Support Agency (USAFISA), Memo, March–May 1995, subject: JROTC Manpower and Organizational Study (JMOS); MG James Lyle, for ASA, M&RA, October 2, 1995, subject: JMOS; LTC Hayes, USACC, FS, March 19, 1996, subject: JROTC Update; Briefing, Tri-service ROTC Conference, Naval ROTC Update, February 2011; S. Hrg. 105–776, 1998, 42–43; F. Holloway, USACC, FS, August 12, 1999, subject: USACC Authorizations; Coumbe et al., *U.S. Army Cadet Command*, 175, 183.

21. *DASUM: FY 2002* (Washington, DC: USACMH, 2011), 6–7.

22. The author witnessed the events described.

23. DOD, *DoDI 1205.13: JROTC Program* (ASD-FMP), December 26, 1995, 1–1; Carol Hetler, USACC, IS, April 1, 2005, subject: MS Associated w/Army JROTC.

24. LaTasha James, "Franklin Military Academy Is Finally an Independent High School," *Richmond Educator*, March 9–15, 2005, 2; Russ Gallagher, "Background: Other Public Military Academies," JROTC Director, Philadelphia Military Academy (PMA), March 30, 2004; Stephanie Horvath, "Spit-and-Polish Schools," *Wall Street Journal*, August 29, 2002; MG W. Winfield, CDR/USACC, to LTG Robert Van Antwerp, CDR/USAAC, April 7, 2007, subject: USACC EXSUM (4/1–7/2007).

25. CPS, HS Programs, Brochure: *JROTC*, n.d.; H. Rept. 106–644, 49, 186.

26. Steve Cork, Commandant, SMA, Daniel Kennedy, CEO/Headmaster, SMA, and Robert Lechner, DO, SMA, interview, September 23, 2005 (hereafter cited as Cork, SMA); Russ Gallagher, D-JROTC, PMA, interview, October 6, 2005.

27. Horvath, "Spit-and-Polish Schools," B-1; Orquedia Price, "Guarded Optimism at OMI: Mayor Brown's Military Charter School Hasn't Flunked Out . . . Yet," *East Bay Express*, January 16, 2002, http://www.eastbayexpress.com/ebx.

28. Christopher Swanson, "Cities in Crisis: A Special Analytic Report on High School Graduation," *Educational Research Center (ERC)*, April 1, 2008, 1, https://epe.brightspot cdn.com/4e/36/359345454d31b91fc69de70e662e/citiesincrisis040108.pdf.

29. A. McDuffie, "No JROTC Left Behind," *In These Times*, September 20, 2008, 1; Dori Turner, "Military Schools on Rise," *Washington Times*, June 9, 2009, 16.

30. McDuffie, "No JROTC Left Behind," 1.

31. Price, "Guarded Optimism at OMI," 24; Cork, SMA.

32. Dirk Johnson, "High School at Attention," *Newsweek*, January 21, 2002, 43.

33. IP, USACC, Arthur Coumbe, September 21, 2007, subject: Army JROTC: Trends & Developments, 1987–2007 (hereafter cited as Coumbe, Trends).

34. Merl Fuchs, C/HSP, email to author, February 13, 2008, subject: NDCC Units; James House, CDR/12BDE/USACC, email, February 11, 2008, subject: NDCC Units; Stan McCallar and Anthony Proulx, interview, October 17, 2007.

35. Coumbe, Trends.

36. MG Wallace, CG/USACC, and James Hayes, President/CEO, Junior Achievement Inc., MOI, July 12, 2000, subject: Agreement between USACC and Junior Achievement Inc. regarding JANMRMP; Donna Rice, USACC, IP, March 9, 2006, subject: Army JROTC Program.

37. Carol Hetler, interview, November 26, 2007; Rick Mills, MAO, CPS, briefing, April 1, 2008, subject: CPS: MS and JROTC; Jennifer Wedekind, "The Children's Crusade," *In These Times*, June 10, 2005, http://www.alternet.org/story/22192.

38. Col Hester, D/JROTC, Wichita PS (WPS), to Donna Rice, May 3, 2007, subject: IP: Middle School Leadership Program.

39. Ibid.

40. WPS, "Schools Honor Veterans," *Express Online* 6, no. 4 (November 3, 2007), http://www.usd259.com/news/express/2007-2008/111307.htm.

41. Allison Wisk, "North Dallas Middle School's JROTC Program Sees Its Efforts Payoff," *Dallas Morning News*, April 4, 2008, 7.

42. Arthur T. Coumbe, Paul N. Kotakis, and W. Anne Gammell, *History of the U.S. Army Cadet Command: Second Ten Years, 1996–2006* (Stillwater, OK: New Forums Press, 2009), 74, 178 (hereafter cited as *Second Ten years*).

43. Ibid., 179–82.

44. Jolanda Kern, "Study of the JROTC" (master's thesis, NPS, 2003), 19, 23–24.

45. Coumbe et al., *Second Ten Years*, 174, 197.

46. Barry Shoop, *Officer Education Reform* (Newport, RI: USNWC, 2002), 2–4.

47. John H. Pryor, et al., *The American Freshman: National Norms Fall 2009* (Los Angeles, CA: HERI, 2009), NSB Table 2-64, 143, accessed December 16, 2024, https://www .heri.ucla.edu/PDFs/pubs/TFS/Norms/Monographs/TheAmericanFreshman2009-Ex panded.pdf.

48. Christine Matthews, *U.S. National Science Foundation* (Seattle, WA: CRS, 2007), 6; Deborah Stine, *The America Competes Act & FY 2009 Budget* (Seattle, WA: CRS, 2008), 1–2.

49. US Commission on National Security/21st Century, *Road Map for National Security* (Washington, DC: US Commission on National Security/21st Century, 2001), 30–38; Richard Cheney and Bill Taylor, *Professional Military Education* (Washington, DC: CSIS, 1997), 5; William Owens, *Lifting the Fog of War*, with E. Offley (Baltimore: Johns Hopkins University Press, 2000), 24.

50. Coumbe et al., *Second Ten Years*, 97; USACC, IP, March 12, 2008, subject: JROTC & NSC Relationship; Arthur Coumbe, "The History of OEMA" (unpublished manuscript, 2016), 73.

51. USAF/AETC, briefing, March 18, 2008, subject: Aerospace & Technology Honors Camp.

52. Coumbe et al., *Second Ten Years*, 234.

53. ICAF, NDU, *2004 Education Industry* (Washington, DC: NDU, 2008), 7; Coumbe et al., *Second Ten Years*, 254.

54. Gary Hoachlander, Steven Klein, and Carol Studier, *New Directions for High School CTE in Wyoming* (Alexandria, VA: MPR Associates, 2007), 2.

55. Thomas McConnell, DAI, Clarksville-Montgomery CS, to Donna Rice, March 20, 2009, subject: Tennessee Issues with JROTC & NCLB (TIJN).

56. Hoachlander, Klein, and Studier, "New Directions," 3.

57. Nicolette Wheeler, DAI, Fulton CSS, to Donna Rice, March 20, 2009, subject: TIJN.

58. NSTC, briefing, n.d., subject: "NJROTC Program Brief."

59. Reese, *America's Public Schools*, 325.

60. Michael Johnson, D/JROTC/USACC, "State of the JROTC: SITREP for CG USACC," November 7, 2008.

61. Robert Gates, SECDEF, to Arnold Schwarzenegger, Gov/CA, May 24, 2008; ADM G. Roughead, CNO, to Arnold Schwarzenegger, Gov/CA, October 24, 2008.

62. Johnson, SITREP.

63. Coumbe et al., *Second Ten Years*, 223.

64. The White House, ExpectMore.gov., "Detailed Information on the JROTC Assessment," 2006, https://obamawhitehouse.archives.gov/sites/default/files/omb/assets/omb/expetmore/detail/10003233.2006.html.

65. Ibid.

66. Ibid.

67. Richard Ragaller, D/AFJROTC, briefing, March 4, 2008, subject: Tri-service Briefing; Hugh Atkinson, "Marine Corps JROTC" (master's thesis, ACSC, April 2008), 13.

68. Ken Ruiz, "School Board, Army Resolve Salary Issues," *Daily Bulletin*, July 11, 2005; Celanie Polinick, "JROTC Training over at Clairton High School," *Pittsburgh Post-Gazette*, July 14, 2005, https://www.post-gazette.com/pg/05195/537299-55.stm-24k.

69. Greg Toppo and Jack Gillum, "Tide Turns against Schools as Home Foreclosures Rise," *USA Today*, March 15, 2009, 1–2.

70. Mickey Powell, "Possible JROTC Cut Concerns Instructor," *Martinsville Bulletin*, February 17, 2009, http://www.martinsvillebulletin.com/article.

71. COL Ronald Elrod, CDR/4BDE/USACC, to MG Arthur Bartell, CDR/USACC, February 23, 2009, subject: Budget Concerns w/JROTC; Missy Wattenbarger, "JROTC

Leaders Speak Out on School Budget," *Crossville Chronicle*, October 15, 2008, http://www.crossville-chronicle.com/local/local_story_289083419.

72. Donna Rice, USACC, IP, July 12, 2008, subject: SFSB Actions concerning JROTC Program.

73. 153 Cong. Rec. S788–798 at 89 (2007), 89.

74. Ibid.

75. Michael Bernick, "Readers' Forum: Joan Buchanan and the Fight to Save JROTC," *Oakland Tribune*, April 11, 2009, 7.

76. Ibid.

77. AB 223—Assemblywoman Fiona Ma et al., FS, n.d., subject: Reinstating JROTC & PE Credits.

78. Jill Tucker, "SF School Board to Vote on JROTC," *San Francisco Chronicle*, May 13, 2009, 15.

79. David Burrelli and Jody Feder, *Military Recruitment on HS and College Campuses: A Policy and Legal Analysis* (Washington, DC: CRS, 2009), 4.

80. S. Rep. No. 107–4, 2002, 71, 84–85.

81. Ibid., 13–14.

82. Ibid., 14–15.

83. Ibid., 15.

84. *TRADOC Congressional Update*, May 12–16, 2008, 3.

85. H.R.3326, *Department of Defense Appropriations Act*, 2010, 111th Cong. (2010), 412–13; Alaska Dept. of Military and Veterans Affairs, *Strategic Plan, 2012–2016*.

86. Lawrence Kapp, *Recruiting and Retention: FY 2011/12* (Washington, DC: CRS, 2013), 1.

87. MLDC, IP 8, *Outreach and Recruiting*, February 2011, 3, 6.

88. MLDC, DP 1, *Outreach and Recruiting*, February 2011, 9.

89. MLDC, IP 9, *Implementation and Accountability*, February 2011, 1.

90. Donna Rice, interview, September 26, 2006.

91. MLDC, DP 1; Donna Rice, interview, 5, 40.

92. S. Hrg. 111–13, 2010, 25.

93. S. Rept. No. 112–176, 2012, 193.

94. Dieter Waldvogel, "The Importance of Foreign Language and Culture Training," *Foreign Area Officer Journal of International Affairs* 16, no. 3 (Fall 2013): 9–10.

95. HASC Rep. 111–68, 2012, 67; HASC 110–71, 2010, 25.

96. *Partnership for 21st Century Skills, Learning for the 21st Century*, 13, accessed December 24, 2024, https://www.omsd.net/site/handlers/filedownload.ashx?moduleinstanceid=2612&dataid=15502&FileName=P21_Report.pdf.

97. DOD, *STEM Education and Outreach Strategic Plan, 2010–2014* (Arlington, VA: DOD, 2009), https://secure.afa.org/ProfessionalDevelopment/AerospaceEducation/ReportsandStudies/RS_PDFs/DoD-wide%20STEM%20Plan%20FINAL.pdf.

98. S. Hrg. 112–25, 2012, 81.

99. S. Hrg. 112–256, 2012, 3, 93; Caryn Mohr and Dan Mueller, *STARBASE Minnesota Long-Term Follow-Up Study* (St. Paul, MN: Wilder Research, 2012), 93; MLDC, DP 1, 7.

100. "Too Fat to Fight," *Mission Readiness*, April 8, 2010 (hereafter cited as TFTF).

101. Randy Smith, *Recruiting the Future Force* (Carlisle, PA: USAWC, 2011), 7, 32.

102. TFTF; Smith, *Recruiting the Future Force*, 4.

103. S. Hrg. 112–256, 2012, 1–4.

104. H.R. Rep. No. 111–66, 2010, 2647; Paul Heaton and Heather Krull, *Unemployment among Post-9/11 Veterans and Military Spouses* (St. Paul, MN: RAND, 2012), 1, 6.

105. H.R. Rept. No. 111–66, 2010, 2647.

106. Donald Williams, "Historical Lessons to Avoid a Hollow Force" (master's thesis, JFSC/JAWS, Norfolk, VA, June 12, 2013), 3–4, 14; Michael Lay, *Avoiding Another Hollow Force* (Washington, DC: NDU/JAWS, 2013), 23.

107. S. Rep. No. 112–73, 2012, 110–11.

108. Ibid., 111; MLDC, DP 1, 6; SASC Rep. No. 112–590, 2012, 515.

109. House Armed Services Committee, *The Impacts of a Continuing Resolution and Sequestration on Defense*, HASC Rep. No. 113–3 (2013), 3–4.

110. USACC, IP, January 25, 2010, subject: Project PASS.

111. Quoted in Jennifer Nastu, "Keeping Students on a Path to Graduation: Early Intervention and Credit Recovery Programs Are Helping At-Risk Students Achieve Success," *eSchool News*, March 2011, 38, http://www.eschoolnews.com/wp-content/blogs.dir/2/files/2011/02/eSNMar11K12.pdf.

112. IP, Project PASS.

113. Ibid.

114. MOI, John Vanderbleek, January 22, 2010, subject: Project PASS Update.

115. John Meyers, for LTG Freakley, CDR/US Army Accessions Command (USAAC), March 19, 2010, subject: Update on Project PASS.

116. "Project PASS: The Goals of Middle School JLC Curriculum," *WIDS Wire* (Spring, 2011): 8.

117. Steve Arel, "Army Unveils Project PASS, Junior Leadership Corps," US Army, March 11, 2011, http://www.army.mil/article/53186/.

118. H.R. Rep. No. 111–66, 299; Charles A. Henning et al., *FY2011 NDAA: Personnel Policy* (Washington, DC: CRS, 2010), 4, 23.

119. Henning et al., *FY2011 NDAA*, 23; S. McManimon, B. Lozenski, and Z. Casey, "Perpetual War(s), Impossible Peace," *Peace Studies Journal*, January 2013, 73.

120. Leo J. Daugherty and Arthur T. Coumbe, *History of the U.S. Army Cadet Command: Third Ten Years, 2006–2017* (Fort Knox, KY: GPO, 2019), 431.

121. Ibid.

122. Ibid., 432.

123. Ibid., 433.

124. Charles Goldman et al., *Geographic and Demographic Representativeness of the JROTC* (Santa Monica, CA: RAND, 2016), xii.

125. Mike Baker et al., "'I Felt Trapped': Sexual Abuse of Teens in the Military's J.R.O.T.C. Program," *New York Times*, July 9, 2022, https://www.nytimes.com/2022/07/09/us/sexual-abuse-jrotc.html.

126. *Defense Primer: JROTC* (Washington, DC: CRS, 2022).

127. House Committee on Oversight and Reform, memo, JROTC: Protecting Cadets from Sexual Abuse and Instructor Misconduct, November 9, 2022, https://docs.house.gov/meetings/GO/GO06/20221116/115190/HHRG-117-GO06-20221116-SD002.pdf.

128. 115 Cong. Rec. S1 (2018).

129. 116 Cong. Rec. S5018 (2020).

130. Ibid.

131. HASC, H.R. Hrg. 117–34 (2023), 6, 24, 27, 36; S. Hrg. *116*–268 (2020), 9.

132. James Wood, USACC, interview, June 29, 2023.

133. *DOD Appropriations: Hearing before the House Committee on Appropriations*, 117th Cong. 400 (2021) (statement of GEN James McConville).

134. CRS, *FY 2024 NDAA: Junior Reserve Officers' Training Corps (JROTC) Matters* (n.p.: IN12205, 2023).

135. Ruth Farmer et al., "Engaging JROTC Youth in CS Pathways: A Community Discussion of K–12 Cyber Security and Data Science Topics," February 26, 2020, https://dl.acm.org/doi/10.1145/3328778.3372516.

136. LTC (Ret) James Wood, USACC JROTC Directorate, interview, February 5, 2024.

Index